BEYOND THE GREAT WALL

BEYOND THE GREAT WALL

Recipes and Travels in the Other China

JEFFREY ALFORD AND NAOMI DUGUID

Studio photographs by Richard Jung
Location photographs by Jeffrey Alford and Naomi Duguid

ARTISAN

PUBLISHED BY ARTISAN

A Division of Workman Publishing Company, Inc.

225 Varick Street

New York, NY 10014-4381

www.artisanbooks.com

Library of Congress Cataloging-in-Publication Data

Alford, Jeffrey.

 Beyond the Great Wall : recipes and travels in the other China / Jeffrey Alford and Naomi Duguid ; studio photography by Richard Jung ; location photographs by Jeffrey Alford and Naomi Duguid.

 p. cm.

 Includes bibliographical references and index.

 ISBN 978-1-57965-301-9

 1. Cookery, Tibetan. 2. Cookery, Chinese—Yunnan style. 3. Tibet (China)—Description and travel. 4. Yunnan Sheng (China)—Description and travel. 5. Silk Road—Description and travel.

 I. Duguid, Naomi. II. Title.

TX724.5.T55A44 2008

641.5951'5—dc22

2007028556

Design by Jan Derevjanik

Food styling by Linda Tubby

Props styling by Roisin Nield

Maps by Rodica Prato

Printed in Singapore

First printing, March 2008

10 9 8 7 6 5 4 3 2 1

ABOVE: *Detail of a traditional Tibetan house in Lhasa.* OPPOSITE: *Two Bai women talking at Xiapin market, west of Dali, in Yunnan.*

CONTENTS

THE OTHER CHINA

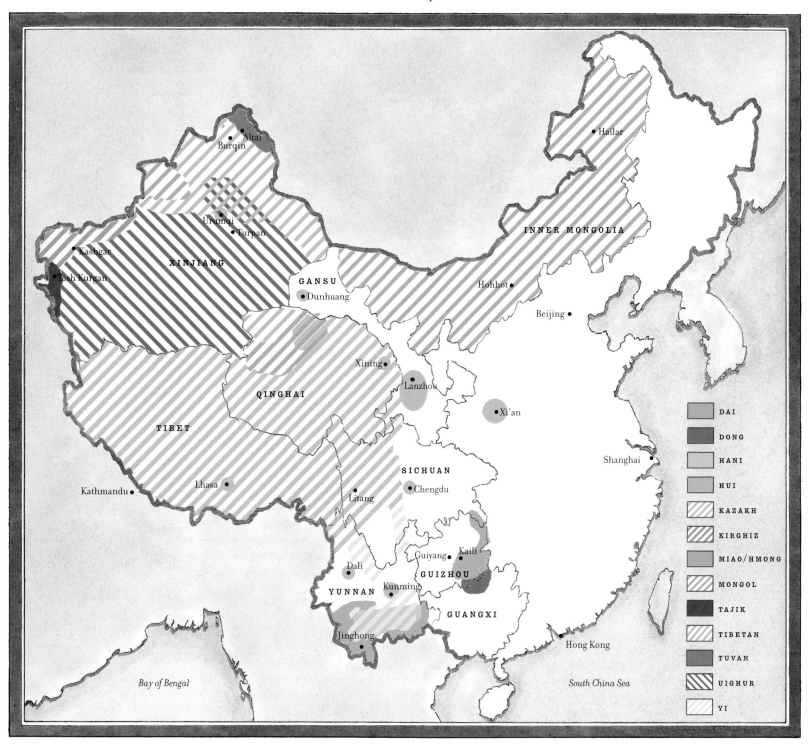

INNER MONGOLIA

XINJIANG

GANSU

QINGHAI

TIBET

SICHUAN

YUNNAN

GUIZHOU

GUANGXI

Altai
Burqin
Hailar
Urumqi
Turpan
Kashgar
Tash Kurgan
Dunhuang
Hohhot
Beijing
Xining
Lanzhou
Xi'an
Shanghai
Kathmandu
Lhasa
Chengdu
Litang
Guiyang
Kaili
Dali
Kunming
Jinghong
Hong Kong

Bay of Bengal

South China Sea

DAI
DONG
HANI
HUI
KAZAKH
KIRGHIZ
MIAO/HMONG
MONGOL
TAJIK
TIBETAN
TUVAN
UIGHUR
YI

By Lake Er Hai, not far from Dali, Yunnan.

INTRODUCTION

A map of the world would look very different if instead of marking political borders we outlined regions based upon food and culture. Spain, Great Britain, India—all would look dramatically different, but of all the countries in the world, the one that might look the most profoundly different is present-day China.

Three-fifths of the land area we now call China is historically the home of people who are not ethnically Chinese. Tibet, for example, was once a Himalayan nation almost equal in size to China. Similarly, the Silk Road region of the far west (present-day Xinjiang), now home to the Uighurs, as well as to Tajiks, Kazakhs, Tuvans, Tatars, Mongols, and Kirghiz, has often been outside China's control, sometimes united, sometimes fragmented into small fiefdoms. Mongols, whose culture is now split between two countries, had at one time the most powerful army in the world. And in the mountainous southwest, particularly in the provinces of Yunnan and Guizhou (which are culturally more closely related to neighboring Southeast Asia than to China), there is a greater diversity of people and cultures than in almost any other place in the world.

In this book our aim is to draw a new map of China, a food map that focuses on the outlying regions of present-day China, an area we refer to as "beyond the Great Wall," and on the peoples who live there. Beyond the Great Wall is a metaphorical term that alludes to the historic attitude of the Han Chinese toward anyone not culturally Chinese, including people of other cultures who live within the borders of China—those the Han Chinese traditionally regarded as uncivilized or barbarian.

We've traveled many times in these regions. In fact, it was in Tibet that we first met each other, in 1985. Long before, even as children, both of us had been fascinated by all the different regions beyond the Great Wall. We'd read about Tibet, its nomads and pilgrims, its rich religious history and culture, and about the mighty rivers that rise in Tibet and flow out in four directions. We'd read about Chinese Central Asia, about the old Silk Road and Marco Polo, and about the early explorers who set out across the Takla Makan Desert. We'd read about the Mongolian steppe and about Genghis Khan and his conquering Mongol army. These were places that easily filled the imagination: intensely blue skies, snow-capped mountains, camel caravans, and welcoming oases.

China opened its borders in the early 1980s, and so, separately and together, we traveled widely beyond the Great Wall over the course of the decade (travels we write about in the early chapters of this book). However, once other projects intervened, we spent little time here for six or seven years.

When we first began this project, we couldn't wait to start traveling, to revisit many of the places we loved, and to go farther afield. In our minds we could already taste the handmade noodles and tandoor flatbreads of the Uighur oases, and the Hami melons and grapes, the cumin-scented lamb kebabs, and the sun-drenched tomatoes and peppers. We could already smell the unbelievably crisp high-altitude air of Tibet and see our way across miles of open land with a deep blue sky above. In our minds we were already sitting cross-legged on the floor in traditional Dai bamboo houses in far southern Yunnan, eating sticky rice with our hands and dipping it into fiery-hot sauces.

But in 2005, on our first two solo trips to China for this book, neither of us was at all prepared for what we found. We were caught completely by surprise. We'd heard all the news about the world's fastest-growing economy. We'd talked with fellow travelers about China's rapid changes. We'd seen documentaries and read books. But still we were unprepared.

China in the twenty-first century was completely different from the China we'd first encountered in the early 1980s.

We realized that we were witnessing the most dramatic social and economic change in the shortest amount of time that we had ever seen. China felt like a raging river, swollen with floodwaters, running fast and furious. On one hand it was mesmerizing, and on the other hand frightening. Because our aim was to look, as much and as often as we could, through the eyes of people living on the periphery, outside central China, what we saw was alarming.

The economic prosperity in China is wildly uneven, and it's non-Han China that is most frequently on the short end. Mass migrations of people from densely populated regions of central China to the more sparsely populated areas of Tibet and Xinjiang have the potential to completely overwhelm local culture.

To give a sense of all this change, we have arranged many of the "story" portions of this book in chronological order, beginning with Naomi's first trip to mainland China in the summer of 1980 (called, "Summer 1980") and continuing with travels up to the present day. We hope that by arranging the stories in this way we can better illustrate just how dramatic the changes are beyond the Great Wall, not only in culture but obviously, too, in food. Each chapter concludes with a profile of a particular people ("The Uighur People," "The Tibetan People," and so on). Of course there isn't room enough to profile everyone, but we hope this gives some idea of the great diversity of peoples who live beyond the Great Wall. Also, for the first time, we've included an "N" or a "J" at the end of those stories where it seems important to distinguish who is writing.

This is a cookbook, not a thesis, but it is probably the most outwardly "political" cookbook we will ever write (though we think of all our cookbooks, and a great many other cookbooks that we most admire, as inherently political). When it comes to food and cooking, China is a very

A street in a small Tibetan town in western Sichuan.

remarkable place. The diversity, the ingenuity, the resourcefulness, the incredible depth of history, tradition, and culture—all of these things make food in China, and eating in China, one of life's great pleasures. But just as food in Spain is not only the food of Madrid or Barcelona, the food of China is much more than the food of Beijing, Shanghai, and Guangzhou. From Tibet to Xinjiang, from Inner Mongolia to Yunnan, food has traveled back and forth across this region, has cross-fertilized, for centuries.

And it's never been traveling faster than now.

This book is about not only the food of people living in the regions beyond the Great Wall, but also cultural survival and the preservation of food and culture in smaller societies faced with the impact of a giant at the doorstep.

THE LAND

Geographically, China is astonishingly like the United States, two big countries with extremely varied landscapes. If you slid one around the globe, it would fit almost perfectly on top of the other. They're like twins, nearly identical in area and latitude, with a densely populated eastern coast and a western region that is relatively arid. The northern areas of China, like those of the United States, are cold in winter and hot in summer; the southern areas are semitropical, with hot, humid summers.

There is, however, one major geographic difference between the two countries: China has only one coast, the east coast, and the country's population and prosperity trail off westward. It's as if the United States ended at Nevada and Arizona instead of at California and the rest of the prosperous West Coast.

The population, wealth, and agricultural fertility of China are concentrated in the east, an area that extends inland from the coast about 800 miles (a little more than the distance from Washington, D.C., to St. Louis). This is the heartland of China, where Chinese culture arose and flourished and where the population is overwhelmingly Han Chinese. (In this book, we call it **central China**.)

Lying outside central China are the areas of the country that we think of as "beyond the Great Wall." They're traditionally home to non-Han peoples of many distinctive cultures, shaped in no small part by their unique physical environments.

Starting in the southern border areas are the provinces of **Guangxi**, **Guizhou**, and **Yunnan**, where the terrain is mountainous, with subtropical vegetation, steep-sided river valleys, and a monsoon climate that brings heavy rainfall in the summer months. The abundant rainfall and mild climate make rice a rewarding crop almost everywhere here, and also result in an abundance of fruit and a year-round growing season for vegetables. Many different ethnic groups live in these valleys, quite isolated from one another until recently.

In **northwestern Yunnan** and in **western Sichuan** provinces, historically Tibetan areas, the terrain gets even more mountainous and elevations greater, finally merging into the Tibetan plateau. Major rivers, including the Salween, Yangtze, and Mekong, flow south through the mountains, cutting deep valleys. Here some places are wooded, with ample rainfall, while others get very little rain, so that very few crops can be grown unless there is a nearby stream or river to provide water. People live by herding livestock and cultivating hardy crops such as barley and potatoes.

Tibet is about 1,000 miles wide from east to west (about the same as the distance from Hong Kong to Tibet's eastern border). In central Tibet, there are high uplands, cut by occasional fertile valleys. The most striking of these is the wide valley of the Brahmaputra River (called the Yarlung Tsangpo in Tibet). The river flows due east across Tibet, along the northern edge of the **Himalaya**, until it turns south, cutting through the mountains, to reach Assam in India. In Tibet, settlements and farms are usually in the valleys, at elevations over 11,000 feet. Villages were traditionally built at the base of the hills for defensive reasons and to avoid using arable land. Winters are very cold and dry; summers are moderately warm, with occasional monsoon rainfall that penetrates the Himalaya from the south. Farther west, the elevation of the Tibetan plateau increases to about 15,000 feet. Most of the sparse population of western Tibet consists of nomads who move with their herds of yaks and goats from grazing ground to grazing ground.

The Tibetan plateau is bordered on the north by the **Kunlun Mountains**. North of them lie the vast **Tarim Basin** and the **Takla Makan Desert**, one of the world's largest desert areas, with fertile agricultural oases at intervals around its northern and southern edges. (The routes linking these oases to central China and to the countries to the west are now collectively referred to as the **Silk Road** or **Silk Routes**.)

LEFT: *The steep hillsides near the Red River (called the Yuan Chiang in China) in southeastern Yunnan have been shaped over the centuries into astonishingly beautiful and productive rice terraces by the Hani people who live there.* CENTER: *Mani stones outside the Tibetan village of Burang, just north of the Himalaya in far western Tibet. The stones have been incised with prayers and piled up to form a large wall. When we were first in Burang in 1976, a small portrait of Mao sat among the mani stones on top of the wall.* RIGHT: *From the Khamba La, a high pass several hours drive from Lhasa en route to the town of Gyantse, there's a breathtaking view of Yamdrok Tso (Yamdrok Lake), and behind it the northern face of the Himalaya. India lies on the other side of the mountains.*

The desert is mostly sand, trackless and thankless. Small rivers flow in and peter out; no water flows out. It's a "vast drainageless basin," as Aurel Stein, a great explorer of the region, described it. The desert itself lies inside the largest province in China, **Xinjiang.** In the Takla Makan, temperatures in winter can drop to zero degrees Fahrenheit, while in summer they can reach over 100 degrees.

The eastern edge of the Tarim Basin is in **Qinghai** province, which rises to higher elevations as it meets the Tibetan plateau. *Qinghai* means "blue lake" in Mandarin; it's also the Chinese name of the huge saline lake called the Koko Nor ("blue lake" in Mongolian) in northern Qinghai.

The western rim of the Tarim Basin is framed by the **Pamir Mountains,** where temperatures are extreme and winds often brutal. Herders and seminomadic agriculturalists eke out a living at higher elevations, and there is a little cultivation in the valley floors. The tallest mountains here are over 20,000 feet, and in the wide U-shaped valleys, yaks and goats graze on the tough summer grasses.

Along the northwestern edge of the Tarim Basin is an east-west range of snow mountains called the **Tian Shan,** or "Celestial Mountains." They divide the Tarim from another dry basin to the north, the **Dzungaria.**

It's a wide, flat area of salt marshes and grasslands, rimmed by hills and mountains, most notably the **Altai Mountains,** which mark the border with Russia and Mongolia. The winters here are harsh and start early. By the third week in September, the leaves are already turning.

East of the Dzungarian Basin is the biggest desert of all, the **Gobi.** Most of it lies in the country of Mongolia, but some is within the borders of the Chinese province of **Inner Mongolia,** a vast inland plateau. Here again, temperatures are extremely cold in winter and hot in summer. There are few trees in most of Inner Mongolia. Where there is enough moisture to support vegetation, there are vast grasslands, though the grass is green and fresh only from mid-June until early September. Apart from some rolling hills and the occasional streambed, the terrain is relatively flat, giving no shelter from the frequent strong winds.

A landscape in which only the hardy and resourceful can survive, Inner Mongolia was traditionally home to only nomads. Over the last few hundred years, Han farmers have moved in to plow the grasslands and grow crops. In the modern era, mining companies and others bent on exploiting and extracting the area's rich mineral resources have created open-pit mines, and towns and cities for those who work them.

LEFT: *The ruins of a fort outside the small frontier town of Tash Kurgan are a reminder that this valley in the Pamirs lies on the historic trade route (one branch of the fabled Silk Road) from Afghanistan and Pakistan into Chinese Central Asia.* RIGHT: *In southwestern Yunnan, a typical Southeast Asian bridge made of bamboo provides passage for people and animals across a tributary of the Mekong River (known as the Lancang in China).*

In this book most place-names are given in the modern standard Chinese form, the Pinyin alphabet that is used in China for transcribing words and names (see note). The Pinyin phonetic alphabet is made up of the twenty-six letters of the English alphabet, but uses some of them differently.

The most difficult of these letters and letter combinations for English speakers are listed here.

Fog and mist in the town of Yuanyang, in southeastern Yunnan.

CONSONANTS

"X"   Used to represent a slightly sibilant "s" sound. The city of Xi'an is pronounced roughly "see-an"; the large western province of Xinjiang is pronounced "sin-jiang"; and the city of Xining is pronounced "si-ning."

"Q"   Used to represent a lightly sounded "ch," as in "children." The landlocked province called Qinghai is pronounced "ching-high"; and the capital of Xinjiang, Urumqi, is pronounced "oo-room-chee."

"C"   Used to represent a "ts" sound. The Lancang, the Chinese name for the Mekong River, is pronounced "lan-tsang."

"Z"   Used to represent a "dz" sound. The large river that rises in northeastern Tibet and flows through central China—often written as Yangtze in English—is written "Yangze" in Pinyin, and pronounced "yang-dze."

"ZH"   Used to represent a "dj" sound, a rather heavy sounding "j." The city of Lanzhou, in Gansu, is pronounced "lan-djoh" and the Dong village of Zhaoxing is "djow-sing."

VOWEL COMBINATIONS

"AI"   Used for the long "i" sound, as in "hi." The mountains in northern Xinjiang, the Altai, are pronounced "all-tie"; the town of Hailar in Inner Mongolia is pronounced "high-lar"; the name of the Dai people is pronounced "die."

"AO"   Used for the sound "ow" as in "cow"; thus Zhaoxing is "djow-sing"; and the name of the people known in China as Miao is pronounced "mee-ow."

"EI"   Used for the long "a" sound, as in "bay"; thus Beijing is "bay-jing."

"OU"   Used for the sound "oh"; thus Lanzhou is "lan-djoh" and the province of Guizhou is "gway-djoh."

"UI"   Used to represent the sound "way"; so the name of the people known as Hui is pronounced "hway" and Guizhou is "gway-djoh." The exception is the name of the Uighur people, which is pronounced "wee-gur."

NOTE: *The exceptions to our use of Pinyin transcriptions are place-names in Tibet. We give those in the spelling that is more familiar to English speakers, and that tends to be those used by Tibetans abroad. Thus we refer to the towns of Gyantse and Shigatse rather than the Pinyin Gyanze and Xigazê; to the Yarlung Tsangpo (the name of the Brahmaputra River in Tibet) rather than the Yarlung Zangbo. In addition, we use the name Tibet for the area that is referred to in Mandarin as Xizang (pronounced "see-dzang" and meaning western treasure), and the name Tibetan for people referred to in Mandarin as "zang-zu" (pronounced "dzang-dzu").*

THE PEOPLE

Most (about 92 percent) of the one and a half billion people who live in the People's Republic of China are ethnically Chinese, Han Chinese, and most of them live in central China, along the densely populated eastern seaboard, an area roughly the size of the East Coast of the United States to the Mississippi River, about a third of the total area of China.

Chinese culture first evolved here in the fertile area between the Yellow and Yangtze Rivers, more than 3,000 years ago. As the Chinese developed sophisticated methods for managing their flooding rivers and irrigating agricultural land, their agricultural wealth increased, permitting the development of large cities such as the ancient capital Chang'an (now the city of Xi'an). Other inventions included paper, a sophisticated writing system, and an elite educational system, as well as gunpowder, porcelain, and silk. Over time, as the population of central China grew and prospered, the Han gradually expanded south of the Yangtze River and north of the Yellow River, as well as westward into what is present-day Sichuan province.

Beyond the relatively homogenous Han-populated area of central China lie the regions "beyond the Great Wall." Here live people of many different cultures and ethnicities: Tibetans, Mongols, Uighurs, Miao, Hui, Dong, Yi, Dai, and others.

These groups have had complex relationships with the Han Chinese over the centuries. Some conquered China (Mongols, Tibetans, Manchus). Some have historically been quite independent of China (Yi, Miao, Hani), some have become relatively assimilated (Manchu, Zhuang), and others (Tibetans, Uighurs) have remained astonishingly distinct.

These days the descendants of all of these cultures are citizens of the People's Republic of China. The five stars on the flag of China represent the country's five major peoples: Han, Tibetan, Mongol, Manchu, and Muslim (a term that encompasses the Uighurs and the Hui). The Han dominate: they are the majority by far, with all non-Han labeled "minority peoples" by the Beijing authorities. There are some fifty-five officially designated minority peoples in China, who currently make up about 8 percent of the population, or about 125 million people.

To Westerners, the most familiar of these non-Han peoples are probably the Tibetans. In the seventh century, starting in central Tibet, not far from Lhasa, the Tibetans were united under King Songtsen Gampo, whose army conquered what is now Xinjiang, and parts of Ladakh (in India) and expanded Tibet's borders north and east in the eighth century, at one time holding the Chinese capital of Chang'an. Tibet became Buddhist and developed a written language. The Tibetan empire lasted for about two centuries. The country then fragmented into smaller areas. It was conquered by the Mongols under Genghis Khan in 1207. A later Mongol khan adopted Tibetan Buddhism, and Kublai Khan (1215–1294) became a great Buddhist patron, creating an important link between the two cultures that still exists. After the Mongols lost power in the fourteenth century, Tibet regained its independence but was again fragmented, this time under the control of various monasteries, centers of Buddhist learning and of economic power. In the seventeenth century, a strong central authority took control of Tibet, a reformed monastic sect (the Gelug or Yellow Hat sect) led by the Dalai Lama. Until the twentieth century, Tibet remained relatively autonomous, with a feudal-type economy and culture centered around the large monasteries, ruled from the center (Lhasa) by a succession of Dalai Lamas or regents.

After the Maoists took control of central China in 1949, the Chinese government embarked on a conquest of the areas beyond the Great Wall, including Tibet and the western desert areas. The following year, the Chinese army conquered the eastern Tibetan regions of Kham and Amdo and assimilated them into the Chinese provinces of Sichuan, Qinghai, and Gansu. In 1959, the fourteenth Dalai Lama fled from Lhasa to India, and the Chinese took complete control of central and western Tibet.

Originally a loose collection of nomadic tribes, the Mongols came to play a pivotal role in the history of China and the rest of Asia. In the early thirteenth century, Genghis Khan led his small nomad tribe to dominance and then fought and eventually obtained the allegiance of the rest of the Mongol tribes. The highly mobile Mongol army, all on horseback, moved out to conquer neighboring lands. Genghis Khan's army subdued what are now Inner Mongolia, Gansu, Xinjiang, and Tibet. His sons and grandsons conquered most of Russia and the area around the Caspian Sea, Iran, Afghanistan, and Iraq, then Turkey and Syria. They also conquered central China, as well as territories to the south in Yunnan, and down into present-day Burma.

Kublai Khan, Genghis Khan's grandson, founded a new dynasty, the Yuan, that ruled the Chinese empire for about a century, from 1280 to 1368. During his rule, as mentioned above, the Mongols converted to Tibetan-style Buddhism. With the defeat of the Yuan Dynasty by the Chinese Ming Dynasty (1368–1644), Han Chinese culture reasserted its dominance, and the Mongols retreated to their homeland. They continued to form political and military alliances from time to time but were never again a great power. Over the centuries, Han settlers gradually moved into Inner Mongolia and encroached on the grasslands, tilling the soil and building settlements.

Because of a longtime trickle of migrants from other parts of China, the population of Inner Mongolia has less than 20 percent people of Mongol descent. Many of the Mongols there live in towns and cities, but some do still live on the grasslands in *gers* (dome-shaped wool tents), their flocks of horses, cattle, or sheep grazing nearby. In northern Xinjiang, and in scattered places in Qinghai and Yunnan, there are also pockets of Mongols. Their ancestry goes back to the invading Mongol armies of the thirteenth century.

The history of the western desert and mountains, an area often referred to as Chinese Turkestan, or Chinese Central Asia, and now Xinjiang province, is complicated, a story of invaders and local wars. The majority population in the oases around the Takla Makan Desert is Uighur (pronounced "wee-gur").

The Uighurs are a Turkic-speaking people (like the Uzbeks, Kirghiz, and Kazakhs) who were originally nomads from the steppes of what is now Mongolia. They moved west, but, unlike other Turkic-speaking peoples, they became settled farmers in the oases and developed a so-

LEFT TO RIGHT: *A Bai woman sells produce in Kunming, capital of Yunnan. A young Tibetan nun, ordained the day before, in Labrang, Gansu. And, at the same nunnery, an older nun, with her life mapped onto her face. A Tibetan boy at the market town of Burang, in western Tibet; in summer, when the passes are open, people come across the mountains from Nepal to trade lowland goods for salt and wool from Tibet. Uighur men, like this man from Kashgar, often wear beautifully embroidered caps. Uighur women usually cover their heads with a colorful scarf, like this blue-eyed woman, also from Kashgar.*

phisticated, literate culture. In the ninth century, the Uighurs controlled the whole of the Takla Makan Desert region. They were conquered by the Mongols in the thirteenth century, in the latter's sweep westward.

Like Samarkand or Venice, though to a lesser degree, the oasis settlements became wealthy because of the trade along the Silk Road, the network of caravan routes that linked China with Persia, India, the Mediterranean, and Europe. The oases were home to many different people—Arabs, Persians, and others, including some Europeans—drawn there by trade. Trade along the Silk Road flourished from the twelfth century until the fifteenth, when the trade shifted to sea routes (less subject to brigands and political problems). The oasis towns fell into relative obscurity, becoming isolated outposts fought over by local warlords and rarely controlled by any central authority.

The Uighurs are still agriculturalists and businesspeople. In recent years, they have become known as entrepreneurs in the cities of central China, selling everything from kebabs and flatbreads to silks and other valuables from Xinjiang.

One of the many consequences of the Silk Road trade was the arrival in the oasis settlements, and eventually in central China, of new religions traveling in from the west—notably Buddhism, Manicheaism,

Christianity, and, later, Islam—brought in by traders, travelers, merchants, and priests. By the twelfth century, most of the population of the oases had converted to Islam.

In China, one nationality is defined by religion rather than by ethnicity, and that is the Hui, who are Muslims. Hui people (today about ten million total) live in many parts of China, but they are a particularly important part of the population near the upper stretches of the Yellow River in northwest China, in the provinces of Qinghai, Gansu, and Ningxia. There are also large communities of Hui people in some central Chinese cities, including Xi'an and Guangzhou, where they have built mosques and often have their own markets. The usual shorthand description of the Hui is that they are Han who converted to Islam, but in fact their roots include people of other ethnic origins: they are the descendants of Arab and Persian traders as well as of Han converts to Islam.

In the mountain areas along the borders of present-day China live people of many different ethnicities and cultures. Few of them have ever formed a state or had a sense of national identity. Some of them originated in more fertile lowlands and over time were pushed to more marginal areas; others seem always to have been uplanders. The most

diverse regions, ethnically speaking, are the southern and southwestern hills and mountains in Guangxi, Guizhou, and Yunnan. Here live large populations of Hmong, known in China as Miao (see page 183), Dong (page 120), Dai (page 237), and Yi and Hani (page 316) peoples, among many others.

During the Long March, when Mao's forces were fighting for control of China, his army traveled through the steep hills of Guizhou and Guangxi. For many villagers, it was their first contact with Han Chinese people, and it was the beginning of the process of incorporating them into the state of China. To this day, many of the peoples in the southern and southwestern hills remain fairly remote from mainstream Chinese life, cultivating rice and vegetables, corn and millet; using animal or people power; and still speaking their own languages, though now some of their children go off to the cities of central China for work or higher education.

In the mountains of western and northern Xinjiang live small numbers of mostly seminomadic peoples: Kirghiz (see page 288), Tajiks (page 343), Kazakhs (page 157), Tuvans (page 255), and some Mongols. Some of them have migrated down to cities such as Kashgar and Urumqi, but most still live in small villages in winter and, in summer—when they travel to higher pastures with their herds of goats, camels, yak, and sheep—in yurts. Larger numbers of each population live across the border in neighboring countries (Kyrgyzstan, Russia, Tajikistan, Kazakhstan, Mongolia, and Afghanistan).

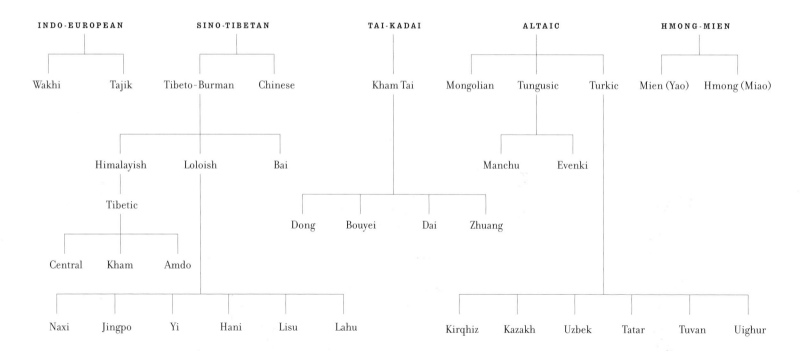

LANGUAGE FAMILIES

LEFT: *A Uighur girl in Kashgar adjusts her head scarf.* RIGHT: *A crowd of Tibetans in Litang, in western Sichuan.*

THE FOOD

From the oases of Xinjiang to the grasslands of Inner Mongolia, Qinghai, and Tibet, from the well-watered semitropical hills and valleys of Yunnan and Guizhou to the rugged mountains in Xinjiang and Tibet, the traditional culinary cultures of the regions beyond the Great Wall reflect local climate and terrain. Along with these, the availability of water and fuel determines what foods can be grown and how people cook.

In the mountains and grasslands, the higher and drier regions, including much of Inner Mongolia, Tibet, Qinghai, and the mountainous edges of Xinjiang, there's a nomadic herding tradition. Nomads live from their herds, eating fresh or dried meat as well as a variety of dairy products. They trade wool or salt (gathered from saline lakes and salt pans) for grain and tea. In Xinjiang, smaller non-Han populations (Kirghiz, Tajik, Kazakh, Tuvan) live a nomadic or seminomadic life in the harsh climate of the Pamir, Tian Shan, and Altai Mountains.

In Tibet, the staple meat is yak (rather like beef), and lamb and goat are also common. A wide variety of vegetables and wheat and rice are available in Lhasa and other towns, but in the countryside, people still eat a relatively traditional diet based on barley, meat, tea, and dairy products (butter, cheese, and yogurt). The staple Tibetan grain, hardy enough to survive high altitude and low rainfall, is barley. Sometimes it's made into puffed barley, but mostly it's roasted as a whole grain, then ground into *tsampa*, a fine flour that is immediately digestible (see page 180). The traditional staple Tibetan meal for herders and travelers, as well as for many living settled on the land, is tea flavored with salt and butter and eaten with tsampa stirred into it.

In Inner Mongolia, meat dishes (usually sheep or goat) are simmered or grilled. Hot pot is a practical and convivial Mongol tradition of simmering meat in broth that has now spread across China to Korea and Southeast Asia. Mongolian barbecue has also become popular in the West. Dairy products are eaten in a wide variety of forms: yogurt, dried milk, fresh and dried cheeses, butter, and much more. In recent times, wheat flour has become available, so that people eat wheat noodles and flatbreads, as well as millet. Rice too is brought in from other parts of China and has become a staple in more prosperous Inner Mongolian towns. Tea is usually drunk with milk.

The oases of the Takla Makan Desert in Xinjiang consist of fertile fields rimmed with trees, as well as small villages and larger towns. The trees help create a cooler microclimate that provides respite from the heat and fiercely dry air. Because water is brought to the oases by underground channels from mountains far away, the microclimate is moist compared to the desert air, and the soil, well watered, produces vegetables, fruits, and grains, primarily wheat. Herds of sheep and

goats graze at the edges of the oases and out into the desert. Staples are wheat-based foods—tandoor-baked flatbreads and wheat flour noodles of many kinds—and meat, grilled over a fire or simmered with oasis-grown vegetables such as tomatoes, peppers, and onions. Rice is eaten at festive occasions in the form of meat *pulaos*, often accompanied by fresh salads or pickles.

The semitropical climate of the hills of Yunnan, Guizhou, and western Guangxi, with its generous rainfall and mild temperatures, produces a much wider variety of fruits and vegetables for local cooks to work with. Though there are seasons, they are not as marked and extreme as in other areas beyond the Great Wall. Pigs flourish, and so does rice, and both are staples, along with a wide variety of greens. Many dishes are stir-fried, and there is also a one-pot cooking tradition that produces simmered stews and family soups. Because these southern areas are populated by a large number of greatly diverse peoples, many of whom have influenced one another to some degree, it's not possible to speak much about food in general terms; the pleasure is in the specifics. Highlights for us include the tart-hot flavors of Dai cuisine, a close cousin of Lao and northern Thai food; the hearty family-style soups of the Dong people; sticky rice; chile pastes flavored with Sichuan pepper; inventive takes on fish; and an array of unusual salads and lightly cooked vegetables.

LEFT TO RIGHT: *A Hui man selling chickens in Burqin, northern Xinjiang. Pink radishes for sale at a Dong village in Guizhou. Morning market noodle stand in the largely Miao market in Chong'an, Guizhou. Small cubes of pressed tofu for sale at the Yi and Hani market in Luchen, Yunnan.*

in your kitchen

Of all our books, this is perhaps the easiest one for cooks from North America to embark on using the equipment they already have and shopping at their usual grocery stores. Ingredients and equipment that may be unfamiliar are described in the Glossary.

Most of the fresh ingredients called for in the recipes are common temperate-climate vegetables, such as carrots, potatoes, spinach, and tomatoes. There are also Asian vegetables such as bok choi, bean sprouts, and daikon (white radish) that have become familiar to North Americans recently and are widely available.

Seasonings are relatively simple, with scallions, ginger, onion, garlic, fresh and dried chiles, salt, and black pepper being most important, though Sichuan pepper also plays a role in some dishes. Liquid ingredients and flavorings such as peanut oil, soy sauce, rice vinegar (two kinds), and chile paste are everyday staples in our kitchen. They can be found in Asian groceries and many of them are available in larger supermarkets. They keep well, so mail order is another option.

Dry ingredients include rice, rice flour, wheat flour, and dried noodles, rice noodles, and cellophane noodles (also called bean threads). These can all be found in Asian groceries and in well-stocked grocery stores, or can be mail-ordered (see page 366).

The cooking methods used in the recipes require little special equipment. The wok is the easiest, most practical tool for stir-frying, but a wide skillet can be substituted. Your usual pots will serve you well for making the simmered soups and stews, though you may want to try cooking with a sand pot (see page 130). You may want to buy a bamboo steamer (see photo, page 153), if you don't already have a steamer of any kind—it's an inexpensive, attractive kitchen tool. Hot pot is a simple way of cooking and eating at the table with friends (see page 269 for more), so you may want to buy a hot pot (available in large Chinese grocery stores).

CONDIMENTS AND SEASONINGS

Great Wall has salsas or sauces or condiments that are put on the table to heighten flavors and to give guests the chance to vary tastes and add intensity to their food as they eat. We love them for their bright flavors and for their simplicity.

The salsas and chutneys make wonderful accompaniments to grilled meats and deep-fried snacks; we also like to serve them as dips for sticky rice or crackers or bread. We've had to restrict ourselves here to just a sampling. There's a bright red chile paste, made of quickly processed red cayennes (page 18); a tart and enticing grilled vegetable salsa from the Dai of southern Yunnan (page 22); a fresh tomato salsa-like sauce from Guizhou (page 18); a simple green herb sauce from the Mongol repertoire (page 23); and two quick chutneys (page 24) now found in Tibetan communities in central Tibet and in Gansu and Qinghai.

In most areas beyond the Great Wall, and elsewhere in the world where winters are hard, autumn is the time for preserving vegetables and drying meat. In a farmhouse in the far north of Inner Mongolia, with a huge brick-and-tile stove in the kitchen, Naomi saw pails of cabbage in brine slowly turning into pickles, and out in the yard another fermented cabbage pickle, this one turning into something more like Korean kimchi. Pickles and preserves originated as a way of coping with scarcity. Now they've become a delicious end in themselves, intense and distinctive ways to bring flavor to a meal.

Many traditional pickled greens, such as pickled mustard greens (see Glossary) and kimchi, are available in Asian grocery stores. We urge you to buy several and sample them. They're a great addition to the table.

We have included two easy brined recipes, one for a Tibetan white radish pickle (page 25), the other for pickled cayenne chiles, bright red and beautiful (page 34). Both have become pantry staples for us, because they can be served as condiments and are also ingredients in other dishes. Among the other pantry staples in this chapter are hot chile oil (page 29) and Guizhou chile paste (page 35).

OPPOSITE: *Cayenne-style chiles growing by a house in the Miao village of Xijiang, in Guizhou.* ABOVE: *A hand of ginger.*

MARKET STALL FRESH TOMATO SALSA

This couldn't be simpler. Like all simple dishes, it requires good basic ingredients; make it whenever you have access to ripe local tomatoes. It reminds us of the topping for *pa amb tomàquet*, the delicious Catalan tomato-smeared bread.

Raw vegetables are a special treat in China, where almost all vegetables are served cooked. I came across fresh tomato salsa in a rural market in Guizhou, in a town called Chong'an. It was one of a number of condiments and toppings at a noodle stand (see Hand-Rolled Rice Noodles, page 142). The fresh flavor of the tomatoes combined with salt and a little sesame oil was like a new discovery.

Serve as a topping for rice noodles or other noodles, as a condiment with any meal, or as a salsa with sticky rice or chips. To use as a topping for noodles, pour over the noodles, either hot or at room temperature, using about 1 cup salsa per serving. To serve as a condiment, put out in a bowl with a spoon.

> 4 medium-large perfectly ripe thin-skinned tomatoes
> 1 scallion, minced, or about 1 tablespoon minced chives
> ½ to 1 teaspoon roasted sesame oil, to taste
> 1 teaspoon kosher salt or sea salt, or to taste

Working over a bowl to catch the juices, cut the tomatoes into bite-sized pieces and drop them into the bowl. Then squeeze the cut tomatoes a handful at a time to soften them and squeeze out even more juice. Add the minced scallion or chives and sesame oil and stir to mix. Add the salt and stir, then taste and adjust the oil and salt if you wish.

Serves 3 to 4 as a topping for noodles, 6 as a condiment or salsa

BRIGHT RED CHILE PASTE

We're accustomed to seeing chile paste, made from dried red chiles and a little oil, set out as a table condiment with noodles and used in kitchens all over China. But we've learned that many cooks in Guizhou, Guangxi, and Yunnan also use a fresh sauce, made from red chiles that are very like cayenne chiles. Whenever you come across ripe red cayenne chiles, make up a batch of this paste. The chiles are ground or pounded to a paste with a little salt and a touch of vinegar. The paste is bright red, a beautiful addition to the table.

> About ¼ pound (8 to 10) fresh red cayenne chiles
> 1 teaspoon salt, or to taste
> Pinch of sugar (optional)
> 1 tablespoon rice vinegar
> 2 tablespoons water, or more to taste

Wash the chiles well, then cut off the stems and coarsely chop the chiles. Place them in a food processor, add the salt, and process to a paste. Add the sugar, if using, and the vinegar and pulse to blend. Turn out into a bowl, using a rubber spatula to scrape the chile paste from the processor bowl, and add water to thin to the texture you desire. With the amount of water suggested above, the paste will be thick and dense with chiles, but it can be made quite thin by adding up to ¼ cup water: it's up to you. If you make it thinner, you may want to add another pinch of salt.

To serve as a condiment, place in a small shallow bowl and put out a spoon so guests can help themselves to a drizzle of the paste as they eat. To use as a flavoring in stir-fries, add either at the beginning, once the oil in the wok is hot, to give an undernote of warmth (try using 1 teaspoon to start with), or when the dish is almost cooked, to give a fresh dash of heat (use less, perhaps ½ teaspoon).

Stored in a clean glass jar with a tight-fitting lid in the refrigerator, leftover chile paste will keep for a week or so.

Makes a generous ½ cup

FROM LEFT: *Market Stall Fresh Tomato Salsa and Bright Red Chile Paste.*

It became a cliché in the 1970s, those photographs of Chinese streets crammed with cyclists in somber-colored jackets and pants. Dark blue, dull green, and gray or black were the only colors you'd ever see in the photos, apart from the brilliant red of the Chinese flag. China seemed to be a country in monochrome, a stage set filled with crowds of people all dressed alike, deindividualized and desexualized.

When I went to China for the first time, in the summer of 1980, it looked like those photos, in places. Independent travel was not permitted for casual tourists, so I went with a tour group from the United States. On our one-month trip we traveled by plane, train, and bus to areas beyond the Great Wall (Xinjiang and Inner Mongolia), as well as to various Chinese cities (Beijing, Xi'an, Guangzhou, Taiyuan). We were fed elaborate meals, mostly Chinese regional food prepared by gifted chefs in banquet style, which meant there were many refined dishes and very little rice.

The wide expanses of Tiananmen Square in Beijing were filled with cyclists at rush hour, and the sight of a car was unusual. The cities were quiet, with few horns, just the jingle of bicycle bells and the rumble of wheeled carts. People were nervous about talking with us, but at the same time intensely curious about foreigners. They'd crowd around, but then if they saw an official or a policeman approach they'd melt away, not wanting trouble. It was my first real experience of a totalitarian state.

For more than ten years, during the Cultural Revolution and after (1966–1976), religious and cultural expression was completely suppressed, academics punished or killed, foreign influences rooted out and destroyed. Once Mao died in 1976, there seemed to be a relaxing of the regime. Our guides told us about the fall of the Gang of Four (they had been arrested less than a month after Mao's death and were blamed for the excesses of the Cultural Revolution) and the Four Modernizations (designed to bring the economy up to speed).

There was talk of greater openness and of greater freedom for private enterprise, religion, and cultural expression. In Xi'an, we visited the main mosque, newly reopened and very beautiful. We learned a little about the Hui (see page 216). In Xinjiang, the Uighur people (see page 90) in Urumqi and Turpan and the Kazakhs in the mountains (see page 157) wore bright colors—the women in skirts and headscarves rather than the drab pants of women in central China, the men still in Mao-style cotton shirts and pants, but with embroidered skullcaps and leather boots that made each person very individual-looking and so unlike the Han.

It was in Xinjiang that we first saw food (mostly stacks of melons, a few vegetables, and flatbreads) for sale in the street. In the cities of Central Asia, the only shopping possibilities were department stores, drab, grim places with not much for sale and very surly government-employed staff with no interest in helping customers. The few well-stocked shelves were those in the foreign-currency section of the stores, where only dollars or other hard currencies were accepted.

I came away from that trip fascinated by my glimpse of the non-Han peoples living in the areas beyond the Great Wall. I wondered how those people felt, dominated by the central government and by the Han majority. I wondered if I would ever be able to travel freely along the Silk Road and in Inner Mongolia, or if I'd ever be able to spend time in Tibet and the tribal areas in the south. It seemed very unlikely at the time. . . . **N**

OPPOSITE: *Uighur men and boys, full of life and curiosity, at the Sunday bazaar in Kashgar.*

DAI TART GREEN SALSA

Like their cousins the Lao and the Shan, the Dai people of southern Yunnan are brilliant grillers. They use fire not only to cook but also to impart distinctive flavor to various dishes. We first tasted this olive-green salsa in a Dai household in Menghan, a market town on the Mekong River about a day's drive from the Lao border.

This salsa is a member of the family of dishes known as *jaew* in the Tai languages. They're made of grilled ingredients that are pounded or processed to a sauce, then served as a condiment or as an accompaniment to rice meals. The traditional ingredient here is *makawk*, a sour fruit known in English as a hog plum (see Glossary for more). A close equivalent in terms of taste and tartness is the North American tomatillo; the recipe gives instructions for both.

The flavors are nicely balanced between the tart-acid of the fruit and the sweetness of the grilled shallots and garlic, and they are anchored by the warm taste of the grill. This is a rare example of a southeast Asian salsa that has no chile heat.

Serve with grilled or roasted meat, such as Dai Grilled Chicken (page 252) or Lisu Spice-Rubbed Roast Pork (page 314), or as a dip for Sticky Rice (see page 162). [PHOTOGRAPH ON PAGE 165]

¾ pound tomatillos (or hog plums, if available; see headnote)

1 cup shallots, preferably Asian shallots (see Glossary),
   not peeled, halved lengthwise if large

1 medium head garlic cloves, separated but not peeled
   (about ⅓ cup)

¼ cup water

1 teaspoon salt, or to taste

2 ounces (¼ cup) ground pork

½ cup chopped coriander

If grilling, prepare a medium-hot fire in a charcoal grill or preheat a gas grill. Place the tomatillos (or hog plums), shallots, and garlic cloves on a grill screen or other fine-mesh surface on the grill. *Alternatively,* place them in two heavy (preferably cast-iron) skillets over medium-high heat. Grill or cook, turning frequently, until well softened and touched with black patches all over, 10 to 15 minutes, depending on your cooking method. Set aside to cool.

Meanwhile, place the water in a small pan and bring to a boil. Add the salt and pork and cook, stirring to break up lumps and to prevent sticking, until all the pork has changed color, about 1 minute. Set aside.

Peel the grilled tomatillos, shallots, and garlic and trim off any very black spots. Place them in a blender or food processor and pulse or process briefly, just until you have a coarse sauce texture. Turn out into a bowl. Add the pork with its cooking liquid, and stir to blend together.

Just before you serve the salsa, stir in the coriander. Taste and adjust the salt if you wish. Serve in a decorative bowl and provide a serving spoon so guests can help themselves.

Leftovers will keep for several days stored in a tightly sealed glass container in the refrigerator.

Makes 2 cups

GRASSLANDS HERB SALSA

For three brief months in the summer the grasslands of Inner Mongolia are like a rolling green ocean under a blue, blue sky. A cyclist rides across the grasslands near Ulan Tokay, north of Hohhot.

In Manzhouli, on the border between Inner Mongolia and Siberia, I shared a convivial meal of lamb hot pot at a small lively restaurant with Driver Lin (see page 307) and another friend. Manzhouli is a wild place, as most border towns are, a place where goods and services, both legal and illegal, are bought and sold and lots of money seems to change hands.

The condiments that came with the hot pot were distinctive, as they often are, for every cook adds a twist. The one I particularly liked at this place was a thick green herb salsa spiked with a little vinegar. Here is our take on that bright-tasting sauce.

Serve this to accompany grilled or roast chicken or lamb. We also like it drizzled on *pulao* or on plain rice.

> 2 cups packed coriander leaves and stems, or substitute
>   mint leaves
> ½ cup coarsely chopped scallions (white and tender green parts)
> 2 tablespoons rice vinegar
> ¼ teaspoon salt, or to taste

Place the herbs and scallions in a food processor or a mini-chopper and process to a coarse paste. Add the vinegar and salt and pulse to blend. *Alternatively*, use a mortar and pestle to reduce the greens to a coarse paste, then add the vinegar and salt and mix well. Taste and adjust the seasoning if you wish.

Transfer to a small serving bowl and serve with a small spoon so guests can help themselves.

Makes about ¾ cup

QUICK TOMATO-ONION CHUTNEY

One day a young Tibetan woman named Tsai and I went out for lunch in Labrang, to a small Tibetan café-restaurant up on the second floor, overlooking the main street. Tsai ordered *sha-pa-le* (see Savory Tibetan Breads, page 214), while I asked for *ping sha* (see Beef with Mushrooms and Cellophane Noodles, page 280). Her deep-fried breads, small and delicious, came with this mildly spiced tomato chutney. It's a new thing, the use of a relish or chutney in Tibetan meals; it seems to be connected with the return of Tibetans from India and Nepal.

This is a wonderful accompaniment for Cheese Momos (page 212) or other deep-fried snacks, and it makes a good condiment for grilled or roast lamb and pork.

2 tablespoons peanut oil or vegetable oil

¼ teaspoon cumin seeds or ground cumin

½ cup minced onion

1 dried red chile

½ to 1 teaspoon salt, or to taste

2 medium tomatoes (½ pound total), chopped

½ cup minced coriander or Chinese celery leaves (optional)

Heat the oil in a wok or heavy skillet over medium-high heat. Add the cumin seeds and let them crackle and get aromatic, about 20 seconds (or just 5 seconds for ground cumin), then add the onion and chile. Stir briefly, then add ½ teaspoon salt. Cook, stirring frequently, until the onion is translucent, about 5 minutes.

Add the tomatoes and stir for a minute or so, until they start giving off their liquid.

Bring to a boil, then lower the heat, cover, and simmer until the tomatoes are soft, about 10 minutes. Remove the cover, lower the heat, and simmer a little longer, to reduce the liquid slightly.

Taste for salt and adjust if you wish. (We like this slightly salty, especially if we're serving it with grilled or roast meat, so we usually add at least another ½ teaspoon.) Just before serving, stir in the herbs, if using.

Makes a generous 1 cup

TIBETAN GINGER-TOMATO CHUTNEY: I encountered another version of this salsa-like condiment in Lhasa. There the touch of heat came from ginger rather than from dried red chile. Substitute 1 tablespoon minced ginger for the dried chile. This chutney pairs especially well with beef dishes. [PHOTOGRAPH ON PAGE 153]

TENZIN'S QUICK-PICKLED RADISH THREADS

We've been struck by how often there's a little radish included in Tibetan dishes (see Tsampa Soup, page 47, for example). The radishes in Tibet are large and mostly white, like high-altitude cousins of the daikon radish (known also as icicle radish, or by its Hindi name, *mooli*). Some have a blush of pink on them, and they are sometimes rounded rather than long and straight. In this book we've called for daikon whenever Tibetan radish is traditionally used.

In Tibet, radishes also come to the table as a condiment, like a concentrated little salad. The radish is grated, then stored with flavorings in a vinegar brine and allowed to stand; in a few days, it's ready to be eaten. Like any household standby, radish pickle can vary a lot, depending on the cook's tastes or family traditions.

We learned our version from our friend Tenzin, in Lhasa. We have known him since the first time we were in Tibet, in 1985, when he ran the travelers' hostel we stayed at near the Jokhang Temple. Each time we planned to stay in Lhasa, we'd write ahead to Tenzin to try to book our favorite room. We'd give him English lessons, sitting out on the roof, looking over the old section of Lhasa, with its flat rooftops, to the golden ornaments on the Jokhang Temple and the hills beyond.

When I returned to Lhasa after a gap of nineteen years, I found Tenzin married and with a good job. It was wonderful to see him so settled and content. I had a lot of food questions for him, and we spent time in his kitchen talking about basics, including this pickle. Tenzin told me that some people also put in garlic or MSG. We prefer to flavor ours with only ginger, Sichuan pepper, scallion, and a little onion.

This pickle is very tart and vinegary (though it mellows over time), and is meant to be eaten as a condiment, an accompaniment to meat and rice, not on its own. (But I also love to eat it a nontraditional way: I start with good bread, perhaps lightly toasted, spread on unsalted butter, then top it with generous clumps of pickled radish.)

The radish is cut into long, thin shreds, which we do using a coarse grater; you could also slice it into julienne using a Benriner or other vegetable slicer. The shreds are placed in a jar with the flavorings, the salt and vinegar are added, and the jar is sealed and shaken to mix all the flavors. Then it's set in the sun to ferment for a couple of days. In warm weather, the pickle is ready in 2 days; in colder weather, or with cloudy days, allow 4 days.

Because daikon radish is available all year round, this quick pickle can be made at any time of year and stored in the refrigerator for weeks. When the jar starts to run low, it's time to make another batch.

1 pound daikon radish, peeled and coarsely grated or thinly sliced (see headnote)
2 medium scallions, minced
½ small onion, cut into thin slices
About 2 tablespoons minced ginger
2 tablespoons kosher salt
1 to 2 tablespoons minced garlic (optional)
1 teaspoon dry-roasted Sichuan peppercorns, ground (optional)
About 3 cups rice vinegar

Place the radish, scallions, onion, and ginger in a large bowl and toss to mix them well. Stuff half the mixture into a sterilized 4-quart jar and add 1 tablespoon of the salt and the garlic and/or Sichuan pepper if you wish. Add the remaining radish mixture and the second tablespoon of salt, and pour on the vinegar, which should cover the mixture completely. Seal and shake the jar to distribute the vinegar well.

Place in a sunny spot by a window for 2 to 4 days (see headnote), giving the jar a shake occasionally to help blend the flavors. It is now ready to use. The pickle will keep indefinitely if well sealed and refrigerated.

To serve, use a clean spoon or fork or chopsticks to lift out a clump of radish strands and place them in a condiment bowl.

Makes 4 cups

OPPOSITE: *Lhasa Yellow Achar (page 28).* LEFT: *An older monk, a man who lived through the turmoil of the Cultural Revolution, sits outside the temple in Gyantse, in central Tibet, reading prayers from the book in his lap.* RIGHT: *At the huge Tibetan Buddhist monastery of Labrang, in the province of Gansu, the walls around the complex are lined with tall prayer wheels. The devout give each prayer wheel a vigorous turn as they walk past, always circumambulating the temples in a clockwise direction.*

HANI CHILE-GARLIC PASTE

This condiment for rice from the Hani people of the hills of southern Yunnan (see page 316) uses garlic and shallots that are quickly grilled, then pounded to a paste with chiles and salt. The sauce is thick and spicy hot, a great condiment for grilled meats of all kinds.

1 medium head garlic, cloves separated but not peeled

2 shallots, not peeled

¼ teaspoon salt, or to taste

3 fresh bird chiles or serrano chiles

Place the unpeeled garlic and shallots in the coals of a fire or in a gas flame (on a stovetop or grill) and cook, turning occasionally, until well blackened; *alternatively*, place on a lightly oiled baking sheet and roast in a 400°F oven until softened, 15 to 20 minutes. Remove and let cool.

Peel off the blackened outer layers, then coarsely chop the garlic and shallots. Place in a mortar or food processor with the salt. Slice off and discard the stems of the chiles, then coarsely chop the chiles and add to the other ingredients. Pound or process to a coarse paste.

Transfer to a small dish and serve with a small spoon.

Makes a scant ¼ cup

MONGOLIAN ROASTED GARLIC PASTE: In northeastern Inner Mongolia, I came across another version of garlic paste, served as a condiment with Beef Hot Pot (page 282). It complements Mongolian Barbecue (page 263) and all kinds of grilled meat very well. Use 1 cup unpeeled garlic cloves (about 2 large heads), ¼ to ½ teaspoon cayenne, ½ teaspoon salt, and ¼ teaspoon roasted sesame oil. Cook the garlic as above. Then cut off the end of each clove, squeeze the flesh from the skin, and mash it in a small bowl or a mortar. Stir in the cayenne, salt, and sesame oil and serve warm or at room temperature.

Makes about ¼ cup

LHASA YELLOW ACHAR

The term *achar* is used in Nepal (and, farther afield, in Malaysia) for any side relish or chutney. It's a word to set your mouth tingling and watering with anticipation. And it's a word that is now quite common in Lhasa, as a number of Tibetans who were once in exile have come back and opened small restaurants, often staffed by cooks from Nepal.

This little side dish is tart from its basic ingredient, Tenzin's Quick-Pickled Radish Threads, and pale yellow from turmeric. It is a wonderful foil for the lushness of deep-fried snacks such as Cheese Momos (page 212) and for meat dishes such as Lisu Spice-Rubbed Roast Pork (page 314), Classic Lhasa Beef and Potato Stew (page 283), or Keshmah Kebabs (page 262). [PHOTOGRAPH ON PAGE 26]

1 to 2 tablespoons peanut, canola, or vegetable oil

1 tablespoon minced ginger

¼ cup minced onion or shallots

1 teaspoon ground cumin

½ teaspoon ground coriander

1 teaspoon salt

½ teaspoon Chile Oil (page 29), Guizhou Chile Paste (page 35), or store-bought chile paste, or substitute ¼ teaspoon cayenne, or to taste

1 cup Tenzin's Quick-Pickled Radish Threads (page 25)

1 teaspoon turmeric

½ cup coarsely chopped coriander

Place a wok or heavy skillet over medium-high heat. Add the oil, then add the ginger and onion or shallots and stir-fry briefly. Toss in the cumin, coriander, salt, and chile oil or paste or cayenne. Stir-fry until the onion or shallots are tender, about 2 minutes. Add the radish pickle and turmeric and cook, stirring frequently to prevent sticking, until the flavors have blended, 2 to 3 minutes. Turn out into a bowl.

Just before serving, stir in the chopped coriander. Store leftovers in a nonreactive container in the refrigerator for no more than 2 days.

Makes 1 cup

CHILE OIL

Chile oil is one of those simple additions to the pantry that you are likely to find yourself using in all sorts of ways. Although you can buy it in Chinese and Southeast Asian grocery stores, the commercial version is usually made with cottonseed oil, which has an unpleasant aftertaste. Better to quickly make up a batch yourself. It keeps well in the refrigerator. Add a dash of it to spike a salad dressing or a stir-fry, or include it in a dipping sauce.

1 cup peanut oil or vegetable oil
5 to 6 tablespoons chile pepper flakes or crushed dried red chiles

Heat the oil in a wok or skillet until just starting to smoke. Remove from the heat and toss in the dried chile flakes or pieces. Let stand until cooled to room temperature.

Transfer to a clean, dry glass jar and store, well-sealed, in the refrigerator. The chiles will continue infusing the oil.

To use, scoop out the oil, or a mixture of oil and chile flakes, with a clean, dry spoon. You can also, after a week or so, strain the chile out, leaving you with a beautiful clear reddish orange oil.

Makes about 1 cup

At a market near Dali, Yunnan, in the drizzle of late monsoon rains, a woman eats a bowl of rice noodles topped with various condiments.

YUNNAN HILLS GINGER PASTE

We've eaten this ginger paste at market stalls in Yunnan, served as a spicy topping for rice-noodle soups or for fermented rice curd. Ginger is pounded to a paste in a mortar with some salt, then blended with a little water to extend it. Dollop it on hot chicken noodle or rice soups to give them an extra spike of flavor, especially in the winter, when warming tastes are most welcome. Put a tablespoon or so of ginger paste on top of your bowl of hot soup, then stir in as you eat. You can also use it as a topping for cubes of fresh tofu.

½ cup chopped ginger
Pinch of salt
Water as needed

Place the ginger and salt in a large mortar or in a food processor and pound or process to a paste. Transfer to a bowl, and stir in a little water to make a smooth paste.

Makes about ⅓ cup

Naomi traveled to China for the first time in 1980 (see "Summer 1980," page 21) but we didn't know each other then, and my first trip was later. In 1982, I was living in Taipei, Taiwan, working as an English teacher, studying some Mandarin, and taking cooking classes. Every once in a while I'd hear a story about someone visiting "the Mainland," traveling independently, but it seemed very hard to believe. The rumor was that a visa could be arranged in Hong Kong from a travel agent in Chungking Mansions, a low-life building full of bottom-end hostels, Indian restaurants, and drug deals. It all seemed a bit unlikely—it was "Communist China," after all.

But the rumor persisted, and before long I met people who'd made the trip. At first, only seven cities in China were open to independent travelers. After that it became thirteen, then twenty-one. If you were traveling on a train or a bus and it stopped in a "closed" town or city, you weren't allowed to get off. No one seemed to know exactly why some cities were closed and others open. One obvious reason was that China had very little infrastructure for foreigners, very few hotels, very few restaurants. But China was also highly xenophobic. The biggest question was really why the Chinese government was allowing independent travel at all.

My first trip came in March 1984. I got my visa in Hong Kong and caught a boat to Guangzhou, another boat overnight up the Pearl River, then a local bus to a town called Yangshuo, in Guangxi, a place other travelers had told me to go. In Yangshuo, I stayed in People's Hotel Number One (not that there was a Number Two). On my second night, there was torrential rain and the whole ground floor flooded with several feet of water, so I was moved to the second floor.

Every day was interesting. I watched fishermen fishing with cormorants on the river, and in the countryside outside town, I walked through intensely gardened fields. Eating was a big puzzle. There was only one restaurant in Yangshuo, the People's Restaurant, and it had very strict hours that weren't immediately obvious to me. Breakfast began at something like six A.M. and finished exactly ninety minutes later. If you missed it by one minute, you wouldn't be served. And the same for lunch and dinner. It was like eating in a school cafeteria, only far more militaristic and several degrees gloomier.

Upon entering the restaurant, I first had to purchase little coupons from a sullen clerk who sat behind a tiny barred window, then take the coupons to another place, where I'd be served. My problem was I had no idea what was available, or what the price was. And, unlike almost anywhere else in the world, the people working there were almost unanimously not interested in helping or in being nice. It was institutional China, something I would learn a lot about in the years to come.

The food itself was great, simple but great. In the morning, I'd have hot soybean milk and flatbreads filled with buckwheat honey. For lunch and dinner, I'd eat a big bowl of rice served with a plate of stir-fried local greens, and another of spicy stir-fried tofu. Beer was available, though it required a separate coupon from a different clerk. It came served in a large soup bowl and cost ten fen, which was about two and a half cents.

From Yangshuo I traveled by train to Kunming, and then by bus to the small walled town of Dali, another place I'd been told to visit. Dali was a Bai town, not a Han town, and the feel was different, more relaxed, and more friendly. J

OPPOSITE: *A Bai woman tries on a bracelet at the market in Xiapin, near Dali. She's wearing traditional clothing, and her basket is supported by a tump line so that her head takes the weight, a method used by many cultures in Yunnan and Southeast Asia.*

ABOVE: *A child explores a huge mortar and its contents of pounded dried red chiles, at the market in the Dai town of Menghan in southern Yunnan.*

OPPOSITE, LEFT: *Pickled Red Chiles (page 34).* OPPOSITE, RIGHT: *Chiles for sale in the mist and fog of Yuanyang, in the hills of southeastern Yunnan.*

PICKLED RED CHILES

Pickling is an age-old way of storing seasonally available ingredients; it's also a way of lengthening the time you can keep any fresh ingredient successfully. Pickled chiles are a staple in many places beyond the Great Wall, as well as in parts of central China. They are, we've discovered, very handy and easy to have on hand. Over time, the heat of the chiles becomes a little muted, and the balance of flavors shifts toward slightly sweet, but the chiles keep their bright color and some texture too. We now rely on them as a staple. You can use them in place of fresh chiles when stir-frying (for example, in Pork with Napa Cabbage and Chiles, page 298) or put them out as a table condiment (especially when serving Hui-style lamb dishes, or any grilled meat).

You can buy jars of bright red "made-in-Thailand" pickled chiles in many Asian groceries, but they are sweeter and hotter than the pickled chiles we've come across in the outlying mountain and desert areas of China, from Yunnan and Guizhou to Qinghai and Xinjiang. And it's very easy to make your own. These Yunnanese-style pickled chiles are less hot than the Thai version and have no added sweetness. They're spiked with a little Sichuan pepper. Make up a batch when you come across very red ripe cayenne chiles. You can increase the yield by scaling the recipe up in proportion. [PHOTOGRAPH ON PAGE 33]

> About ¼ pound red cayenne chiles (about eight 6-inch-long
>   chiles) (see Note on Chile Alternatives, below)
> 1 cup rice vinegar
> 1 tablespoon kosher salt
> ¼ teaspoon Sichuan peppercorns
> 1 star anise, whole or in pieces (optional)

Wash the chiles, and cut off the stems. Cut into approximately ½-inch slices. Measure out 1 cup and set aside.

Heat the vinegar in a nonreactive pan. Add the salt and stir until it dissolves. Add the peppercorns and star anise, if using. Bring to a boil, then lower the heat and simmer for 30 seconds or so. Remove from the heat and let cool to lukewarm.

Meanwhile, sterilize a 1-cup canning jar, lid, and ring.

Stuff the sliced chiles into the jar, pressing down to compact them a little. Transfer the vinegar and spices to a cup with a spout and then slowly pour the liquid and spices into the jar, filling it right to the top. (You may have several tablespoons of vinegar left.) Put on the lid and then screw the ring on tightly.

Set the jar in a sunny spot for 2 days, then refrigerate. The pickles will be ready in 2 weeks and will keep well for 3 months.

Makes 1 cup

NOTE ON CHILE ALTERNATIVES: If you can't find cayennes, you can use serranos, which are smaller than cayennes and have more chile heat. To balance that, we suggest that you strip out their seeds before slicing them: cut off the stem ends, then cut a slit lengthwise in each chile, strip out the seeds, and discard.

NOTE ON PICKLING METHOD: The method here and for Tenzin's Quick-Pickled Radish Threads (page 25) calls for the vinegared and brined raw ingredients to be set out in the sun. It's a traditional method we have seen in Tibet, Guizhou, and Yunnan. Perhaps the warmth or the sunlight encourages fermentation, but we don't know the why, only that it's the usual way. The pickled chiles need more time to soak and soften than the radish threads, and we call for refrigeration for that process, though they could also be stored in a cool cupboard.

QUICK PICKLED CHILES: To make up a last-minute version, say for use in a recipe, or to put out as an improvised condiment, start with fresh red cayennes. Strip out the seeds, then slice as above and place in a bowl. Bring the hot vinegar, salt, and spice mixture to a boil, then pour over the sliced chiles. Put a small plate or lid on top to weight the chiles down so they stay immersed. Let stand for half an hour or more before draining and serving.

GUIZHOU CHILE PASTE

We love chile pastes and condiments of all kinds. They highlight the tastes of the foods they accompany and complement them, and they give each person a chance to custom-flavor every mouthful. Once you've made chile paste, it sits handily in the refrigerator, ready to add heat and dimension to any meal.

We've encountered all kinds of chile pastes in our wanderings beyond the Great Wall. As with chile pastes from other parts of the world (such as North African *harissa* and Lao *jaew*), the basic ingredient is dried red chiles. After that, the options are many. In Guizhou, a hilly province in southern China bordered by four other provinces—Sichuan, Yunnan, Hunan, and Guangxi—Sichuan pepper is used a great deal (though not in the overwhelming way it often is in Sichuan). So the chile pastes we've encountered there usually have a hint or more of Sichuan pepper, as this recipe does, and no sweetness at all.

1 cup dried red chiles, stemmed

1 cup boiling water

1 teaspoon salt

2 tablespoons peanut oil or vegetable oil

2 tablespoons minced shallots

1 teaspoon Sichuan peppercorns, ground (see Note)

1 tablespoon rice vinegar

Place the chiles in a bowl and pour the boiling water over. Weight the chiles down with a small lid or plate to keep them immersed in the water. Let soak for an hour, or until softened.

Transfer the chiles and soaking water to a food processor. Add the salt and process to a puree. Return the puree to the bowl.

Heat a wok over high heat. Add the oil and lower the heat to medium, then toss in the shallots and Sichuan pepper and stir-fry until the shallots are translucent, 2 to 3 minutes. Add the chile puree (watch out for spattering) and bring to a boil, then reduce the heat and simmer, stirring frequently, for about 5 minutes, until the liquid is reduced by half or so.

Transfer to a bowl and stir in the vinegar. Let cool before transferring to a clean, dry glass jar, and tightly seal with a clean lid. Store in the refrigerator.

Makes a generous ½ cup

NOTE ON SICHUAN PEPPER: Sichuan pepper has a distinctive taste and effect on the mouth. If you love it, then do feel free to increase the quantity here to 1½ or 2 teaspoons. The chile paste will then have, besides chile heat, some of the tongue-numbing powers of Sichuan pepper, as well as a stronger hit of flavor.

ALL-PURPOSE GUIZHOU BASTING SAUCE FOR THE GRILL: If you are grilling meat, fish, or vegetables, Guizhou Chile Paste diluted with oil makes a dynamite basting sauce. Use 1 teaspoon chile paste for every 2 tablespoons peanut oil or vegetable oil. Whisk well to blend them together, then brush lightly onto your meat or fish or vegetables before you grill. Brush again with the flavored oil (whisk just before you do) shortly before you remove the food from the heat.

TRIBAL PEPPER-SALT

People who grill meat know that a simple spice rub can transform flavors, and textures too. Beyond the Great Wall, a simple pepper-salt (a roughly 3 to 1 blend of salt and ground toasted Sichuan pepper) is often used as a seasoning and spice rub. But a number of the peoples who live in the hills and valleys of southern Yunnan and of Guizhou provinces have a more chile-hot take on the classic.

We learned this version of pepper-salt when eating in a Dai household (see page 237) in southern Yunnan. Later we met it again in the food of the Miao (page 183) and the Dong (page 120) in Guizhou, as well as among the Yi (page 316) near the Vietnamese border in Yunnan. Use it as a dry rub on meat before roasting or grilling; put it out on the table as a condiment; add it to oil (see Pepper-Salt Basting Oil, below); or use in other recipes as suggested.

Consider the recipe proportions here as a guide. You may choose to alter them once you've tried the pepper-salt. Another option is to substitute black peppercorns for the dried red chiles.

3 dried red chiles or 2 teaspoons black peppercorns
2 tablespoons kosher salt
1 teaspoon Sichuan peppercorns

If using dried chiles, dry-roast them in a small heavy skillet over medium-high heat until they soften, about 1 minute. Turn out and coarsely chop; discard any tough stems. Transfer to a spice grinder or clean coffee grinder, or to a mortar, add 1 tablespoon of the salt, and grind or pound to a powder. Turn out into a bowl and set aside.

Place the Sichuan peppercorns, and the black peppercorns, if using, in the skillet and dry-roast until just aromatic, 1 to 2 minutes. Transfer to the spice or coffee grinder or mortar, add the remaining 1 tablespoon salt (or the 2 tablespoons if you aren't using dried chiles) and grind or pound to a powder. Add the powder to the ground chile-salt. Let cool completely before storing in a clean glass jar.

Makes about 3 tablespoons

PEPPER-SALT BASTING OIL: Use the pepper-salt to flavor oil, for basting when you are grilling food. Stir about 1 tablespoon powder into ¼ cup oil (we like it in olive oil, as well as in more traditional peanut oil or lard). Brush onto vegetables or meat just before you grill and/or as they are grilling.

LEFT: *Outside the Dong village of Zhaoxing, in Guizhou, on a path leading up a hillside past rice terraces and small streams, we came upon a shrine presided over by these totemic figures. Offerings of flowers and of rice and water were in front of them. The Dong are animists, with different villages and areas worshipping slightly different beings, so we don't know exactly who these figures represent.*
OPPOSITE: *Two kinds of heat: on the left are Sichuan peppercorns and on the right, flakes of dried red chile.*

LEFT: *Tibetan families sit watching a school event in Litang. In this town in western Sichuan, as in most majority-Tibetan areas outside the Tibetan Autonomous Region, Tibetan culture feels relatively strong and vibrant. The woman on the right is spinning a prayer wheel as she talks to the baby. Inside the wheel are printed prayers.* RIGHT: *An older woman in Lhasa smiles at us as she makes her way around the Barkhor, the circular route around the Jokhang temple, a place of pilgrimage and prayer in the center of Lhasa. She holds her string of prayer beads in her left hand.*

THE TIBETAN PEOPLE

If you look for Tibet on a current map of China, what you will find is an area labeled Tibet Autonomous Region. The TAR, as it is often referred to, is a province of the People's Republic of China. Following the Revolution in China, in 1949, the Beijing government took military control of Tibet's eastern areas in 1950, and then of central and western Tibet in 1959, when the Dalai Lama fled to India along with many monks and other Tibetans. The borders of Tibet were redrawn so that most of its eastern region (Kham) and northeastern region (Amdo) became part of the neighboring provinces.

Ethnographic (or cultural) Tibet is much larger than the TAR. More than half the Tibetans in China live outside the TAR, primarily in neighboring areas in the provinces of Qinghai, Sichuan, and Yunnan. (It is difficult to find accurate population figures for all Tibetans living in China; published estimates vary from four to six million.)

It is in the majority Tibetan areas adjacent to the TAR, as well as in far western Tibet, that we've encountered Tibetans living most traditionally. Lhasa and nearby areas of central Tibet are the focus of a huge amount of Chinese military control. The Tibetan population there has been swamped by masses of Han (Chinese) and Hui (Chinese Muslim) migration for two generations, and Tibetan life there has been closely monitored and restricted by the authorities since 1959. There are still Tibetan political prisoners in China.

Because Tibetan-inhabited areas range over a vast and diverse region, Tibetan food varies widely. In the fertile valleys of central and eastern Tibet, many kinds of vegetables and several grains (wheat and barley) are grown, as well as rapeseed (canola), raised for its oil.

Houses are usually built of stone, beautiful and solid, with small multipaned windows. In some forested parts of the Kham region (in the Tibetan areas of Sichuan and Yunnan provinces), houses are traditionally built of wood. The livestock (yaks; yak-cow crossbreeds called *dzomo*, used for milk; and goats and sheep) occupy the ground level, while the living quarters are upstairs, where it is warmer and sunnier. The flat rooftops are used for drying vegetables, meat, chiles, and firewood, possible because most of Tibet is high desert with relatively little snow or rain.

In the high-altitude regions of western Tibet and Qinghai, Tibetan nomads move with their herds from grazing ground to grazing ground. The nomads are known as Drogpa, or Golok, and live in wool-felt tents (canvas in the summer) that can be packed up onto the yaks when it's time to move camp. The nomads live from their herds, selling the wool from the sheep and goats to traders and using the money to buy tea as well as barley. Some gather salt from the saline lakes of the high plateau, which they sell to traders; others gather medicinal plants to sell.

The government restricts the areas in which the nomads graze their herds, especially in the eastern and northeastern regions, arguing that the nomads will have better access to education and health care if they settle into fixed communities, and that there will be less overgrazing. But this idea is highly controversial, because it involves changing a lifestyle that has been in place for generations, and one that is uniquely adapted to the environment. No matter which side one agrees with, it is deeply disturbing to see lines of wire fencing running across what for centuries was wide-open grassland.

SOUPS

MANY OF THE DISHES IN THIS CHAPTER, NOTABLY the ones from cold-weather climates, are like Central Asian cousins of the traditional soups, broths, and stews of northern and eastern Europe (Irish stew, for example) and the related pioneer dishes of North America. They are made with potatoes and carrots, a touch of greens when available, and meat for depth of flavor. Cooking is often in one pot and involves long, slow simmering of meat, bones, and vegetables.

The broths give wonderful flavor to other dishes: hot pots, noodle dishes, soups, and stews. And the soups are distinctive, from Tsampa Soup (page 47), with its seductive flavor of roasted grain and its smooth texture, to the delicate balance of tomato and lamb in Hui Tomato-Lamb Noodle Soup (page 59), to the hearty and satisfying Hui Vegetable Soup (page 48), made with no meat at all.

There are recipes here as well from the subtropical hills and valleys of southern Yunnan and Guizhou, where soup is at the heart of the family meal, eaten with rice and an assortment of other dishes, often stir-fries. Even in these milder climates, people turn to soup for comfort and sustenance. The soups are quickly made and have a wonderful inventiveness; see Family Soup Dong-Style (page 49) and Dai Chile-Fish Soup with Flavored Oil (page 54).

OPPOSITE: *"Mongol moto": a motorcycle tailored for cold weather with fur-muffed handlebars, in Hailar, Inner Mongolia.* ABOVE: *Chinese chives: chive flowers (buds) on the left and chives with flat leaves only (also called garlic chives) on the right.*

KAZAKH GOAT BROTH

This is so simple it's hardly a recipe, but it was new to us. In the Altai Mountains in northern Xinjiang, I was invited several times into a Kazakh yurt, where, sitting on carpets and leaning against padded quilts, I watched as meals were cooked over a small portable iron stove fueled with wood. The meals were some of the simplest and best I have ever eaten, often prepared with just a pressure cooker.

Goat shank was simmered in the cooker to make a broth, and while it was cooking, a noodle dough was rolled out (see Kazakh Noodles, page 133). When the broth was ready, the steam was released from the pressure cooker and the meat taken out of the pot, leaving the hot broth on top of the stove. The noodles were then stretched by hand and dropped into the hot broth. It all happened quickly and deftly and looked effortless, with people chatting all the while.

I came home from northern Xinjiang determined to buy a pressure cooker. But in the end, we just cooked the goat shanks in a large soup pot. It was so easy, and so good.

We've come to love goat as a less expensive and very delicious alternative to lamb. Good goat meat, from a reasonably young animal, has a mild lamb flavor. It is becoming more available in North America, and we recommend it highly; look for organic or naturally raised meat (see Glossary for more).

Serve the broth as a clear soup, or use it the traditional way to cook Kazakh Noodles or other homemade or store-bought noodles. Then serve the noodles in the broth, or serve the broth as a side dish to a platter of the noodles, as you please.

1½ pounds goat shank or lamb shank, cut into 1-inch lengths (have the butcher do this)
4 quarts cold water
Salt

Place a cast-iron or other heavy 8-quart pot over low heat. Add the pieces of shank to the dry pot and brown all over, turning occasionally, approximately 15 minutes.

Add the water and raise the heat to bring it to a vigorous boil, then lower the heat and simmer, partially covered, for about 2 hours.

Remove the bones and meat from the broth. Cut the meat into bite-size pieces and put out on a plate, so guests can add it to their soup as they wish. Add salt to taste to the broth (we normally start with ½ teaspoon salt for 2 cups broth), and ladle into bowls.

Makes about 8 cups broth; serves 8 as a clear soup, 4 to 6 as a one-dish meal with noodles

A Tibetan man drives a small tractor in the center of Litang, a large Tibetan town in western Sichuan.

TIBETAN BONE BROTH

This useful broth is called *ruthang* in Tibetan. It's traditionally made by simmering yak bones, for which we substitute oxtail or beef shank. It gives many Tibetan recipes great depth of flavor (see, for example, Tsampa Soup, page 47, and Stir-Fried Stem Lettuce Lhasa-Style, page 103), and we find ourselves happy to always have a stash of it in the freezer, especially in the colder months of the year.

> 2 pounds oxtail or bone-in beef shank, chopped into 8 to 12
>   pieces (have the butcher do this)
> About 9 cups water
> 1 tablespoon minced or crushed ginger
> 1 star anise (optional)
> 1 teaspoon salt

Rinse the beef thoroughly in several changes of lukewarm water. Place in a large heavy pot and add enough cold water to cover by an inch or two. Bring to a boil and skim off the foam. Add the ginger, star anise, if using, and salt, reduce the heat, and simmer, partly covered, for 1 hour.

Pour the broth through a sieve or strainer into a bowl. (Set the bones and meat aside if you wish, to be served with rice or noodles, or discard them.) If not using the broth immediately, let it cool completely, then store it in a well-sealed container in the refrigerator, or freeze in 2-cup containers.

Makes about 8 cups

TSAMPA SOUP

There is something very soothing and sustaining about *tsam-thuk*, as this classic soup is called in Lhasa dialect. It is another take on the freshly-baked-bread-with-meat idea that characterizes the food of central Asia (and, in fact, much of the traditional cooking of northern Europe as well). Here, instead of flatbreads wrapped around fire-cooked kebabs, the meal is soup, a beef broth thickened with tsampa, the roasted barley ground into flour that is a Tibetan staple. There's a seductive taste, almost nutty, from the roasted grain, and a smoothness on the tongue from the blend of tsampa and the butter added at the last moment. *"Shin-bu-du!* (Delicious!)"

This is a Lhasa version, made with strips of steak that we substitute for the traditional yak meat. In other more rural places, where fresh meat is not often available, cooks would usually include small pieces of dried yak meat.

1¼ cups Tsampa (page 180), or substitute 1 cup barley flour,
    dry-roasted in a skillet until golden

¼ pound daikon radish (about ½ small radish)

6 cups Tibetan Bone Broth (page 45) or beef or chicken broth

2 tablespoons peanut oil, vegetable oil, or butter

½ medium onion, thinly sliced

½ to ¾ pound boneless beef round or sirloin steak, cut into
    strips about 1½ to 2 inches long and ¼ inch wide

2 to 3 cups water

2 to 2½ teaspoons salt, or to taste (see Note)

1½ to 2 cups baby spinach leaves or coarsely chopped regular
    spinach

2 tablespoons butter

To make sure your tsampa or roasted flour is fine enough, pass it through a fine sieve. Set aside.

Peel the daikon radish, then grate it on a coarse grater into long strands. Set aside.

Pour 3 cups of the broth into a wide heavy pot (4 quarts is a good size) and bring to a boil. Add the tsampa or roasted flour and stir until smooth. Add the remaining 3 cups broth and bring to a boil. Add the radish strands and simmer until tender, about 10 minutes.

Meanwhile, heat the oil or butter in a heavy skillet over medium heat. Add the onion and sauté gently for several minutes. Add the meat strips and ½ teaspoon salt, raise the heat to medium-high, and cook, turning once, just until the beef has changed color, about 3 minutes total. Use tongs to lift out the meat and set it aside on a plate. Add the onion and oil or butter to the soup.

To deglaze the skillet, place the pan over high heat, add 1 cup water, and bring to a boil. Scrape the bottom of the pan with a spatula to detach any browned bits or caramelized juices, then add the flavored water to the soup. (*The recipe can be prepared ahead to this point and set aside for up to 1 hour. Or let cool, and refrigerate for up to 36 hours. Bring the soup to a simmer before proceeding.*)

Add 1 cup more water to the soup and bring back to a simmer. Add the meat and bring back to a simmer. Add extra water if you wish a thinner broth. Taste for salt and add up to 2 more teaspoons if necessary. Add the spinach leaves to the simmering broth. When they turn bright green, after a minute or two, add the butter and stir to blend it in.

Serve the soup hot in large bowls, with bread, or with rice if you prefer.

Serves 4 or 5 as a main course, 6 to 8 as a soup course

NOTE ON SEASONING: A number of recipes in Lhasa cooking use soy sauce. These tend to be wealthy people's versions of traditional dishes. People in the country, or those with less money, would usually not include city refinements, such as soy sauce and a greater variety of vegetables. If you'd like, instead of using salt to adjust the seasoning, add 1 to 2 tablespoons soy sauce; it gives an extra depth of flavor.

HUI VEGETABLE SOUP

I learned this easy soup at a tiny hole-in-the wall eatery in a town called Labrang in Tibetan, Xiahe in Chinese, in the southern part of Gansu province. The town is home to a huge Tibetan monastery, also called Labrang, and is surrounded by hilly grasslands. Apart from the majority Tibetan population, there are a large number of Hui people (see page 216).

Three people ran the little eatery: a Hui brother and sister, and the brother's wife, who was about six months pregnant. I watched her early one morning as she prepared the vegetable soup that they would be using all day. It can be served as a hearty cabbage and potato soup or strained and used as a broth or wonderful all-purpose stock, or as the liquid in a vegetarian hot pot. The Hui café owners serve it as a broth over noodles.

The basic flavor and nutrition come from tofu sticks (available in Asian groceries; see the Glossary for more about these useful pantry staples). They're soaked briefly in water to soften, then chopped and stir-fried. The other essentials include a couple of potatoes, peeled and sliced, and plenty of grated or thinly sliced cabbage.

This simple dish is easy to make if you have the right tools: a good sharp cleaver or chef's knife (we prefer a cleaver here) and a heavy stockpot.

A generous handful of tofu sticks (6 or 7 lengths of about
    8 inches; see headnote)
¼ cup peanut oil or vegetable oil
1 tablespoon minced ginger
2 teaspoons salt, or to taste
¼ teaspoon Sichuan peppercorns, ground
½ teaspoon cumin seeds, ground, or ground cumin
¾ pound (2 medium-large) Yukon Gold potatoes or red
    potatoes, peeled and thinly sliced
About ½ pound Napa cabbage (½ small cabbage), thinly sliced
    crosswise (4 cups loosely packed)

About 6 cups water
1 teaspoon Guizhou Chile Paste (page 35), Bright Red Chile
    Paste (page 18), or store-bought chile paste
2 cups loosely packed coarsely torn spinach leaves or chopped
    greens such as amaranth leaves, pea tendrils, or dandelion
    greens

Place the tofu sticks in a large wide bowl, add warm water to cover, and let soak for 15 minutes. Drain, squeeze out the excess water, and chop the sticks into 2-inch lengths. You should have about 1½ cups. Set aside.

Heat the oil in a medium heavy stockpot (about 6 quarts) over medium-high to medium heat. Add the tofu sticks and stir-fry for 2 minutes (if they start sticking, lower the heat a little). Add the ginger, salt, Sichuan pepper, and cumin and stir well. Add the potato slices and cabbage. Cook, stirring and turning the vegetables to expose all surfaces to the flavored oil and the heat, for several minutes, until you see the cabbage starting to wilt a little.

Add 2 cups water and the chile paste and stir to mix. Bring to a boil, cover, and cook at a gentle boil until the vegetables are very soft, about 10 minutes. Add about 4 more cups water and bring to a boil. Cover, reduce the heat, and simmer for 10 minutes. (The soup will look like a fairly thick cabbage soup at this point.)

Add the spinach or other greens and cook, stirring occasionally, just until tender.

Ladle into bowls and serve, perhaps with hunks of bread and some cheese, Western-style.

Serves 4 as a one-dish meal

HUI VEGETARIAN BROTH: Cook the soup for an extra 20 minutes, without adding the greens, then strain it, discarding the solids. Serve as a clear broth, with some greens floating in it if you wish, or use as an ingredient in stir-fries or other dishes. Or dilute it with more water to use as the cooking broth for Hui Vegetable Hot Pot (page 117).

FAMILY SOUP DONG-STYLE

At family suppers in Dong culture (see page 120), the soup goes in the center of the table, with a hot charcoal fire under it to keep it bubbling. The round table has a hole cut in the center to accommodate the pot, which has a rounded bottom and looks like a deep wok. A ladle is set out, and diners use it to scoop some soup into their bowl of rice. Then, using their chopsticks, they help themselves to a bite or two from another dish—say, a stir-fried vegetable or slices of grilled meat.

We like to serve this in a heavy pot that holds the heat. Another option would be to place the soup in a hot pot (see page 269) or an electric rice cooker (as I saw done in a less traditional Dong household), or in a pot over a small portable stove at the table. Put out a ladle so guests can help themselves to broth now and then throughout the meal. Apart from rice, we'd suggest serving a side with some crisp texture, such as Jicama–Tofu Sheet Stir-Fry (page 105) or Green Papaya Salad with Chiles (page 78), as well as a simple grilled meat or fish dish, such as Grilled Pickerel from Burqin (page 228) or Mongolian Lamb Patties (page 272).

2 tablespoons peanut oil

3 dried red chiles

2 tablespoons minced ginger

1 tablespoon minced garlic

½ teaspoon Sichuan peppercorns, coarsely ground

½ pound boneless pork shoulder or butt or fresh ham, thinly
    sliced and cut into pieces approximately 1½ inches by 1 inch

4 cups water

1 teaspoon salt, or to taste

2 tablespoons minced scallion greens or chives (optional)

Heat a large wok or heavy skillet over high heat. Add the oil and swirl gently to coat the pan. Toss in the chiles, ginger, garlic, and Sichuan pepper and stir-fry for 5 to 10 seconds. Add the meat and stir-fry to expose all surfaces to the hot pan until all surfaces have changed color. Add the water and salt and bring to a boil. Reduce the heat and simmer, partially covered, for 10 minutes.

Just before serving, add the scallion greens or chives and simmer just until wilted. Taste for salt and adjust if necessary. Serve hot.

Serves 4 with rice and one or two side dishes

NOTE: When I watched this soup being made in a Dong household, the cook added the water to the stir-fried seasonings, and then the pork went into the boiling water. We prefer to stir-fry the pork slices first, to sear them and give them more flavor, then add the water and simmer.

A Dong woman sits under a drum tower in Zhaoxing, a large Dong village in eastern Guizhou. In the background, the neighborhood's lusheng (large panpipe-like instruments) *are leaning against a wall. Dong drum towers, tall pagoda-like structures made of fir and constructed without nails, are gathering places where children play and older people meet to chat. There are usually wide comfortable wooden benches under the towers, where women work on their embroidery while men play some form of chess or checkers.*

I reached Lhasa for the first time in March 1985. I had flown from Chengdu, in Sichuan, on a very early flight. I remember arriving at the airport hours before dawn, nervous that somehow the flight wouldn't happen. I had my ticket, I even had a special permit for Tibet issued by the Public Security Bureau (a branch of the police), but somehow I thought I'd get stopped: I'd wanted to go to Tibet for as long as I could remember, and had never thought it would be possible. Tibet had been absolutely "closed" all my life, and for all my parents' lives. Several times while in Nepal, I'd trekked near the border, Tibet feeling like a wild, vast unknown on the other side of the mountains.

There were a couple of other Westerners in the queue, but the flight was almost entirely military, PLA (People's Liberation Army). I had no idea why the Beijing government had opened Tibet to foreigners.

At dawn the plane took off, and almost immediately we were over mountains. As far as I could see, there were mountains covered in snow. The mountains were incredibly high, and the narrow valleys amazingly deep. The plane kept heading west, crossing one ridge of mountains, then a cleft of valley, then another ridge of mountains, one after the next. It was like nothing I had ever seen before (or anywhere else since).

We arrived at Gonggar Airport, south of Lhasa, in midmorning. We walked over from the plane to a one-room concrete-block building, the terminal, to pick up our bags. The sun was bright and harsh (at 11,000 feet above sea level), and the wind was cold. I could see for miles in all directions, and there was barely a tree on the landscape. There wasn't a bus or a car in sight. I slept that night in a simple hotel near the airport. The next day a bus appeared and a couple of hours later I was in Lhasa.

I stayed in the dormitory of the Banak Shol Hotel, one of two hotels in Lhasa at that time. There was a restaurant on the ground floor. To order, I'd go into the kitchen and point to ingredients that I wanted, and then a cook would stir-fry them in a large wok set over a roaring wood fire. Stir-fry and rice—the selection wasn't much, but it was hot and good.

After a week or so in Lhasa, I felt as if I knew almost every foreigner in town, at least by sight. There weren't many of us. Everyone exchanged information, because we were all equally ignorant. There were no guidebooks, no local maps. At last someone found a Bank of China office in a tiny house far from the city center, where we could change money, and a sigh of relief went through the hotel.

Lhasa was a bit surreal for me then, and raw. The cold wind blew constantly. My traveling companion, a woman, was assaulted at knifepoint by a Tibetan man. Some of the foreigners in the hotel didn't believe her; they didn't want to know anything bad about Tibet. Tibet was tough, no doubt about it.

It was also extraordinarily full of life. People laughed and joked, and at night they'd eat, drink, sing, and dance. In the market, Tibetans would pull at the hair on my arms and then giggle, or a stranger might give me a piece of dried cheese just to be friendly. Having come from central China, where I'd grown accustomed to suspicious or sullen-looking faces, I was suddenly in a place where people happily engaged with me, where people were more apt to smile than to stare. J

OPPOSITE: *On the bank of the Yarlung Tsangpo (the Tibetan name for the Brahmaputra River), a Tibetan man waits in a sandstorm, spinning his prayer wheel. Samye Gompa, the first Buddhist temple in Tibet (built over 1,100 years ago) and a place of pilgrimage, is four hours walk away. The Tsangpo rises by Mount Kailas, the sacred mountain in western Tibet, and then flows due east for about 800 miles before turning south through the Himalaya and flowing into India and Bangladesh.*

In 1979, long before I ever traveled to China, I sat in on a sociology of China class at the University of Pittsburgh taught by Professor C. K. Yang, a wonderful teacher. The reading list was huge, and it was such great reading, I read every word.

But I am often reminded that much of what we read I later discovered to be relatively untrue. For example, the Cultural Revolution (1966–1976) had been over for several years when I took the course. We now know that it was a terribly destructive time in China, yet the only book we read about it described it positively, as a recharging of the batteries of revolution. Academics in the West, including Professor Yang, remained determined to see China through rose-tinted glasses, and in part for good reason. China had, after all, made a remarkable transition from the utter depths of poverty, although at a price.

Now, in the twenty-first century, I wonder if we in the West are again sometimes deliberately blind when it comes to China, only this time it's not the academics, but the business world. China is a totalitarian state with a terrible human rights record, but it's also an enormous market. Perhaps Western business interests, like the Western academics of the 1960s and '70s, see only the parts of China they want to see. J

ABOVE: *A subtropical streetscape in southern Yunnan, in the town of Menghan.*
OPPOSITE: *Dai Chile-Fish Soup with Flavored Oil (page 54).*

DAI CHILE-FISH SOUP
WITH FLAVORED OIL

Behind most Dai houses in the villages of southern Yunnan, there's a small pond. Fish live there, and when the cook wants fresh fish, she can just go to the pond and scoop one out, or send a child to get one for her. As a result, there's a large Dai repertoire of dishes using fresh fish.

This is one of the easiest soups we know, a pleasure whether served as a fish course in a Western-style meal or as one of several dishes in a rice-centered Southeast Asian–style meal. It reminds us of the fish soups from farther south in the Mekong Valley, in Laos and Cambodia. As in those soups, there is acidity, in this case from tomato, and coriander leaves are used to flavor the broth rather than simply as a garnish.

The soup has a fair amount of chile heat. To cut back on it, reduce the number of chiles. The secret ingredient is the Dai Flavored Oil, which tempers the soup, bringing flavors together. Assemble the ingredients for the oil before you start the broth. That way, you can quickly make the oil while the broth is cooking, then add it to the soup, hot and aromatic, straight from the pan. [PHOTOGRAPH ON PAGE 53]

> 1¼ to 1½ pounds firm-fleshed fish steaks or fillets, such as
>   tilapia, striped bass, or lake trout, or an ocean fish
>   such as snapper or cod
> 4 cups water
> 3 dried red chiles
> 2 fresh green bird chiles or serrano chiles
> 1 tablespoon ginger, cut into small matchsticks
> 1 garlic clove, smashed
> 1 large or 2 small scallions, sliced lengthwise into ribbons,
>   then crosswise into 2-inch lengths
> 1 cup coriander leaves and stems, coarsely chopped
> 1 medium tomato, ripe or green, as you wish, finely chopped
> 2 tablespoons Dai Flavored Oil (page 55), or to taste
> 1½ to 2 teaspoons salt, or to taste
> Freshly ground pepper (see Note on Pepper)

Cut the fish into 1- to 2-inch pieces. Place in a small pot, add the water, whole chiles, ginger, garlic, scallions, and coriander, and bring to a boil, then immediately lower the heat and simmer for 5 minutes.

(Meanwhile, prepare the flavored oil.)

Add the tomato, the oil, including the garlic slices, and 1½ teaspoons salt to the hot broth and simmer for another 5 minutes or so. Taste for salt and adjust if necessary, then add pepper to taste.

Serve hot or warm.

Serves 4 as a soup course or as part of a rice meal

NOTE ON SERVING: The soup is traditionally served with all the flavorings still in it. The chiles and garlic clove are not meant to be eaten, but are just put aside by each diner as he or she eats. If you wish, you can strain the soup before serving it, so that it comes to the table as a broth. In that case, though, we'd suggest that you remove the garlic slices from the flavored oil before adding it to the soup and set them aside, then add them to the broth when you serve it.

NOTE ON PEPPER: Both white and black pepper are used in Southeast Asian cooking. White tends to be used in pale dishes such as this, partly for aesthetic reasons. But we find we always prefer the rich taste of black pepper to that of white; suit yourself.

WHOLE FISH OPTION: We suggest that you use fish steaks or fillets, but you could start with a whole fish weighing close to 2 pounds. Trim off the head and fins, lift the meat off the bone, and cut it into 1- to 2-inch pieces. Then simmer the trimmings and bones in 3 cups water, and use the strained broth as part of the liquid for the soup.

Dai Flavored Oil

Flavored oils are the cook's best friend. In Southeast Asia, these oils—others include scallion oil, chile oil (see page 29), garlic oil, and combinations thereof—are added at the last moment, just before the dish is served. Sometimes they are floated on the surface of a soup when it is served, as olive oil or butter might be on a Mediterranean or European soup, to give a subtle extra richness. Other times, as in this soup, they are added near the end of cooking to pull all the flavors together and accentuate them. Try adding this oil at the last minute to other soups to give them another layer of flavor and heat.

> 2 tablespoons peanut oil or vegetable oil
>
> 4 dried red chiles
>
> 1 tablespoon thinly sliced garlic

Heat the oil in a small heavy skillet. When it is hot, toss in the chiles and garlic and wait several seconds, until they start to brown, then remove from the heat and remove the chiles. Add the oil and garlic to the hot soup, or put out as a table condiment.

Makes a generous 2 tablespoons

NOTE ON SCALING UP: To multiply the recipe, increase the oil and garlic in the same proportion, but the chiles by less than half as much again. For example, to triple the recipe, use 6 tablespoons oil, 3 tablespoons sliced garlic, and only 6 to 8 chiles.

Earthenware containers of rice liquor and pickled vegetables are stored under traditional Dai houses in southern Yunnan.

CELLOPHANE NOODLE SOUP
WITH FISH BALLS

This delicate soup was served at a party, a sit-down banquet for about eighty people that I was invited to in the Dong village of Zhaoxing in eastern Guizhou province. It may look a bit demanding because of the fish balls, but it is surprisingly easy to put together.

You can buy fish balls, fresh or frozen, in most Chinese and Southeast Asian grocery stores, but homemade ones are quick to make and usually better. Start with fish fillets from any white-fleshed fish you like. You can also begin with a whole fish, in which case you'll want one that weighs 2 pounds or a bit more. Use the trimmings to make your broth.

Cellophane noodles are also known as bean threads. They're manufactured from a paste made of processed mung beans that is extruded as very thin noodle strands. They are sold dried, in small cellophane packages weighing 100 grams (less than 4 ounces) or in larger ones weighing 500 grams (about 1 pound). Cellophane noodles must be soaked briefly in hot water before they can be cut into lengths and cooked. When cooked, they are tender and transparent.

SOUP

6 cups water

2 scallions, minced

1 tablespoon minced ginger

About ½ pound fish heads and/or bones or fish steaks or fillets

¾ teaspoon salt, or salt to taste

Half a 100-gram package cellophane noodles (use sharp kitchen scissors to separate the noodles from the larger bundle)

1 teaspoon rice vinegar

1 teaspoon roasted sesame oil

About ¼ cup chopped Chinese celery leaves or coriander leaves (optional)

Dried noodles for the pantry: on the left and right, two versions of cellophane noodles (bean threads) tied with the traditional twine; and in the middle, an opened bundle of rice sticks (dried rice noodles).

FISH BALLS

1 pound boneless, white-fleshed skinless fish fillets
(see headnote)

½ teaspoon minced ginger

½ teaspoon cornstarch

¼ teaspoon salt

Up to ¼ cup water

To make the broth, place the water in a medium pot, add the scallions, ginger, and fish heads and bones, and bring to a vigorous boil. Add the salt, partially cover, and cook at a strong boil for 20 minutes. Lower the heat, cover, and simmer for another half hour or so.

Meanwhile, place the bean threads in a bowl and add hot water to cover. Let soak for 15 to 20 minutes, then drain. Use scissors to cut them into shorter lengths if you wish. Set aside.

To make the fish balls, use a cleaver or sharp knife to finely chop the fish, or pulse in a food processor. Place in a medium bowl, add the minced ginger, cornstarch, and salt, and use your fingers or a fork to mix and blend well. Add 2 tablespoons water and mix well. Scoop up about 1 teaspoon of the mixture and try to press it into a ball. If it is too crumbly to stick together, add a little more water (some fish require a little more or a little less water than others) and squeeze the mixture between your fingers to blend it.

Lightly oil a plate. With moist hands, shape a fish ball by scooping up a scant tablespoon of the fish mixture and lightly rolling it into a ball between your moistened or lightly oiled palms. Set the ball on the plate. It will be a little bumpy perhaps, especially if you hand-chopped the fish; don't worry. Repeat with the remaining fish mixture. You will have 30 to 35 balls. Set aside.

Strain the fish broth through a fine-mesh sieve and discard the solids. You should have between 3 and 4 cups broth. Add water if necessary to bring it up to 4 cups. Pour the broth back into the pot, add the vinegar, and taste for salt. Adjust the seasoning if you wish.

About 10 minutes before you wish to serve the soup, bring the broth to a rapid boil. Add the soaked bean threads and the fish balls and bring to a boil. Reduce the heat slightly and cook at a strong simmer for 5 to 7 minutes, or until the fish balls are cooked through; use a slotted or mesh spoon to turn the balls over so all sides are exposed to the hot broth. They will turn white and expand a little as they cook.

Remove from the heat, add the sesame oil, and serve immediately, topped with a sprinkling of celery leaves or coriander leaves if you wish. Put out the pot or a large serving bowl of the soup, with a ladle and tongs or chopsticks, so guests can help themselves. Or serve in individual bowls, allotting about 5 to 6 fish balls to each, as well as noodles and broth, and top each with several leaves of celery or coriander if you wish.

Serves 4 generously as a soup course, 6 as part of a rice meal

HUI TOMATO-LAMB NOODLE SOUP

I'm in Rekong, a small town in Qinghai, tired from the journey here and wanting only to send a quick e-mail, eat a warm meal, and sleep a long sleep. I ask at my little hotel for directions to the *wan-ba*, as e-mail places are known in China. And there it is, just along from where I'm staying, crowded with young people and thick with cigarette smoke. When I'm finished, and paying for my half hour, I ask the guy at the cash register where to eat. He sends me down the street to a little Hui restaurant that's steamy with the aromas of hot soup and noodles. I sit at a table and soon a huge bowl arrives, a tomato-lamb broth with small tender pieces of lamb and tomato floating in it, served over slippery square-cut noodles. It's completely delicious and satisfying, a warm welcome on a chilly rainy evening.

Dough for Amdo Noodle Squares (page 128), or substitute
¾ pound store-bought wide egg noodles cut into 2- to
3-inch lengths
2 tablespoons peanut oil, vegetable oil, or rendered lamb fat
(see Glossary)
1 tablespoon minced ginger
1 tablespoon minced garlic
¾ pound lamb or goat meat, trimmed of fat and cut into
bite-sized pieces (about 1½ cups)
½ to 1 teaspoon salt, or to taste
2 medium tomatoes, chopped (about 1½ cups)
5 cups hot water
1 cup packed coarsely chopped spinach or other greens (see Note)
About ¾ cup minced coriander

CONDIMENTS
Jinjiang (black rice) vinegar, cider vinegar, or rice vinegar
Soy sauce (optional)

Make the noodle dough, if using, and set aside to rest, covered with plastic wrap.

Heat the oil or fat in a large heavy pot over medium heat. When it is hot, add the ginger and garlic and cook, stirring occasionally, until softened, about 5 minutes. Add the meat, raise the heat to medium-high, and brown it all over. Stir in ½ teaspoon salt, then add the tomatoes. Lower the heat to medium and cook, stirring occasionally, for 5 minutes.

Add the hot water and bring to a vigorous boil, then lower the heat and simmer, partially covered, for 10 minutes. Taste for salt, and adjust if you wish. Remove from the heat. (*The soup can be prepared ahead and reheated just before serving. Refrigerate, covered, if not serving within 1 hour.*)

Shortly before you wish to serve the soup, bring a large pot of salted water to a boil. If you made the dough, roll out and cut the noodles. Cook the noodles until tender; drain.

Meanwhile, bring the soup to a boil. Stir in the spinach and let cook for 1 minute, or until softened.

Divide the noodles among four large bowls. Ladle the hot soup over the noodles, distributing the meat, spinach, and tomatoes evenly as you do so. Top each serving with a generous tablespoon of minced coriander.

Put out the remaining coriander along with the other condiments so guests can adjust their soup to taste. Encourage them to drizzle a little vinegar into their soup, or put out a small condiment bowl for each guest, so they can make a dip of vinegar and soy to use as a flavoring for the pieces of meat as they eat.

Serves 4 as a one-dish meal

NOTE ON GREENS: You can substitute chard leaves, stripped from the stems, or other tender leafy greens for the spinach; cooking time will be a little longer for chard than for spinach. Or you can omit the greens entirely.

OPPOSITE, LEFT: *A line of* chortens *(the Tibetan word for stupa) outside Kumbum Monastery. Kumbum lies a short distance south of the town of Xining, in Qinghai province, and is an important center of pilgrimage. It is here that the present Dalai Lama was first taken as a child—after he was recognized as the reincarnation of the preceding (thirteenth) Dalai Lama—for his family home is in a nearby village.* OPPOSITE, RIGHT: *Hui Tomato-Lamb Noodle Soup.*

As is the case with Tibet, the ethnographic and cultural borders of Mongolia are larger than the present-day political borders of the country of Mongolia (also known as Outer Mongolia) and the Chinese province of Inner Mongolia. Ethnographic Mongolia extends both farther north, into Siberia, and farther south and west, to the Great Wall and into Xinjiang province. If you also include the many pockets of Mongols who have survived even farther afield, as far west as Afghanistan and as far south as Yunnan province, then the Mongolian "world" is a very large one.

The Mongols were once a force that conquered China, most of Central Asia, and beyond (see page 7), but they were driven out of central China in the fourteenth century and largely returned to their homeland. They continued to form alliances but were never again a great power.

There are approximately five million Mongols in China today, almost four million of them in Inner Mongolia. They make up less than 20 percent of the population of the province; the Han majority there numbers about twenty million. Inner Mongolia became a political part of China in the twentieth century, though it remained (and remains today) culturally linked to the People's Republic of Mongolia through shared customs, language, and religion.

The Mongols converted to the Tibetan form of Buddhism at the time of Kublai Khan. *Oboos* (stones piled into cairns) topped with prayer flags mark significant places in the landscape in Inner Mongolia and the temples are very like Tibetan temples (see photo, page 268). Mongol pilgrims visit temples in Lhasa and other significant Tibetan Buddhist temples on pilgrimage.

The Mongols in Inner Mongolia today can be roughly divided into three groups. One is still semi-nomadic, living relatively traditionally, keeping herds of sheep and goats, cattle and horses (see "Mongolia out of Season," page 244). Their dome-shaped dwellings, built on light wooden frames, are called *gers*, though outsiders often refer to them as yurts, the Turkic name. Another group, a relatively small one, is also rural but is engaged in cultivation rather than raising animals. However, most farming in Inner Mongolia is done by Han people whose parents and grandparents settled there. They grow grain (barley, millet, buckwheat, and corn), as well as hardy vegetables such as cabbage and root vegetables. The third group consists of Mongols who work in mining, or in industry or other urban occupations, and live in cities and towns such as the capital, Hohhot, and the industrial city of Baotou.

In Mongol tradition, foods are categorized into white foods (eaten more in the summer and fall) and red foods (more associated with cold weather). White foods are milk and dairy products, processed or dried or fermented, including various forms of yogurt, dried milk strips, cheese, and more. (Settled Mongols traditionally eat more grain, such as parched barley, and hardy vegetables, in place of the white foods of nomadic animal herders.) Red foods are, of course, meat, mostly sheep, usually simmered, then eaten with the broth that results. Traditionally all parts of the animal are eaten. Tea is a staple, drunk with milk, sometimes with butter and salt added too.

LEFT: *Inside a Mongol ger: the smoke-hole flap is partly open, letting in light, there's a kettle on the wood stove, and Saren (see "Mongolia out of Season," page 244) carries a large thermos of tea. Beds are placed against the walls and stacked with folded quilted bedding.* RIGHT: *A horseman rides across the Hulun Buir Plain in late October, the season when Mongol herders move their gers (yurts) from up on the hills to campsites in the valley near the river. The ger is made of canvas and felt lashed to a dome-shaped wooden frame, where the one entrance, a painted wooden door, is set. On the ground, rolls of folded felt and canvas lie ready to cover another ger.*

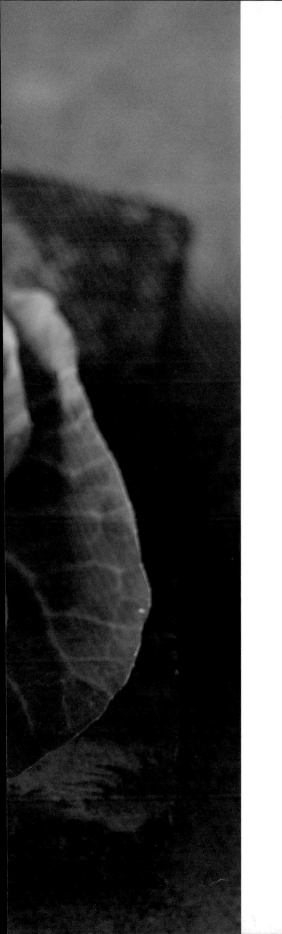

S A L A D S

central China, except the occasional wedge of cucumber, in the areas beyond the Great Wall there are plenty of crisp raw vegetables and herbs.

Salad traditions in these cultures and regions vary enormously. In the mild subtropical climate areas of Yunnan and Guizhou, salads are intensely flavored, tending to the tart and chile-hot (see Green Papaya Salad with Chiles, page 78, and Pea Tendril Salad, page 66). Sprouts, dried kelp, and the dried fungus known as tree ears all find a place in salads: see Hani Soy Sprout Salad (page 73), and Cucumber–Tree Ear Salad (page 79). Up north on Inner Mongolia's border with Russia there's a *salat* tradition that seems like fusion food: Napa and Red Onion Salad (page 86) and Beef-Sauced Hot Lettuce Salad (page 67) are delicious examples. Farther west, along the border with Siberia, lies the Kazakh area of northern Xinjiang, where there are similar salads (see Sprouts and Cabbage Salad Kazakh-Style, page 72). In Tibet, where greenery and fresh vegetables have not traditionally been available (though they are now being grown in greenhouses near many towns), salads don't have much meaning. Freshness comes from condiments and pickles (see the Condiments and Seasonings chapter).

In the oases of Xinjiang, where tomatoes, peppers, melons, cucumbers, and greens grow in abundance in the desert heat, chopped or sliced tomatoes and cucumbers are the basis for many simple refreshing assembled salads that are similar to those across the border in Uzbekistan and Tajikistan. Along with a generous sprinkling of salt, salads here are flavored with fresh herbs such as coriander or dill, and scallion greens, and/or pomegranate seeds in season (see Cooling Oasis Salad with Tomatoes and Herbs, page 89). Vinegar is on the table as a condiment for cooked dishes, not for dressing these salads.

Curiously, in China the words "raw" and "cooked" carry other meanings. They have long been used to distinguish between different groups of non-Han people. "Cooked" refers to people considered somewhat civilized in Chinese terms— i.e., people who are more sinicized—while "raw" refers to people and cultures viewed as very uncivilized.

OPPOSITE: *On the banks of the Mekong River, just outside Jinghong, in southern Yunnan, a man waters beds of green vegetables. Each year in October, as the water level in the river drops at the end of the rainy season, people who live along the river, from Yunnan to Thailand, cultivate freshly exposed areas along its banks for planting garlic and scallions and green vegetables.* ABOVE: *Tree ears: on the left, dried tree ears; on the right, soaked, and thus ready to be cooked and eaten.*

PEA TENDRIL SALAD

Pea tendrils, also known as pea shoots or pea sprouts, are the top 6 to 12 inches of the growing tips of green pea plants. We love pea tendrils, and we're happy to see them appearing fresh in more and more markets each year. There are two kinds: a finer version, where the shoots are very young and tender, with a delicate texture, and a more vigorous version, which is what we call for here, with twining stems, developed small leaves, and sometimes white pea flowers.

This attractive warm salad comes from the Dai people in southern Yunnan province. As in many Dai dishes, flavors combine tart-sour (the sesame oil–vinegar dressing) with chile heat (the garnish of slivered red cayenne chile) and mild sweetness (the pea tendrils) in a nice balance. [PHOTOGRAPH ON PAGE 308]

Pea tendrils, the tender finer version.

1 pound pea tendrils (see headnote)

DRESSING

2 tablespoons rice vinegar

1 teaspoon salt

1 teaspoon roasted sesame oil

1 small red cayenne chile or ½ large

2 tablespoons peanut oil or vegetable oil

½ cup thinly sliced shallots

Wash the pea tendrils well; drain and set aside.

Place the vinegar, the 1 teaspoon salt, and the sesame oil in a small cup and stir well; set aside.

Strip out and discard the seeds from the red chile, then thinly slice it. Set aside.

In a large pot, bring 3 quarts salted water to a boil. Toss in the pea tendrils and stir to immerse them in the water. Cook for 3 minutes, or until just tender to the bite—because pea tendrils vary considerably in terms of toughness, the cooking time may vary a little. Drain thoroughly in a colander and refresh briefly under cold water, then drain and press out excess water. Turn the greens out onto a cutting board and pull together into a mound. Chop with a chef's knife or cleaver into about 1-inch lengths, so that they will be easier to eat. Press out the excess liquid again.

Place the tendrils on a wide serving plate. Stir the sesame oil dressing again, pour it over the tendrils, and toss gently to coat.

Place a wok or heavy skillet over high heat. When it is hot, add the oil and swirl gently, then add the sliced shallots, lower the heat to medium-high, and fry until the shallots are pale to medium brown, about 2 minutes. Use long chopsticks or a spatula to keep the shallots moving so that they don't burn. Take the pan off the heat and pour the oil and shallots over the pea tendrils.

Sprinkle on the sliced red chile and serve.

Serves 4 as a salad or side dish

BEEF-SAUCED HOT LETTUCE SALAD

We came across this warm salad in Inner Mongolia, a place where Siberian and Mongolian worlds meet and are cross-blended with the traditions of the people who have moved into the region from many other parts of China. We don't know if this is a fusion dish of some kind, perhaps showing a Russian influence, but we do know that it's unusual and very appealing. Torn romaine is tossed in a hot dressing flavored with ground beef and warm seasonings. The crunch of the barely wilted lettuce is a beautiful contrast to the full-flavored warmth of the vinegar-spiked sauce. [PHOTOGRAPH ON PAGE 69]

About 4 packed cups coarsely torn romaine lettuce
   (see Note)

DRESSING

1 tablespoon peanut oil or vegetable oil

1 tablespoon minced garlic

1 tablespoon minced ginger

½ pound (1 packed cup) ground beef

½ teaspoon salt, or to taste

1 tablespoon soy sauce, or to taste

1 tablespoon Jinjiang (black rice) vinegar, or to taste

½ cup warm water

2 teaspoons cornstarch

1 tablespoon cold water

½ teaspoon roasted sesame oil

Place the lettuce in a wide salad bowl or serving dish and set aside.

Place a wok or heavy skillet over medium-high heat. When it is hot, add the oil and swirl to coat the bottom of the pan. Toss in the garlic and stir-fry for 10 seconds, then add the ginger. Stir-fry over medium-high to medium heat until slightly softened and starting to turn color. Add the meat and use your spatula to break it up so there are no lumps at all, then add the salt and stir-fry until most of the meat has changed color. Add the soy sauce and vinegar and stir to blend. Add the warm water and stir. (*The dressing can be prepared ahead to this point and set aside for up to 20 minutes. When you are ready to proceed, bring to a boil.*)

While the dressing mixture is coming to a boil, place the cornstarch in a small cup or bowl and stir in the cold water to make a smooth paste. Once the liquid is bubbling in the pan, give the cornstarch mixture a final stir, add to the pan, and stir for about 1 minute; the liquid will thicken and become smoother. Taste for salt, and add a little salt or soy sauce if you wish. Add the sesame oil and stir once, then pour onto the lettuce. Immediately toss the salad to expose all the greens to the hot dressing. Serve immediately (or see Note).

Serves 4 as a salad or side dish

NOTE ON TEXTURE: If you use romaine lettuce, the salad will have good crunch as well as some wilted softer textures when you first serve it. We love the contrast. If you prefer a softer texture, either let the salad stand for 5 minutes before serving it, to give the greens more time to soften in the warm dressing, or use leaf lettuce instead of romaine.

It poured nearly every day of my first visit to Sipsongpanna, the southernmost area of Yunnan. I took a plane from Kunming south to a town called Simao, and from there it was a day's bus ride on winding mountain roads to reach the town of Jinghong. I was thrilled to get there and to have my first glimpse of the Mekong River, flowing south out of China and into Southeast Asia, connecting two worlds.

In Sipsongpanna, I felt as if I was no longer in China. Some women wore sarongs instead of cotton jackets and pants in dull colors. They were Dai women (see page 237), distinctive and graceful. Other women were in short tunics of handwoven hemp, their legs bare, and their men were in loose hemp trousers, very like tribal people I had seen in northern Burma some years earlier. Many of the streets were unpaved, slick with mud in the September rain, and my flip-flops made a muddy spatter on the back of my legs as I walked.

There was a regular boat service from Jinghong to villages downstream, so one day I took the boat to the village of Menghan, sharing the boat with an assortment of people, everyone loaded with produce and equipment, with chickens in bamboo cages, and lots of children. We made several stops at small landings along the way. The boat waited for an hour in Menghan, unloading and taking on new passengers and cargo, so there was a little time to wander around and explore. The houses in the village were made of wood, graceful large structures built on stilts. Colors were brilliant in the overcast light, and whenever it stopped raining, the green of rice paddies glowed in the distance.

Too soon, it seemed, we were heading slowly back upstream, the boat engines working hard against the flow of the monsoon-swollen river. I had no idea then that in twelve years I'd be back in Menghan, traveling with a family of my own (see Dai Spicy Grilled Tofu, page 111). N

ABOVE: *At a street market in Menghan, in southern Yunnan, a Dai woman wearing a traditional sarong and blouse trims sugarcane; others sit waiting with their bags of produce.* OPPOSITE: *Beef-Sauced Hot Lettuce Salad (page 67).*

The tall blue-eyed woman staying in the dormitory of the Kunming Hotel caught my eye. She wore lots of chunky silver rings set with Tibetan turquoise. She was over sixty years old, I thought, very unusual in a dorm full of twentysomethings, but she had a vigor to her that was younger than her age. I asked her where she was from, and how long she was staying in Kunming.

"From Switzerland," she replied. "I'm taking the overnight train tomorrow to Chengdu, then I fly straight to Tibet."

I had a ticket on the same train to Chengdu, so we shared a taxi to the station the next day. The station was crowded, and as we stood in an echoing noisy tunnel under the tracks, waiting in a crowd to board the train, we almost had to shout to each other to be heard.

"Do you know the book *Forbidden Journey*?" she asked me.

"A wonderful book! I've always wondered what became of her, the author," I said.

"Well," she said with a smile, "I'm Ella Maillart. It's my book."

I was stunned. I'd read many of her books, extraordinary books. She had lived as a student in Moscow in 1932 and then traveled through Soviet Central Asia, experiences she describes in her first book, *Turkestan Solo*. In 1934, she went to Beijing, and from there she made an epic six-month journey on foot and horseback west across China all the way to Hunza (in present-day Pakistan), a trip she describes in *Forbidden Journey*. Her books are classics, travel literature about a kind of travel that is unimaginable now in the age of e-mail, cell phones, and rapid airplane connections.

On the train, we spent much of the twenty-three-hour ride talking.

Ella told me about driving overland from Switzerland to India in 1938 with a friend who was a morphine addict; about spending the war years in India; and about her long friendship with Nehru, India's prime minister from independence, in 1947, until 1964.

"I haven't talked about these things in years!" she said. "This will be my first time to Tibet," she went on. "I didn't get there in the thirties, and then for many years, because of the Chinese invasion of Tibet, I thought that it would be wrong to go, but now I'm getting old [she was in fact eighty-two when we met] and I might never have another chance."

"I'm also headed to Tibet," I told her, "but by bus, from Golmud."

"Then hopefully I'll see you again."

Two weeks later, I got to Lhasa and found Ella at the Snowland Hotel. She was packing. It was her last night in Lhasa. We went out for supper at a nearby eatery. Ella was a vegetarian, so we shared plates of stir-fried cabbage, stir-fried bean sprouts with slivered scallions, boiled potatoes with coarse salt, and a plate of chile-hot tree fungus.

"Why didn't you ever marry?" I asked Ella as we ate.

"I never found a man who was interested in the same questions I was," she replied, her blue eyes gazing straight at me.

"I've decided not to return to my job," I followed, perhaps looking for advice, looking for approval.

"'*Il faut suivre ta boussole*' [You must follow your compass], as we say in French. Do what feels right to you, then figure out how to earn a living at the same time."

We finished eating and exchanged addresses, and the next morning she was gone. **N**

OPPOSITE: *A Tibetan nomad walks on the vast plain below Mount Gurla Mandata, in the Mount Kailas area of western Tibet. The plain is at an elevation of about 15,000 feet.*

SILK ROAD TOMATO–BELL PEPPER SALAD

Long ago, Bahargul, a Uighur woman who had come to Toronto to complete her master's degree and was a friend of a friend, taught us how to make Uighur *pulao*. We included that *pulao* in *Seductions of Rice*. When the *pulao* was done, Bahargul quickly chopped up a salad just like this, to eat alongside as a cooling accompaniment to the flavored rice and meat. We love it still.

1 medium-large bell pepper, preferably yellow or orange

1 large or 2 medium ripe tomatoes

½ teaspoon salt, or to taste

About ¼ cup chopped coriander, mint, or dill

Remove the core, seeds, and ribs from the pepper. Slice lengthwise in ¼-inch-wide strips and cut the strips into 1-inch lengths. Place in a shallow bowl. Chop the tomato into small chunks and add to the bowl.

Sprinkle on the salt, add the herbs, toss gently, and serve.

Serves 4 as a small salad

YOGURT DRESSING: You can add a yogurt dressing to the salad if you like. Whisk 2 tablespoons well-chilled full- or reduced-fat yogurt with ½ teaspoon salt and a pinch of cayenne, then pour over the salad. Toss gently to mix well, sprinkle on a little chopped coriander, mint, or dill, and serve immediately.

SPROUTS AND CABBAGE SALAD KAZAKH-STYLE

In the mountains of northern Xinjiang, I spent a night sleeping alongside six other men in a Kazakh yurt, one of several dozen yurts set up together near Kanas Lake. The yurts functioned like guesthouses for Kazakh workers in the region, and the cost of a night's sleep included breakfast. For breakfast that morning we had steamed breads, this simple bean sprout and cabbage salad, and hot tea. We ate at a small table outside, surrounded by snow-capped mountains. All around us was activity, people riding horses, shoeing horses, packing packs. (Many of the Kazakh men make money leading Han Chinese tourists on horseback treks, sometimes several days in length.)

2 cups shredded or coarsely grated Napa cabbage

1 cup bean sprouts

3 red cayenne chiles, seeded and minced

2 tablespoons rice vinegar

1 teaspoon salt, or to taste

Place the cabbage and bean sprouts in a large bowl. Pour boiling water over to cover, and let stand for 3 to 5 minutes. Drain and place in a salad bowl.

Add the chiles to the cabbage and sprouts and toss.

Whisk together the vinegar and salt and pour over the salad. Toss to blend, taste for salt, and serve.

Serves 4 to 5 as a salad or side dish

HANI SOY SPROUT SALAD

My favorite parts of the Hani markets in southeastern Yunnan (see page 316) were the long aisles piled high with sprouts. There were chickpea sprouts, soybean sprouts, mung bean sprouts, and several others I couldn't identify. They were in giant piles, in beautiful shades of white, brown, and yellow, all bursting with freshness.

This salad is like one I ate at Luchen market. It makes a bright-tasting side dish.

SALAD

1 pound soybean sprouts (see Note)

2 tablespoons soy sauce

1 teaspoon finely chopped seeded red cayenne chile

2 tablespoons minced scallions (white and tender green parts)

¼ cup coriander leaves

DRESSING

1 tablespoon vegetable oil

1 tablespoon rice vinegar

½ teaspoon salt

¼ teaspoon roasted sesame oil

Wash the soybean sprouts and drain them. Bring 8 cups of water to a boil in a medium saucepan. Add the sprouts and soy sauce and bring back to a boil. Reduce the heat to a simmer and let the sprouts cook, uncovered, for 1 hour, or until tender.

Drain the sprouts in a colander (if you like, drain them over a bowl and save the cooking water for a vegetarian broth), and put them in a shallow bowl or on a plate.

Place the dressing ingredients in a cup and use a fork or small whisk to blend them together well. Pour the dressing over the sprouts and toss gently to mix. Add the red chile, scallions, and coriander leaves and gently toss again. Serve warm or at room temperature.

Serves 4 as a salad or side dish

NOTE ON SOYBEAN SPROUTS: Unlike the more commonly available mung bean sprouts, soy sprouts, which have larger green or yellow half-beans attached to them, can take long cooking without turning to mush. Look for them in Chinese grocery stores and specialty produce markets.

In the Yi and Hani markets of southeastern Yunnan there are piles of bean sprouts of many kinds for sale; these soy sprouts are in the market in Luchen.

kaili minced tofu rice sandwiches

In the small city of Kaili in eastern Guizhou, there's a lane of street vendors who set up around sunset. During the day, the same lane is a small produce and fish market, but down another lane to one side, by some steps, there are stalls that offer a street version of hot pot: You choose skewers of fish or squid or vegetable or tofu, and they are then immersed in a vat of hot broth to cook or reheat before being handed to you. At the bottom of the steps, there's a woman selling what I called in my diary "sticky rice sandwiches," a Miao specialty, we've since learned. The "bread" is two small disks of sticky rice, each the diameter of a small hamburger bun. Pressed between the disks is a dollop of minced dressed firm tofu very like Pressed Tofu with Scallions and Ginger (opposite). The sandwiches cost about fifteen cents, and they're delicious, with a tender texture.

Tofu portraits: on the left, two pieces of pressed tofu lie on top of a block of fresh tofu, the firm Chinese version. On the right, pieces of frozen tofu: the cube in the front has been thawed, the water squeezed out, and the tofu torn in half to show its sponge-like open structure, ideal for absorbing flavor.

PRESSED TOFU
WITH SCALLIONS AND GINGER

We think of ourselves as unofficial promoters of certain foods, and pressed tofu is one of them. We'll often take a pressed tofu dish, such as this one from the Dai people in southern Yunnan, to a potluck supper so that friends who haven't tasted it can have a chance to try it. At one such potluck, I happened to be standing by the buffet table when an eight-year-old boy came up with his father.

"What's that?" he asked his father.

"I think it's tofu," his father replied.

The boy crinkled his nose and looked unimpressed. His father served himself and took a bite, and then another bite, and then his son decided to try it. Then he too took another bite. The rest of the evening, every once in a while, I'd notice the boy pop over to the table and take a little more pressed tofu. Success!

Pressed tofu is now available in most East Asian groceries. It comes in white, pale brown, and dark brown, depending upon whether or not it has been flavored with soy and other seasonings, and it is always inexpensive. It is extremely versatile: it can be grilled, stir-fried, or simmered. It has the consistency of a firm-soft cheese (such as unripe camembert) but no cheese flavor, just a mildly salty subtle taste of bean.

This particular dish is a cross between a chopped salad and an appetizer. It has chile heat, like so many Dai dishes, and it is traditionally served with small wedges or sections of cabbage that diners can use to scoop up mouthfuls of salad. Serve with sticky rice if you wish.

⅓ pound pressed tofu

½ cup lightly packed chopped scallions
   (white and tender green parts)

1 tablespoon soy sauce

1 tablespoon water

½ teaspoon crushed dried red chile or chile pepper flakes

2 tablespoons minced ginger

ACCOMPANIMENTS

6 to 8 small cabbage wedges (green or savoy cabbage) or
   wedges of iceberg or other head lettuce or about 12 leaf
   or Bibb lettuce leaves

1 lime, cut into small wedges

Rinse the pressed tofu, then cut it into very small pieces (¼-inch or smaller cubes) and place in a medium bowl. Add the scallions to the tofu, and set aside.

In a small bowl, stir together the soy sauce, water, and dried red chile. Let stand for 5 minutes to allow the flavors to blend.

Add the ginger to the tofu and scallions and toss to mix well. Pour the dressing over. Serve with the cabbage or lettuce leaves, and invite your guests to squeeze on a little lime juice as they eat, mouthful by mouthful.

Serves 4 to 6 as a salad or appetizer

In early October 1985, I arrived in Golmud on the slow train overnight from Xining. Golmud lies in what looks like the middle of nowhere on a map, in a featureless dry plateau in the province of Qinghai, not far from the edge of the Takla Makan Desert. Camels roam outside town, the wind blows, and in fall and winter, straggles of Tibetan nomads pass through, headed to Lhasa on pilgrimage.

Golmud was for a long time a transportation hub of a kind, for until recently the railway from Beijing and central China ended there (see Note). Anyone who wanted to go farther, say south to Lhasa, or northwest to Dunhuang, had to find space in a truck or a bus (in earlier times they'd have searched out a horse or a camel).

When I got to the bus stand, several families of nomads (pilgrims headed to Lhasa) sat waiting, leaning against a mud-brick wall for shelter from the wind and the dust it brought. I asked around, but no one knew when or even if a bus might leave that day. So I set my pack down and joined the pilgrims by the wall. Eventually a man came and opened the door of one of the two rackety-looking buses parked in the lot. Luggage was tied on the roof with ropes, tickets sold, and then we headed out across the flat, bare landscape.

It was an amazing trip, that journey with the pilgrims. Many of them spent the whole time praying, saying prayers rapidly under their breath and sliding their prayer beads between thumb and forefinger. There were lots of older men and women, each with a small prayer wheel, which they kept spinning as we drove along. There were several women with babies and small children, their hair in many long gleaming braids down their back, all joined at the bottom and threaded with turquoise beads in the Amdo (northeast-Tibetan) style. Most people had brought food for the journey, so every once in a while, someone would offer around pieces of dried yak or goat meat; then we'd all chew slowly, making it last. All I had to share were some rather tasteless hard candies, but they too were a welcome break.

Despite its apparent barrenness, the landscape had life in it. Every so often a few of the men would get very animated and point out the window. Sometimes I could eventually make out what they had spotted long before—a herd of wild asses, a fox, a wild yak—but most often I couldn't see the animals at all.

Late on the afternoon of the second day, we started heading up the Kyichu River Valley to Lhasa. Everyone was keyed up and expectant. The hum of prayer in the bus grew louder. When the Potala Palace at last came into sight, high on its hill, all gleaming roofs and fantastical, the bus came alive with chanting, prayers, and joy. **N**

NOTE: Since July 2006, the railway has been opened all the way to Lhasa, to the dismay of Tibetans, who feel it will encourage an influx of settlers from central China (see "Lhasa Tensions," page 205).

OPPOSITE: *A Tibetan woman, her hands clasped behind her back, keeps her prayer beads moving while she prays.*

GREEN PAPAYA SALAD WITH CHILES

It's no wonder that green papaya recipes pop up frequently throughout Asia, because almost anywhere papaya trees grow, they grow easily and produce abundantly. Green papaya is eaten as a vegetable from India to Thailand, Yunnan, and Vietnam. And green papayas are easy to transport, not nearly as fragile as ripe ones, making them inexpensive in the market.

This dish comes from a tiny no-name restaurant on a back lane in Jinghong, in the far south of Yunnan province. At the restaurant, it came with almost every meal, like an appetizer or a palate refresher. The salad is lightly pickled, but the green papaya remains slightly crunchy. It reminds us a little of the lightly pickled carrots and white radish that come as side condiments in Vietnam.

When we make the dish, we julienne the green papaya as people do in Thailand and Laos for *som tam* (pounded green papaya salad). We peel off the dark green skin, then use a cleaver to chop and slice the papaya, as described below. The process may sound complicated, but it's not. It's easy and fun, especially if your cleaver (or chef's knife) is sharp.

Make the salad a couple of hours, or as long as 6 hours, before you wish to serve it.

One 2-pound green papaya

2 tablespoons ginger, cut into small matchsticks

1 to 2 tablespoons thinly sliced seeded red cayenne chile

FOR PICKLING

4 cups water

½ cup rice vinegar

1 tablespoon salt

1 teaspoon sugar

Peel the papaya using a vegetable peeler, and cut off the hard stem end. Rinse the papaya to make it easier to hold on to. Hold the papaya in one hand, and use a sharp cleaver or chef's knife to make repeated lengthwise shallow cuts straight into the surface of the papaya, making many, many parallel cuts. When you have covered the first side of the papaya with lengthwise cuts, stand the papaya on end on a cutting board and then shave off the julienned strips of papaya by sliding your cleaver down the cut side of the papaya (in the same way you slice kernels off a cob of corn), trimming off all the long narrow slivers.

Repeat on the other side of the papaya, then continue until you have cut most of the papaya into julienned strips. (Be sure not to cut too far down into the center of the fruit, because you don't want any papaya seeds mixed in with your shreds. Papaya seeds have an incredibly strong taste that is not what you want in your dish!) You should have 4 cups.

Put the shredded papaya in a bowl, add the ginger and red chile, and mix well.

In a nonreactive saucepan, bring the water to a boil. Add the rice vinegar, salt, and sugar, stirring to make sure the salt and sugar dissolve. Bring back to a boil, then pour the brine over the papaya. Let sit for 1½ to 2 hours.

Drain the salad just before serving. Put it out in a bowl so guests can help themselves, or serve individually in small condiment bowls.

Serves 4 to 6 as a condiment/salad

PRESERVED VEGETABLE OPTION: You can also add up to ½ cup finely chopped preserved green vegetable, such as pickled mustard greens (see Glossary), to the salad.

CUCUMBER-TREE EAR SALAD

This Dong salad is made with crisp chopped cucumber and small pieces of well-soaked tree ear fungus, which are a beautiful shiny black against the cucumber's pale green. They are dressed with warm and sharp flavors (ginger, vinegar, pickled chiles, sesame oil), and the salad tastes mildly pickled, a flavor characteristic of Dong cuisine (see page 120). Serve as a foil for hearty main dishes.

If you don't have any pickled chiles handy, you can substitute a sliced fresh red cayenne chile, as described below. Start making the salad 45 minutes to an hour before you wish to serve it.

¼ cup dried tree ears (see Glossary)

About 2 tablespoons ginger, cut into fine matchsticks

1 tablespoon thinly sliced Pickled Red Chiles (page 34) or store-bought pickled chiles, or substitute 1 small red cayenne chile, seeded and very thinly sliced

2 tablespoons rice vinegar

1 tablespoon water

½ teaspoon salt, or to taste

1 medium English cucumber (about ½ pound)

1 teaspoon roasted sesame oil

Soak the tree ears in boiling water to cover for 20 minutes.

Place the ginger in a small bowl. If using a fresh chile, add it to the ginger.

Heat the vinegar and water together in a small nonreactive pan over medium heat, and stir in ½ teaspoon salt to dissolve it. When the mixture comes to the boil, pour over the ginger. Let stand for 10 to 15 minutes.

Drain the softened tree ears and chop into small pieces (nickel- to quarter-sized), discarding any tough sections. You will have about ¾ cup. Place in a medium bowl and set aside.

Peel the cucumber and cut lengthwise in half. Chop into irregular chunks no more than ½ inch by ¾ inch. Add them to the bowl with the tree ears. If using pickled chiles, add them to the bowl.

Pour the vinegar-ginger mixture over the cucumber mixture. Toss to mix well. Add the sesame oil and toss again. Let the salad marinate in its own juices for 30 minutes, giving it a stir several times to distribute the flavors.

Just before serving, stir the salad again, then taste and add a little salt if you wish.

Serves 4 as a salad or side dish

OPPOSITE: *Dai Carrot Salad (page 83).* LEFT: *At a bus stop in southern Yunnan two Dai women on cell phones supervise a streetside grill.* RIGHT: *In the early morning, a Dai noodle soup vendor sets up at the market in Menghan, in southern Yunnan. Morning market noodles, usually fresh rice noodles bathed in broth, are sold at small stalls like this one in all the local Dai markets. Customers sit on small benches at the table, help themselves to condiments, and get a warming start to the day.*

KOMBU WITH DARK SOY AND SCALLION RIBBONS

I was so surprised to find dried kombu seaweed in mountainous land-locked Yunnan province. I saw it not only in "cosmopolitan" Jinghong, but also in the remote mountain town of Yuanyang. In China, kombu is called *hai dai*. You can generally find it here in North America in East Asian supermarkets, as well as in natural food groceries, sometimes labeled kelp, other times kombu, its Japanese name (see Glossary).

Once soaked, kombu has a great texture, a firm chewy bite that melts into tenderness. It's sold in rectangular sheets about 8 inches by 4 inches or in long fronds that are folded. If the long sheets are what you have, unfold them and figure out what will give you the square inches called for in the recipe.

We've adapted this appetizer/salad a bit from the one I first tasted in Jinghong market. We use a thick soy sauce, a store-bought sauce that we have enjoyed for years at home; a brand from Taiwan called Kimlan, it has a distinctive orange label (see Glossary for more). Here in Toronto it is widely available in Chinese groceries. Don't try substituting other "thick soys"—their taste is entirely different. If you can't find Kimlan, substitute a regular soy sauce.

Serve this as a salad or as an appetizer with drinks.

2 sheets (each about 6 by 9 inches) kombu

About 2 tablespoons thick soy sauce (see headnote)

1 large or 2 small scallions, cut lengthwise into ribbons and crosswise into 1-inch lengths

Rinse the kombu well, then soak the sheets in warm water to cover for 20 minutes, or until well softened.

Drain the kombu and remove and discard any hard bits. Cut lengthwise into 2-inch-wide panels, then stack them and cut them crosswise into ¼- to ½-inch strips. You should have about 1 cup packed kombu.

Place in a wide bowl, immediately add the soy sauce, and toss well. Sprinkle on the scallion ribbons and serve.

Serves 4 as a salad or appetizer

NOTE ON TIMING: Kombu/kelp has a slightly mucilaginous texture after it has been soaked, so it should be dressed right away after soaking, so the ribbons don't start to stick to one another.

LHASA SEAWEED SALAD: It's hard to be more landlocked than in Tibet. But dried kombu is lightweight and keeps well, so it has become a useful vegetable in Lhasa and other Tibetan towns. We've seen it there shredded into soups, and we've also had it as a kind of intensely flavored salad, dressed with chile paste and scallions. With its red and green and black, its chile heat, and its faint tang of the faraway ocean, it's an attractive and delicious addition to a dinner table. Whisk together about 2 teaspoons Guizhou Chile Paste (page 35) or Bright Red Chile Paste (page 18) with ½ teaspoon roasted sesame oil and a scant ½ teaspoon salt. Pour the dressing over the soaked kombu as soon as it is sliced, as above, and toss well to coat, then sprinkle on the scallion ribbons and serve.

CUCUMBERS IN BLACK RICE VINEGAR

Cucumbers are one of the mainstays for people living in the oases of Xinjiang. They're used as a cross between a salad and a condiment. This is one of the easiest ways we know to brighten a weeknight supper. It also complements deep-fried treats such as Cheese Momos (page 212) or Giant Jiaozi (page 210) beautifully.

1 English cucumber (about ½ pound)

About 2¼ teaspoons salt

2 tablespoons Jinjiang (black rice) vinegar

1 teaspoon roasted sesame oil

Peel the cucumber completely, or remove lengthwise strips of peel, leaving some of the cucumber unpeeled, to give the slices an attractive look. Slice lengthwise in half and then in half again. Use a knife or sharp spoon to clean out the seeds. Cut each piece lengthwise in half, then cut crosswise into ¼-inch slices.

Place the cucumber in a bowl. Add 2 teaspoons of the salt and let stand for 10 minutes, then transfer the cucumber to a sieve or colander and rinse thoroughly under cold water. Squeeze gently to remove excess water, and place in a shallow bowl.

Whisk the vinegar and sesame oil together and pour over the cucumbers. Toss to blend. Set aside until ready to serve (no longer than 30 minutes).

Just before serving, taste, and add about ¼ teaspoon salt, or to taste, if you wish.

Serves 4 as a salad or side dish

CUCUMBER-VINEGAR SAUCE: If you mince the cucumber, this becomes more like a condiment than a salad. It's a standard item at noodle stalls in Xinjiang and Qinghai provinces. Serve it with noodle dishes and pulaos, putting it out in a bowl, with a spoon, so guests can help themselves.

Serves 6 to 8 as a condiment

DAI CARROT SALAD

There is so much good cooking in the small city of Jinghong (see page 227) in southern Yunnan province that it would take a long time to feel well acquainted with all that is there. Restaurant-hopping in the warm tropical evenings of Jinghong is lots of fun, but even better are the morning and afternoon markets, where there is an incredible variety of prepared foods to choose from. This carrot salad is one such dish: colorful and full of flavor. [PHOTOGRAPH ON PAGE 80]

1 pound large carrots

About 2 tablespoons Pickled Red Chiles (page 34) or store-
    bought pickled chiles, cut into ½-inch slices

3 scallions, smashed and sliced into ½-inch lengths

1 tablespoon soy sauce

1 tablespoon rice vinegar

1 teaspoon roasted sesame oil

½ teaspoon salt, or to taste

2 to 3 tablespoons coriander leaves, coarsely chopped

Peel the carrots. Using a cleaver or chef's knife, slice them very thin (⅛ inch thick if possible) on a 45-degree angle. You should have 3 cups.

In a medium saucepan, bring 4 cups of water to a boil. Toss in the carrot slices and stir to separate them. Cook just until slightly softened and no longer raw, about 3 minutes. Drain.

Transfer the carrots to a bowl and let cool slightly, then add the chiles and scallion ribbons and toss to mix.

Whisk together the soy sauce, rice vinegar, and sesame oil. Pour over the salad while the carrots are still warm. Stir or toss gently to distribute the dressing, then turn the salad out onto a serving plate or into a wide shallow bowl.

Serve the salad warm or at room temperature. Just before serving, sprinkle on the salt and toss gently, then sprinkle on the coriander and toss again.

Serves 4 as a salad or appetizer

We met in Lhasa, Naomi and I, in early October 1985. We were both staying in the Snowland Hotel, both in dormitories. At night, a lot of people would meet on the rooftop of the hotel because the nights are beautiful in central Tibet in October, clear and mild, and because the roof was a far better place to sit than the dorm rooms. That's where we first met, on the roof in the dark.

We started to talk about books, about "Himalayan" literature, and realized that we'd read many of the same books, several of them somewhat obscure (see page 129). And we'd both spent months in Nepal, and Naomi had traveled in Ladakh, the Tibetan region of India. To be traveling in Tibet was a dream for both of us, and for many of the same reasons. So it was easy to talk.

The next day, we went on a bicycle ride together. I was in Lhasa with five friends from my hometown in Wyoming, and we all had bicycles. We were hoping eventually to bicycle across the Himalaya from Lhasa to Kathmandu. A company had given us the bicycles, and another company had given us gear. I'd had the idea for the ride during my Jeep ride to the border six months before (see page 51), but it wasn't as if we were avid cyclists.

Naomi borrowed a friend's bike, and we rode outside town, then sat by the river and talked. When we got back to the hotel, we discovered a flat tire on Naomi's bike. She said she'd help me patch the tire, but I said she should go, I could do it. I didn't want to tell her, but patching tires wasn't one of my strong points. I'd gotten myself all the way to Tibet with a bicycle, but knew very little about bicycle repair.

Two days later, we went on a three-day trip in a Jeep, together with two Italian guys Naomi had met earlier in her travels. We were hoping to get to Samye Gompa, the first Buddhist temple built in Tibet (over 1,100 years ago). But as we were walking to the monastery, Naomi and I stopped to talk. And we talked and talked. We never made it to the temple. But by the end of the day, we were talking about having a family together.

My bicycle trip to Kathmandu began ten days later. Six of us rode out of town, imposters all, excited and fearful at the same time. Would we find water on the way? Would we be stopped by the police? Would we be able to cross the passes? When we camped the first night, many of us had flat tires from a nasty kind of thorn that we came to know too well. The following morning, we started the long all-day climb to the top of our first pass, Khamba La, 15,820 feet in elevation (see photo, page 4).

A week later we reached the town of Shigatse in southern Tibet, and there was Naomi! She was traveling by Jeep with a friend named Amy Kratz and two Himalayan anthropologists, Corneille Jest and Gabriel Campbell. That night she and I took our sleeping bags to the roof of the two-story caravanserai-style hotel where we were staying. Across the way was a large monastery, Tashilhunpo, and just outside its gates a crowd of pilgrims, mostly nomads, had set up camp. In the middle of the night, we were awakened by the howling of dogs. When we opened our eyes, we saw that the full moon was going into total eclipse. The dogs went on howling, and the pilgrims began chanting. . . .

Naomi and I will never forget October–November 1985. We rendezvoused again when I got to Kathmandu. We hung out at tea shops and little restaurants, talking and eating apple pie and cinnamon buns. And we planned our next trip back to Tibet. J

OPPOSITE: *Tibetan family with young child, in western Sichuan.*

NAPA AND RED ONION SALAD

The summers in Inner Mongolia are brief, and during the rest of the year, fresh green vegetables are in short supply. Like people in Tibet and in northern places (the Russians who live just across the border in Siberia, for example, or the Koreans), people in Inner Mongolia have figured out solutions. Cabbages and other vegetables that have been pickled or dried, dried mushrooms, and easily stored root vegetables such as potatoes, carrots, radishes, and turnips, along with cucumbers grown under glass, do stand-in duty for all that is not available.

This crunchy late-autumn salad has beautiful curving shards of red onion tossed with fine shreds of Napa cabbage. One of many salads that we ate in the cold days of late October in Inner Mongolia, it includes elements from both sides of the border: Chinese flavorings are used to dress a Siberian/Russian-style salad, just the thing to add fresh bite to a winter meal. Because it can be made ahead and keeps its flavor and texture, it's a great dish to take to a potluck dinner.

1 small or ½ medium-large red onion (¼ pound)

2 teaspoons salt, or to taste

2 cups shredded Napa cabbage (see Note)

2 teaspoons roasted sesame oil, or to taste

1 tablespoon minced ginger

1 tablespoon rice vinegar, or to taste

About ½ cup coriander leaves

Slice the onion lengthwise into quarters, then very thinly slice each quarter lengthwise. You should have about 1 cup. Place in a sieve, add 1 teaspoon of the salt, and toss well. Set over a bowl and let stand for 10 minutes to drain.

Meanwhile, place the cabbage in a bowl and pour over boiling water to cover (about 4 cups). Let stand for a minute or two, then drain in a colander. Place back in the bowl and set aside.

Rinse the onion with cold water, then squeeze dry and add to the cabbage. Set aside.

Heat the 2 teaspoons sesame oil in a small wok or small skillet over medium heat. Add the ginger and cook for about 1 minute, stirring frequently to prevent sticking. Add the vinegar, and once it bubbles, pour the mixture over the salad. Toss to blend, then add the remaining 1 teaspoon salt and toss again. The salad can be served immediately or left to stand for up to an hour so flavors can blend.

Just before serving, taste and add a little more sesame oil if you want to bring that flavor forward, as well as more salt if you wish. Add the coriander leaves and toss.

Serves 4 as a salad or appetizer

NOTE ON SHREDDING CABBAGE: To shred the cabbage, slice crosswise into very thin slivers with a cleaver or chef's knife.

opposite, left: *Napa and Red Onion Salad.* opposite, right: *A Mongol woman outside her ger (yurt) in Inner Mongolia.*

LEFT: *Pomegranates, an unexpected reminder of easier milder climates, on sale in the market in Hailar, Inner Mongolia.* RIGHT: *A young Uighur girl chats with a goat at the busy Sunday bazaar in Kashgar, in western Xinjiang.*

ONION AND POMEGRANATE SALAD

In this classic Central Asian salad, onions are salted briefly, then rinsed to wash away their sharpness. It's like an instant pickling, making them sweeter and more tender. They're dressed with salt, sugar, and vinegar, then sprinkled with coriander leaves and pomegranate seeds.

Pomegranates come into season around October and are usually available until late January or early February. There are both sweet and tart pomegranates. The sweet ones are much more widely available in North America, and that's what you want to buy.

> 2 medium red or white onions (about 1 pound), thinly sliced
>
> 1 tablespoon salt, or to taste
>
> 3 tablespoons rice vinegar
>
> 1 teaspoon crushed rock sugar or regular sugar
>
> ½ teaspoon chile pepper flakes (optional)
>
> ½ cup chopped coriander
>
> ½ cup pomegranate seeds (see Note)

Place the onions in a colander set over a bowl or in the sink, sprinkle on the 1 tablespoon salt, and toss to mix well. Let drain for 15 minutes or so, then rinse well with cold water and gently squeeze out excess liquid. Separate the slices as you place the onions in a shallow bowl.

In a small bowl, mix together the vinegar, sugar, and chile flakes, whisking well to blend them, then pour over the onions. Toss to distribute the dressing. Taste, and add a little salt if needed. Add the coriander and toss, then sprinkle on the pomegranate seeds.

Serves 4 as a salad or side dish

NOTE ON POMEGRANATE TECHNIQUE: To get at the seeds, use the tip of a sharp knife to make a 2-inch square cut in the skin, cutting just through the skin. Lift the cut piece from the rest of the fruit; some seeds will still be attached. Repeat with another section of skin. Now you have easy access to the seeds in the center of the fruit. Separate them from the astringent-tasting pith and heap in a bowl. They're beautiful, a great garnish for salads and *pulaos*, and a nice little snack on their own.

COOLING OASIS SALAD WITH TOMATOES AND HERBS

When it's hot and dry, as it is in summertime in the deserts of Xinjiang province, a moist salad is very welcome. The only "dressing" is minced herbs and salt. The salad pairs beautifully with rich *pulaos*, and with grilled kebabs.

> About 1 pound ripe tomatoes
>
> About ½ pound English cucumber
>
> ½ pound daikon radish, peeled, or red radishes
>
> 2 tablespoons minced scallion greens
>
> ¼ cup packed minced herbs: dill, coriander, flat-leaf parsley, or mint, or a mixture
>
> 2 teaspoons salt, or to taste

Chop the tomatoes into ½-inch dice or smaller, and place in a bowl. Peel the cucumber, chop into small dice, and add to the tomato. Chop the radish(es) into small dice and add. Add the herbs and salt, and toss to mix well.

Transfer to a wide shallow bowl, and serve immediately.

Serves 6 as a salad or side dish

THE UIGHUR PEOPLE

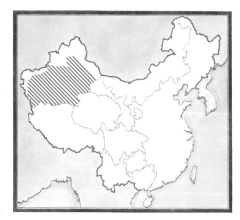

Uighurs (sometimes written Uygurs) are a Turkic people whose language is related to Uzbek, Kirghiz, and Kazakh. They are the majority non-Han population in Xinjiang. Their current population in China is approximately eight million (smaller groups live in Afghanistan, Kazakhstan, Uzbekistan, Turkey, and Mongolia). Nearly 85 percent of Xinjiang is desert and/or uncultivatable land, so most Uighurs live in desert oases or in the foothills of the Tian Shan Mountains.

Uighurs have been an important culture in this part of the world since well before the eighth century. (When Genghis Khan took control of a large chunk of Central Asia in the thirteenth century, it was Uighur scribes he relied upon to develop a system for writing and keeping accounts. Although that Uighur script is still the Mongolian alphabet, the Uighur language is now written in a modified Arabic script.) At various times since then, Uighurs have had sovereignty over their homeland or have made alliances with neighboring peoples, enabling them to have local autonomy. For a short period in the 1930s, they formed an independent republic, but it fell back under Chinese rule in 1944.

Prior to the tenth century, Buddhism, Nestorian Christianity, Manicheaism, and Animism were all practiced in Xinjiang, but in the tenth to twelfth centuries, Uighurs converted to Islam, and they are now primarily Sunni Muslims. They have a sense of national identity, and there is a vocal Uighur nationalist movement, despite efforts by the government in Beijing to suppress it by imprisoning or sometimes even executing Uighur nationalists.

The Uighurs are primarily farmers and traders. In the desert oases, they farm vegetables, wheat, and fruits (they're famous for their sweet melons, and for their long sweet grapes and the raisins that are made from them), as well as cotton. The oases are watered by irrigation systems built long ago, which transport water from faraway mountains underground, a system invented by the Persians. Uighurs can also be found in the cities of central China, where they sell street food (kebabs and flatbreads), run Uighur restaurants, and trade traditional Xinjiang products.

Traditionally, Uighur men wear a small flat embroidered cap. Uighur women cover their heads with colored scarves or brown veils and wear dresses of brightly patterned cotton (see photo, page 209). The fabric is printed with multicolored ikat designs that mimic the ikat-woven silk for which Uighurs have been famous for centuries. (In ikat weaving, the weft threads are dyed before being woven, which results in distinctive soft-edged patterns in the fabric.) Uighurs are also known for their wool-felt rugs.

Everyday foods in the oases are anchored by tea and bread. The breads are leavened flatbreads of various kinds, called *nan* (see Uighur Nan, page 190) and baked in tandoor ovens. The tea is usually drunk clear, from bowls. The other daily staple is noodles, made of a wheat-flour dough that is stretched and flung in a very distinctive method (see "Uighur Flung Noodles," page 152). These are usually served in a broth or topped with meat and vegetables (see Laghman Sauce for Noodles, page 135). For feasting and special occasions, the main dish is *pulao*, rice flavored with meat and vegetables and served on a large platter, family-style (see Chicken Pulao with Pumpkin, page 174).

LEFT: *An older Uighur man stands by a kilometer post in the Altai Mountains, in northern Xinjiang.* RIGHT: *Two Uighur children play outside a traditional Central Asian–style house built of sun-dried brick, in Kashgar, western Xinjiang.*

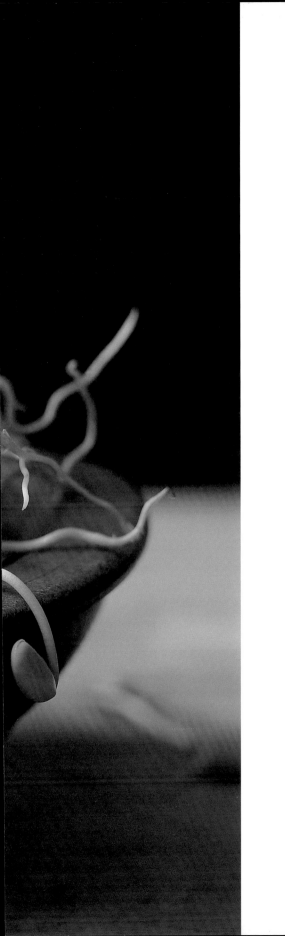

MOSTLY VEGETABLES

IN THE SOUTHERN PROVINCES OF YUNNAN AND Guizhou, with their milder climates and abundant rainfall, cooks have a wide array of vegetables to choose from year-round, but in Inner Mongolia and Tibet, and in Gansu, Qinghai, and Xinjiang, during the long, cold winter, the word "vegetable" comes to mean potatoes, carrots, radishes, and other hardy root crops, as it did until recently in northern Europe. And, as in European tradition, in these colder areas beyond the Great Wall, a little meat or meat broth is often part of the recipe, giving it depth and succulence. Sometimes, especially in dishes from the mountain tradition, we have the impression that the vegetables are just there as a way of extending the flavor of the meat (see Kazakh Cabbage Stir-Fry with Lamb, page 100). In Yunnan and Guizhou provinces, as in much of central China, the vegetable dishes are often flavored with a little pork (see Ginger and Carrot Stir-Fry, page 96, for example). Alternatively, tofu sticks or other forms of tofu are added to vegetable stir-fries and simmered dishes, to give more substance (see Jicama–Tofu Sheet Stir-Fry, page 105).

With the recent influx of Han and Hui people from central China into Tibet, there is a much greater variety of vegetables in the markets there, especially in the larger towns. There are also more vegetables available now in Qinghai and Gansu provinces (see Hui Vegetable Hot Pot, page 117). Some are being shipped in, but many are grown locally in greenhouses in the valleys near the towns.

You'll find vegetable dishes in the Salads chapter too, of course, and also in Condiments and Seasonings, in the form of fresh sauces and chutneys, as well as pickles.

OPPOSITE: *A street in the predominantly Bai town of Dali, by Lake Er Hai in Yunnan. A man walks by a house where cabbage greens (a winter vegetable) are strung on a line under the eaves to dry in the cool winter sun. The next step will be to pickle them.* ABOVE: *Napa cabbage, also known as Chinese cabbage or Chinese lettuce.*

GINGER AND CARROT STIR-FRY

I first tasted this root vegetable stir-fry at a little eatery in Xijiang, a large Miao village (see page 183) in Guizhou. It's an ideal fall and winter dish, and a great way to prepare carrots. They are cut into strips, then stir-fried with lots of ginger cut the same way.

The chopping takes a little attention. Start with two "fingers" of firm, nonfibrous ginger. Peel them and cut lengthwise in half before cutting them into narrower lengthwise sticks. Do the same with the carrots.

There's great depth of flavor from the small amount of pork that flavors the cooking oil, and plenty of sauce to spoon onto your rice. Ever since the first time we tried to reproduce the dish in our kitchen, it's been a big weeknight supper favorite.

2 tablespoons peanut oil or lard

1 tablespoon minced garlic

⅓ pound boneless pork butt, shoulder, or loin, thinly sliced and cut into ½-by-1½-inch strips

2 whole green cayenne chiles or 3 dried red chiles

About ⅔ pound carrots, peeled and cut into matchsticks (1¾ cups)

About ⅓ pound ginger, peeled and cut into matchsticks (1 cup)

½ teaspoon salt

1 cup water

10 to 12 Sichuan peppercorns, lightly crushed or coarsely ground

2 tablespoons soy sauce, or to taste

Heat a wok or wide heavy skillet over high heat. Add the oil or lard and swirl to coat the bottom of the pan. Toss in the garlic and stir-fry for 10 seconds or so, then toss in the pork and chiles. Stir-fry, separating the pieces of meat so all get exposed to the hot pan, until they have started to change color all over, less than 2 minutes.

Toss in the carrots and ginger and stir-fry for about a minute. Add the salt and stir-fry for another minute. Add the water, cover, and boil vigorously for about 3 minutes, then remove the lid and let the liquid boil down for a minute or two. Add the Sichuan peppercorns and soy sauce. Stir-fry for another minute, or until the carrots and ginger are tender but still firm.

Turn the stir-fry out onto a shallow bowl and serve hot or warm.

Serves 4 as a side dish or as part of a rice meal

A pile of yellow carrots at the market in the Turpan oasis in Xinjiang; we've also seen dark purple and burgundy-colored carrots in markets beyond the Great Wall.

Before traveling in Tibet, we'd thought of ourselves as pretty good with campfires. We'd both grown up in places where campfires were a treasured part of summer and fall, Naomi in Ontario, and I in Wyoming. We both knew how to build a fire, how to get a fire going in the rain, all the normal sort of stuff. And we'd also been around hearths and fires in many places around the world, watching people cook. But Tibet was a different experience altogether.

In April 1986, we hired a driver and a bare-bones Toyota Land Cruiser to make a trip from Lhasa, in central Tibet, to Mount Kailas, in far western Tibet. The first few nights along the way, we stopped in towns where there were hotels with little "restaurants" attached, really sort of truck-stop versions of Lhasa hotel eateries, where cooks prepared food in large woks set over massive wood fires. By the third and fourth nights, we were in sparsely populated areas, and the "truck stops" became small, single-floor concrete-block buildings with dorm beds, thermoses of boiled water, and piles of dried yak dung for making a fire.

We hadn't had much experience building fires with dung, but we'd watched a lot of people cooking over dung fires, so we were ready to have a try. It was relatively easy, especially if we had a little paper to get the fire going. What we could cook was limited by the altitude (water boils at a lower temperature at high altitudes, so white rice was edible after an hour; potatoes took longer). In any case it was pleasant, as it always is, to have a fire going. Nights are cold in April in Tibet.

A few days later, we were in the Changtang area of western Tibet, a high desert plateau dotted with small lakes, most of them salt lakes. The only people around were nomads or the very occasional Chinese truck driver or Tibetan trader, and the "road" was more like traces in the dirt (something like following the Oregon Trail one hundred years too late). We traveled fifteen to twenty miles per hour, always holding on to something in the car to brace against the constant bumps. At the end of a long day, we welcomed the sight of a truck stop. But we were now at fifteen thousand feet. And for some reason, there was no more yak dung. Instead, there were enormous piles of dried goat dung.

Still, we were feeling confident by this time. We built a little tower with paper and dung, and then lit a match. The paper burned, but not the dung. We just couldn't get it to catch fire. Finally we went to ask a truck driver, a guy standing around outside. He looked at us with a mix of pity and disgust, then walked over to his truck, took off a large gas can (in the Changtang, everyone has to travel carrying extra gas), and brought it into the room. He poured some gas onto our pile of goat dung and lit a match. Whoosh! Suddenly we had a fire. The best thing about goat dung, we learned, is that there's usually plenty of it.

A few days later, we came across a man out in the middle of nowhere whose truck had gotten stuck in the sand of a dry riverbed. We stopped, and everyone worked, pushing and digging. Once the truck was freed, it was time for lunch. As we started eating our dried yak jerky and our 761 bars, the truck driver dug around in his cab and then appeared with a couple of cans of preserved meat (they were somewhat ubiquitous at that time in China). He put the cans on the ground in front of his truck, went around back, and reappeared with a blowtorch. He took aim, then lit up the scene with a flash of flame, sizzling the cans for about ten seconds. A minute later, when they'd cooled a little, he cut them open and offered us some meat. Cooking with fire, high-altitude-trucker-style.

OPPOSITE: *A Tibetan woman pilgrim in the Mount Kailas region of western Tibet places a stone on a cairn topped with prayer flags and other offerings.*

KAZAKH CABBAGE STIR-FRY
WITH LAMB

The day after Serik and I had our fall on the motorbike (see page 300), we drove back along the same mountain road and stopped in at the house of the people who had been so nice to us the day before. The small log house sat all by itself just off the road, miles from the nearest settlement. A big dog barked as we arrived, and soon the couple (and their daughter) came out to see who'd driven up. They smiled to see us, then they looked closely at Serik's wounds and made sure that he was okay. They asked us to come in.

Near the door there was a cast-iron wood-burning stove, fully stoked, so the house was warm and cozy. Cigarettes, which are still a big thing all across China, were passed around, and then cups of hot salted tea. The husband, a tall, friendly Chinese man, put Uighur music on a small stereo, and his wife, a Kazakh, set about chopping onions and slicing cabbage. They showed me photographs of their house in winter (a long, hard winter, just a stone's throw from Siberia in Russia), and I showed them photographs from Canada. We talked about horses (they have twelve), and about Uighur music, and Kazakh music.

Then lunch was ready. We ate this simple, delicious stir-fry, Kazakh bread (see page 195), several different jams, and yogurt, and drank bowls of salty butter tea.

Since we first worked on this recipe at home, we've gotten into the habit of buying just a little bit of lamb, several small chops, for example. We cut the meat off the bone, then mince it with a cleaver. Its delectable flavor goes a long way, not just in this dish, but in other stir-fries too.

1 tablespoon peanut oil, vegetable oil, or rendered lamb fat (see Glossary)
A scant ¼ pound boneless lamb, finely chopped or ground
½ red onion, thinly sliced
1 red cayenne chile, seeds and membranes removed and thinly sliced
1 green cayenne chile, seeds and membranes removed and thinly sliced
1 pound Napa cabbage, thinly sliced crosswise (about 5 cups)
½ teaspoon salt, or to taste

Place a wok over high heat, and once it is hot, add the oil and swirl a little. Toss in the lamb and red onion and stir-fry for 1 minute. Add the chiles and stir-fry for 15 seconds, then add the cabbage. Stir-fry briefly, then add the salt and continue to stir-fry for 3 to 4 minutes, or until the cabbage is wilted and tender. Taste and adjust the salt if you wish.

Turn out onto a plate and serve.

Serves 3 to 4 as one of several dishes

TIBETAN RATATOUILLE

On a recent trip to Lhasa, I had several versions of this simmered tomato-eggplant stir-fry in small Tibetan-run restaurants and in one private home. The dish was new to me, a sign perhaps of the greater availability of vegetables in Lhasa and a greater preparedness among younger Tibetans, at least those in the larger towns, to eat more vegetables. Make it in mid- to late summer when vegetables are at their peak; or substitute canned tomatoes in other seasons. Serve with plenty of rice to absorb the full-flavored ginger-garlic broth. There's no chile or chile paste in the dish, but there is a small taste of China: a touch of Sichuan pepper and a hit of soy sauce.

> 2 long or 4 short Asian eggplants (about 1 pound total)
> 2 to 3 medium tomatoes (¾ to 1 pound), or substitute
>   2 cups canned tomatoes
> 2 scallions
> 2 tablespoons peanut oil or vegetable oil
> 1 tablespoon minced garlic
> 1 tablespoon minced ginger
> 2 teaspoons salt, or to taste (less if your broth is salty)
> ¼ teaspoon ground Sichuan pepper, or to taste
> ½ to ¾ cup **Tibetan Bone Broth** (page 45) or mild vegetable,
>   chicken, or meat broth
> 1 tablespoon soy sauce, or to taste

Trim the stems off the eggplants. Cut lengthwise into long narrow slices (about 15 per eggplant), then cut these crosswise into 2- to 3-inch-long strips. Set aside. Cut the tomatoes into thin wedges, about 12 to a tomato, or chop canned tomatoes into coarse dice. Set aside. Trim the scallions, and reserve the greens. Cut each scallion lengthwise into ribbons, then cut into 1½- to 2-inch lengths. Set aside. Mince the scallion greens; you should have about 2 tablespoons greens. Set aside.

Place a large wok or heavy skillet over high heat. When it is hot, add the oil and swirl to coat the bottom of the pan. Toss in the garlic and ginger and stir-fry briefly. Add the eggplant and stir-fry for a minute; press it against the hot sides of the wok (or bottom of the pan) to try to scorch all surfaces. Add 1 teaspoon of the salt and stir-fry for another minute, then add the tomatoes. Stir-fry for 2 minutes, or until the tomatoes are softened. Add the scallion ribbons and stir-fry to mix. Add the Sichuan pepper and the remaining 1 teaspoon salt and stir-fry for another minute.

Add ½ cup broth and continue to stir-fry until it comes to a boil. Cover and boil hard for 3 minutes, then uncover and stir. Cover again and cook for another 2 minutes. Uncover, stir, and taste the eggplant for doneness. Cook it a little longer if necessary.

Stir in up to ¼ cup more broth if you'd like a more saucy texture. Add the soy sauce and the minced scallion greens, stir, and taste for seasonings. Turn out into a shallow bowl and serve hot.

Serves 4 as a side dish, 2 as a main course with rice and a side dish

CHILE-HOT BRIGHT GREEN SOYBEANS WITH GARLIC

This attractive dish from the Bai people, who live in western Yunnan province around Lake Er Hai, is traditionally made with fresh fava beans, also known as broad beans, but we prefer to make it with soybeans. We love their bright green color and tender texture, and their availability. We usually buy them already shelled, frozen, in one-pound bags. They're often labeled *edamame*, the Japanese name.

> 1 pound (2 cups) fresh or frozen shelled soybeans (see headnote)
>
> Scant 2 tablespoons peanut oil
>
> 2 tablespoons thinly sliced Pickled Red Chiles (page 34) or
> store-bought pickled chiles, or substitute 5 dried red chiles
>
> 5 garlic cloves, thinly sliced
>
> ½ teaspoon star anise pieces
>
> 1 teaspoon salt
>
> About 1 cup mild chicken broth or pork broth or water
>
> 2 teaspoons cornstarch, dissolved in 2 tablespoons cold water
> (optional)

Rinse the beans under cold water, drain, and set aside.

Heat a wok over high heat. Add the oil and swirl it a little, then add the chiles and garlic and stir-fry for about 30 seconds. Add the soybeans and the star anise and stir-fry for about 1 minute. Add the salt and broth or water and bring to a boil, then reduce the heat and simmer until the beans are very tender, about 7 minutes. (Fresh and frozen take about the same time.)

If you wish, thicken the broth: Give the cornstarch mixture a stir and add it to the wok. Stir-fry for a moment, until the liquid thickens. Turn out and serve.

Serves 4 as a side dish

OPPOSITE, LEFT: *A Bai woman in Dali, Yunnan.* OPPOSITE, RIGHT: *Chile-Hot Bright Green Soybeans with Garlic.*

STIR-FRIED STEM LETTUCE LHASA-STYLE

We don't know why stem lettuce, usually called celtuce in North America and known as *osun* in Lhasa, is so widely available there. Perhaps because it grows mostly underground it's better able to survive the cold than other green vegetables. We do know that this easy stir-fry makes a delicious vegetable side dish, warming on a cold day, with its soupy broth and hint of Sichuan pepper.

Celtuce came to Europe from China in the late 1800s and to the United States in the 1930s. The stem is about 12 inches long, like an elongated broccoli stalk, and it grows underground, with a tuft of leaves at the top.

Prepared celtuce, with the stems peeled or sliced into long fine light green strips, is now sold in markets in Lhasa, and piles of celtuce can also be found in Sichuan and Yunnan food markets. However, it's very hard to come by in North America unless you grow your own. We suggest that you substitute broccoli stalks, which have a very similar texture once sliced, or use the whiter bottom part of Napa cabbage. (Instructions for both are included; for leafy greens options, see Lhasa-Style Leafy Greens on page 104.)

The vegetable strands are stir-fried, then briefly simmered in broth. Traditionally a little Tsampa (page 180) is used to thicken the broth, but you can use cornstarch dissolved in cold water.

> About ½ pound celtuce stems, broccoli stems, or whiter stem
> ends of Napa cabbage (see headnote and Note)
>
> 2 tablespoons peanut oil or canola oil
>
> 2 garlic cloves, smashed into chunks
>
> 1 shallot or ½ small onion, thinly sliced
>
> 1 tablespoon minced ginger
>
> 1 teaspoon salt, or to taste
>
> 2 tablespoons minced scallion greens (optional)
>
> ½ teaspoon ground Sichuan pepper
>
> 1 cup Tibetan Bone Broth (page 45) or meat, chicken, or
> vegetable broth

(continued)

1 to 2 tablespoons Tsampa (page 180), or 1 tablespoon
cornstarch, dissolved in 2 tablespoons cold water

To prepare celtuce or broccoli, peel off the tough outer skin. Cut lengthwise in half and then lengthwise into very thin slices about 4 or 5 inches long, rather like short wide noodles. If you have a Benriner or coarse grater, use it to make long, slender lengthwise slices. You should have about 3 cups. Set aside.

To prepare Napa cabbage, detach the leaves one by one from the stem. Trim off the coarse base, then stack them 4 at a time and cut lengthwise into very narrow strips. Cut the strips crosswise in half. You should have about 4 loosely packed cups; set aside.

Heat a wok over high heat. Add the oil and swirl it around. Toss in the garlic, shallot or onion, and ginger and stir-fry for a minute or so to soften them a little. Toss in the celtuce, broccoli, or Napa and stir-fry briefly, then add the salt and stir-fry for about a minute. Add the scallion greens, if using, and Sichuan pepper and stir, then add the broth and bring to a vigorous boil. Cover and cook for 1 minute. Check for doneness: the vegetable strands should be tender but still firm. If necessary, let boil a little longer, uncovered. Taste for salt and adjust if needed.

If you wish, thicken the broth by adding the tsampa or dissolved cornstarch and stir-fry until the broth thickens, about 15 seconds. Turn out and serve.

Serves 4 as a side dish

TOFU-CELTUCE STIR-FRY: The first day we were in the Dai village of Menghan with our kids (see Dai Spicy Grilled Tofu, page 111), our host, Mei, prepared a very different stem lettuce stir-fry, a Dai version, for lunch. The celtuce strips were seared in a hot wok, then stir-fried with about ½ cup pressed tofu (see Glossary), chopped small, and small chunks of tomato. She didn't use broth; the only liquid came from the tomato. Flavorings were mild—a little Sichuan pepper, a little dried red chile, and salt.

LHASA-STYLE LEAFY GREENS: The technique used in Lhasa for stem lettuce can also be used for leafy greens, including dandelion greens, pea tendrils, and bok choi. For dandelion greens or tender pea tendrils, begin with 1 pound greens. Wash well, drain, and cut crosswise into 1-inch lengths. Cook as above, but cooking time in the broth will be a little shorter. For bok choi, begin with 1 pound small Shanghai bok choi or regular bok choi. Cut them lengthwise in half, and wash thoroughly in a bowl of water. Follow the cooking directions above, but increase the cooking time after you add the broth to about 4 minutes, covered.

NOTE ON NAPA CABBAGE: Use the whiter stem end of a medium to large Napa cabbage (also known as Chinese cabbage; see Glossary). We often use the leafier pale green parts, cut crosswise, for a stir-fry or for Napa and Red Onion Salad (page 86), then use the stem ends for this Lhasa dish. If starting with a whole cabbage, cut off the bottom 8 inches. Set the leafy top aside for another purpose.

JICAMA-TOFU SHEET STIR-FRY

This Yunnanese stir-fry, with its touch of chile and ginger heat, is a simple dish, but one or both of the two main ingredients may be unfamiliar.

Dried tofu sheets are a wonderful pantry staple. They are sold in Chinese groceries (see the Glossary for more). They must be soaked in lukewarm water for 20 minutes or so before using and then can be stir-fried quickly. They absorb flavors beautifully, so they are great in soups and in well-sauced stir-fries like this one.

Jicama (the Mexican name) is often known as yam bean or white tuber in Asia. A pale tan tuber with a crisp white interior, it is native to the Americas but now widely used in China as well as in Malaysia, Indonesia, and Thailand. It stays crunchy when cooked, providing a lovely contrast to the soft texture of the simmered tofu.

1 dried tofu sheet, about 2 ounces (see headnote)

1 small jicama (about 1 pound)

2 tablespoons peanut oil

5 dried red chiles

2 thin slices ginger

1 teaspoon salt, or to taste

1/2 cup vegetable broth, meat broth, or water

1 to 2 tablespoons soy sauce, or to taste

2 teaspoons cornstarch, dissolved in 1 tablespoon cold water

2 to 3 tablespoons minced scallion greens, chives, or coriander (optional)

Break the tofu sheet (it's brittle and will shatter when squeezed) into smaller pieces, about an inch or two in size. Place in a bowl, add warm water to cover, and soak for 20 minutes.

Meanwhile, use a sharp knife to peel the tan outer layer off the jicama, cut the jicama into 1/4-inch slices, then cut the slices into approximately 1-inch squares. You should have about 4 cups. Set aside.

Heat a wok or large heavy skillet over high heat. Add the oil and swirl it around, then toss in the chiles, ginger, and salt. Add the jicama and stir-fry for about 20 seconds. Lift the softened tofu sheet pieces out of the water with your hand, without squeezing them, and add to the pan. Stir-fry for about a minute. Add the broth or water, bring to a vigorous boil, and cook for about a minute.

Add 1 tablespoon soy sauce to the pan and stir to blend it in. Stir the cornstarch mixture, add to the pan, and stir-fry for 30 seconds or so, until the sauce thickens a little. Taste for seasoning, and adjust if you wish by adding salt or soy sauce.

Turn out into a wide shallow bowl and sprinkle on the minced greens, if using. Serve hot or at room temperature.

Serves 3 to 4 as part of a rice meal

Tibetan nomads and shepherds, like nomads every-where, have figured out how to be portable. Their wealth is in their herds, yaks and goats primarily. The animals feed on pasture, and they help transport the family belongings from one grazing ground to the next. Nomad "houses" are tents made of wool from their animals. Belongings are minimal but always include a kettle for boiling water and various containers of stored foods. Yet these too are minimal: butter, tea, salt, tsampa, dried cheese. Drying is the primary technique for storing and preserving food, not just cheese, but also meat. In Tibet's very dry high-altitude climate, drying is quickly done, and it has the advantage for nomadic people of making foods weigh less. No heavy jars of pickles here, just dried or freeze-dried foods.

On our first trip out to Mount Kailas in southwestern Tibet, we came upon a nomad encampment in a striking place. A nearby lake, beautifully framed by low snow-covered hills, was still frozen despite the intense spring sun. The extended family consisted of a couple and their three children, who lived in one tent, and an auntie (we understood her to be the husband's unmarried older sister), who lived in a nearby tent on her own. Sheep and goats and yaks were dotted all over the bare-looking landscape, moving slowly as they searched for something to eat.

The husband invited us into the family tent, made of brown-black yak wool woven into a thick fabric. We sat down and began to exchange the basic information that always gets aired among strangers: age, marital status, number of children, etc. His wife poured tea into small bowls for us, fresh hot butter tea, and we sat sipping it and looking around at the tent. She reached up, untied a leg of dried lamb or goat that was hanging from the cross-pole, and handed it to her husband. He took out a large knife and cut a thin sliver of meat from the place where some meat had already been sliced off, then passed the leg and the knife to me. I cut off a slice and then passed them both on to Jeffrey. The meat was delicious, not tough as I had expected, and almost sweet, like prosciutto, with a melting texture on the tongue.

After tea, we went over to the auntie's tent and found her bottle-feeding several young kids, baby goats that were too weak to nurse from their mothers. Before leaving, we gave the family the only thing we had to offer: a color photograph of the Dalai Lama. The wife murmured a prayer as she touched the photo to the top of her head, reverently, then tucked it away in a safe place. When we passed by that way two weeks later, heading back to Lhasa, the family was gone, moved on to another grazing ground. N

OPPOSITE: *Every year at the busy summer market of Burang, in western Tibet, Nepalis come from the other side of the Himalaya to trade lowland goods for Tibetan wool and salt, and old friends like these two Tibetan men meet again with pleasure.*

He was tall, skinny, and about twenty-five years old, the guy at the "poste restante" in the post office in Kashgar. We'd go in occasionally to check for mail, in those days before e-mail, and there he'd be, awkward and friendly, and very underemployed. He always wanted us to hang around so he could practice his English.

One day when we stopped by, he smiled broadly at us. "Your parents are very well, and your sister is moving to California," he said to Jeffrey. "What?" we said, not understanding. "Yes, yes," he said happily, "they wrote you a postcard. Yes, here it is!" He held it up, looking pleased, then handed it to us.

"You read it?" we said.

"Oh yes, I read all the postcards in English. It is good practice for me!"

We said nothing; there was nothing to say, really. So we just thanked him for our mail and headed off down the street.

Not far from the post office a gigantic Mao statue still stood, carved from pale pink stone and the tallest thing around. Was he smiling to himself at the eagerness of the young postal worker?

ABOVE: *Pakistani traders at a* chai khana (*informal tea shop and restaurant) in Kashgar sip tea as they wait to be served a lunch of noodles with* laghman *sauce. The traders travel along the Karakoram Highway from Pakistan to do business, modern versions of Silk Road travelers of centuries past.* OPPOSITE: *Tofu Batons with Hot Sesame Dressing (page 110).*

TOFU BATONS
WITH HOT SESAME DRESSING

We first tasted these tofu batons in the Jinghong market in southern Yunnan, sold by Dai women (see page 237). There, as in nearby Thailand to the south, vendors come to the market each day with a vast array of cooked and prepared dishes, ready to be taken home and served as part of lunch or dinner. It's like "gourmet take-out," only inexpensive.

As in so many dishes in Dai cooking, there's chile heat combined with a bit of sour. It's an easy dish to prepare, and if you've never cooked before with tofu sticks, they're a fun discovery and a good pantry item. When rehydrating them, make sure that they are totally submerged in the soaking water. [PHOTOGRAPH ON PAGE 109]

3 ounces tofu sticks (4 to 6 sticks)
  (see Glossary)

1 tablespoon peanut oil

1 teaspoon roasted sesame oil

½ teaspoon chile pepper flakes, or to taste

1 tablespoon rice vinegar, or to taste

2 tablespoons soy sauce, or to taste

½ teaspoon sugar

¼ cup coriander leaves

Bring 2 inches of water to a boil in a medium pot. Add the tofu sticks, breaking them if necessary to make them fit, and use a wooden spoon to push them under the surface of the water. Turn off the heat. Weight down the sticks with a plate that fits inside the pot to keep them submerged. Cover and let sit for 30 minutes.

Remove the plate and drain the tofu well. Cut the sticks into 2-inch lengths, trimming off and discarding any tough bits. Cut the sticks lengthwise in half or into quarters, to make narrow batons. Set aside.

Heat a wok or wide heavy pot over medium-high heat. Add the peanut oil and sesame oil. When the oil is hot, add the chile flakes and tofu batons and stir-fry for 2 minutes, stirring and pressing on the batons to expose them to the hot surface of the pan.

In a small bowl, combine the vinegar, soy sauce, and sugar and whisk well, then pour over the tofu batons. Stir-fry briefly to distribute the flavors, then bring the liquid to a boil. Immediately lower the heat to medium-low, cover, and simmer for 5 minutes.

Turn out into a wide shallow bowl. Taste and add a little more soy or vinegar if you wish. Sprinkle on the coriander leaves, and serve warm or at room temperature.

Serves 4 as a side dish

DAI SPICY GRILLED TOFU

This grilled tofu always reminds us of our first time traveling in Yunnan as a family. One afternoon, when Dom was nine and Tashi was six years old, we arrived in the town of Menghan and checked into a small family-run guesthouse that another traveler had told us about. The family had two very nice teenage daughters who immediately whisked Dom off to explore the neighborhood. He was delighted.

And then an hour or so passed, and we began to wonder about him. We weren't particularly worried, just wondering. Suddenly we heard the sound of a motorbike and up pulled the girls, with another friend, and with Dom, all four squeezed on the motorbike. Dom was eating spicy grilled tofu, happy as could be with his new friends.

¾ pound pressed tofu (see Glossary)

2 teaspoons lard (see Note)

1 teaspoon crushed dried red chile or chile pepper flakes

½ teaspoon salt

1 cup Soy-Vinegar Dipping Sauce (page 151)

Prepare a fire in a charcoal grill or preheat a gas grill. Soak 4 thin bamboo skewers in water for 30 minutes.

Cut the tofu into 8 squares, 2 inches by 2 inches. Set aside.

Combine the lard with the chile pepper and salt, and blend together with a fork. The lard should be soft, but not melted. Set aside.

Thread the pressed tofu onto the skewers, putting 2 squares on each skewer and threading them on a diagonal, so they look like diamonds. Lay out on a platter, and use a basting or pastry brush to brush on one side with the flavored lard.

Place brushed side down on the grill and grill for 2 to 3 minutes, until nicely browned. As they grill, brush the top sides of the squares with the remainder of the lard mixture. Turn and grill the second side until nicely browned, another 2 to 3 minutes.

Serve on the skewers, arranged on a plate. Serve with the sauce in condiment bowls, so guests can dip their tofu squares as they wish.

Serves 4 as an appetizer or as part of a meal

NOTE: We learned from the Dai what good flavor a little pork fat can give. We trim the fat off pork roasts or other cuts when we bring them home, then freeze it in a plastic bag, in small quantities, so it's there when we need to render more lard (see Cooking Oils and Fats in the Glossary for instructions). You can also buy lard from many butchers.

A market scene in the Dai area of southern Yunnan, in the town of Menghan, on the Mekong River.

Kashgar, an old oasis town and important stop on the Silk Road trade routes, lies in the far west of China's Xinjiang province (in some older books, in fact, the whole of western Xinjiang is called Kashgaria). In 1986 Kashgar was a predominantly Uighur town. Unlike Urumqi, the major city and capital of Xinjiang province, which could be reached by train and already had a majority Han population, Kashgar was much more remote and had retained its Uighur identity. In Kashgar in 1986, central China still felt very far away.

Our plan was to bicycle from Kashgar through the desert and mountains and eventually over the Khunjerab Pass to the Hunza Valley in Pakistan. The road we would take, known as the Karakoram Highway, had been under construction for almost twenty years, a joint project between China and Pakistan, and it was scheduled to open to foreign travelers in May 1986.

We'd come a long way to get here. We'd brought bicycles, tools, a tent, and sleeping bags, as well as a month's supply of freeze-dried food to Lhasa, where we'd been based for several months. From Lhasa, with the help of three kind friends met there, we'd traveled overland to Kashgar with all our gear.

That trip took eleven days. First we traveled by bus for two days north from Lhasa to Golmud, and from there it was another long day's bus ride northwest to the town of Dunhuang. Then we had a two-day train ride to Turpan, another day and night of train to Korla, and three more days by bus to Kashgar. This was the modern version of traveling the Silk Road. We weren't traveling with camels or donkeys, as in days of old, but the trip was still a long one, and we were happy to arrive.

We were staying at the Chini Bagh Hotel, which had been the British consulate from about 1890 to 1947. We'd read about the Chini Bagh in books by travelers who had stayed there, such as Ella Maillart (see "Ella," page 70) and Peter Fleming, and also in memoirs by men who had been posted there as consuls, including C. P. Skrine and the famous climber Eric Shipton (see Bibliography). The building had seen better days, but it was still full of charm. The other people staying there were mostly businessmen and traders from Pakistan who were seizing the opportunity to explore China's then-new experiment with free enterprise.

In Kashgar we ate as if we might never be able to eat again. There were incredible flatbreads (nan) baked fresh in tandoor ovens several times a day. There were melons from the oasis, watermelons and Hami melons, and sweet perfumed melons we'd never tasted before. There were many kinds of lamb kebabs and rich intricate *pulaos*. But almost best of all were the homemade noodles, hand-stretched noodles (see "Uighur Flung Noodles," page 152), one of the food world's most amazing cooking feats.

Every evening we would have a plate of noodles with laghman sauce (see page 135), fresh tomatoes stir-fried with green peppers, a little lamb, and slices of onion. Simple, but beyond delicious. We'd drink a beer or two and watch donkey carts pass on the street in front of us. Sometimes we'd even have a second plate of noodles. And all this in the desert air, in an ancient Silk Road town.

Then one day it was time to leave. We loaded up our panniers and set out on our bicycles across the desert. Like so many travelers before us, we were heading for the snow-capped mountains we could see, like a mirage, far away on the western horizon: the Pamirs, and beyond them the Karakoram.

OPPOSITE: *A small horse caravan in the Pamirs, below Mount Kongur.*

Town square in Yuanyang, with several Yi women and morning fog.

YUANYANG GRILLED POTATOES

These grilled potatoes are part of a typical Yi noodle stand (see Yi Market Noodles, page 126), and a common street food in the Hani areas of southeastern Yunnan. They are just delicious on their own, but they also pair well with grilled meat and a salad. We often make them when we're cooking beef, pork, or chicken on the grill; then all that's left to do is prepare a salad or green vegetable to serve alongside.

The potatoes are first boiled until almost cooked through, then peeled and cut into chunks. The chunks go on the grill, and soon they have a wonderful grilled flavor and chewy skin. They are not seasoned or oiled before grilling, but once cooked, there's an array of flavors that can accompany them, from coarse salt to chile paste to chopped cucumbers. In the end, we find them most delectable eaten plain with salt. Allow about half a pound of potatoes per person.

> Large potatoes, such as Yukon Gold, preferably local and
>   organic
> Coarse salt
> Tribal Pepper-Salt (page 36) or ground dry-roasted Sichuan
>   pepper (optional)
> Soy-Vinegar Dipping Sauce (page 151; optional)

Place the potatoes in a large pot of water and bring to a boil. Boil until the potatoes are barely cooked through. Drain and let cool. (The potatoes can be boiled as long as a day ahead; once cooled, store covered in the refrigerator.)

Prepare a charcoal grill or preheat a gas grill, with the rack about 5 inches above the coals or flame.

Strip the peels off the potatoes and cut them into 1½-inch chunks. The more cut surfaces they have, the more taste of the grill they'll absorb during cooking. Place them on the grill (either directly on the grate or in a grilling box) and grill, turning occasionally, until golden on all sides; resist the urge to season them while they cook.

Serve plain, accompanied by coarse salt and, if you like, a choice of seasonings put out in small bowls.

EASY LHASA FRIED POTATO SLICES

This deep-fried street-food snack comes from Lhasa. The potatoes are peeled, sliced, and slipped into hot oil. When they are lifted out several minutes later, they are golden and crisp on the outside and tender in the center. The vendor dusts them with a little cayenne, if you want, and a sprinkling of salt.

I wanted to see if making Lhasa-style fried potatoes was as easy as all the vendors there made it look. The first time I tried it, I was working on a wood stove, so the temperature varied, and I had only a small wok for deep-frying. We had a crowd for supper, but the meal itself would not be ready for another hour. I hoped the fried potatoes would fill the appetizer gap and keep everyone happy.

They did: the slices cooked to a beautiful golden brown, it was easy to tell when they were ready, and I found deep-frying them a pleasure. The only complication was deciding what flavorings to add: salt is a given, but options include chopped fresh mint (a nontraditional idea inspired by the mint in our garden; ground roasted Sichuan pepper; cayenne, which is quite common in Lhasa; and/or a pepper-salt.

These are best eaten hot and fresh, as an appetizer or a snack. We've found that when we fry them, some people like the thinner, crispier slices, while others prefer the tender, paler, thicker ones. So when you slice your potatoes, remember that you don't have to cut them to the exact same thickness—variation means your guests have choices, and that's a great thing.

About 3 pounds Yukon Gold or other firm potatoes, peeled

Peanut oil for deep-frying (2 to 4 cups)

Coarse salt

OPTIONAL TOPPINGS

Cayenne pepper or Tribal Pepper-Salt (page 36)

Ground dry-roasted Sichuan pepper

About 1 cup mint leaves, coarsely chopped

Cut the potatoes into ¼-inch slices and set aside in a large bowl. Put out a slotted spoon or a long-handled mesh skimmer. You may also want to use a long-handled spatula. Have a shallow wooden or ceramic bowl ready for serving the potatoes.

Place a large wok or deep heavy pot on the stovetop; make sure it is stable. (Or use a deep fryer.) Pour 2 inches of oil into the wok or pot and heat over medium-high heat. You want the oil to be between 350° and 375°F; use a deep-fry thermometer to monitor the temperature. Or test it in the following way: Slide a slice of potato into the oil. It should sink and fizz and then slowly start to rise to the surface. If it bobs right up and starts to brown very quickly, the oil is too hot—lower the heat slightly. If it sinks and rests on the bottom for a while lethargically, the oil is not yet hot enough.

When the oil is at temperature, slide in a handful of potato slices, without crowding; there should not be so many that they are above the level of the oil. Use a spatula or the slotted spoon or skimmer to move the potatoes around; separate any slices that are sticking together. After about a minute, move them again and gently turn them over, to ensure all sides are cooked in the hot oil bubbling up from the bottom. After another minute or two, you should see them browning.

Lift one slice out with a slotted spoon, and transfer it to a plate. Cut it and taste it, being careful not to burn yourself. If the potato is tender all the way through, use the slotted spoon or skimmer to lift the rest of the potato slices out of the oil, pausing for a moment to let excess oil drain off them, then transfer them to the serving bowl.

Repeat with the remaining potato slices, handful by handful. You'll quickly learn to judge when the potatoes are done the way you like them. Once you have cooked several batches, sprinkle on salt and any other toppings you wish and put them out for your guests. Repeat until all the slices are cooked and served (see Note).

Serves 6 as an appetizer with drinks or as a snack

NOTE ON STORING OIL: Set the wok or pot of oil aside in an out-of-the-way place to cool. Pour the cool oil through a fine-mesh strainer into a clean, dry jar. Seal with a tight-fitting lid and store in the refrigerator. You can reuse the oil several times for deep-frying or stir-frying. Once it gets dark or has a strong smell, discard it.

HUI VEGETABLE HOT POT

The cliché image of Central Asian food is of kebabs or other grilled meat, perhaps with some dairy products on the side. But, like many clichés, the image needs adjusting. In Xining, an old trade-route town just east of the Koko Nor with a large Hui population, I came upon a brilliant vegetarian hot pot.

It was late on a Friday afternoon. Men were just coming out of the mosque after prayers, and the markets were lively. There were skewers of lamb's liver and tongue grilling over charcoal, tended by bearded men; there were stacks of flatbreads and vegetables of all kinds; there were noodle makers cutting and stretching batches of pale smooth dough; and in several stalls, frequented mostly by women or families, there was this Hui version of hot pot.

I couldn't resist. I went in and found a seat, but then I had real trouble deciding what to order. There were skewers of raw vegetables of all sorts: four different types of mushrooms, several kinds of lettuce leaves, eggplant slices, potato slices, zucchini, mustard greens, pea tendrils, pressed tofu slices, and more. You chose the skewers you wanted and they were cooked to order and served to you with a bowl of noodles and hot broth.

The great thing about this approach is that because there is only one kind of vegetable on each skewer, they can be cooked to a beautifully exact doneness, with no compromise. The vendor took the skewers I'd chosen (oyster mushrooms, zucchini, a romaine-like lettuce, and mustard greens) and plunged them into the vat of boiling broth. He used a mesh colander to scoop up some parboiled noodles and placed them in hot water to heat up and soften. They came out first, steaming and soft, and were tipped into a large bowl. As each skewer of vegetables was cooked, it was lifted out and laid across the bowl. Finally he poured hot broth onto the noodles and sprinkled on some chopped Chinese celery and scallion greens.

On the table was a cruet of black rice vinegar, along with small dishes of soy sauce, chile paste, and a vinegar-cucumber sauce. I took a sip of the broth with my spoon, then added a little vinegar and a little soy to it. I made up a small blend in the condiment dish they gave me: a dab of chile paste stirred into the dark vinegar. Then I used my chopsticks to slide a zucchini slice off its skewer and dip it into the chile-paste blend. Delicious! The noodles had great bite, the mushrooms were poached to perfection, and the lettuce was too. Altogether it was a wonderful meal.

To reproduce this style of hot pot, all you need is a choice of vegetables and wooden skewers (30 or so for 6 people) to thread them on; some noodles, homemade, or store-bought fettuccine or egg noodles; a broth; a large pot; and some condiments. Serve as a main course, perhaps followed by a grill such as Uighur Lamb Kebabs (page 260) or Dai Grilled Fish (page 222), with cooling slices of sweet melon to finish the meal.

1½ to 2 pounds Amdo Noodle Squares (page 128), long Tibetan
   noodles (see page 144); or Tuvan noodles (see page 246)
   or 1 pound store-bought fettuccine or egg noodles
2 tablespoons peanut oil or vegetable oil

VEGETABLES
3 medium zucchini, cut into ¼-inch slices
20 to 30 leaves of leaf lettuce
About 6 leaves Napa cabbage, cut crosswise into 2-inch-wide strips
1 pound mixed mushrooms (such as oyster and white), cut in
   half if large
2 cups large cauliflower florets and/or large broccoli florets
2 cups mustard greens or bok choi leaves

(continued)

About 1 cup Jinjiang (black rice) vinegar

Soy sauce

½ cup Guizhou Chile Paste (page 35) or store-bought chile paste

2 cups Cucumber-Vinegar Sauce (page 83)

8 to 10 cups Hui Vegetarian Broth (page 48) or other vegetable
    broth or light chicken stock

Bring a large pot of water to a boil. Add the noodles or pasta and cook
until barely cooked through and still firm. Drain and transfer to a
bowl. Drizzle with the oil and toss to coat. Set aside.

Prepare the skewers, filling them only one-half full, leaving both
ends clear (see photo, page 116). Thread 3 to 5 zucchini slices each on
6 to 8 skewers. Thread 6 skewers with the lettuce leaves, piercing each
leaf several times so it is secure. Thread 6 skewers with the Napa
cabbage. Thread 6 skewers with 3 or 4 mushrooms each. Thread 6
skewers with 3 or 4 cauliflower or broccoli florets each. Thread 6
skewers with mustard greens or bok choi leaves.

Put out the condiments in bowls, as well as two small condiment
bowls for each guest, so they can serve themselves and make their own
combinations of dipping sauces.

Bring the broth to a rolling boil in a large pot. Place the vegetable
skewers into the broth in order of firmness, so, for example, the
cauliflower and broccoli go in well ahead of the lettuce.

Meanwhile, divide the noodles among six soup bowls.

As the vegetables on each skewer are done, lift the skewer out of
the broth and lay it on a platter. Once all the skewers are out, ladle the
hot broth over the noodles in each bowl and set out the bowls. Place
the platter in the center of the table and let guests help themselves
to skewers of vegetables. They can use chopsticks to slide cooked
vegetables off the skewers and into their soup as they wish. Invite them
to make a blend of condiments in their condiment bowls for dipping
or for pouring into their soup.

Serves 6 as a main course

*On our trip along the Silk Road (see "Kashgar, 1986," page 112), we were invited to
a Uighur home in Aksu, a small oasis town at the time that has now grown into a
bustling small city. The family were bakers and noodle-makers. Here, in the
courtyard behind their clay-brick house, the father stretches noodles in the classic
Uighur style while his young daughter watches. Notice the trellises overhead,
which less than a month later (we were there in late May) would be lush with
grape vines, giving welcome shade from the intense desert sun.*

SILK ROAD CHICKPEA-CARROT FRITTERS

The first and only time I tasted these chickpea fritters in China was in a tiny restaurant (using the word "restaurant" makes it sound bigger than it was) just off the main intersection in the town of Turpan (see "Turpan Depression," page 200) in Xinjiang. I'd been invited to the restaurant by two fellow travelers, Stephane and Thanya, whom I had met a few days before. We had rented a car together to go on a morning's outing, and for lunch we ended up in this little place they'd discovered earlier. The fritters were served with a hot chile pepper paste; like falafel, they were moist and soft rather than crunchy, and they were beautiful with their strands of orange carrot.

As remarkable a pleasure as the restaurant was, Stephane and Thanya were even more remarkable. They had been on the road for three years, teaching English in Sichuan, Taiwan, and Inner Mongolia. It was through their excellent recommendations that Naomi ended up spending time in Hailar (see "Mongolia out of Season," page 244).

Stephane and Thanya are from Timmins, Ontario. They're both bilingual in French and English, as well as working toward fluency in Mandarin. As travelers, they were immediately friendly and open, and they were unwaveringly appreciative of the opportunity to live, work, and travel in China. They were the opposite of jaded, and it was so refreshing to be with them. They are also among the most adventurous eaters—on the road—that I have ever known, always looking for something new to try. I felt very lucky to meet them.

For the next few months, we corresponded by e-mail. They journeyed into northern Pakistan, got caught in the middle of a local war in Gilgit, and then traveled all around the coast of India before finally returning home.

Serve the Fritters with Guizhou Chile Paste (page 35) or Bright Red Chile Paste (page 18) or a store-bought chile paste; Jinjiang (black rice) vinegar (see Glossary) or Soy-Vinegar Dipping Sauce (page 151); and/or a chutney or relish, homemade (see Index) or store-bought.

1 cup dried chickpeas
1 tablespoon water
1 teaspoon salt
¼ teaspoon freshly ground black pepper
2 cups coarsely grated carrots (about ¾ pound)
Peanut oil for deep-frying (2 cups)

Wash the chickpeas and soak overnight, covered, in 4 cups water.

Drain the chickpeas and transfer to a food processor. Add the 1 tablespoon water, the salt, and pepper and process until the chickpeas are finely ground. Transfer to a bowl, add the carrots, and mix well.

Scoop up 2 tablespoons of the mixture, squeeze it together in your hand, and shape it into a ball between your palms. It will be about the size of a golf ball. Flatten it into a disk about 2 inches across and set aside on the counter near your stovetop or on a lightly floured baking sheet. Repeat with the remaining mixture. You will have about 14 disks.

Set out a platter or two plates lined with paper towels or brown paper beside your stovetop. Also put out a slotted spoon or mesh skimmer. Place a large wok or large deep wide pot on your stovetop; make sure that the wok or pot is stable. (Or use a deep-fryer.) Pour in 2 inches of oil and heat the oil over medium-high heat. To test the temperature of the oil, hold a wooden chopstick vertically in the oil, with the end touching the bottom of the pot. If bubbles come bubbling up along the chopstick, the oil is at temperature. The oil should not be smoking; if it is, turn the heat down slightly and wait a moment for it to cool, then test again. (A deep-fry thermometer should read 325° to 350°F.)

Slide 3 or 4 chickpea disks into the oil and cook for 2½ to 3 minutes, using the slotted spoon or mesh skimmer to turn them over partway through, until they are nicely browned on both sides. Lift the fritters from the oil, pausing to let excess oil drain off them, and place on the paper towels or brown paper. Repeat until all the fritters are cooked.

Transfer the fritters to a serving plate. Serve hot or warm, with the condiments of your choice.

Makes about 14 fritters; serves 4 to 6 as an appetizer or as a side dish

THE DONG PEOPLE

The Dong live mostly in eastern Guizhou and western Guangxi. They number about three million. Like the Dai (see page 237), the Dong are one of many branches of the Tai-Kadai linguistic and ethnographic family, which also includes Thai and Lao. Their languages are distinct but have common roots.

Different villages in the Dong area have distinctive clothing and embroidery designs, so that villagers can distinguish at a quick glance where a stranger is from. Dong women are famed for their textiles, not just woven cotton and hemp, but also the technique of indigo dying—the fabric is pounded so that it absorbs a dark, rich color, almost purple-black, and has a sheen to it. The women also do very fine embroidery, some groups more than others, and are rarely without handwork in their spare time.

The Dong are known for two types of special timber-frame structures, drum towers and covered bridges. The drum towers are pagoda-like with an open area at the bottom, where the villagers can sit and visit and children can play, protected from the sun and rain, beneath a multilayered roof that tapers to a point. The whole structure is timber frame, a complex set of crosspieces of decreasing size. Similarly, the covered bridges are roofed timber-frame structures with railings but no walls. They may have been developed as a practical way to have a place to sit and to work sheltered from the wind, rain, and hot sun, but they've evolved into extraordinary structures, less common than the towers (not every village has a bridge).

Older women and men can be found at any hour in the shelter of the neighborhood tower or covered bridge, chatting, playing chess, embroidering, or keeping an eye on small children. The drum towers also shelter the village collection of *lusheng*, instruments made of parallel lengths of bamboo that look like large panpipes and sound like very reedy bagpipes.

The Dong areas of Guizhou and Guangxi have plentiful rains most years, and rice, the staple crop, is grown on steeply terraced hillsides, with sophisticated stone barriers and small waterways for managing water flow. Though sticky rice seems to be a cultural marker for the Dong, as it is for all Tai peoples that we know of, regular aromatic rice is also grown. On the steepest hillsides are carefully tended groves of the fir trees the Dong use to build their timber-frame houses, towers, and bridges.

Rice growing demands community cooperation and a lot of hard work, especially in hilly landscapes. Harvesttime is late September to late October. The sheaves of rice are hung on distinctive latticed scaffolding to dry, then carried home and hung under the eaves, like a hanging golden curtain. Some households also have sheaves of millet drying in the same way. By early November, there are chiles, some medium-hot (cayennes) and some sweet-hot (certain Turkish or Spanish chiles), drying in the sun alongside soybeans, chopped greens, and mustard seeds. There's a delicious tradition of pickled greens, and meat and fish are often pickled too.

LEFT: *An aerial view of Zhaoxing village, taken from up on one of the steep hillsides that rim the town. At the lower left is one of the town's covered bridges, airy yet sheltering, and in the upper right is a drum tower (there are five in Zhaoxing, more than in any other Dong village). The houses are tall wood structures built of fir, with no nails used in their post-and-beam construction. A new house is being erected in the upper left. Recently, tourism has brought more prosperity to the town; notice the occasional satellite dish on the rooftops.* RIGHT: *Also in Zhaoxing, a grandmother, her hair bound up in the distinctive black-and-white handwoven scarf worn by older Dong women in this part of Guizhou, sits at her loom weaving. The loom is inside her house, by an opening that gives her natural light to work in and a good view of people passing by on the footpath outside.*

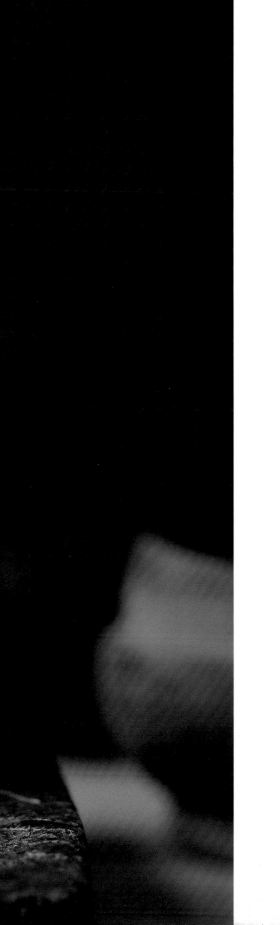

NOODLES AND DUMPLINGS

WE'VE COME TO SEE NOODLES AS YET ANOTHER way people mark cultural identity. There's a huge noodle world beyond the Great Wall, delectable, sustaining, and wonderfully varied. This chapter is a selective noodle map of that world. All the techniques here are relatively easy, and forgiving too. There are wheat noodles and rice noodles, noodles made with egg and those without. There are long noodles and square ones; noodles that are rolled out and cut, Italian-style; noodles that are stretched by hand; and noodles just quickly torn off a dough. There are noodles made of steamed wheat flour batter as well as hand-rolled rice noodles.

Beyond the Great Wall, noodles are most often eaten in a meat broth, making a one-dish meal. While working on this book, we encountered many variations on the morning-market noodle theme. One of the most memorable was at a small stand run by a Ge woman in the little market town of Chong'an, in Guizhou (see Hand-Rolled Rice Noodles, page 142). Another was in the steep terraced landscape of southeastern Yunnan (see Yi Market Noodles, page 126). We've also included a classic Central Asian take on morning noodles in broth, Central Asian Morning Market Noodles with Lamb (page 148). Noodles can instead be dressed with sauce (see Noodles with Sesame Sauce, page 149, and Laghman Sauce for Noodles, page 135), or added to a stir-fry.

We think of steamed and boiled dumplings as an extension of the noodle tradition: they are made of noodle dough and are often served in a broth, as noodles are. So we've included in this chapter recipes for *jiaozi*, succulent filled dumplings (page 150), and for *momos*, classic Tibetan meat-filled steamed dumplings (page 154).

OPPOSITE: *A Uighur noodle-maker stretches a batch of noodles in classic style, in the market in the Turpan oasis.* ABOVE: *A small stack of Hand-Rolled Rice Noodles (page 142).*

YI MARKET NOODLES

I discovered these noodles in the town of Yuanyang on a cold, foggy February morning. The street-side noodle stand where they were being made was crowded with people, and there were good smells and lots of steamy pots, so I stepped up and ordered a bowlful. The two people running the stand were mother and daughter, and though they were working frantically to keep up, they happily answered my questions and tolerated my camera. Each bowl of noodles was prepared individually in a sand pot over a low gas flame. The various ingredients (ground pork, dried tofu, and vegetables) were added one by one and cooked together, and then in went a huge handful of fresh rice noodles and some broth, and the dish was done.

They took each bowl over to a small table nearby that was surrounded by many small stools, where patrons could sit to eat. Also at the table was another woman vendor who was grilling chunks of potatoes and small squares of tofu, which could be eaten with the noodle soup.

A few days later, in the town of Luchen, a five-hour bus ride away, I was walking through the central market, and there were noodle stands serving a very similar dish. The broth and several of the ingredients were not the same, but the noodles were once again fresh round (like spaghetti) rice noodles, and the squares of tofu in both places were halfway between firm and regular tofu in texture, with a mild flavor. And at each stand there were cooks busy grilling potatoes and tofu, just as in Yuanyang.

The people who were preparing the noodles in Yuanyang were Yi, while the people preparing them in Luchen were Hani (see page 316). This particular version is our take on the noodles I had in Yuanyang, so we call them Yi market noodles, but we don't know their exact origin. Since fresh round rice noodles are hard to find in North America, we substitute dried rice noodles, known as rice sticks (see Glossary), soaked briefly in warm water.

It is fun to prepare these noodles in a sand pot, and if you haven't ever used one, it's a great excuse to buy one and to get a feel for this kind of one-dish cooking; see "Sand Pot Notes," page 130, before you start. Otherwise, just use a heavy 3- or 4-quart saucepan.

Start soaking the tofu sheets and noodles, and the dried mushrooms, if using them, about 30 minutes before you want to serve the dish.

8 dried shiitake mushrooms or 2 cups thinly sliced
    fresh shiitake or other mushrooms
2 cups hot water
4 dried tofu sheets or 6 tofu sticks (see Glossary)
One 1-pound package rice sticks (dried rice noodles)
6 to 8 scallions
6 cups Quick Pork Broth (below) or chicken or vegetable broth
2 to 3 tablespoons lard or vegetable oil
2 tablespoons chile bean paste (see Glossary)
½ pound ground pork
3 cups thinly sliced green cabbage
4 teaspoons salt, or to taste

Rinse the dried mushrooms if using, place them in a small bowl, and add the 2 cups hot water. Put a small plate or lid on top to weight the mushrooms so they are immersed, and set aside to soak for 10 minutes.

Break or cut the tofu sheets or tofu sticks into several pieces each. Place in a bowl with hot water to cover and let soak for 10 minutes.

Place the rice sticks in a wide bowl with hot water to cover, and set aside to soak for 10 minutes.

Drain the mushrooms, reserving the soaking water. Measure it and add enough hot water to make 2 cups liquid; set aside. Trim off and discard the tough stems and thinly slice the mushrooms. Set aside.

Drain the tofu and cut it into strips or batons about ½ inch wide and 2 inches long, discarding any tough bits. Set aside.

Drain the rice sticks and set aside.

Trim the scallions. If they're large, cut lengthwise in half. Cut the white and enough of the tender green parts into 1-inch lengths to make 1 packed cup. Mince enough of the remaining green parts to make about ¼ cup for garnish. Set aside.

Place the broth in a pot over low heat to warm.

Place a wide 3- or 4-quart saucepan over medium heat, add the lard or oil, and swirl to coat the bottom of the pan. Toss in the chile bean paste and stir to blend it into the oil. Add the pork and cook, using a spoon or spatula to break up any lumps, until it has changed color all over, about 2 minutes. Toss in the mushrooms (soaked or fresh), tofu, and cabbage, add the salt, and stir. Cook for about 1 minute. Add the scallion lengths and the reserved mushroom soaking water or 2 cups hot water, raise the heat, and bring to a boil. Cook at a strong boil for 3 to 4 minutes, or until the cabbage and mushrooms are tender.

(*Alternatively*, if you have a sand pot, use a wok to do the initial frying of the bean paste, pork, mushrooms, tofu, and cabbage, then transfer to the sand pot. Add the scallion lengths and the reserved mushroom soaking water or hot water, place over medium heat, and bring to a boil. Cook as above until the cabbage and mushrooms are tender.)

Add the soaked noodles and the warm broth. Bring to a boil, then reduce the heat and simmer for 2 to 3 minutes. Serve topped with a generous sprinkling of the minced scallion greens.

Serves 4 as a main course

QUICK PORK BROTH: We often decide to make these noodles at the last minute. To make up a quick broth, we put about 1 pound fresh pork roast or loin or whatever we have on hand in a pot with 8 cups water, a bay leaf, and a grinding of black pepper. We bring it to a boil, then simmer it until the pork has cooked through and we have a lightly flavored broth, about 20 minutes. We use the broth to make the noodles and save the pork to slice for sandwiches the next day.

A Yi market noodle stand in Yuanyang, Yunnan.

AMDO NOODLE SQUARES

The noodles in the area that was once the Amdo region of greater Tibet (and now is part of Gansu and Qinghai provinces) tend to be flat squares rather than long strips. People in Lhasa, in central Tibet, refer to square noodles as "Amdo noodles" (in English), and in Amdo (where I heard them called *than-te* in Tibetan and *mian par* in Mandarin), both Tibetan and Hui (see page 216) eateries seem to feature square noodles.

We find them very attractive, and very easy to make. They have no egg, just flour, water, and a little salt. The food processor makes light work of the kneading, and the rolling out is very forgiving. All you need is a rolling pin and a knife or pizza cutter for cutting the noodle sheets into squares. (In many Tibetan households, the dough isn't cut, but instead small squarish pieces are simply torn off the rolled-out dough.)

The texture of these, like that of most homemade noodles, is wonderful, with a pleasing resistance as you bite in, yet a silky smoothness on the tongue, especially noticeable with the wide surface of noodle squares. Serve them topped with a hearty soup or stew. Hui Tomato-Lamb Noodle Soup (page 59) is classically served over square noodles, but they also pair well with Laghman sauce (see page 135) or with Hui Vegetable Soup (page 148). Or serve them as a pasta course, topped with a favorite sauce or flavoring, or floating in a clear broth as a soup course. [PHOTOGRAPH ON PAGE 58]

2 cups all-purpose flour, preferably unbleached, plus extra
    for surfaces
½ teaspoon salt
Generous ½ cup water

Place the flour and salt in a food processor and pulse to mix. With the blade spinning, slowly add the water through the feed tube—at about the ½-cup mark, a ball of dough will form. Transfer the dough to a lightly floured surface and knead for several minutes. Cover with a cloth or with plastic wrap and let rest for at least 30 minutes or as long as 3 hours.

Turn the dough out onto a lightly floured surface and, with a sharp knife, cut it into 4 equal pieces. Flour each piece on both sides, then flatten each lightly under the palm of your hand. Set 2 pieces aside while you roll out the others. Roll out each piece to a 9-inch square or slightly larger. Use a pizza cutter or sharp knife to cut each square into 1-inch strips and then cut the strips crosswise to yield square noodles about 1 inch on each side (with some odd-shaped ones near the corners). Dust lightly with flour, and transfer to a flour-dusted plate or bowl. Repeat with the remaining dough pieces. (*The squares can be made up to a day ahead. Cover them loosely with a cloth to keep them clean. The noodles will dry out a little as they wait, so they will take slightly longer to cook.*)

When you want to serve the noodles, bring about 8 cups of water or broth (Tibetan Bone Broth, page 45; or chicken broth) to a boil in a wide pot; if using water, add 1 teaspoon salt. Sprinkle the noodles into the boiling liquid. They will sink and then within a minute slowly rise to the surface. Let cook for about another 2 minutes, or until they are tender (test them as you would test pasta).

Drain the noodles, place in individual serving bowls, and top with soup or stew (see headnote).

Makes about ¾ pound noodles; serves 3 to 4 as a main course if topped by a hearty soup or stew, 6 served in broth as a soup course

NOTE ON COOKING THE NOODLES AHEAD: If not serving the noodles immediately, place them in a large bowl, add a little broth or oil, and toss them gently to coat all surfaces and prevent them from sticking. If you want to reheat them before serving, place them in a colander or sieve and immerse in hot water for about 30 seconds, then drain and serve immediately.

NOTE ON DOUBLING THE RECIPE: If you wish to double the recipe (for example, if your guests include ravenous teenagers), make the dough in two separate batches in the processor, then combine them to knead. Once the dough has rested, cut it into 8 equal pieces and proceed as above.

Chu Gompa, a Tibetan Buddhist temple built on a rocky crag overlooking Lake Manasarowar, at dawn. A small plume of smoke declares that morning tea is brewing. Behind, on the horizon to the north, is Mount Kailas (called Kang Rimpoche by Tibetans), a sacred mountain and holy destination for not only Buddhist pilgrims but also Hindus, Jains, and Bons (believers in the pre-Buddhist religion of Tibet). Four of the major rivers of Asia rise near here: the Brahmaputra (called the Yarlung Tsangpo in Tibet), the Karnali, the Indus, and the Sutlej.

literature of the periphery

We both started reading about Tibet and Xinjiang, about the Silk Road, and about Yunnan's tribal territories, long before we had the chance to visit. When we first met in Lhasa (see "Falling in Love," page 85), we had many books, and travel ambitions, in common.

"The literature of the periphery," as we've come to call it, is a world unto itself, peopled by explorers, religious ascetics, anthropologists, historians, linguists, etc. These are some of the books that have moved us, for whatever reasons. (For a longer list, see the Bibliography.)

Before we knew each other, we'd each been entranced by Lama Anagarika Govinda's account in *The Way of the White Clouds* of his conversion to Tibetan Buddhism and his travels in the Mount Kailas region in 1949. We'd both read Heinrich Harrer's classic *Seven Years in Tibet*. We'd also read Marco Polo's *Travels*, and *The Monkey's Tale*, a partly mythic story about how the Buddhist scriptures were brought eastward along the Silk Road to the ancient Chinese capital Chang'an. John Keay's books about the Great Game, when Russia and Britain jostled for power in Chinese Turkestan in the late nineteenth and early twentieth centuries, had given us a sense of the geopolitical importance of Central Asia.

Naomi had been captivated by Ella Maillart's book *Forbidden Journey* (see "Ella," page 70) and its complement, *News from Tartary*, by her traveling companion Peter Fleming.

We've read accounts by archaeologists, such as Aurel Stein and Albert von Le Coq about their Silk Road discoveries, which describe finds and digs and theories about the region's history, but they don't give us a picture of daily life. So we were delighted to find a recent book, *Life along the Silk Road* by Susan Whitfield, which is a reimagining of the lives of a number of people based on archaeological finds and old texts, and which breathes life into the rather chaotic history of Chinese Central Asia. We highly recommend it.

ABOVE: *The Tuvan village of Hom sits in a valley in the Altai Mountains. The wood house is Tuvan, the yurt Kazakh. The autumn mist is heavy in the early morning.* OPPOSITE, LEFT: *Kazakh Noodles (page 133) in broth, topped with chopped scallion.* OPPOSITE, RIGHT: *Kazakh and Tuvan men in the Altai Mountains of northern Xinjiang.*

Sand pots go way back in Chinese tradition. They're made of clay, glazed on the inside but usually with a rough sandy unglazed surface on the outside. The most commonly available ones here in North America are shaped like saucepans with a thick handle and a lid. Sometimes they are reinforced with wire mesh on the outside. They are traditionally used to make slow-simmered dishes, hearty soups, and stews, in the same way Spanish *cazuelas* are used. Unlike the individual sand pots the Yi and Hani were using at the market (see photo, page 127), most of the ones available here are large enough for 4 or more servings.

Sand pots are sensitive to abrupt changes in temperature, so they should not be placed on a cold surface, for example, or placed in the re-frigerator when they come off the heat, but they can take direct heat (in China they are usually set over an open flame). *They should not be placed over heat when they are empty*, or they will crack. Fill your sand pot at least a quarter full before placing it over low to medium heat.

If you have a new sand pot, wash it thoroughly and let it soak in cold water to cover for 24 hours. Drain and let dry for a day, then fill the pot with water, place over medium heat, and bring to a boil. Simmer for about 20 minutes, then turn off the heat and let stand until cooled to room temperature; drain. Your pot is now ready for use.

Shaping Kazakh Noodles: (1) a cut length of noodle dough, after resting; (2) a first gentle stretching of the dough; (3) pulling the dough longer by pulling the hands apart (notice the already stretched noodles on the floured work surface); (4) several stretched noodles, coiled together.

KAZAKH NOODLES

My first introduction to these noodles was in Serik's sister's yurt (see "Motorcycle," page 300). It was one of several yurts set up somewhat haphazardly in a large open field, close to a large construction project. The project, which appeared near to completion, was a government hotel venture in Kanas Lake National Park. The hotel looked a little bit like a Colorado ski area, with a fancy lodge and many surrounding condos, but it was not yet up and running.

The Kazakh yurts were a definite contrast. I assumed that the yurts were there for the project's workers, but I'm not sure. I rode up on the back of Serik's motorcycle, and when his sister came out and discovered that he had been in a motorcycle accident (his face and hands were badly scraped), there wasn't a lot of small talk. She was furious with him because, after all, Kazakhs ride horses, not motorbikes! We all went into the yurt and drank hot salty tea, and they talked back and forth in Kazakh. Someone came in from another yurt, and the whole story of the crash was told again, and there were more loud words, not angry, just deeply felt.

And all the while, Serik's sister cooked. She had a pressure cooker (see Kazakh Goat Broth, page 44) on the wood-burning stove at one end of the yurt, and bits of goat shank were cooking away in a broth. She briefly kneaded an egg noodle dough on a small table, then stretched the dough out into several long thick strips, each a foot and a half long, 4 inches wide, and about ½ inch thick. She cut them crosswise into ½-inch-wide strips and covered them with a cloth until the broth finished cooking.

When the broth was done, she took out the meat and bones and then deftly stretched the dough strips into noodles by hand, one by one, tossing each into the broth once it was stretched. Almost instantly, it seemed, she had all the noodles formed and cooking. She made it look incredibly easy. When they were al dente, she strained the noodles from the broth, piled them on a large platter, and sliced a raw onion on top. She put the big pieces of bone (with a smattering of meat) on top, and we all dug in. We ate with our right hands only, as is the rule in Islamic cultures when eating by hand. About midway through the meal,

she poured the broth into small soup bowls, and we drank it alongside the noodles.

As we ate, the tone of the conversation relaxed a bit. Everyone was alive. And we were eating good food, great food.

I got to enjoy these noodles several more times in Kazakh homes, and as soon as I was back home in Toronto, I started trying to make them. We've been playing around with this recipe for three years now. It's been one of those food encounters that is both humbling and exhilarating. There are mysteries, but that makes playing with them all the more fun. Sometimes the dough is easy to work with, sometimes not. But we always come out with noodles, and they always taste great.

You can make the noodles shortly before you want to cook them or make them as long as several days ahead and hang them to dry (see Dried Kazakh Noodles below). It's just a matter of what is most convenient for you. The dough should be made at least half an hour, or as long as 2 hours, before you want to shape the noodles.

3½ cups all-purpose flour, preferably unbleached, plus extra for surfaces

1 teaspoon salt

2 large eggs

About ¾ cup lukewarm water

About 8 cups Kazakh Goat Broth (page 44) or chicken broth

At least an hour before you want to serve the noodles, place the flour, salt, and eggs in a food processor and process briefly. With the blades spinning, slowly pour the lukewarm water through the feed tube until a ball of dough forms (you may need slightly less or slightly more than ¾ cup). Turn out onto a lightly floured surface and knead briefly.

Alternatively, place the flour, salt, and eggs in a medium bowl and whisk or stir to combine them. Add ¾ cup lukewarm water and stir to mix it in. If the dough is still dry or stiff, mix in a little extra water. Turn out onto a lightly floured surface and knead until smooth, about 3 minutes.

(continued)

Cut the dough into 4 equal pieces on a lightly floured surface. Flatten each piece under the palms of your hands into a rectangle approximately 12 inches long and 3 to 4 inches wide. Use a sharp knife or a metal dough scraper to cut the rectangles crosswise into strips just under ½ inch wide. Cover the dough with a cloth or plastic wrap and let rest for at least 30 minutes, or for as long as 2 hours.

Before starting to stretch the noodles, lightly dust a large work surface with a little flour. You will then be able to dust the stretched noodles with a little flour to keep them from sticking, and you can lay the stretched noodles on the floured surface when they're shaped. (You could instead drape them on a rack or over the back of several wooden chairs.)

Stretching the dough the Kazakh way is amazingly easy. Our description of the technique may look long, but once you pick up a piece of dough and see how it yields and thins with the pressure of your fingers and thumbs, you'll find your own technique. We often make these with one of our kids or with a guest, so the work goes quickly, and everyone gets to practice noodle stretching. Pick up a dough strip and touch both sides of it to the floured surface, then pinch it gently near one end between the thumb and forefinger of one hand, holding it nearer the center with the thumb and index finger of your other hand. You'll be stretching it both by pinching it along its length and by pulling the pinched section gently away from where you're holding it in your other hand. Gradually work your way along the strip, pinching it and gently pulling your hands apart a little as you do, to flatten and stretch it. When the strip is 12 to 15 inches long, touch it again to the floured surface to dust it with flour, then lay it to one side of the floured surface. Repeat with the remaining dough strips.

Once all the noodles are shaped, bring the broth to a vigorous boil. Add the noodles, bring back to a boil, and cook until tender but still firm to the bite, about 6 minutes.

Use a mesh basket or tongs to lift the noodles out of the broth and into wide individual soup plates. Ladle broth over the noodles, and serve.

Makes a generous 1½ pounds noodles; serves 4 as a main course, 6 as a hearty soup course

Cut long wheat noodles, rather like long Tibetan noodles (see page 144), hanging to dry in the sun, in Dali, Yunnan.

DRIED KAZAKH NOODLES: If you'd like to make the noodles ahead, so you won't feel rushed, make the dough and let it rest for 30 minutes. Before starting to shape the noodles, dust a work surface generously with flour and set up a rack or other arrangement so you can hang the noodles to dry. We use the backs of wooden chairs or, if we're making a large quantity, a wooden clothes rack. (In China, you'll often see wheat flour noodles set out to dry on clotheslines or clothes racks.) Shape the first noodle and touch it on the floured surface to flour it before hanging it to dry. Repeat with the remaining noodles. Let them dry for at least an hour, or as long as several days. Cook as above. Dried noodles take a little longer to cook (about 10 minutes, in our experience) but are just as successful as the fresh ones.

ROLLED-OUT KAZAKH NOODLES: Instead of hand-stretching the noodles, you can roll the dough out with a rolling pin and then cut the noodles. Cut the dough into 8 pieces rather than 4, and let it rest for 30 minutes or longer before rolling. Press both sides of one piece onto a well-floured surface, then roll out to a thin rectangle about 6 inches wide by 14 inches long. Use a pizza cutter or a sharp knife to cut lengthwise into ¼-inch-wide noodles, and then drape them on a lightly floured surface or over the back of a chair. Repeat until all are rolled and cut. Cook as above.

LAGHMAN SAUCE FOR NOODLES

Every day in Turpan (see "Turpan Depression," page 200) I ate lunch in the same place, a noodle shop in the heart of the market. It's something I really like to do, eat in the same place, whether it is for three days in a row or for ten, because it's one way I can connect with people even though I am essentially just passing through.

This particular noodle shop was like many Uighur noodle shops all across the province of Xinjiang. Four large tandoor ovens stood out in front of the shop, as well as fireplaces for several super-large woks. The cooks would make *samsa* (see page 198) and many different kinds of nan in the tandoors. Over the fires, they'd cook noodles and noodles and noodles, all day long.

I'd always ask for *laghman*, noodles with stir-fried lamb and vegetables, and if I could, I'd sit at the front table so that I could watch the cooks. There was never a moment when something wasn't happening, morning till night. The cooks worked hard, really hard, and they fed a huge number of people.

Right after I'd sit down, a pot of hot black tea would arrive, and about ten minutes later, a plate of fabulous fat homemade noodles topped with a stir-fry fresh from the wok: tomatoes, green peppers, red peppers, onions, and a little lamb. I'd drizzle a little black rice vinegar on top and leap in. [PHOTOGRAPH ON PAGE 136]

SAUCE

½ pound boneless lamb or goat (chops, shoulder, or leg)

2 tablespoons oil

1 medium onion, thinly sliced

1 tablespoon minced garlic

1 large red bell pepper, cored, seeded, and sliced into
　¼-inch-wide strips

1 large green bell pepper, cored, seeded, and sliced into
　¼-inch-wide strips

1½ pounds ripe tomatoes, roughly chopped

2 teaspoons salt

Earlobe Noodles (page 145), Lhasa Egg Noodle Shells (page 138), ½ recipe Kazakh Noodles (page 133), or 1 pound dried egg noodles or fettuccine

Jinjiang (black rice) vinegar for the table

Put a large pot of water on to boil.

Cut the meat into small pieces, approximately ¾-inch squares. Have all your seasonings and vegetables ready to stir-fry.

Heat a large wok or wide heavy pot over high heat. Add the oil and swirl it around a little. When the oil is hot, add the onion, garlic, and meat and stir-fry for about 4 minutes, or until the meat has changed color and the onion is translucent. Add the peppers and stir-fry for 2 minutes. Add the tomatoes and the 2 teaspoons salt and mix well. Lower the heat to medium and cook for approximately 7 minutes, until the peppers are soft but still retain their shape. (Your wok or pot will be quite full, so this cooking becomes more of a simmer than a stir-fry.)

Meanwhile, add 1 tablespoon salt to the pot of water, and drop the noodles into the boiling water. Cook until tender but still firm to the bite. Drain, and distribute among four plates or large wide bowls.

Ladle equal portions of sauce over the hot noodles. Serve immediately. Invite guests to season the dish with black rice vinegar as they wish.

Serves 4 as a main course

OPPOSITE: *Laghman Sauce for Noodles (page 135) over Lhasa Egg Noodle Shells (page 138).* ABOVE: *Shaping egg noodle shells: a cut lump of rested noodle dough, held in the palm, waiting to be flattened with the thumb of the other hand; a noodle shell, just flattened, and ready to be set aside on a lightly floured surface.*

LHASA EGG NOODLE SHELLS

These days home cooks in Lhasa often include an egg or two in their noodle dough, so that's what we've done in this recipe. However, traditionally eggs would have been more of a luxury (and many Tibetans still don't eat eggs). The egg does make the dough stronger and helps it keep its shape, but, like the other Tibetan homemade noodles, these, a rough shell shape, can also be made from the plain noodle dough for Amdo Noodle Squares (page 128). Serve them under a stew or in a hearty soup, such as Kazakh Stew (page 277) or Hui Vegetable Soup (page 48), or with Laghman Sauce for Noodles (page 135). [PHOTOGRAPH ON PAGE 136]

About 2 cups all-purpose flour, preferably unbleached,
plus extra for surfaces
½ teaspoon salt
1 large egg
About ½ cup lukewarm water

Place the flour and salt in the bowl of a food processor and pulse briefly to mix. Add the egg and pulse; then, with the blade spinning, slowly add the water through the feed tube until a ball of dough starts to form.

Turn out onto a lightly floured surface and knead until very smooth. The dough will be quite stiff and strong. Set aside, covered, to rest for at least 30 minutes, or for as long as 12 hours, whatever is convenient.

Cut the dough into 8 pieces. Roll each piece between your palms into an 8-inch cylinder. On a well-floured surface, cut the pieces in half, then cut each 4-inch length into 8 to 10 pieces. Toss them in the flour on your work surface. Flour your left palm (if you are right-handed), place one piece of dough on it, and, with your floured right thumb, press the center of the piece against your palm, sliding it a little, to flatten and thin the center and make a curled thicker outside edge. (Reverse the instructions if you are left-handed.) Set aside on a lightly floured tray or platter and repeat with the rest of the pieces. Although the shaping may sound elaborate or fiddly, after the first few, you will find the process goes quickly. The shells can be cooked right away in boiling water or broth, or left to dry a little.

To cook, bring a large pot of water or broth to a rapid boil. (If using water, add salt, as you would for pasta.) Sprinkle the noodles into the boiling water. Cook until just tender but still with a little bite, about 5 minutes if freshly made. Drain and serve.

Makes about ¾ pound dough, or about 150 shells; serves 4 as a main course when topped with a stew or added to a soup

STEAMED WHEAT NOODLE RIBBONS

We'd seen these noodles for a while, especially among the Hui people in Qinghai, without understanding what they were. Then we discovered that they are one of the simplest ways of preparing wheat flour noodles, and they've become a favorite in our kitchen. They're utterly unlike stretched or cut boiled noodles, in a class of their own.

The noodles are made using the traditional technique for rice noodle sheets: A batter (of wheat flour and water) is poured into a wide shallow pan and placed in the steamer. Once the noodle sheet has steam-cooked and then set, the whole sheet is lifted out of the pan and sliced into ribbons.

The pans and steamers used in noodle stalls are large, perhaps 16 to 18 inches in diameter, and so the noodle sheets are large and the cut noodles long. In our kitchen, we use a steamer about 15 inches across, and we steam the batter in a standard metal pie plate, only 8 inches across. If you have a larger steamer and pan, you'll be able to cook a larger sheet of noodle batter at one time than we do.

In noodle stalls in the provinces of Qinghai and Xinjiang, in western China, the steamed noodles sit in loosely coiled piles, slightly gleaming, thick ribbons. Then someone places an order, and the vendor plucks a handful of noodles from the pile and puts them in a bowl. A little broth may be poured over. The customer tops the noodles with chile paste, dark vinegar, and soy sauce, and perhaps some pickled vegetables, before starting to eat, mouthful by delicious mouthful.

2 cups all-purpose flour
2 cups lukewarm water
Vegetable oil for surfaces

Place the flour in a bowl or the bowl of a food processor. Stir in the water, or add the water through the feed tube with the blade spinning, and stir or process until the batter is very smooth. Transfer to a jug or bowl with a spout. You will have 2½ cups batter.

Set a steamer rack over a pot or wok filled with about 2 inches of water. Find a shallow metal pan, such as a pie plate, that will fit in your steamer (see headnote). Rub the pan with a lightly oiled paper towel, put it in the steamer, and bring the water to a hard boil. Pour ¾ cup (or more if your pan is wider than 8 inches) of batter into the pan. It will flow out to the edges on its own. Cover tightly and steam for 10 minutes or until set firm (though the top of the batter will be a little sticky).

Remove the pan from the steamer, taking care not to burn yourself, and let stand for 5 minutes, uncovered. Brush the top of the noodle circle with a little oil, turn out onto a plate or cutting board, and let stand for another 10 minutes or so, to firm up, then slice into ribbons (¼ to ½ inch wide) with a lightly oiled pizza cutter or a cleaver or sharp knife. Meanwhile, repeat with the remaining batter, getting one batch cooking while you're waiting for a previous one to cool and set.

Makes about 1 pound noodles; serves 4 as breakfast or for a midafternoon snack, 2 as a one-dish meal for lunch with a dressing or sauce

Around a curve of the road, we came upon a Tajik encampment (see page 343) high in the Pamir Mountains. There were three dark-brown yurts on the grassy hillside, a herd of goats scattered nearby grazing, and a handful of children, who came running to the road as soon as they caught sight of us.

Laughing and chattering, they urged us to come up to the encampment. We slowly rolled our heavy bicycles (their full panniers making them look like shiny alien versions of laden donkeys) up the hill and laid them down on the grass by one of the yurts. Several women had come out to see what was going on. We nodded hello to them, then one of them suddenly smiled and gestured to us to come inside. It was beautiful in her yurt. Light came through the smoke hole in the dome of the roof, giving a softened sculpted outline to everything.

Smoke from the tandoor oven in the center of the yurt drifted up and out the hole. We'd spent time with Kirghiz nomads farther north, but this was the first group of Tajik nomads we'd encountered. We were thrilled, as delighted as the children were.

We sat down on low stools and accepted bowls of clear tea. Brightly flowered quilted bedding was folded in piles against the yurt walls. The women and children settled onto stools and the edges of low beds, and we talked, using a blend of gesture, mime, and basic Mandarin. Meanwhile, one woman shaped a soft-textured bread dough into small rounds and another added fuel to the oven to raise the heat. In a little while, with the tandoor oven now very hot, she slapped the shaped flatbreads onto the inner walls of the oven. Soon they were done, stacked and wrapped in a cloth before being set out for us to eat. A bowl of yogurt appeared too, and our bowls of tea were topped up.

The women wouldn't eat with us (it was Ramadan, the Muslim fasting month), but the children happily reached for the breads and yogurt, dipping pieces of fresh bread into the cool whiteness of the yogurt, which was made from the milk of their goats.

OPPOSITE: *In the open landscape of the high Pamirs, not far from the Khunjerab Pass at the China-Pakistan border, a young Tajik girl walks out of her family's yurt. Notice the heavy boulder that weighs the yurt down against the strong winds of the Pamirs, the exposed wooden frame where the flap is open over the smoke hole, and the deep color of the wool felt that covers the yurt and keeps out the weather.*

HAND-ROLLED RICE NOODLES

In Chong'an market in central Guizhou, I watched as a steady stream of customers came to perch on a bench at a noodle stall and slurp down a quick bowl of noodles before heading back to the hustle of market day. Some ordered noodles in soup, others had them plain; all made generous use of the array of condiments out on the table. The condiments were the usual chile pastes and cucumbers in vinegar, as well as a delicious fresh tomato salsa lightly flavored with sesame oil (see Market Stall Fresh Tomato Salsa, page 18).

In the pauses between serving customers, the woman running the stall shaped fresh rice noodles. The dough was white and soft, and she shaped each noodle by rolling a small piece of dough between her palms until she had an irregular cylinder with a fatter middle and skinny ends. When she had a batch shaped, she'd drop them into boiling water to cook for a minute or two, then lift them out (using a mesh skimmer) and set them aside in a pile until needed.

Though she also had more familiar-looking noodles—flat rice noodles, both narrow and wide—on offer, I wanted to try the hand-rolled ones. She scooped up some of the noodles in a bowl, poured on a little hot broth, and topped them with a little of the tomato salsa. The noodles had wonderful bite and yet were tender and cooked through. After eating, I hung around for a good long while watching her technique, hoping I could figure out how to make them at home. And here they are, made of a simple dough of rice flour (*not* glutinous rice flour), boiling water, salt, and oil. We find they work best if you make the dough at least an hour ahead. You can cook them beforehand, then reheat them in boiling water at the last minute if you wish.

Serve them traditionally, freshly cooked and hot, or reheated, or at room temperature, bathed in hot broth if you wish and topped with Market Stall Fresh Tomato Salsa and a drizzle of Soy-Vinegar Dipping Sauce (page 151). We especially love the firm yet yielding texture of the noodles once they've cooled to room temperature. You can also use them as a substitute for pasta. (Because the surface of the noodles is very smooth and slippery, sauce does not cling in the same way as it does to semolina pasta. [PHOTOGRAPH ON PAGE 125]

2 cups rice flour

½ teaspoon salt

Scant 1 cup boiling water

2 tablespoons peanut oil or vegetable oil, plus extra for surfaces

Place the flour in a bowl with the salt. Pour the boiling water over and stir with a wooden spoon until all flour is moistened. Stir in the oil. Knead and mix with your hands or the spoon until very smooth. The dough will be quite stiff. Cover tightly with plastic wrap and set aside for at least 1 hour, or for as long as 3 hours, whatever is convenient.

Before starting to shape the noodles, put out a tray or several large plates. Put a pot of water on to boil (you can also cook the noodles in chicken broth or pork broth). Once it boils, lower the heat and let it simmer so it's ready when you finish shaping the noodles.

Dry your hands thoroughly (the dough sticks to wet skin), then lightly oil your palms (if you use a lightly oiled paper towel, you will be able to use it again to re-oil your palms later if necessary). Pinch off a teaspoon of dough, not more, and roll it into a ball between your palms. Once it's round, still working between your palms, press them slightly closer together as you roll the dough back and forth. This will squeeze the ball of dough and cause it to lengthen. After rolling the dough back and forth several times, you will have a noodle about 3 inches long with a fatter bulge in the middle and pointed tapered ends. All these words may make the process seem difficult, but in fact the shape of the noodle is created by the shape of your palms, with the thicker part in the middle, where there's a hollow in your palms, and two thinner ends where the dough is pressed more tightly by the edges of your palms.

Place the noodle on the tray or a plate and repeat. After you've rolled two or three, the sequence will come automatically and easily. And once you have the knack, you can get all the dough shaped in about 10 minutes (more quickly, of course, if you have a friend helping you).

Bring the water (or broth) back to a vigorous boil. Roll the noodles off the tray or plates and into the boiling liquid. They will sink, then eventually rise to the surface, but (unlike gnocchi) they are not yet done at this point: let them boil for another couple of minutes after they rise. Usually they start sinking again when cooked through—test one or two for doneness at their thickest points. Timing will vary, but it generally takes 5 to 7 minutes, depending on thickness. These noodles are very forgiving, so even if they cook a little too long, they keep their shape and firmness.

Use a mesh skimmer or slotted spoon to lift the noodles into a serving bowl or individual bowls. If serving in broth, immediately pour the hot broth over the noodles. If serving later, you can set the noodles aside for up to 2 hours, until ready to use. In our experience, they don't stick to one another as they cool, but we toss them with a little sesame oil or peanut oil just to make sure.

Makes a scant 1 pound noodles; serves 3 to 4

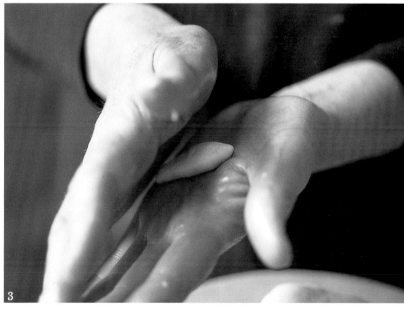

Shaping hand-rolled rice noodles: (1) a piece of dough ready to be rolled into a ball; (2) a rolled ball of noodle dough, ready to be shaped; (3) rolling the ball into a longer shape.

Then thuk is the Lhasa dialect name for what we call Amdo Noodle Squares (see page 128). Some Tibetans roll the dough out and cut it, as described in that recipe, while others just tear off roughly square pieces, tossing them straight into the boiling water. *Then thuk* are associated with Tibetans from Amdo, the northeastern part of greater Tibet, now in Qinghai and Gansu provinces. Perhaps it's logical that the Hui community in that same area makes similar noodle squares (see Hui Tomato-Lamb Noodle Soup, page 59).

Gya thuk is the Tibetan name for long fettuccine-like noodles. They are widely found in Lhasa but are now more likely to be bought at the market than homemade. To make these long noodles at home, use the recipe for Amdo Noodle Squares or for Lhasa Egg Noodle Shells (page 138). Once the dough has rested, cut it into 4 equal pieces and flatten with your palm on a lightly floured surface. Use a rolling pin to roll out one piece at a time to a thin rectangle about 6 inches by 14 inches. Use a pizza cutter or a sharp knife to cut lengthwise into strips about ½ inch wide. Dust lightly with flour, then coil loosely and set aside (you can drape them over the back of a chair or rack to dry a little). Cook in boiling water or broth until cooked through.

The third noodle we've come across in Tibet is known as *gu-ze-ri-tu*, a shell-shaped noodle that looks very like the Puglian pasta called orecchiette (little ears). In Lhasa, our friend Tenzin showed me how to shape *guzeritu* by hand, using the thumb of one hand to press pieces of dough against the opposite palm; see Lhasa Egg Noodle Shells.

A Uighur man at the Kashgar Sunday bazaar enjoys a bowl of noodles.

EARLOBE NOODLES

We first saw someone preparing these noodles in the tiny town of Ngari (also known as Ali) in the far west of Tibet, near the Nepali and Indian borders. A Uighur truck driver was sitting outside his room in a truck-stop hotel with a pot of water boiling over a gas burner. He had a soft dough in one hand, and with the other he was tearing off bits of dough and tossing them into the water.

Earlobe noodles are amazingly simple to make, and so they are a good introduction to the whole noodle idea. They have an irregular shape, which makes them interesting to eat, and because they're homemade, the texture is silky.

Serve them topped with Laghman sauce (see page 135) or in a chicken or lamb or beef broth.

> 2 cups all-purpose flour, preferably unbleached,
>> plus extra for surfaces
>
> ½ teaspoon salt
>
> 1 tablespoon vegetable oil or peanut oil, plus 2 to 3 tablespoons
>> oil for surfaces
>
> 1 large egg
>
> ½ cup lukewarm water

Place the flour and salt in a food processor and process for 10 seconds to mix thoroughly. Add the 1 tablespoon oil and the egg and process for 30 seconds, or until mixed in well. With the motor running, add the water in a steady stream, then process for 10 seconds. The dough should have formed into a large ball. Feel the dough. If it feels very sticky, add 1 to 2 tablespoons more flour and process briefly. If the dough feels dry and floury, start the processor, add 1 to 2 tablespoons more water, and process just until a ball of dough forms.

Turn the dough out onto a lightly floured surface and knead for a minute or so. Cover with plastic wrap and let rest for at least 30 minutes, or as long as 2 hours.

When you're ready to make the noodles, bring a large pot of water to a boil. Add 1 teaspoon salt.

Meanwhile, divide the dough into 8 pieces. Work with one piece at a time; set the rest aside. Roll the dough back and forth on the counter under your palms to shape a cylinder 8 to 10 inches long. Put a little oil on your hands or on another part of the counter and roll the dough to coat it. Place it on a tray and repeat with the remaining pieces of dough. Cover with plastic wrap.

Standing by the pot of boiling water, start shaping the noodles: Hold one end of a cylinder of dough in one hand (your left hand if you are right-handed, or vice versa). With the thumb and forefinger of your other hand, pinch the end of the cylinder, squeezing or pinching a bit of dough into a piece the size of a quarter, then tear the pinched piece off and immediately throw it into the water. Squeeze again, tear, and toss. At first it will feel awkward, but soon you'll get a feel for the process and be able to work very quickly. Try to work as quickly as you can so that the noodles cook fairly evenly. When you've finished with one cylinder, pick up another. To help the process along, enlist a friend or family member so it moves double quickly.

The first time you make the noodles, use only 4 cylinders at once, and cook the noodles for about 7 minutes, timing them from the last noodle you put in (once you have become adept at the process, you can shape and cook all the noodles at once). Test for doneness: you want them cooked through but still with some bite. Use a wire mesh skimmer or a sieve to lift the noodles from the pot, draining them well. Put them in a bowl, oil lightly, and toss to ensure they don't stick together.

Repeat with the other 4 dough cylinders. Drain, combine with the other noodles, and toss so they are all lightly oiled. Serve in soup or topped by a sauce, as you please.

Makes about ¾ pound noodles; serves 3 to 4

On our last night in Chinese territory, we camped some miles below the Khunjerab Pass, the border between China's Xinjiang and Pakistan's Hunza Valley. That evening, over a supper of freeze-dried brown rice simmered in water, we imagined the next day: we'd have a hard climb to the pass, but by evening we'd be in Pakistan, maybe we'd even find a tea shop and chai. It was an exciting thought.

The next morning, we awoke to blinding whiteness. A heavy wet snow had fallen in the night, burying our bicycles and transforming the landscape. So much for chai, we thought. But the hot June sun was intense and soon there were small trickling sounds as the snow melted, the only sounds apart from the soft hum of the wind and the rustle of the tent and sleeping bags as we packed them into stuff sacks.

Slowly we pedaled up the road, feeling the elevation a little. We'd heard that somewhere along the way there was a final Chinese checkpoint. We couldn't imagine where it might be, for as far as we could see there was nothing but the snow-and-melt pinto of the landscape, with the dark line of the road making hairpin curves as it climbed toward the pass. We couldn't even see the tops of the tall peaks that we knew lay all around.

Then on a hillside up ahead, we saw a low green building by the road: the checkpoint. As always when dealing with the authorities in China, we were a little nervous: Would they stop us? Would they fine us for being on bicycles?

The soldiers in their drab green uniforms came out to meet us as we pedaled up. They looked at everything: the bicycles, the panniers, our clothing. Several of them got on the bicycles, laughing as they tried to get steady on the slope of the road. "Come inside," they said. "Have you eaten? Have lunch with us."

We'd been late starting out, and we wanted to get safely down from the pass before dark, but it wasn't an offer we could refuse. What *were* they eating up there anyway? we wondered. They put on rice to cook in plenty of water—congee at 15,000 feet—and took out some jars of preserved vegetables, flavorings for the rice.

There were six men staffing the post, not Tajiks or Kirghiz locals, as you might expect, but lowlanders, Han men from the Chinese heartland: Shanghai, Beijing, Xi'an. It is a two-year posting. We asked them how they liked it up here on their own in this huge high-altitude landscape. It's beautiful, they told us, but they get lonely and homesick. We asked if they had seen any animals, snow leopards, for example (we had to sketch one to make ourselves understood). Yes, twice, was the answer, once really close up.

After we'd all eaten the congee, using chopsticks to help ourselves to the vegetables, and slurping down the soup, they said, "We have something more." They brought out a large, shiny unmarked tin can and cut it open. Inside were mandarin segments floating in syrup. Their brilliant orange color was a startling reminder of warm places far away. We ate the fruit family-style straight from the tin, all of us standing around the guy who held it in his hand, reaching in with our chopsticks to pick up segments of the fruit, one by one. They tasted wet and sweet, with a hint of tin can, but most of all they tasted of generous hospitality.

We've never forgotten those soldiers at the outpost of empire, their warmth, their pleasure at having guests.

OPPOSITE: *Chinese border guards check out our loaded bicycles at their post below the Khunjerab Pass, some miles from the actual border with Pakistan.*

CENTRAL ASIAN MORNING MARKET NOODLES WITH LAMB

The day I was leaving Xining, in Qinghai province, I went for my last Central Asian meal of the trip. It was early morning, and the sharp slanting light gave me an elongated shadow that kept me company as I walked over to the row of noodle stalls near the river. Most of the cooks were women, their heads covered with modest scarves, as is the custom for Hui women here. There were small tables set out on the sidewalk by each stall. Steaming tall pots of soup, tangled piles of cooked wheat noodles, pieces of tender-looking boiled meat, and little bowls of condiments: these advertised breakfast.

I walked past the stalls, checking them out, then opted for the one with an amiable-looking cook and several tables of customers already eating. The others might have been just as good—I have no idea. All I can say is that when the cook placed my bowl in front of me, the noodles bathed in hot broth and topped with a few slices of cooked lamb, it looked wonderfully inviting.

The meat was delicious. I ate it first on its own, then lightly flavored with some of the condiments on offer (a small jug each of vinegar and soy sauce, a little plate of chopped coriander leaves, a bowl of chile paste). I tried them each in turn, then in combination. In between bites of meat, I slurped up mouthfuls of the long smooth noodles (like Tibetan *gya thuk*; see page 144) and sipped spoonfuls of broth. The broth was mild, a neutral backdrop for all the condiment flavors, ideal for washing down the meat and noodles.

Back home, I wondered whether simmering a lamb or goat shoulder in water with minimal flavorings would yield the same delicious result. We've discovered that it does. A side benefit is that the cooked meat makes great sandwiches the next day, like cold roast beef but more tender (and particularly good topped with Quick Tomato-Onion Chutney, page 24). We use shoulder, because it has such good flavor, but you could also use leg, which has proportionately more meat and less bone.

A 1½- to 2-pound bone-in lamb or goat roast (shoulder or leg)

8 cups water

1 medium-large onion (about ¾ pound), cut into large chunks

½ to 1 star anise

1½ to 2 teaspoons salt, to taste

Hand-cut Tuvan noodles (see page 246) or Tibetan long noodles (see page 144) or ¾ pound dried fettuccine or linguine

1 cup minced coriander (optional)

CONDIMENTS AND TOPPINGS

About ½ cup soy sauce

About ½ cup Jinjiang (black rice) vinegar or cider vinegar

Bright Red Chile Paste (page 18) or chile oil, homemade (page 29) or store-bought

Cucumber-Vinegar Sauce (page 83; optional)

½ cup minced scallions (white and tender green parts)

½ cup minced coriander (optional)

Rinse the meat and trim off excess fat. Place in a large pot with the water, onion, and star anise. Bring to a boil and skim off the foam; then reduce the heat and simmer, partially covered, for about 1 hour.

Remove the meat from the pot, and strain the broth. (If you have time, you can put the broth in the refrigerator to chill it, then skim off the fat; store the fat in a well-sealed glass or plastic container in the refrigerator so you have it handy for making *pulaos*. If keeping the broth for more than 48 hours, store in the freezer.)

Pour the broth back into the pot. Add salt, starting with 1 teaspoon and then adjusting to taste. The broth should be underseasoned, if anything, because as they eat, diners will add seasoning in the form of soy sauce and/or vinegar, as well as chile paste and other condiments.

If using fresh handmade noodles, bring the broth to a boil. If using dried pasta, bring a large pot of water to a boil for the pasta and salt it. Bring the broth just to a simmer. Add the noodles or pasta to the boiling broth or water and cook until tender but still with some bite.

Lift the noodles out of the broth, or drain the pasta, and distribute among four large soup bowls. Slice the meat off the bone and place a few slices on top of each serving. Pour the hot broth over, sprinkle on the coriander if you wish, and serve.

Put out a small condiment dish for each diner and place the condiments on the table, together with a plate of the remaining slices of meat, so guests can help themselves as they wish.

Serves 4 as a substantial one-dish meal or main course

BOTTOMLESS-POT CENTRAL ASIAN BROTH: At the stalls in Xining, the broth pot needs to be "bottomless" to feed customers all day. The cooks include bones as well as meat in the broth pots, and then, when the meat is tender, lift it out, leaving the bones. When and if they need to, they top off the broth pot with more hot water. If you are feeding a crowd, you may want to do the same. Use about 1 pound goat or lamb bones, 1 coarsely chopped onion, and 1 star anise for every 8 cups water you use beyond the water called for above. Bring the water to a boil, then reduce the heat and simmer for 10 minutes before adding the meat and continuing as above. When seasoning the broth, use about 1½ teaspoons salt per each 8 cups water. Any excess broth can be stored, once completely cooled, in well-sealed containers in the freezer—a handy stash for when you wish to make hot pot or get a flavorful noodle soup on the table quickly.

NOODLES WITH SESAME SAUCE

Noodles are an important part of Uighur cooking, so it stands to reason that they're enjoyed at room temperature (especially in summer) as well as hot; this dish can be served either way. The sesame (tahini) dressing goes beautifully with noodles and is a snap to make.

The recipe has only moderate chile heat, from minced fresh cayenne chiles. For more heat, increase the fresh chiles or add dried cayenne powder to taste. We like it very chile-hot, the way we've encountered it in Xinjiang, with a cucumber salad served alongside for a cooling contrast.

SAUCE

1 cup tahini (sesame paste)

¾ cup warm water

¼ cup cider vinegar

¼ cup soy sauce

1 pound homemade noodles, such as Tuvan noodles (see page 246) or Tibetan long noodles (see page 144) or dried linguine or other pasta

GARNISH

4 to 5 scallions, finely chopped

3 to 4 tablespoons red cayenne chiles, seeded and finely chopped

In a medium bowl, whisk together the tahini and warm water, mixing vigorously until well blended. Add the vinegar and soy sauce and stir well. You will have about 2 cups sauce. Let sit for 1 hour.

Bring a large pot of lightly salted water to a boil. Add the noodles and cook until cooked through but still firm to the bite. Drain.

If you want to serve the noodles hot, place in a large bowl, stir the sesame sauce and pour it over them, and toss to blend well. *Alternatively*, if you want to serve the noodles at room temperature, rinse them with cold water to cool, then toss with the sauce.

Garnish with the scallions and chiles just before serving.

Serves 4 as a light meal with a salad or a vegetable dish

SAVORY BOILED DUMPLINGS

Jiaozi (pronounced "jáo-dze"), as these succulent juicy dumplings are known in Mandarin, are quick to make and oh-so-easy to eat in quantity. They're cousins of the boiled, steamed, or baked filled dumplings of Central Asia. The filling we use here is ground pork, mixed either with finely chopped leek or with carrot diced small. You can substitute ground lamb for the pork, as people do in Qinghai and Xinjiang, if you wish.

Somewhat untraditionally, we make the wrappers with a basic egg noodle dough, but you could also use the (more standard) basic noodle dough for Amdo Noodle Squares (page 128). The egg dough is especially easy to roll out and shape into *jiaozi*.

Once filled and pinched closed, the dumplings are tossed into boiling water to cook until they float to the surface, like ravioli, about 1 minute. The meat cooks through as the dumplings boil, and the filling is succulent and full of flavor. In Inner Mongolia and in Qinghai, we've seen the cooking water for *jiaozi* enhanced by the addition of dried wolfberries, listed below as an option. The dried orange-colored berries are about the size of raisins. They are sold in Chinese herb stores, and you can also now find them in some health food stores, usually by their Tibetan name, *goji* (see the Glossary for more).

A steamer full of country-style jiaozi *(dumplings) accompanied by dipping sauce, at a small eatery in Jiangche, in southern Yunnan.*

This recipe makes 64 dumplings, 32 with each filling. They can be served on plates or in broth, as you please. Serve hot and fresh, with generous amounts of the dipping sauce set out in individual condiment bowls.

> **1 recipe of dough for Kazakh Noodles (page 133),**
>   **2 recipes dough for Amdo Noodle Squares (page 128), or**
>   **75 store-bought wonton wrappers (see Glossary)**

LEEK AND PORK FILLING

1 small leek

¼ pound (½ cup) ground pork (or ground lamb)

½ teaspoon salt

1 teaspoon soy sauce

½ teaspoon roasted sesame oil

CARROT AND PORK FILLING

1 medium carrot, peeled and cut in half

¼ pound (½ cup) ground pork (or ground lamb)

2 teaspoons minced garlic

½ teaspoon salt

1 teaspoon soy sauce

½ teaspoon roasted sesame oil

About ½ cup wolfberries (see headnote; optional)

Soy-Vinegar Dipping Sauce (page 151)

Keep the dough covered while you make the fillings.

For the leek filling, trim off the tough root end of the leek and the tough ends of the leaves. Cut lengthwise into quarters, then thinly slice. Place in a large bowl of cold water and let stand briefly, then lift out, leaving any grit behind. Repeat with several changes of water, then drain well. Measure out 1 loosely packed cup sliced leek and place in a medium bowl. (Use any extra for another purpose.)

Add the remaining filling ingredients to the leeks and stir with a fork, breaking up any lumps in the meat and blending the ingredients well. Set aside.

For the carrot filling, bring a small pot of water to a boil. Add the carrot and parboil for about 5 minutes. Remove from the heat and refresh under cold water (save the cooking water to use in soup, if you like). Cut the carrot into small dice. Measure out ½ cup, and place in a medium bowl. (Use any remaining carrot for another purpose.)

Add the remaining filling ingredients to the carrot and blend together with a fork. Set aside.

The fillings can be prepared as long as 12 hours ahead and stored, covered, in the refrigerator.

Place the bowls of filling by your work surface. Line a baking sheet with wax paper or parchment paper, dust with a little flour, and place near your work surface.

Place the dough on a lightly floured surface and cut it into 8 equal pieces. Set 7 pieces aside while you work with the first one. On the floured surface, roll the dough under your palms to make a smooth, even cylinder 8 inches long. Cut into 8 equal pieces (cut it in half and then in half and half again). Flatten each piece into an oval about 2 inches by 3 inches.

Place a scant 1½ teaspoons of one of the fillings on one oval (or wrapper), fold the dough over to make a half-moon shape, and pinch the edges closed (the dough is soft, so the edges will stick when pinched lightly; if necessary, moisten one edge lightly before pinching). Set the shaped dumpling on the lined baking sheet. Repeat with the remaining 7 pieces and then with the remaining dough (or wrappers) and fillings. Don't worry if some of the dumplings are irregularly shaped; shape does not matter, and all will cook through in the same time.

Bring a large pot of water to a vigorous boil. Toss in the wolfberries, if using, and boil for 5 minutes. Toss in 10 dumplings and watch as the water comes back to the boil. About a minute later, the dumplings will slowly bob to the surface. Let cook for another 15 seconds, then use a mesh skimmer or slotted spoon to scoop them out of the water, letting them drain over the pot, and into a bowl. Repeat with the remaining dumplings—you can cook a larger number at a time once you feel comfortable with the method.

Serve hot, with the dipping sauce on the side.

Makes 64 dumplings; serves 8 as an appetizer or part of a meal, 4 to 6 for lunch with soup or a vegetable side dish

NOTE ON FREEZING DUMPLINGS: The dumplings also freeze well once shaped. To cook frozen dumplings, drop them straight into boiling water; they will take about 3 minutes to cook through.

Soy-Vinegar Dipping Sauce

This classic condiment is a must-have if you are serving *jiaozi* (boiled dumplings). It is also a great accompaniment for noodle soups. Make it just before you wish to serve it.

> ½ cup soy sauce
> ¼ cup Jinjiang (black rice) vinegar or rice vinegar
> 2 tablespoons fine ginger shreds (see Note)

Combine all the ingredients in a bowl and stir. To serve, divide among two or more small condiment bowls and put out a small spoon for each, so guests can dip their dumplings into the sauce or else drizzle it on, to taste.

Makes about ¾ cup

NOTE ON GINGER SHREDS: To make the ginger shreds, peel a piece of ginger about 2 inches long and slice lengthwise very thin. Stack the slices and cut into very fine matchsticks.

uighur flung noodles

We have not included a recipe for Uighur flung noodles. They're extraordinary, and we have tried, a lot, but we must confess we've been unable to make them with much success. For this traditional technique, there's kneading, but no rolling out of the dough. Instead, a piece of well-kneaded dough is stretched a little, then the dough is held like a rope, one hand at each end, and flung so it stretches to a loop about four to five feet long (see photo, page 124). The ends are then held in one hand and the loop in the other. The double strand is flung again, and again the weight of the dough stretches the loop longer. So it goes, the noodles getting thinner each time they are "multiplied" by stretching.

We've spent hours watching Uighur noodle-makers knead and fling dough. We're fascinated by the method, such an ingenious way of transforming a wheat flour dough into food. And we love the texture of the cooked noodles, but we've not made enough headway with them in our own kitchen, so we can't give instructions. Instead, here is a progress report: we've worked with hard-wheat bread flour and ordinary all-purpose. We've made soft doughs and stiffer ones. We've kneaded the dough for a long time and kneaded it less. In each case, we could get some stretch, even several loops, but soon the dough would break rather than stretch. Finally we'd give up and instead hand-stretch the dough (as we do for Kazakh Noodles, page 133) or roll it out into thin sheets and cut it (as we do for Tuvan noodles; see page 246). The noodles were always delectable, but we still hope that someday we'll break through and solve the mystery of flung noodles for ourselves.

ABOVE: *A young man flings Uighur noodles in the background, while another stirs a huge wok of boiling broth over an open fire, at the market in Kashgar, in western Xinjiang.* OPPOSITE: *Steamed Tibetan Momos (page 154) in a bamboo steamer, with Tibetan Ginger-Tomato Chutney (page 24) alongside.*

STEAMED TIBETAN MOMOS

Momos are succulent filled dumplings Tibetan-style. They're most often made using yak meat (for which we substitute beef), but we've also come across lamb *momos*. Both options are given below.

The meat is usually chopped by hand, rather than ground, which gives the dumplings good bite. We suggest that you start with reasonably lean meat, chill it well, and grind it yourself, using the food processor (or you could chop it using two cleavers). The filling is flavored with minced scallion, ginger, a little hot chile, and fresh herbs—either Chinese celery or coriander.

The *momos* steam in a Chinese-style bamboo or metal steamer topped with a tight-fitting lid. If you have several steamer baskets, then you can get all the *momos* cooked at once by stacking the steamers. If not, each batch takes about 15 minutes to cook through. [PHOTOGRAPH ON PAGE 153]

DOUGH

2 cups all-purpose flour, preferably unbleached

½ teaspoon salt

½ teaspoon baking soda

A generous ½ cup lukewarm water

FILLING

1 pound boneless lean beef or lamb, preferably a little fatty, cut into 5 pieces and well chilled

6 scallions, coarsely chopped (1 cup)

¾ cup chopped Chinese celery leaves or coriander

2 tablespoons minced ginger

1 teaspoon Guizhou Chile Paste (page 35) or store-bought chile paste, or 2 dried red chiles, stemmed and crushed

2 teaspoons salt

½ teaspoon freshly ground black pepper

Soy-Vinegar Dipping Sauce (page 151), Tenzin's Quick-Pickled Radish Threads (page 25), or Guizhou Chile Paste (page 35)

Place the flour, salt, and baking soda in a food processor and pulse to mix. With the blade running, slowly add the lukewarm water through the feed tube until a ball of dough forms. *Alternatively,* place the flour, salt, and soda in a medium bowl and mix together. Add the water and stir and turn to make a rough dough.

Turn the dough out onto a lightly floured surface and knead briefly, until smooth. Cover with plastic wrap and let rest for 20 to 30 minutes.

Meanwhile, make the filling: Place the meat in the food processor along with the scallions and process until coarsely chopped. Add the remaining filling ingredients and process briefly to blend them together. Turn the filling out into a bowl and set aside.

Lightly oil a steamer basket.

Place the dough on a lightly floured surface and cut it into 3 equal pieces. Set 2 aside, loosely covered. Cut the remaining piece of dough into 8 equal pieces, by dividing it in half and half and half again. Pat, roll out, or stretch one piece to a 4-inch round. Place 1 level tablespoon of filling in the center and pull the sides up around the filling, then pinch them together over the filling and twist slightly to form a kind of topknot. Place in the steamer basket, topknot side up. Repeat with the remaining dough and filling until the steamer is full.

Place the steamer over a wok or pot of boiling water, cover tightly, and cook until done, 12 to 15 minutes. (Cut one dumpling in half to see if the meat has changed color, indicating that it is cooked.) Meanwhile, shape the remaining dumplings.

When they are done, remove the cooked dumplings from the steamer, and cook the rest in batches.

Serve hot or warm, with the accompaniment of your choice.

Makes 24 dumplings; serves 6 as part of a meal with a soup and a vegetable, or 8 as an appetizer

MONGOLIAN DUMPLINGS: In Mongolia, there's a boiled or steamed dumpling that's called *jiaozi* in Mandarin but is more like a *momo*. It's substantial rather than refined, a great addition to the noodle repertoire, made of noodle dough wrapped around herb-flavored ground lamb or beef. The dough is much thicker than *jiaozi* dough, and the dumplings are hearty. To make boiled lamb dumplings, use the *momo* dough, but substitute the filling from Mongolian Lamb Sausages (page 272). Divide the dough into 12 equal pieces. One at a time, roll out or flatten each into a round about 5 inches in diameter. Place 3 tablespoons filling onto the round, fold over to make a half-moon shape, and pinch closed. Roll the edge over itself and pinch again to seal well. Set aside on a lightly floured baking sheet or work surface near your stovetop. Bring a large pot of water to a boil. Add the dumplings one by one, bring the water back to a rolling boil, and cook until the dumplings and filling are cooked through, about 10 minutes. Use a mesh skimmer or slotted spoon to lift them out. Serve hot or at room temperature, with an array of condiments, as above.

Serves 6 as a hearty snack, 6 to 8 as part of a meal with soup and a vegetable dish

Stacked bamboo steamers sit over a huge wok at a small restaurant open to the street, in Hailar, Inner Mongolia.

LEFT: *Two Kazakh men shoeing a horse, near Kanas Lake, in the Altai Mountains of northern Xinjiang.* RIGHT: *A Kazakh street-food vendor in the town of Altai, in northern Xinjiang.*

THE KAZAKH PEOPLE

Approximately one and a half million Kazakhs live in China (out of roughly eighteen or nineteen million Kazakhs worldwide). After the Uighurs (see page 90), they are the second largest non-Han population in Xinjiang (the very large, sparsely populated province in the far west of China). Like the Uighurs and the Kirghiz (see page 288), the Kazakhs are a Turkic people. They live primarily in the Tian Shan Mountains in the central part of Xinjiang (north of the Takla Makan Desert), and in the Altai Mountains in the far north, where the borders of Kazakhstan, Russia, and Mongolia meet.

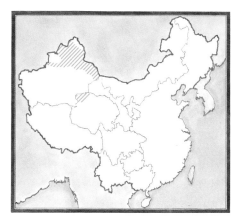

Kazakhs have always been a fiercely independent people, living mainly as nomadic or seminomadic pastoralists. In their native homeland, what is present-day Kazakhstan, they lived under Mongol rule from the thirteenth to the early fifteenth century, then under the Tatar *khanates* (states) that succeeded the Mongol domination, and eventually under Russian rule from the eighteenth century onward. In the 1920s they suffered tremendously under Stalin's oppressive policies of forced collectivization. During that period, many fled to neighboring China. (Kazakhstan, an area almost the size of all of Western Europe, had a reported population of 3.6 million people in 1926; ten years later, because of outmigration and famine, it was only 2.3 million.)

But for the Kazakhs who fled to China, life didn't get much better. There they suffered through forced collectivization again in the 1950s, and then through the Cultural Revolution (1966–1976). As it has done with other nomadic peoples, the Chinese government has always encouraged—and/or forced—the Kazakhs to abandon their nomadic lifestyle. In China today, many Kazakhs live and work in cities and towns, but a significant number still lead a relatively traditional lifestyle, keeping camels, horses, herds of sheep and goats, and living, at least in the summer months, in dome-shaped yurts.

Kazakhstan is now an independent republic, and in 2000 an enormous oil deposit was discovered on its Caspian Sea coast, making the economic future of the country look bright. But even though the economy is booming and the government has declared that all Kazakhs are welcome to return, a very small percentage of the Kazakhs in China have actually done so. We don't know why, and can only guess that they want to wait and see whether life really does look better in Kazakhstan.

The cooking of the Kazakhs is a reflection of their traditional lifestyle. Meat, bread, and milk and dairy products are all important elements of the cuisine, as is rice brought in from central China. Food is very seasonally based, and food preservation, through the use of salting and drying, is important, given the long, cold winter season.

Meat soups and stews are at the heart of Kazakh cooking, and most meals are simmered one-pot or one-platter dishes (see Kazakh Noodles, page 133, and Kazakh Pulao, page 177).

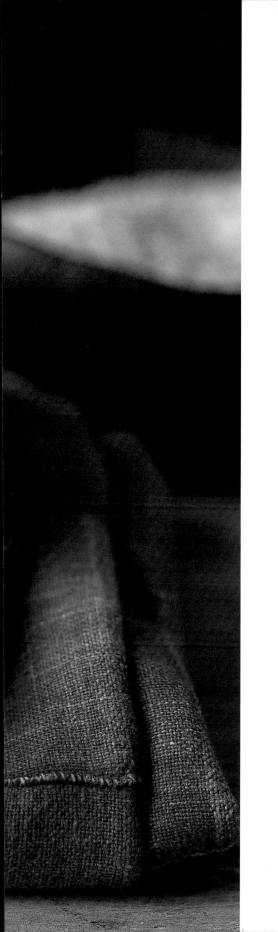

RICE AND GRAINS

An assortment of rices—including several grades of jasmine rice, white sticky rice, and red and black rice—for sale at the market in Jinghong, in southern Yunnan. The colored rices may be used for congee or sweets, or as the basic mash for making rice liquor.

WE LOVE BEST THE FOODS WE CAN RELY ON AND eat with pleasure day after day, the comforting, undemanding flavors and textures of staple grains. For some, that translates into a passion for bread, but for people living beyond the Great Wall, it often means an intimate relationship with rice, millet, or barley, or with noodles. (The noodle connection is so huge that noodles have their own chapter, as do breads.)

We begin with instructions for cooking plain rice of two kinds: sticky rice, the traditional staple for many peoples living in southern Yunnan and in Guizhou and parts of Guangxi province, and jasmine rice, which is our everyday rice.

An alternative to plain steamed rice is rice—or another grain—cooked to a thick porridge texture. It can be eaten to anchor a meal, as plain rice is, or instead served with toppings and condiments for breakfast or a snack. The word used in English for grains cooked with lots of water to a soupy texture is sometimes "porridge," or it may be "soup." Another word often used is "congee," from the Hindi *kañci*, meaning a rice porridge. Rice congee is a staple food in many places in Asia

(Japan and Thailand, for example, as well as China), usually made very plain, sometimes cooked up with mung beans, as we have it here (see page 173). At breakfast or as a late-evening snack, it's served with an array of savory toppings and flavorings, from chopped pickled vegetables to salted peanuts, chopped grilled meat, and seasonings. Though many North Americans may not be used to the idea of pickled greens and other strong savory tastes for breakfast, for those who love it, congee is comfort food, easy to spoon down and warming. Other grains have their place in the congee world too, especially in areas where rice is a luxury. We've included a millet congee (see page 172), which we like as an accompaniment at supper in place of plain rice, and also a dramatic-looking black rice congee (see page 167).

In Xinjiang, many people, including the Kazakhs (see page 157) and Uighurs (page 90), have a tradition of festive rice dishes in the *pulao* tradition (see Chicken Pulao with Pumpkin, page 174; and Kazakh Pulao, page 177). Flatbreads and noodles are the everyday staples, made with wheat grown in the oases,

but *pulaos* are the dishes for special occasions, served on large platters, family-style. The rice is simmered in broth with meat and vegetables and aromatics, absorbing flavor as it cooks. These *pulaos* are part of the flavored rice tradition that extends from Central Asia to the *pulaos* of Mogul India and the eastern Mediterranean, the paellas of Spain, and the pilafs, *pulaos*, and perloos of West Africa and South Carolina. They are best made with Mediterranean varieties of rice; we suggest baldo or arborio or Valencia, which have a generous capacity to absorb the flavored broth and yet keep their shape.

The last section of the chapter is devoted to tsampa, the amazing Tibetan staple that is an ingenious solution to the challenge of making edible food from hard grain. Barley grows only in the valleys of Tibet, so the high-altitude nomads trade meat and salt for barley tsampa. Tsampa is lightweight, keeps well, and needs no further cooking, no further fuel, to make it digestible. With access to a good coffee grinder or, better still, to a flour mill, we've found we can make it at home, a great discovery.

STICKY RICE

The Dong (see page 120), like the Dai (page 237) and many other Tai peoples, are traditionally sticky rice eaters. Even though sticky rice is now more often a festive food than an everyday staple for some families, it's still an important mark of identity.

This was brought home to me when I stayed in the Dong village of Zhaoxing, in eastern Guizhou. The schoolteacher daughter of one of the families I met there had married a Han man, also a schoolteacher. He was one of very few non-Dong in the village. And one of the ways that he kept his separate identity, apart from not speaking the Dong language (he and his wife spoke Mandarin together), was that he did not eat sticky rice. The family made large batches of sticky rice while I was there, once for the name-giving party for a cousin's baby, the other time for a celebration that marked the opening of their new guesthouse. On both occasions the daughter was very careful to say to me, "My husband and I don't eat sticky rice."

Sticky rice is a special variety of rice (also known as glutinous rice), with opaque white grains rather than the translucent grains of most raw rices. It's now widely available in Asian grocery stores. The sticky rice in Japan is short-grain, but the rice used by the Dong and Dai is like Thai and Lao sticky rice, medium- to long-grain. Look for bags labeled "sweet rice" or "glutinous rice" and "product of Thailand" (for more, see Glossary). Sticky rice has relatively little capacity to absorb moisture (unlike risotto rices, for example, or basmati) and is usually cooked by steaming after being soaked in water overnight.

With the increasing popularity of Southeast Asian cuisines, especially Thai and Vietnamese, more and more people in North America have now eaten sticky rice, at least in a restaurant. What many people don't realize is how easy and forgiving it is to cook: no measurement of water and rice, just a long soak in water and about 35 minutes steaming.

The Dong and the Dai, like many people in northern Laos, steam their rice in wide bamboo cylinders over boiling water. In North America, you can steam the soaked rice in a regular Chinese bamboo steamer, after lining the rack with a tea towel to prevent the rice from falling through the slats, or you can use a Lao-style conical basket placed on the rim of a pot.

Show your guests how to pick up a small clump of sticky rice in one hand and then tear off a little of it, as you'd tear a bite-sized piece from a slice of bread. Shape it into a firmer ball and scoop it through a savory sauce, such as Dai Tart Green Salsa (page 22), or use it to pick up a small piece of grilled fish or meat. [PHOTOGRAPH ON PAGE 165]

3 cups Thai sticky rice (see headnote)

Rinse the rice briefly to wash off any dust. Place in a large pot and add about 6 cups tepid water. Cover and set aside for 10 to 12 hours to soak. (If you are in a rush, you can hurry the rice by soaking it in warm water: don't make the water boiling hot, just very warm, and reduce the soaking time to 4 hours. Longer soaking produces a slightly better texture.)

Drain, then place the rice in a steamer—a conical or round sticky rice steaming basket if you have one (see headnote), or a regular Chinese bamboo steamer lined with muslin, cheesecloth, or a loose-weave tea towel so the rice doesn't fall through (see photo opposite).

In either case, you need 2 to 3 inches of water in the pot under the steamer, and the rice in its basket must be above, not in, the water. A conical or cylindrical basket should fit tightly into the pot (so the steam can't escape around the sides). A regular steamer works best resting in a wok; otherwise, it should fit tightly over a pot of water.

Bring the water to a boil. If you are using a Lao steaming basket, then just cover the top loosely (it will cook uncovered, but we find covering it makes it cook a little more quickly and evenly) and steam for about 35 minutes. If you are steaming in a wide round steamer, cover tightly and steam for 20 minutes; remove the steamer and use a wooden spoon to turn the rice over, then place the steamer back over the boiling water and continue to steam for about 15 minutes. The rice should be tender but still firm when done.

Turn the rice out onto a counter or other surface and use a long-handled wooden spoon or spatula to spread it out and then to lift the sides in toward the center, to create a round lump of rice (this evens out the texture). Transfer to one or more covered baskets, or place in a bowl and cover with a well-moistened cloth to prevent the rice from drying out. Serve warm or at room temperature.

Makes about 6 cups; serves 4 to 6

STICKY RICE WITH CURED SAUSAGE: As the rice steams, flavorings can be cooked or heated on top of it. In Jinghong, we've seen Chinese sausage cut into pieces, steam-cooking on top of a large batch of sticky rice. To try this, buy about ½ pound Chinese sausage, rinse it, and cut it into ½-inch lengths. Once the soaked rice is in the steamer, scatter the sausage on top, cover, and steam until the rice is done, as above. Serve the sausage separately, or mix it into the rice after steaming.

Sticky rice, once soaked, can be steamed in a number of ways. Here it is placed in a cheesecloth-lined steamer that is in turn placed over water in a wok (the water must not touch the rice). The steamer is then covered, the water brought to a boil, and the rice cooks to an even doneness in about half an hour.

ABOVE: *In late autumn the rice has been harvested in these rice terraces not far from the Miao village of Xijiang in Guizhou province. What remains is the stubble, already flooded with water so that it can be plowed under and the ground readied for the next planting. The method of storing rice straw by stacking it on a pole to repel the rain is used by the Miao and Hmong we encountered, whether in China or in Southeast Asia.* OPPOSITE, LEFT: *Sticky Rice (page 162) with Dai Tart Green Salsa (page 22).* OPPOSITE, RIGHT: *Baskets of newly harvested rice, in the Dong village of Zhaoxing, also in Guizhou.*

BASIC RICE

Most rice in the south of China is consumed very close to where it is grown. People have a strong feeling of attachment to the rice they grew up with, and though its flavor is subtle, everyday rice can vary a lot in flavor from place to place and variety to variety.

We use Thai jasmine as our everyday rice. You may have another favorite; use whatever medium- to long-grain rice pleases you. You will need a heavy straight-sided relatively wide (rather than tall) 3- to 4-quart pot, with a tight-fitting lid, or a rice cooker.

> 2 cups Thai jasmine rice
> About 2½ cups water

To wash the rice, place it in a bowl or pot and add plenty of cold water. Stir the rice and water round and round with your hand, then pour off the water. Repeat two or three times, until the water runs clear after you have swished it around.

Transfer the rice to your rice-cooking pot or rice cooker. Add enough water to cover the rice by about ¾ inch. Test the depth of the water by placing the tip of your index finger on the top surface of the rice; the water should come up to the middle of your first knuckle. (This is the usual way of measuring water for plain rice in Southeast Asia and in the cultures we've been in in southern China. If you prefer a cup measure, drain the washed rice thoroughly in a strainer, then place in the pot with 2½ cups water.)

If using a pot, place the pot over high heat. When the water is boiling, cover tightly, lower the heat to medium-low, and cook for 10 minutes. Reduce the heat to the lowest setting and cook, covered, for another 6 to 7 minutes. Remove from the heat and let stand for 5 minutes, still covered.

If using a rice cooker, put the lid on and turn it on. (The cooker will automatically bring the water to a boil and then lower the heat and cook it until done. You will see an indicator light change color or turn off when the rice is done.) Once the rice is cooked, let stand for 5 minutes, covered.

When you remove the lid from the pot or rice cooker, you will see that the grains on top have fluffed and are standing on end.

Rinse a wooden rice paddle or wooden spoon with cold water and slide it down the side of the pot, then tilt to lift up some of the rice gently and turn it over. Repeat all around the sides of the pot.

Serve hot or warm. Leave the lid on, to keep in warmth and moisture.

Makes about 4 cups; serves 4 to 6

NOTE ON SCALING UP: To make a larger quantity, to serve 6 to 8, or because you'd like leftovers, use 3 cups rice. Add water using the same fingertip measure as above, or add 3¾ cups water to the well-drained rice. Cook as above.

BLACK RICE CONGEE

This purplish black version of rice porridge/congee can be served for breakfast or as a rice dish at any time. It's especially attractive when sprinkled with a fresh green herb, such as chopped coriander leaves. Black rice congee is made of black sticky rice mixed with either rice brokens (broken rice grains; see Glossary) or white rice such as jasmine. The black rice stains the white rice grains a beautiful purple. In China, black sticky rice is grown in the southern provinces of Guangxi and Guizhou. Black sticky rice from Thailand is widely available in North America.

Chinese red dates, also called jujubes, are available at Chinese grocery stores and at some health food stores. Like wolfberries, they've recently come to the notice of Westerners because of their health properties. Cooks in China add them to soups because they are believed to be good for circulation and for the skin. (See Glossary for more on Chinese dates.) They have a slight sweetness and are pleasant little nuggets of flavor to discover as you eat the congee, but they can, of course, be left out.

Serve black rice congee with savory flavors such as a chopped cucumber salad or, nontraditionally, chopped avocado dressed with fresh lime juice. For a sweet alternative, see Coconut Milk Black Porridge below. [PHOTOGRAPH ON PAGE 170]

About 6 cups water

½ cup black sticky rice, washed and drained

¼ cup rice brokens or medium-grain rice such as Thai jasmine, washed and drained

¼ cup Chinese red dates (see headnote; optional)

Bring 6 cups water to a vigorous boil in a wide pot. Sprinkle in the rices and bring back to a vigorous boil. Lower the heat and cook at a medium boil, partially covered, for 15 minutes, then add the dates, if using, and cook for another half hour or until the rice is very soft and starting to break down. Stir occasionally to prevent sticking, and gradually lower the heat as the congee cooks, to prevent scorching. If it is getting very thick but is not yet cooked, add another cup or so of water, bring back to a boil, and continue cooking.

Serve hot.

Serves 4 as part of a meal

COCONUT MILK BLACK PORRIDGE: For a lusher version, and one more like our Western idea of porridge, cook the congee as above, but serve it with sweetened coconut milk: Heat 2 cups canned or fresh coconut milk and dissolve about ½ cup packed brown sugar in it. Put the sweetened coconut milk in a small jug and invite your guests to pour it generously onto their congee (or you can stir some of it into the rice before serving it). You might also want to offer slices of fresh fruit (bananas or pears, for example) or berries.

OPPOSITE: *A fairly prosperous Han woman farmer in Inner Mongolia, north of the town of Yakishi and not far from the border with Siberia. She and her husband are tenant farmers who grow barley, millet, and vegetables and raise chickens. In the summer they also have a small farm-stay business, where guests come to stay for up to several weeks. When we dropped by in late October, she was busy pickling cabbage in preparation for winter. In her kitchen was a large tiled stove fueled by charcoal that is used for cooking and also for heating the house. The family's electricity comes from a small solar panel; it's enough to power the television and several lightbulbs.*

We were in China three times in the 1990s, twice in Yunnan. The first time was in March 1994. I was in Vietnam, visiting a friend. He had heard that the China-Vietnam border—so long inaccessible—was now "open" for foreigners. I got a Chinese visa in Hanoi, then caught a train into the mountains of northern Vietnam. I stayed in Sapa, a village with an amazing mix of tribal cultures. It was rainy there, and I was carrying heavy camera equipment as usual. One day my knee went out and swelled up like a pumpkin. Ice bags didn't exist in Sapa, so I used cold beer bottles to reduce the swelling, Chinese beer.

A young man gave me a ride on the back of his motorcycle, four hours down a muddy winding road, from Sapa to the China border. There was a train waiting on the other side, across a long bridge over a big river. It felt like a scene from a World War II movie: my bad knee, the rain, the bridge, the train waiting on the other side. But the Chinese border officials told me the train wouldn't leave until the next day and that I should stay in the hotel overnight. And so I did.

But it was not like any Chinese hotel I'd ever stayed in. I had a room to myself, not a bed in a dorm, a nice clean room. I turned on the television (a television, in China!) that night, and from deep in the mountains of the China-Vietnam border area, where just a few years earlier a war had been fought, I watched an NBA basketball game.

The next day, I caught the train to Kunming. It was a spectacular ride. The track followed the course of the Red River, through deep mountain gorges. High up on the mountainsides, I could see rice terraces on a huge scale, as vertical as any rice terraces I have ever seen. I knew that we were passing through entirely tribal areas, but I had no idea who the peoples were and getting off to explore was not an option.

Kunming, the capital of Yunnan, was a city I was familiar with, but it had changed a lot in the ten years since my last visit. A decade earlier, the large main streets had been jam-packed with bicycles, with only the very occasional car or truck. Now it was just the opposite. There were still a million bicycles, but they had their own lane on the side, and the street was crowded with vehicles. It was the same attractive city, with tree-lined streets and with great food, but quite transformed.

A few years later, we were traveling with our kids from northern Yunnan down to the Lao border, working on our Southeast Asian cookbook, *Hot Sour Salty Sweet*. In Jinghong, in southern Yunnan, we stopped in at a little travelers' café run by a group of young Hani women (see page 316). It was a café that you might expect in Kathmandu, or by a beach in southern Thailand. The young woman waiting on our table spoke to us in English far better than our Mandarin. After our food arrived, she pulled up a chair and chatted with us. She was twenty, or maybe not quite, from Guangxi, far to the east. She'd come to Yunnan to work. She'd heard that Dali (a small charming town in Yunnan, 300 miles west of Kunming) was a "cool" place to work, but so was Jinghong, and Jinghong had a better climate, so here she was.

For decades, it had been impossible for Chinese citizens to choose where they lived. The Beijing government changed all that in 1993, probably to facilitate the movement of labor from the poorer north to the booming south. People immediately started to relocate from poorer areas to more prosperous ones. Some say it was the largest movement of people in history.

The China of the 1990s was a world away from the China of the '80s.

OPPOSITE: *A village set in the steeply terraced landscape of Yunnan, about one day's drive south of Dali. In the rainy season the terraces will be green with growing rice plants.*

OPPOSITE, CLOCKWISE FROM THE TOP: *Millet by the Bowlful (page 172) topped with pickled mustard greens; Black Rice Congee (page 167) cooked with Chinese red dates; Rice Congee with Mung Beans (page 173) with Bright Red Chile Paste (page 18) and roasted salted peanuts.* LEFT: *A large steamer full of sticky rice from the amazing terraces just outside town, in Yuanyang, southeastern Yunnan.* RIGHT: *Rice for sale at the market in Jinghong, in southern Yunnan.*

MILLET BY THE BOWLFUL

Millet, like sorghum, was once a very important staple in northern China, eaten as a toasted grain or cooked like porridge. Although these days wheat has largely displaced it as a staple food, millet is still eaten as a toasted grain by many rural people in Inner Mongolia, we're told. And some homely traditional millet dishes, such as this simple porridge, or congee, can still be found in contemporary China, even in the cities.

There was a particularly good millet congee in the northern Inner Mongolian city of Hailar. It was part of a breakfast buffet, and I found it wonderfully soothing food for a cold morning. Alongside were an assortment of pickles and spicy flavors to eat on or with the congee. We suggest putting out roasted salted peanuts, some chopped pickled mustard greens or Tenzin's Quick-Pickled Radish Threads (page 25); a chile paste or some chile oil; and perhaps some Cucumbers in Black Rice Vinegar (page 83). Or instead you can treat the congee like Western-style porridge and top it with slices of banana or some berries, milk or yogurt, and perhaps a drizzle of honey.

Millet congee can also be served as a substitute for rice in a main meal, just as it was traditionally eaten in parts of northern China and in poorer mountain areas. We've become very fond of eating it this way, especially when we're tired on a chilly evening, because it's real comfort food, and solidly sustaining. [PHOTOGRAPH ON PAGE 170]

½ cup millet

5 cups water

OPTIONAL ACCOMPANIMENTS (see headnote)

About ¼ cup chopped pickled mustard greens (see Glossary)

About ¼ cup roasted salted peanuts

Bright Red Chile Paste (page 18), Guizhou Chile Paste (page 35), or store-bought chile paste, or Chile Oil (page 29)

Cucumber-Vinegar Sauce (page 83)

Wash the millet well in several changes of water.

Place the water in a large heavy pot and bring to a boil. Add the millet and return to the boil, then lower the heat to medium, cover, and cook until very tender, about 45 minutes.

Serve for breakfast with some or all of the suggested accompaniments. Or serve in place of rice to anchor a meal.

Makes 4 cups; serves 3 to 5 for breakfast or as part of a meal

MILLET POLENTA: If you cook the millet ahead, or if you have leftovers, you'll notice that as it cools, it thickens into a solid mass. To reheat, place it in a pot, add about ½ cup water, and stir until the millet is hot. Millet was the staple in many of the areas of Italy that later turned to a New World crop, corn, for their staple grain, and we think that this property millet has of thickening to a bread-like texture when cooled must be the origin of polenta. For millet polenta, cook it as above, then spread it in a lightly greased baking pan. Drizzle on a little olive oil and bake in a 350°F oven for 30 minutes. Serve cut into slices as you would serve polenta.

RICE CONGEE WITH MUNG BEANS

This blend of white rice and whole mung beans (the small dried dull-green beans that are sprouted to make mung bean sprouts) is another classic version of porridge/congee. It's an old and healthy combination, rice with legumes, easy to prepare, and reminiscent of the *kitchree* of the Indian Subcontinent, in which rice and dal are cooked and served together. We've come across rice-mung congee in various places, from Inner Mongolia to Guizhou.

It makes a great breakfast porridge, but we also like it for supper, served in place of plain rice and accompanied by savory dishes, just as we do with millet (see Millet by the Bowlful, page 172). The small tender beans are like darker dots in the pale rice and have a slightly firmer texture. Put the beans and rice on to cook an hour or more before you wish to serve the congee. Or, to make it for breakfast, cook it the night before, then reheat it quickly in the morning. The texture is like a thick porridge. [PHOTOGRAPH ON PAGE 170]

¼ cup dried whole mung beans

About 6 cups water

½ cup medium- or long-grain rice (jasmine or other—but not parboiled rice)

OPTIONAL TOPPINGS

Roasted salted peanuts

3 tablespoons chopped pickled mustard greens (see Glossary)

2 to 3 tablespoons Guizhou Chile Paste (page 35) or Bright Red Chile Paste (page 18) or store-bought chile paste

Soy-Vinegar Dipping Sauce (page 151)

About ¼ cup dry-roasted sesame seeds

Rinse the mung beans, put them in a large heavy pot, and add 4 cups water. Bring to a vigorous boil, then lower the heat to maintain a medium boil, partially cover, and cook until the beans are softened but not yet cooked through, about 30 minutes.

Wash the rice, and add it to the pot with 2 more cups water. Bring to a vigorous boil, then lower the heat, partially cover, and simmer for about 25 minutes, until the rice is very soft. Check the pot occasionally to ensure that there's enough water and that the rice and beans are not sticking to the pot; add more hot water if necessary.

Serve the traditional way, with an assortment of the suggested toppings. Or serve in place of plain rice with a meal.

Makes about 6 cups; serves 4 with toppings, 4 to 6 as part of a meal

RICE-MUNG BEAN SOUP: This congee transforms easily into a flavorful winter soup: When it is done, add an extra cup of water to thin the congee, and bring almost to a boil, then lower the heat to keep it at a low simmer, partially covered. Heat 2 tablespoons peanut oil in a wok or heavy skillet over medium-high heat. Toss in 1 tablespoon minced garlic and stir-fry briefly, then add 1 tablespoon minced ginger and 1 or 2 dried red chiles and stir-fry for 10 seconds. If you'd like a meatier soup, add about ¼ pound ground pork or lamb and stir-fry until it has changed color. Add 1 cup diced tomato (fresh or canned), 1 tablespoon soy sauce, and 1 teaspoon salt and stir-fry until blended in. Add 2 teaspoons toasted sesame oil, then add to the hot rice soup. Taste for seasoning and add a little salt if needed. Pour into bowls and garnish each bowlful with about 1 tablespoon minced scallion greens or chopped coriander leaves. Serve hot.

Serves 4 to 6 as breakfast or as part of a meal

CHICKEN PULAO WITH PUMPKIN

The Uighurs (see page 90) share with their close cousins the Uzbeks a delicious *pulao* tradition. *Pulao* or *pilaf* is the name for a rice dish that is cooked together with flavorings, most often including meat, and water, to make a generous one-dish main course. It's a dish of celebration, for rice is a luxury food in the oases of western China, while bread and noodles are the everyday foods.

The *pulao* idea seems to have spread out from the sophisticated cuisine of Persia (Iran), radiating east along the Silk Road and west into Arab-held lands (and eventually through the Arabs to Spain, where it became *paella*). It also traveled south into Afghanistan and eventually to the Indian Subcontinent with the Mogul invaders. Along the way, it was adapted to local conditions in interesting ways.

In Uighur hands, *pulao* is most often cooked in a *q'azan*, a wide shallow wok-like pan. We use a wide heavy pot or sometimes a very large wok. As with paella or risotto, the flavor base cooks first, in oil, then water is added to make a broth. Finally the rice is added and cooks in the broth, absorbing flavor, to make a wonderful backdrop for the chicken and pumpkin here. Serve with a salad or two, say Onion and Pomegranate Salad (page 89), Cucumbers in Black Rice Vinegar (page 83), or Napa and Red Onion Salad (page 86).

2½ cups medium-grain Mediterranean-style rice,
  such as arborio, baldo, or Valencia

1 tablespoon salt, or to taste

About 4 pounds whole chicken legs and/or breasts

About ½ pound daikon radish

¼ cup peanut oil or vegetable oil

2 medium onions (¾ pound), coarsely chopped

2 medium tomatoes, coarsely chopped

4 cups water

About 1 pound peeled pumpkin or winter squash,
  cut into 1½-inch cubes

ACCOMPANIMENTS

¾ cup Jinjiang (black rice) vinegar or cider vinegar, diluted
  with ¼ cup water, or to taste

2 lemons, cut into wedges (optional)

Freshly ground black pepper

Rinse the rice well with cold water. Place it in a medium bowl with enough lukewarm water to cover it by an inch, stir in 1 teaspoon of the salt, and set aside to soak.

Remove the excess fat from the chicken. Finely chop about 3 tablespoons fat and set aside. Traditionally the skin is left on, for extra flavor and succulence; remove and discard it if you wish. Use a cleaver to chop the chicken into approximately 2-inch pieces, leaving the bones in. Rinse and set aside.

Peel the daikon and grate it on a coarse grater, or cut it into matchsticks (thinly slice it on a long diagonal, then stack the slices and cut into matchsticks). You will have about 2 cups. Set aside.

Heat the oil in a large wide heavy pot over medium heat. Add the reserved chicken fat and render it (over medium heat, the fat will gradually melt into the oil, leaving some small crispy cracklings). Once the fat has melted, scoop out the cracklings and save for another purpose (such as a topping for congee or for flatbreads). Raise the heat to high, and when the oil and fat are nearly smoking, add 1 teaspoon of the salt. Carefully slide the chicken pieces into the oil and start to brown them, turning occasionally. (If your pot is not wide enough, you may have to brown the chicken in 2 batches; then return all the chicken to the pot.) After several minutes, add the onions. Cook until the chicken is browned on all sides, then add the daikon and tomatoes and stir well. Lower the heat slightly and cook for about 5 minutes, stirring if the vegetables are sticking at all. The daikon should have softened and the tomato will be starting to disintegrate.

Add the water and the remaining 1 teaspoon salt, raise the heat, and bring to a vigorous boil. Lower the heat to medium and boil gently, partly covered, for 10 minutes. Taste the broth and adjust the seasoning if necessary.

(continued)

Drain the soaked rice and sprinkle it into the broth. The liquid should cover the rice by ½ inch; add a little hot water if necessary. Bring to a boil, then cover tightly, lower the heat to medium, and cook for 5 minutes. The water will now be just level with the top of the rice. Distribute the pumpkin pieces over the rice. Cover tightly once more, lower the heat to very low, and cook for 30 minutes.

Remove the pot from the heat and let stand for 10 minutes before removing the lid.

Traditionally *pulao* is served on a platter, the rice mounded and then the pumpkin and chicken pieces placed on top, but we like to serve it straight from the pot. If you serve it on a platter, use tongs to lift out the chicken pieces and the pumpkin (the cooked cubes of pumpkin are very tender, so be careful not to mash them), and set them aside. Use a wooden spoon or spatula to mound the rice on the platter, then place the pumpkin and chicken pieces on top. Traditionally guests, after washing their hands, eat with their hands, helping themselves directly from the platter. If your guests are not comfortable eating this way, serve them individually, or put out several serving spoons so they can serve themselves from the platter, and provide spoons and forks to eat with.

Put out several condiment bowls of the vinegar, together with small serving spoons. Invite guests to drizzle a little vinegar onto their rice. If you like, put out wedges of lemon to be squeezed over the chicken and rice to taste, and put out a pepper mill.

Serves 6 as a main course

CHICKEN-QUINCE PULAO: Quinces are a common fruit in the Silk Road oases in the autumn. They look like knobby yellow apples and are very hard (see Glossary). They have a delicious sweet-acid flavor when cooked and, when available, are often used in Uighur *pulaos* as a foil for the meat. You can include 1 or 2 small quinces, peeled, cored, and cut into 1-inch chunks, instead of the pumpkin or in addition.

A Uighur man sits in the shade with his teapot and bowl of tea, in Kashgar, in western Xinjiang.

KAZAKH PULAO

The Kazakhs who live in the northern part of Xinjiang make a simple *pulao* that is full of flavor. We call for 3 tablespoons fat or oil—festive *pulaos* are made with more fat, but this is a plain, almost everyday *pulao*, hence the restraint. (If you feel you must, you can reduce the quantity even further, to 2 tablespoons.)

We have really come to appreciate goat meat in the last few years for its clean lamb taste and reasonable price. If you can't find goat, use lamb instead, as directed below. Have your butcher chop the meat into 2-inch chunks. Accompany the *pulao* with a simple chopped salad such as Cucumbers in Black Rice Vinegar (page 83).

2 cups medium-grain Mediterranean rice, such as arborio,
    baldo, or Valencia

1½ pounds goat shank or lamb back ribs, trimmed of excess
    fat and cut into 2-inch chunks, or bone-in stewing lamb,
    cut into chunks

3 tablespoons rendered lamb fat (see Glossary) or
    vegetable oil (see headnote)

1 large onion, diced

3 large carrots, peeled and cut into julienne or coarsely
    grated (2 cups)

1½ teaspoons salt

½ teaspoon freshly ground black pepper

3 cups hot water

Place the rice in a sieve and rinse three or four times with cold water. Set aside.

Rinse the meat with cold water. Pat dry. Set aside.

Place a wide heavy pot over medium heat. Add the fat or oil, and when it is hot, add the meat and brown, using a wooden spoon to turn it so all sides are exposed to the hot oil, for about 6 minutes. Add the onion and cook for 4 minutes, or until mostly translucent and starting to brown. Add the carrots and cook for 4 minutes. Add the salt and pepper and stir in.

Sprinkle on the rice and stir it in. Add the water, raise the heat, and bring to a boil. Cover the pot tightly (use aluminum foil if necessary to seal it well), reduce the heat to very low, and cook for 40 minutes. Remove from the heat and let stand for about 10 minutes to firm up.

Serve on a platter, the rice mounded in the center and the meat on top.

Serves 4 as a main course

Late May. The rain was coming in sheets straight at us, blown by a fierce north wind. We were in the grasslands south of Labrang, in Gansu, riding sure-footed Tibetan ponies, with miles still to go before we got back to town. A small, low house appeared, barely visible, about a hundred feet off the track we were following. We decided to seek shelter until the worst of the storm had passed, so we rode up, sending the two dogs chained outside into a frenzy of barking. The woman of the house appeared and gestured to us to tie up the horses and come inside.

She led us through the outer room, where stacks of brush and dried yak dung (for fuel) were stored, and into the house, shutting the door firmly behind us. The house was a single room, a long rectangle with a stove in the middle, a sleeping platform at one end with a stack of folded thick covers on it, two benches by the stove, and shelves on one wall for bowls and utensils. The roughly plastered walls were very thick, and the room was snug and warm, an oasis, a haven. I was shivering uncontrollably in great shudders as I sat down by the stove. It was narrow, with a stovepipe at one end and a top surface large enough to hold two kettles.

As her slender fourteen-year-old son sat staring at the unexpected visitors, and the wind whipped the rain about outside, our hostess got down four bowls from a shelf and set them on a ledge. From a wooden box, she dolloped a generous two or three tablespoons of butter into each bowl. Then she lifted one of the kettles off the stove and poured hot tea over the butter. The tea was a mix of brick tea (fermented coarse black tea) steeped with a little salt, with a little butter already in it. The woman handed me a bowl, curves hot to my numb hands, steam rising from the pale liquid.

I'm not a huge fan of butter tea; I can drink it, but it's an effort. And I knew that soon the butter she had put in the bowl so generously would melt and make the tea even more difficult for me to get through, so I hurried to take a few scalding-hot sips before that happened. The tea was a little salty, with a cheesy aged-butter undertaste.

But she hadn't finished: She brought out a wooden box and opened it. Inside was tsampa, roasted barley ground into very fine flour. She gestured to me to hold my bowl out toward her, then added some tsampa to my tea. I stirred it in with my fingertips, slowly moistening all the dry, powdery tsampa. The butter smoothed it beautifully, and soon I had a ball, like a stiff dough, but ready to eat. Holding the warm tsampa ball in my left hand, I broke off small bite-sized pieces and slowly ate my fill. And it was filling.

As I warmed up, I felt so grateful, not only for the hospitality, but also (in the self-absorbed way of the traveler) because the butter tea had been transformed into food that I could eat with pleasure. As I looked around the spare low-ceilinged room, I was brought back to basics. All that was needed for life was in that space: simple food, fuel, and fire, and human warmth and welcome.

A while later, during a lull in the storm, we headed back out into the rain, ready for the rest of our journey. **N**

OPPOSITE: *Butter is consumed in great quantities in the Tibetan-populated areas beyond the Great Wall. It's used in tea and in cooked dishes, as lamp oil and as an offering at the temple, and also, in wintertime, as a way of protecting the skin and hair against the cold. Here in the market in Lhasa, near the Jokhang Temple, butter is displayed for sale alongside boxes of incense and some prayer flags.*

TSAMPA

We've seen fields of barley growing all over Tibetan-inhabited landscapes, from Burang, in western Tibet, to the valleys of Gansu province. We can't tell one kind of barley from another, but we've been told that Tibetans grow several varieties. Barley is their staple grain, for it can survive the short growing season, cold winters, and relatively dry summers of Tibet. Only in a few lower-elevation valleys in eastern Tibet can wheat be grown successfully.

We don't know when it was first made, but *tsampa* (sometimes written *tsamba*, or, in the modern Chinese Pinyin transcription, as *zamba*), the traditional Tibetan mainstay, is a very inventive and adaptable food. Whole barley grains are roasted (often in hot sand) and then ground to a fine powder, as fine as flour. Raw flour, like raw grain, is not edible, but because tsampa is made from cooked grain, it needs no further cooking. (We've learned that other crops, including some legumes, are sometimes used the same way as barley to make a form of tsampa: they're roasted until they're cooked through, then ground into a fine flour-like powder.)

Tsampa has a wonderful toasted grain aroma and flavor. Tibetans traditionally eat it dissolved in hot tea. The tea moistens it completely. And since Tibetan tea is made with butter and salt, the dissolved tsampa becomes like a kind of instant bread.

Because tsampa is lightweight, it's a very portable food. Tibetan nomads and travelers usually carry only a cloth sack of tsampa, some tea, salt, and butter as their provisions; wherever they find themselves, they can boil water and make tea and tsampa. The combination has enabled Tibetans to survive in an extreme landscape for centuries (see "Tsampa in a Storm," page 179).

In parts of Tibet where there are more food choices, of course, in towns and lower-elevation valleys, people have more varied diets. But tsampa is still an important food, and it also finds its way into other dishes (see Tsampa Soup, page 47). We've come to love having a good supply of it on hand. We eat it for breakfast, stirring its warm toasted grain flavor into yogurt (see Morning Tsampa, opposite), and also enjoy the smoothness and depth it gives when used to thicken soups or stews.

If you happen to live near a Tibetan Buddhist monastery or community, you may be able to buy tsampa ready-made, but most of you will be, like us, obliged to buy barley berries (whole grains), and dry-roast and grind them for yourselves at home. Here's what we suggest: Buy a pound of barley berries, preferably organic. Start by roasting 2 cups berries, as directed below, which will yield about 3¾ cups tsampa. You'll find out how the process works, and then you'll be able to see if you want to make larger batches or just make it in 2-cup lots, as we do.

2 cups barley berries (whole grains), preferably organic

Place the barley berries in an 11- to 12-inch heavy skillet (cast iron works very well) and dry-roast over medium-high heat: Stir constantly with a flat-ended spatula or wooden spoon, moving the grains off the hot bottom surface and rotating them from the center to the outside, to ensure an even roast with no scorching. The grains will crackle a little as they expand in the heat, will start to give off a toasted grain aroma, and will change color. Keep on stirring and turning until all the grains have darkened to more than golden, about 10 to 14 minutes. Test for doneness by trying to bite into one of the grains—it should yield easily (times will vary depending on the amount you are roasting, the size of your pan, and the heat). Remove the pan from the heat and keep stirring for another minute or two to prevent scorching.

If you are using a coffee or spice grinder to grind the grain, you will need to work in batches. (A flour mill works well if you have one: no need for small batches, and your grind will be finer and more even.) Transfer about ½ cup of the toasted grains to a clean, dry coffee or spice grinder and grind to a fine flour-like texture (you will hear the sound change as the granules get reduced to a powdery texture). Turn out into a bowl and repeat until all the grain has been ground to flour. If you want to perfect your grind, pass the milled powder through a fine sieve and then regrind any remaining larger pieces.

Let cool completely, then store in a well-sealed wooden or glass container in a cool place. We've found tsampa keeps indefinitely in the refrigerator.

Makes about 3¾ cups

ROASTED BARLEY FLOUR: We experimented with barley flour too, wanting to see whether we could use it as a substitute for tsampa by roasting it in a skillet. We found that the roasted flour had a completely different texture from tsampa, though a similar taste. With tsampa, because the whole grains are cooked first, when they are ground into flour, each fleck of flour is very soft. When we roasted barley flour in a hot skillet, it became gritty, as each separate fleck of flour toasted and dried out. We were forced to conclude that there is no quick answer to making tsampa. However, the roasted flour is an adequate substitute for tsampa in cooked dishes where it is used as a thickener, as, for example, in Tsampa Soup (page 47) or Stir-Fried Stem Lettuce Lhasa-Style (page 103).

MORNING TSAMPA

With a generous supply of tsampa in the pantry, all sorts of treats become easily available. We like tsampa stirred into good whole-milk yogurt, for the taste of the roasted grain is wonderfully welcoming with the yogurt's lush smoothness. Start with your favorite yogurt, and add fruit if you'd like. Sweeten it with a little honey or sugar or maple syrup if you wish. Eat with pleasure for breakfast, or anytime.

> About ½ cup whole-milk yogurt, plain or sweetened
> 3 tablespoons Tsampa (opposite), or to taste
> A handful of berries or chopped fruit (optional)
> Honey, sugar, or maple syrup to taste (optional)

Place the yogurt in a bowl and stir in the tsampa thoroughly so it's all moistened. Add fruit and a sweetener if you wish.

Serves 1

Jars of yogurt and stacks of local flatbreads, in the Tibetan quarter of Lhasa.

LEFT: *Miao (Hmong) men in traditional indigo-dyed clothing play the* lusheng, *a bagpipe-sounding instrument like a large panpipe, at a ceremony in the village of Lande, in Guizhou.* RIGHT: *This woman's distinctively shaped headdress indicates she is Ge, a subset of the Miao (Hmong) that is not recognized as a separate "minority people" by the Beijing government. The Ge people live in the area around the town of Chong'an, where this photograph was taken, as do many Miao.*

THE MIAO/HMONG PEOPLE

Long before we met Miao people in China, we'd spent time in Hmong communities in Thailand and Laos. (There they call themselves Hmong; in Southeast Asia the name Miao has pejorative roots, but in present-day China, people refer to themselves as Miao, at least to outsiders, so we'll use both terms here.) We'd read a remarkable ethnography written in 1976 by W. R. Geddes, called *Migrants of the Mountains*, about the traditional lifestyle of the Hmong, and we'd also seen a moving piece of documentary film about the Hmong coming as refugees to the States after the Vietnam War, *The Best Place to Live* (by anthropologist Louisa Schein). A large number of Hmong from Laos fought as U.S. allies in the Vietnam War. Afterward, many Hmong from Laos fled to refugee camps in Thailand; several thousand of them were eventually resettled in the United States.

We were aware that the traditional Miao/Hmong homeland was in China. We'd read that there were as many as four million Miao living in China, but it was very hard to imagine the population on that scale, for in Southeast Asia they live as slash-and-burn agriculturalists in very remote areas, in communities of less than three hundred people.

Now, twenty years later, we've had a chance to visit many Miao communities in China, and we have a much better sense of where and how they live. But still for us they remain a remarkable people. Like the Yao, another non-Han population, closely linked linguistically to the Miao, they are widely dispersed through southern and southwestern China, as well as through mainland Southeast Asia. More than half of

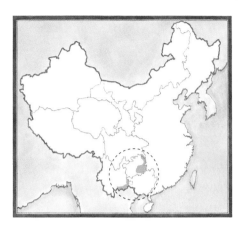

the population of Miao living in China live in the very poor mountainous province of Guizhou, but large numbers also live in Hebei, Sichuan, Yunnan, Hunan, and Guangxi provinces. We've even seen Miao women selling vegetable seeds and herbs on a sidewalk in Lhasa, in Tibet, a thousand miles from where we would expect to see them.

The Miao have an incredibly rich textile tradition, especially for embroidery and appliqué and batik, as well as for indigo-dyeing. All Miao women traditionally embroider: baby carriers, hats for babies, aprons, and jackets that are part of the traditional dress. Within the Miao grouping, there are many subcategories (some say more than eighty), mostly based on distinctive elements in their traditional dress. Each group can be distinguished, by those who know, by the details of the embroidery and the design of the jewelry.

Like other non-Han people who lived in the remote valleys and mountains in southern China, the Miao were historically thought by the Han to be uncouth barbarians. They are still fundamentally disdained and viewed as uncultured by many outsiders, but now, ironically, they also have a curiosity value as "exotic" in the new China. Tourists come from other parts of China (and from Japan, Taiwan, and Western countries) to marvel at their traditional festivals, their traditional clothing, their distinctiveness.

Nowadays, most Miao are settled farmers, tilling the terraced landscapes around their villages; growing rice and corn, vegetables, tea, rapeseed (for oil), and more; and raising pigs.

BREADS

THERE ARE MANY REASONS THAT WE LIKE TRAVELING in the regions beyond the Great Wall, and bread is definitely one of them. Baking traditions here are still very locally based, and bread, in the places where it's common, is still very much a staff of life.

Xinjiang, the large province in the far west of China, is a flatbread lover's paradise. No matter where you are, and no matter what time of day, there's a Uighur baker nearby with a tandoor oven who is just about to bake, or has just finished baking, or is baking as you wait. The breads (nan) fly in and out of the hot tandoor, and stacks of fresh hot flatbreads quickly begin to grow. One customer carries away six, another buys ten, and someone else buys one and eats it on the spot. In the dry desert air of Xinjiang, the smell of the bread is almost as good as the bread itself.

The Tajik people in the Pamirs have their own versions of tandoor nan, and so do the Kirghiz. The Kazakhs make a bread that's unusual for Central Asia, in that it's a domed loaf, not a flatbread (see Kazakh Family Loaf, page 195). Like Home-Style Tajik Nan (page 191), it's made tender with yogurt.

One of the pleasures of travel beyond the Great Wall is the chance to discover a world of delicious and ingenious filled breads, including Cheese Momos (page 212) and Savory Tibetan Breads (page 214), as well as Succulent Lamb Samsa (page 198) and the greens-filled half-moon breads of Turpan (page 208). They're like baked or deep-fried versions of the dumplings in the Noodles and Dumplings chapter.

Filled breads are eaten as snacks, while nan and other plain breads are present at every meal.

OPPOSITE: *A Uighur woman in Kashgar, buying nan (flatbreads).* ABOVE: *A well-seasoned wok holds an array of useful cooking tools, including a mesh skimmer, a rice paddle, a spatula for stir-frying, and a tea strainer made of woven bamboo.*

I'm in Altai, a town of thirty or forty thousand people up in the far northern part of Xinjiang province, after not having been in China for quite some time, five years or so. From the large window in my third-floor hotel room, I look out at a range of tall hills—over those hills lies Mongolia. If I stretch my head out the window and look north, I see a range of even taller hills, almost mountains, and beyond them is Siberia.

I flew here two days ago from Hong Kong, more or less directly. I awoke at our friends' apartment in Hong Kong at five a.m., took a taxi to the subway and then the subway under the harbor to Kowloon. I walked through Kowloon Park past people practicing tai chi just as the sun was coming up. On the other side of the park, I found my way to the China ferry docks, where I went through Hong Kong immigration and officially entered China. By seven-thirty I was on a comfortable ferry traveling at high speed through the harbor, passing in a heavy morning mist through a vastness of container ships and loading cranes; on land, the horizon was banked with towering apartment blocks, one after another after another. Sixty-six million people now live and work in the Pearl River Delta (the triangle of Hong Kong, Guangzhou, and Shenzhen), the most intensive manufacturing region in the world.

By midmorning I was in Shenzhen Airport (Shenzhen is now a city of over seven million people), looking for the gate for my flight to Xinjiang. Everything around me was modern and bright, with that quintessential new airport feel. And on the airplane everyone around me (all Han Chinese from South China) was dressed in twenty-first-century clothing, Western clothing, with plenty of Gore-Tex, aqua, red, and yellow. But near the end of the five-hour flight, in case I might have forgotten, I was reminded that I was in China. The flight attendants stood in the middle of the aisles and led the way as everyone, in perfect unison, obediently did calisthenics in their seats. "Yi, er, san" (one, two, three), roll your head to the left, roll your head to the right. Lift your left arm up and twirl it in a circle. "Yi, er, san."

I couldn't do it. I was the only one on the plane not to do it. It wasn't that I have a problem with stretching, but the coerciveness pushed all my buttons. One China = one way.

Here in Altai there are Tatars, Uighurs, Kazakhs, Mongols, even some Tuvans. There's plenty of space and clear air to breathe. There are several banks and department stores along the main street, and many small shops selling cell phones, just like a main street anywhere in China. But people don't look the same, and they walk with a freer stride. At night I can choose between Uighur noodles or a Tatar or a Kazakh *pulao*, and for dessert I can have thick, creamy Kazakh yogurt with sugar on top, or suck on a chunk of hard Kazakh cheese.

I'm very far from the Pearl River Delta.

I'm not sure how many people here would have joined in the calisthenics on the airplane. I have a feeling I wouldn't have been the only one abstaining. **J**

OPPOSITE: *Uighur men in Turpan, playing a board game in a local café.*

UIGHUR NAN

Uighur nan are flatbreads. In Xinjiang they're cooked in tandoor ovens, but at home we bake them on a baking stone or unglazed quarry tiles.

Tandoor baking is fascinating to watch: The barrel-shaped oven is preheated with a hot fire, then the fire is damped down and the shaped flatbreads are slapped onto the hot inside clay walls of the oven. They stick because they're moist and uncooked. When they've cooked through (usually in three or four minutes), they come unstuck—the baker uses a stick to lift them off the side of the oven just before they fall. Then he slaps on more breads, and so it goes.

The distinctive thing about tandoor breads in this part of Central Asia (in Xinjiang, and also among the Uzbeks, Kazakhs, Kirghiz, and Turkmen across the border in the former Soviet republics) is that the center of the bread is stamped with a nail-studded device, called a *chekitch* or a *durtlik*, depending on the language (see photo, page 206). The stamping prevents the central part of the bread from puffing up during baking, though often it will still puff in spots. The result is a bread with a flatter center and a puffed rim, like a pizza, but instead of a sauced topping that weighs the center down, the stamping makes it flatter.

Bread stamps aren't yet sold in North America, at least we haven't seen them, so we suggest that you stamp the center of the breads all over with a fork. If you enjoy making the breads, you might try making your own bread stamp.

Flavorings for Uighur nan vary, and so do shapes and sizes. These breads are 9 to 10 inches across, with a soft rim and a flattened slightly crisper center lightly sprinkled with cumin, salt, and (optional) minced scallion.

> 3 cups lukewarm water
>
> 1 teaspoon active dry yeast
>
> About 7 to 8 cups all-purpose flour, preferably unbleached,
>   plus extra for surfaces
>
> 1 tablespoon plus 1 teaspoon salt
>
> About 1 teaspoon cumin seeds
>
> 2 tablespoons minced scallions
>   (white and tender green parts; optional)

Place the warm water in a large bowl, sprinkle the yeast over, and stir to dissolve it. Add 3 cups of the flour and stir to make a batter, always stirring in the same direction, to develop the gluten. If you wish, you can set the batter aside in a cool place, covered, for up to 12 hours; this pause helps it gain flavor. You can also just proceed without a pause, and the breads will still be a pleasure to eat.

Sprinkle on 1 tablespoon of the salt, then add another 2 cups or so flour and stir and turn to incorporate it. Sprinkle on a little more flour, and put a generous 1 cup flour on your work surface. Turn the dough out onto the flour and let rest for a moment while you wash the bread bowl and dry it.

Knead the dough, incorporating flour as needed and adding more to your work surface if necessary, until it is no longer sticky, but smooth and elastic and still somewhat soft, about 7 minutes.

Place the dough back in the bowl and cover with a damp kitchen towel or plastic wrap. Set aside to rise until doubled in volume: If you put it in a cool place, you can leave it for at least 6 hours or overnight, and the dough will develop more flavor. At room temperature (about 70°F), the rise will be quicker, about 2 hours.

Dust your work surface with flour. Pull the dough together and turn it out onto the work surface. Use a sharp knife or a metal dough scraper to cut the dough into 8 pieces (cut it in half and then in half and half again).

Roll each piece under your cupped palm on the counter, or between both palms, to form a firm ball. On a well-floured surface, with a floured palm, flatten each ball into a thick disk 5 to 6 inches wide. Turn and press the top side into the flour as well, then set aside to rest, covered, for 20 minutes.

Meanwhile, place a rack in the top third of your oven and put a baking stone or unglazed quarry tiles or a large baking sheet on it, leaving a 1-inch gap between the stone or tiles (if using them) and the oven walls so the air can circulate. Preheat the oven to 450°F.

Ten minutes after the oven has come to temperature (this wait gives the stone or tiles time to heat up completely), start shaping the breads on a floured surface. Press one disk of dough out with your fingertips into a large round, 9 to 10 inches in diameter (or use a rolling pin if you wish). The rest will have softened the dough, so the bread will flatten and stretch easily.

Place one stretched round on a flour-dusted baker's peel or on the flour-dusted back of a baking sheet. Use a bread stamp (see headnote) or fork to prick the center of the round very thoroughly all over, leaving a ½-inch rim all around. Spritz or lightly brush it with a little water (use a sprayer or a pastry brush), then sprinkle on about ⅛ teaspoon cumin seeds and the same amount of salt. Sprinkle on a little of the scallions if you wish.

Use the peel or baking sheet to transfer the bread onto the hot stone or tiles or baking sheet: Open the oven and hold the peel or sheet over the hot surface, then quickly slip the peel away, leaving the dough round on the surface. Repeat with the other stretched round, placing it beside the first bread. Bake for 8 or 9 minutes, until nicely touched with golden brown. While the breads bake, stretch the next pair of dough rounds.

Remove the breads to a rack, or if you want to soften them, stack them and wrap the stack in a cotton cloth. Slide the next pair of breads into the oven, and repeat with the remaining dough and flavorings until all 8 breads are baked.

Makes 8 large round flatbreads, about 10 inches in diameter

Up in the Pamirs, tandoor ovens are permanent features that mark the camping places of Tajik and Kirghiz nomads. Each tandoor, looking small in the open landscape, is surrounded by a circle of bare ground, the traces of the yurts that are occasionally set up around it. The tandoors we saw in the villages are of the same style, small dried-clay cylinders about three feet tall, with open tops.

The Tajiks cultivate a little wheat in the valleys near their villages. The breads we had there, in the village of Dafdar, and in the Tajik yurts (see "The Pamirs, June 1986," page 141), were not just plain white, but had some whole wheat taste of the grain to them. We guessed that there was a little yogurt or whey in the dough, as well as a lower-gluten flour, for they were tender and oh-so-good. We call for a little pastry or cake flour to reproduce those softer-textured breads, and we include some yogurt.

Because the dough is made with a slow-rise technique, and also because of the yogurt, the breads will stay soft and fresh for much longer than quickly risen plain white flour nan. They're smaller, home-style breads, like flattened rolls, if you will. We like making the dough the night before, then baking them for breakfast.

[PHOTOGRAPH ON PAGE 193]

1½ cups lukewarm water

½ teaspoon active dry yeast

1 cup whole wheat or white pastry flour or cake flour

About 3½ to 4 cups all-purpose flour, preferably unbleached,
    plus extra for surfaces

½ cup plain full-fat or reduced-fat yogurt

2 teaspoons salt

(continued)

Place the water in a large bowl and add about 8 granules of the yeast. Add the pastry or cake flour and 1 cup of the all-purpose flour and stir, always in one direction, to develop the gluten, until you have a smooth, thick batter. Cover and set aside to ferment for at least 4 hours, or as long as 24 hours, whatever is convenient. You will see small bubbles at the surface of the batter, showing that fermentation is taking place.

Sprinkle on the remaining dry yeast and stir it in. Add the yogurt and stir, then add ½ cup of the all-purpose flour and stir thoroughly until smooth. Sprinkle on the salt and stir in, then add another 1 cup all-purpose flour and stir and turn to blend it into the dough.

Flour a work surface generously with about 1 cup all-purpose flour and turn the dough out. Knead until smooth and no longer sticky, incorporating flour as needed and adding extra if necessary. You want a fairly soft dough rather than a stiff one.

Wash out and dry your bowl, place the dough in it, and cover with plastic wrap. Set aside at a cool room temperature to rise until more than doubled in volume, for at least 6 hours, or overnight. This slow rise helps give the bread flavor.

Lightly dust your work surface with flour and turn the dough out. Use a sharp knife or a metal dough scraper to cut the dough into 12 pieces: cut it in half and then in half again, then cut each quarter into 3 pieces.

Roll each piece under your cupped palm on a work surface, or between both palms, to form a firm ball. On a well-floured surface, with a floured palm, flatten each ball into a thick disk 2½ to 3 inches wide. Turn and press the top side into the flour as well, then set the disks aside to rest, loosely covered with plastic wrap, for 30 minutes, or for as long as 2 hours, if that is more convenient.

Meanwhile, place a rack in the top third of your oven and put a baking stone or unglazed quarry tiles on it, leaving a 1-inch gap between the stone or tiles and the oven walls so the air can circulate. Preheat the oven to 450°F.

Ten minutes after the oven has come to temperature (this wait gives the stones or tiles time to heat up completely), start shaping the breads. On a floured surface, press one round of dough out with your fingertips into a thin round about 6 inches in diameter, pressing into it firmly and leaving flattened dents. The rest will have softened the dough, so the bread will flatten and stretch easily. Don't worry too much about dimensions: thicker breads are softer (and may puff while cooking), thinner ones are less likely to puff; both are pleasing. Repeat with another 4 or 5 breads, as many as will fit in the oven at once.

Use a flour-dusted baker's peel or the back of a baking sheet lightly dusted with flour to transfer the breads onto the hot stone or tiles, or work by hand. *If using a peel,* place one dough round on the peel or sheet, then open the oven, hold the peel or sheet over the hot surface, and quickly slip it away, leaving the dough round on the stone or tiles. Repeat with the remaining shaped breads, setting them beside each other but not touching. *If working by hand,* you may find it easier to bake only 3 breads at a time, placing them nearer the front, rather than reaching all the way to the back of the hot oven. Place the breads one by one onto the hot surface.

Bake until the breads are lightly touched with brown and the bottom crust is firm, about 10 minutes. Use a long-handled spatula to lift the breads out of the oven as they are ready. Stack on a wire rack, or keep soft by wrapping the stack in a cotton cloth.

While the first breads are baking, shape the next batch. Continue baking the remaining dough rounds until all 12 are baked. Serve warm or at room temperature.

Makes 12 small flatbreads, about 5 inches in diameter

OPPOSITE: *Home-Style Tajik Nan (page 191) with Market Stall Fresh Tomato Salsa (page 18).*

In this first decade of the twenty-first century, China's fast-growing economy is the third largest in the world. The greatest economic growth is in the south, near the cities of Hong Kong and Guangzhou; in Shanghai and areas on the east coast; and in parts of Sichuan province.

With more money, and more freedom to spend it, the rapidly expanding Chinese middle class has begun to travel to the outlying areas of China, to the regions beyond the Great Wall. In the same way that Americans travel to Yellowstone National Park, the Grand Canyon, and the Navajo areas of Arizona and New Mexico to see exotic landscapes and the people who live there, the Chinese are flocking to northern Xinjiang and Tibet, to the Tibetan areas of Yunnan and Sichuan, and to the tribal villages in Yunnan.

This domestic tourism is in full flood during the three annual "Golden Weeks": at Lunar New Year (late January to mid-February), around May 1, and around October 1. In 2001, the central government declared that these weeks would be national holidays, and as a result, that's when the whole country, anyone who can afford to, is on the move.

In late September 2005, just at the start of the October Golden Week, I was in the Kanas Lake area in the far north of Xinjiang, a stone's throw from the border of Siberia. One morning there were more than sixty tour buses filled with Chinese tourists from Shanghai and Beijing. A short time later, at 14,000 feet in the mountains of western Sichuan, I got caught in a traffic jam, moving nowhere for two hours. As far as I could see, there were Chinese tourists in BMW SUVs, brand-new Honda Odysseys, and Volvo station wagons, all heading out from the city of Chengdu to visit the mountainous Tibetan-inhabited areas of western Sichuan. The new face of tourism in China. J

Golden Week traffic jam in the middle of the mountains in western Sichuan, between Litang and Kanding.

KAZAKH FAMILY LOAF

We've found that the easiest way to reproduce this wonderful Kazakh family loaf from the mountains of northern Xinjiang is by baking it in a moderate oven in a straight-sided pot that is 8 inches in diameter and at least 6 inches deep, with a lid. (We use the 3½-quart Calphalon pot that is our family rice pot, and the risen bread doesn't quite come up to the lid; see instructions for a larger loaf, the Large Kazakh Fusion Loaf, below. If your pot is not as large as the dimensions set out here, then cut off ¼ of the dough and bake it separately, perhaps using it to shape some Home-Style Tajik Nan, for example.) Once the dough has done its first rise in a bowl, we shape it into a round and it rises in the pot with the lid on, then goes into the preheated oven, still with the lid on. This modified version of clay-pot baking keeps the bread surface moist as it bakes and produces a fine crust and tender, moist crumb. Near the end of baking, we remove the lid, which allows the top crust to brown a little (the sides brown against the hot metal pot).

The top crust has a few shallow little rips in it that are created when the loaf expands during baking. The classic way to avoid these tears in a top crust is to slash the loaf before baking, but the Kazakhs don't, so we're just mentioning it here as an option. When the bread is first out of the oven, the crust has a fine crisp texture, almost like that of a baguette cooked in a steam-injection oven, but because the loaf is so moist, the crust soon softens.

The yogurt in the dough makes the bread very tender and quite close-textured, ideal for sopping up flavorful meat stews, and for sandwiches. It also makes superb toast. [PHOTOGRAPH ON PAGE 196]

1½ cups lukewarm water

1 teaspoon active dry yeast

4 to 5 cups all-purpose flour, preferably unbleached,
    plus extra for surfaces

½ cup plain full-fat yogurt

2 teaspoons salt

Oil or butter for greasing surfaces

Place the water in a medium bowl and sprinkle on the yeast. Add 1 cup of the flour and stir to make a batter. Add the yogurt and stir it in, then add another cup of flour and stir to incorporate it. Sprinkle on the salt and another cup of flour. Stir and turn the dough to incorporate the flour.

Flour a work surface with about 1 cup flour, then turn the dough out. Knead, incorporating flour as you fold and turn, fold and turn, for about 5 minutes, or until the dough is smooth and still a little soft, but no longer sticky; add more flour to your work surface if necessary.

Wash and dry the bowl. Place the dough in the bowl, cover with plastic or with a lid, and let rise for 3 hours, or until more than doubled in volume. (When the dough is fully risen, you can poke it with a finger and the indentation will stay; if it is not yet ready, the dough will rebound when dented.)

Rinse an 8- or 9-inch cast-iron or other heavy straight-sided pot that is 6 inches or more deep and has a heavy ovenproof lid (see headnote) with hot water to warm it, then wipe dry. Place a circle of parchment paper several inches wider than the pot in the bottom of the pot. Lightly grease the sides of the pot.

Turn the dough out onto a lightly floured surface and flatten it gently under your hand. To shape it into a round, lift one edge of the dough and pull it over to the center, then move along the edge a little and repeat. Continue all around the dough (this creates a stretched surface on the other side of the dough) until you have a circular loaf, then pinch the center well to hold it together. Turn the shaped loaf over gently and place it in the prepared pan, seam side down. Press lightly on it to flatten it out toward the edges of the pan.

Put on the lid and set aside to rise for an hour in a warm spot (we put our rising loaves on the counter and turn on the overhead lights, which give a little extra warmth). The loaf may not quite double.

Meanwhile, place a rack in the middle of the oven and preheat the oven to 385°F.

Bake the loaf with the lid on for 40 minutes. Remove the lid and bake for about another 20 minutes. The sides should be golden brown,

the top well touched with brown. Turn out onto a rack. The bottom of the loaf should sound hollow when tapped and the bottom edge of the bread should be firm when pinched. Let stand for at least 30 minutes to firm up before slicing.

Makes 1 large round domed loaf, 8 inches in diameter and 4 to 5 inches tall

LARGE KAZAKH FUSION LOAF: The first time we made the Kazakh Family Loaf, our kids, now in their late teens, decided they loved its texture, and the loaf vanished. So we thought we'd better figure out a larger loaf than the traditional one Jeffrey had encountered in the mountains of northern Xinjiang. To do that, we used our big old number 26 cast-iron Le Creuset casserole, which is 10 inches in diameter and about 5 inches deep, and we began with a dough half again as large. Since we were already being untraditional, we also wanted a slashed top crust, and a crisper, browner one, in this bread, so we tried baking it at a higher temperature. It takes about 1 hour to bake.

Here are the proportions and instructions: 2¼ cups lukewarm water, 1 teaspoon yeast, about 6 cups all-purpose flour (you can substitute whole wheat pastry flour for 1 or 2 cups of the all-purpose), ¾ cup yogurt, and 1 tablespoon salt. Do the first rise in the bowl, for about 3 hours. Line the bottom of the pot with parchment paper as above, and oil or butter the sides. Proof the shaped loaf in the pot with the lid on, as above, and preheat the oven to 425°F, with a rack in the upper middle. Just before the loaf goes into the oven, slash it two or three times with a very sharp knife. Bake with the lid on for 40 minutes, then remove the lid and bake for another 10 to 15 minutes. Check for doneness as above, tapping on the bottom of the bread and pinching the bottom edge. Let stand to firm up before slicing.

The bread is gorgeous, a 3-pound domed loaf with a fine crust and a lovely golden top and sides, about 10 inches in diameter and 5 inches high.

OPPOSITE: *Kazakh Family Loaf (page 195).* ABOVE: *Uighur men at a tandoor oven, in Altai, northern Xinjiang. The man on the left has a tray full of* samsa *that he's about to slap onto the hot oven walls.*

At the lively Kashgar market, a samsa *baker hands several breads to a customer. In the background men are cutting up meat and preparing the filling.*

SUCCULENT LAMB SAMSA

In the oases of Xinjiang, Uighur bakers fire up their barrel-shaped clay tandoor ovens, then damp down the fires so they can slap flatbreads against the oven walls to bake. Though nan are the most common breads in Kashgar, Turfan, Aksu, Hotan, and the smaller places in between, the bakers also make filled breads, the Central Asian equivalent of the Indian samosa. Chopped lamb flavored with a few seasonings is wrapped in a simple unleavened flatbread dough and baked. The rectangular packages are known as *samsa*, not just in Uygur, but also in Uzbek, on the other side of the mountains, and they are delicious.

Samsa are baked either on the hot walls of a tandoor or on a wide wok-shaped clay surface set over an open fire. When they come out of the oven, they have a delectable aroma and are succulent and satisfying to bite into. In Xinjiang, *samsa* are made by the hundreds and thousands every day. And once you have one, you want another, they're that pleasurable to eat.

Make the dough about 2 hours before you wish to serve the bread. (They take just over half an hour in the oven.) If you have a lot of people to feed, you can double the recipe: double all the ingredients. Serve as a snack or appetizer, allowing 1 or 2 per person. Or serve as part of a light meal, allowing 3 per person, accompanied by a chopped salad such as Cooling Oasis Salad with Tomatoes and Herbs (page 89) or a green salad. A light soup—for example, the chicken broth for Chicken and Noodles Tuvan-Style (page 246), or Hui Vegetable Soup (page 48)—will complement the breads nicely.

DOUGH

2½ cups all-purpose flour, preferably unbleached,
    plus extra for surfaces
1 teaspoon sugar
1 teaspoon salt
About 1¼ cups water

½ pound coarsely ground lamb or about ¾ pound bone-in lamb
    leg, shoulder, or chops (see Note on Texture)

¼ cup lamb fat if using ground lamb

1 packed cup coarsely chopped onion

2 tablespoons plain full-fat yogurt (see Note on Texture)

2 teaspoons minced garlic

⅛ teaspoon cayenne (optional)

1 teaspoon salt

¼ teaspoon freshly ground black pepper, or to taste

Place the flour, sugar, and salt in a food processor and pulse to mix. Then, with the blade running, pour the water slowly through the feed tube until a ball of dough forms. (*Alternatively*, make the dough by hand: mix the dry ingredients in a medium bowl, then stir in the water to make a rough dough.)

Turn the dough out onto a floured surface and knead until very smooth, about 4 minutes. Wrap well in plastic and set aside.

If using bone-in lamb, cut the meat off the bone and trim off most of the fat; set the fat aside. Measure out ½ pound of meat (1 tightly packed cup) and use a cleaver to finely chop it. (You can use the processor, pulsing, but you will get more of a paste rather than the chopped or minced texture that is both traditional and desirable; see Note.) Finely mince ¼ cup of the reserved fat. Add the ¼ cup fat to the chopped or ground meat in a bowl.

Mince the onion by hand or by pulsing it in a food processor. Add to the meat, then add the yogurt and stir in thoroughly. Add the garlic, cayenne, if using, salt, and black pepper and blend in well. You'll have 2 packed cups filling. Set aside.

Place a rack in the upper third of the oven. Put a baking stone or unglazed quarry tiles on the rack, if you have them. Preheat the oven to 400°F. Lightly butter a baking sheet or line it with parchment paper.

Turn the dough out onto a lightly floured surface. Use a metal dough scraper or sharp knife to cut the dough in half. Set one half aside, loosely covered. Cut the remaining half into 8 equal pieces

(cut it in half and then in half and half again). Roll each into a ball under your cupped palm on your work surface or between your palms. Flatten each ball slightly, flour both sides, and let rest for 10 minutes.

Roll out one dough piece to a round 5 to 6 inches in diameter. Repeat with a second dough round. Place a scant 2 tablespoons filling in the center of one of the rounds. Lift two opposite edges up to meet over the dough and pinch to join them. Then lift the open ends up to meet over the center and pinch them together, making a ridged seam across the top of the shaped bread. Flatten gently to make a neat rectangular package. Set the shaped bread seam side up on the prepared baking sheet. Repeat with the second round and place it next to but not touching the first bread. Repeat with the remaining 6 dough balls, and then with the other half of the dough, to make 16 breads in all.

Place the baking sheet on the baking stone or tiles or directly on the oven rack and bake for 35 minutes, or until touched with golden brown. Use a spatula to lift the breads off the baking sheet and onto a plate. They are very hot when they first come out of the oven; wait 5 minutes for them to cool slightly before serving them. Guests can eat them out of hand, as they'd eat a sandwich.

Makes 16 small filled breads; serves 6 for lunch, 12 as an appetizer

NOTE ON TEXTURE: The best *samsa* have a succulent, moist texture that comes from the inclusion of a little fat and from the texture of the meat. If the meat is chopped by hand or coarsely ground, then it won't clump into a tight patty as it cooks inside the dough and it will stay moist and tender, but if it is processed to a paste, then it clumps. Adding yogurt to the mixture gives it extra moisture as well as a subtle acidic tang.

NOTE ON SHAPING: *Samsa* shapes differ from oasis to oasis and baker to baker. They also depend on the oven being used. Often the ends of the packages are overlapped under the breads, so they will cook on the hot wall of the tandoor. Sometimes there is a Y-shaped seam on the top instead. It all depends on local custom and on the baker's preference. We have found that the breads bake best if the dough seam is on the top.

Every day here in Turpan, I've been walking back and forth between two worlds, Uighur and Han. My hotel is in the center of town, which is Han, while the large bazaar where I go to eat and to hang out is almost entirely Uighur, as are the neighborhoods that surround the center. When I first arrived in Turpan, I was confused and a little disappointed because everything around me looked much like any other town in China, with Soviet-style cement buildings and white-tile facades. I had been expecting a legendary desert oasis on the old Silk Road, with wind-sculpted adobe walls and narrow laneways with donkey carts and tinkling bells, the Turpan Naomi had visited in 1980.

The first few days, I kept searching for what I'd come expecting. I'd brought with me an ethnography, *Oasis Identities*, written by anthropologist Justin Jon Rudelson. Most of his fieldwork was done here in Turpan in 1989–1990. At night I'd read about Turpan's remarkable system of irrigation (the *karez*) that channels water deep underground more than ten kilometers, from the Flaming Mountains to the oasis. The oasis lies in the bottom of the Turpan Depression, the second-lowest (500 feet below sea level) human settlement in the world. I'd read about the grape harvest, and the drying of the grapes to make golden raisins, the basis of the prosperous economy here.

Each morning—day two, day three, day four—I'd hit the streets eagerly, but by evening I'd be walking with slumped shoulders back to my hotel. The Han world and the Uighur world are very different from each other, but both are modernizing at a rapid rate. There are no more donkey carts, and so many motorbikes, trucks, and buses, all of them with blasting horns. But of course they are modernizing, I would tell myself, and that's a good thing, not a bad thing.

Day five was a little different. An English teacher, a Uighur man, asked if I would come and talk with his class, and so I did. The students, all Uighur, and all in their mid-teens to early twenties, were outspoken and full of life. On day six, I was invited to a circumcision, and now on day seven, I've been invited to a wedding.

Each day I've walked the same streets. I've gone to the same place for lunch, the same place to drink a beer at night, the same place to buy fruit and juice for morning. My original expectations are beginning to blur. Every day that passes, I've come to see more detail, more life. I see the beautiful clothes of the Uighurs, and the flair with which they dance. I see Han kids playing tag on their way home from school, laughing and teasing.

I'm glad to have come to Turpan, donkey carts or no donkey carts. **J**

OPPOSITE: *Trucks and buses dominate the center of Turpan, but here on the edge of the oasis, donkey carts still rule.*

FLAKY FRIED SESAME COILS

These delectable savory breads, known as *guo cui* (pronounced "gwo tsway") are a fried stovetop Sichuanese version of the Chinese bread known as *shaobing*, a flaky oven-baked sesame-coated flatbread. They're flavored with sesame seeds and Sichuan pepper. The *guo cui* we first encountered in Sichuan had a few shards of fine ham in them that melted into the breads as they cooked; we've included the meat in the variation.

We thought the breads had to be eaten hot from the pan, but we were wrong. As we tested and retested them, we came to prefer them when they had cooled, for then they became a little crisper and somehow the warm taste of the sesame seeds was more pronounced. You may discover, though, that your guests find the breads so delicious that they never get a chance to cool down. . . .

Serve whole or cut into quarters, with a soup and a salad such as Cooling Oasis Salad with Tomatoes and Herbs (page 89) or some sliced cucumbers. Cut into wedges, these also make a great appetizer to accompany drinks.

> 2 cups all-purpose flour, preferably unbleached
>
> 1 cup white or whole wheat pastry flour
>
> 1 teaspoon salt
>
> About 3 tablespoons lard
>
> About 1¼ cups lukewarm water
>
> About ¼ cup sesame seeds
>
> About 1 tablespoon Sichuan peppercorns, ground
>
> About 1 cup peanut oil for shallow-frying, plus extra for surfaces

Place the flours and salt in a food processor and pulse to mix. Add 1 tablespoon of the lard and process for about 30 seconds to blend it in. With the blade running, slowly pour the lukewarm water through the feed tube until a ball of dough forms. Turn the dough out onto a lightly oiled surface and knead for several minutes, until very smooth. Place

the dough in a plastic bag and tie loosely or cover well with plastic wrap. Let rest for at least 1 hour, or up to 3 hours, whatever is convenient.

Cut the dough in half. Set one half aside, in the plastic bag or covered with plastic, while you work with the other half. Cut the dough in half and then cut each half into 4 equal pieces by cutting it in half and half again. Loosely cover 4 pieces with plastic wrap. Working on a lightly oiled surface, roll each of the other 4 pieces out into a 12- to 15-inch-long strip 1½ to 2 inches wide.

Use your fingertips to spread ¼ teaspoon lard onto the top of each dough strip. Roll each strip up fairly tightly, stretching the dough a little as you do so. Without turning it onto its coiled side, flatten each coil to a rectangular bundle under your palm and then use the rolling pin to flatten it out again to a strip about 12 inches long and 1½ to 2 inches wide. The strips may seem a little bumpy or uneven; don't worry.

Once again, spread about ¼ teaspoon lard on the top of each strip. Roll one up loosely, with no stretching of the dough, then lay it on its side on the work surface and flatten gently with the palm of your hand to about 3 inches across (don't worry about dimensions, because you will be rolling it out a little more later). Repeat with the remaining 3 strips. Set aside for a moment, loosely covered.

Put out two small flat plates. Place about 1 tablespoon sesame seeds on one and about 1 teaspoon Sichuan pepper on the other.

Place a large heavy skillet over high heat and add oil to a depth of about ¼ inch (for our 10-inch cast-iron skillet, we use about 1 cup oil). When the oil is very hot (you should see it start to smoke slightly), lower the heat to medium-high.

Meanwhile, lightly press one side of one of the flattened rounds onto the sesame seeds and then touch it lightly to the Sichuan pepper. Place the dough, seed side up, on your work surface and press down on it with your palm to press the seeds in well, then use a rolling pin to roll it out to an approximately 4-inch-diameter round. Repeat with a second round.

Place the breads into the hot oil, seed side up. Cook on the first side for 2 minutes, then use a wide spatula to flip the breads over, being careful not to splash yourself with hot oil. While the breads cook for another 2 minutes on the second side, finish flavoring and shaping the other 2 dough rounds; set aside. After 2 minutes, turn the breads over one more time and give them another minute or so on the first side, pressing down with the spatula to ensure that the center of the breads gets exposed to the heat. They will be a deep golden brown before they are done. Don't worry about overcooking them: they need a good 5 minutes to cook through. When the breads are done, transfer them to a rack or plate, then add the next 2 breads to the oil, seed side up, and cook as above.

Once you get used to the timing, you will be able to shape the remaining breads while the first batches are cooking. Until you're comfortable though, you may want to lower the heat to medium-low once the first 4 breads have cooked and shape and flavor another 4 breads (you'll need to add more sesame seeds and Sichuan pepper to the plates). Once you've shaped the first 2 breads of this next batch, raise the heat under the skillet to high again; then, once the oil is starting to smoke, lower the heat to medium-high and start cooking 2 breads, as above. Repeat with the remaining dough and flavorings.

Makes 16 crispy round flatbreads

HAM SESAME COILS: One version of this bread uses small shreds of ham, along with the lard, to flavor and enrich the breads. If you'd like to try this version, use fine shreds of ham or prosciutto, the fattier the better. Spread a few strips (a scant teaspoon) on each strip of dough along with the lard the second (last) time you spread it with lard. You'll need about ¼ cup thin fine shreds of ham or prosciutto, along with the lard, to make this version.

HUI TWO-LAYER CREPES

I came across these in Qinghai province, in the market in Xining, being made by a fresh-faced, friendly young Hui woman. Her breads were about ten inches across and she cooked them on a large cast-iron griddle. They're made with two batters, a plain flour-and-water batter for the first layer, and a second one with egg and a little sugar for the sweeter, richer pale yellow top layer.

We've adapted the recipe to make slightly smaller (and thus easier to shape and cook) crepes than the originals. (Also see the Mini-Crepe Alternative, on page 204, for appetizer-sized crepes.) Whatever the size, they're very attractive, and supple and pleasurable to eat. Make them as a snack, or to accompany any meal. They'll steal the show. . . .

FIRST BATTER
1¼ cups all-purpose flour
1½ cups lukewarm water
1½ tablespoons vegetable oil
Generous 1 teaspoon salt

SECOND BATTER
1 cup all-purpose flour
2 large eggs
1 cup water
3 tablespoons sugar

About ¼ cup peanut oil or vegetable oil for cooking

Make the batters at least 1 hour, or as long as 3 hours, before you wish to make the breads.

To make the first batter, place the flour in a medium bowl, add the water, and whisk until smooth. Add the oil and salt and whisk to blend. Cover and set aside for 45 minutes to 1 hour.

(continued)

To make the second batter, place the flour in a medium bowl. Whisk the eggs in a small bowl and add to the flour, together with the water. Whisk the mixture vigorously until you have a very smooth batter. Whisk in the sugar. Cover and set aside for 45 minutes to 1 hour (refrigerate if leaving for longer).

About 10 to 15 minutes before you want to serve the breads, place a griddle or a 10- to 12-inch cast-iron skillet, preferably with low sides (see Note), over high heat. When it is hot, lower the heat to medium-high. Add about ½ teaspoon oil and rub it all over the pan with a wadded-up paper towel.

Whisk the first batter. If it seems a little thick (you want a pourable texture, like a crepe batter), whisk in 1 to 2 tablespoons water. Scoop up a scant ¼ cup of batter and pour it onto the hot pan in a spiral, working from the center outward. Use an offset spatula or the back of a large wet spoon to smooth and spread it as thin as possible, to a round about 7 inches in diameter. Let cook briefly, about 1 minute, while you whisk the second batter. Again, if it has thickened, whisk in a little water to thin it to a pourable crepe-batter texture. Scoop up a scant 3 tablespoons of the second batter and pour it on top of the crepe in the pan, using the back of a wet spoon to smooth it out to the edges. Let cook for another minute, or until the surface has turned from liquid to matte. Drizzle on a thin spiral of oil (just over 1 teaspoon), then flip over. Let cook for about 1 minute on the other side, then fold in half and transfer to a plate. Repeat with the remaining batter, stacking the breads as you make them, to keep them soft and supple.

Makes 7 or 8 crepe-like breads about 7 inches in diameter; allow 1 or 2 per person

NOTE ON TECHNIQUE: We've discovered that, as with any crepe, it's easier if your pan has low sides so you can work with a spatula without running into the walls of the pan. If you have trouble spreading the batter very thin, there are two things to try: thin the batter a little more, to make it more liquid and easier to spread, and lower the heat slightly, so the batter doesn't set too quickly.

HUI CREPE WRAPS: These breads were sold plain in Xining, to be eaten out of hand, but we think they are ideal for fillings of all kinds. To use them as sandwich wraps, place tender leaf lettuce on the breads, top with slices of cheese and/or roasted or grilled meat, or else salami or prosciutto, and roll up. Or try a soft filling like tuna salad, egg salad, or guacamole, on tender greens.

MINI-CREPE ALTERNATIVE: We sometimes make nontraditional smaller versions of this bread: Scoop up 1 tablespoon of the first batter and spread into a thin round about 3½ inches across. Use about 2 teaspoons of the second batter. These smaller versions are easier to shape, and they make an attractive base for appetizers. They hold moist toppings well—spread them with a little Lhasa Yellow Achar (page 28) or a nontraditional topping such as tapenade or smoked salmon. They stay supple and fresh for several hours if covered.

Makes about 30 mini-crepes; allow 3 or 4 per person

HUI GREEN ONION CREPES: You can also use the first batter as a base for scallion crepes, beautiful flatbreads that the woman in the Xining market was selling alongside her two-layer crepes. Make only the first batter. Just before cooking the crepes, add ¼ cup minced scallions (white and tender green parts) to the batter and whisk in. Lightly grease a griddle or heavy skillet as above and preheat over medium-high heat. Then pour in ¼ cup of batter in a spiral, starting at the center of the pan, and smooth, as above, with an offset spatula or the back of a wet spoon, to a round just over 6 inches in diameter (the crepe will be a little thicker than the first layer of the Two-Layer Crepes because of the scallions). Once the top turns from shiny to matte and small bubbles appear, after about 1 minute, drizzle a thin spiral of oil, about 1 teaspoon, onto the crepe, then flip it over and cook on the other side for another minute or so, until lightly touched with brown on the underside. Serve these as a savory bread or snack, perhaps with a little salsa or a sharp cheese.

Makes 7 or 8 crepes about 6 inches in diameter

Late fall and winter is pilgrim season in Lhasa, when the city fills with pilgrims from all over. In this line waiting in the courtyard to get into the Jokhang Temple are many nomads and herders; they're recognizable by their thick, long sheepskin coats. They've traveled here from the high-altitude grasslands of western Tibet, western Sichuan, and Qinghai.

When I returned to Lhasa after nineteen years away, it felt so familiar and yet so different too. There were lots more cars and many people looked more prosperous. The most obvious change was the huge growth of the city's non-Tibetan population. The city now stretches down its fertile valley ten miles from its old boundary, and it seems that almost all the population growth is Han Chinese and Hui. These non-Tibetans settle here because they see economic opportunities, for the central government is investing money in Tibet, especially in industry and mining; the large army population also generates business for service industries. The recent opening of the train connection between Lhasa and central China promises to bring even more outsiders to Lhasa.

I was curious, so I conducted an informal survey: I asked every Han Chinese I met where he or she was from, how long he or she had been in Tibet, and finally I would say, "Do you like it here?" The people I spoke with (more than twenty-five in all) came from many different provinces of China. They'd all been living in Tibet a long while, from eight to eighteen years, and they all were very firm: "No, I don't like it."

It's a bit of a grim picture, this majority population disliking the place they live. They don't know or appreciate Tibetan culture, which has a centuries-old literary and philosophical tradition, and they don't learn the language. For them, Tibet is a hardship post, like taking a job on the oil rigs in Saudi Arabia.

You can feel the resentment in both directions: the Tibetans, of the Chinese, who took over Tibet and have controlled it absolutely since 1959 (see page 39); and the Han, of the "barbaric" Tibetans among whom they find themselves. "If they didn't spend so much time praying, they'd have more money," said one Han woman to me, pointing disdainfully at an older woman prostrating herself in prayer in front of the Jokhang Temple. **N**

ABOVE: *Large, densely stamped versions of Uighur nan topped with sesame seeds are stacked and displayed for sale at a small bakery in the Turpan oasis. On the left is a close-up of one of the breads, with a bread stamp. The bread stamps are usually made of wood and have sharp nails on their stamping surface (we've also seen them made of sharp quills tied into a bundle). The center of the bread is stamped repeatedly all over just before it is placed on the hot wall of the tandoor oven. This prevents the bread from puffing, except around the rim.* OPPOSITE: *Uighur Pastries with Pea Tendrils* (page 208).

UIGHUR PASTRIES WITH
PEA TENDRILS

These deep-fried Uighur pastries are made in the Turpan oasis (see "Turpan Depression," page 200), in a little shop in the center of town. We haven't seen them anywhere else. The half-moon turnovers are filled with chopped greens flavored with onion and cumin, and they are very succulent. We use pea tendrils, not the fine delicate pea tendrils that are now sometimes available, but the heartier ones that come in large plastic bags in Asian grocery stores (see Glossary, page 354, for more). You could instead use other firm leafy greens such as Taiwan bok choi, with its long leaves (see Glossary), dandelion greens (add 1 teaspoon sugar to the cooked dandelion greens if you aren't a fan of their enticing bitter edge), or amaranth greens. Serve these on their own or with a dipping sauce such as Soy-Vinegar Dipping Sauce (page 151) or, less traditionally, Quick Tomato-Onion Chutney (page 24). They're a great treat to accompany drinks. [PHOTOGRAPH ON PAGE 207]

DOUGH

1 cup all-purpose flour, preferably unbleached,
     plus extra for surfaces

½ teaspoon salt

Scant ½ cup lukewarm water

FILLING

½ pound pea tendrils or other leafy greens (see headnote)

¼ cup grated onion

¼ teaspoon ground cumin

Pinch of cayenne

½ teaspoon salt

Peanut oil for deep-frying (2 to 4 cups)

Make the dough an hour or more before you wish to fry the breads. Place the flour and salt in a food processor and pulse briefly to mix. With the blade running, slowly add the lukewarm water through the feed tube until a ball of dough forms. Turn the dough out onto a floured surface and knead for several minutes, until smooth and elastic. Let rest, covered with plastic wrap, for at least 30 minutes, or as long as 12 hours.

Meanwhile, prepare the filling: Bring a large pot of water to a rolling boil. Add the pea tendrils and stir with a wooden spoon to push them into the water so they are all immersed. Cook until tender, 4 to 6 minutes (timing will depend on the thickness of the pea tendrils, or other greens). Drain well in a colander and let cool for a moment.

Place the greens on a cutting board and chop them with a cleaver or chef's knife, chopping first in one direction at ¼-inch intervals and then in the other direction until finely chopped (you should have a generous 1 cup packed chopped greens). Place the greens in a bowl, add the onion, cumin, cayenne, and salt, and use a fork to blend well. Set aside. If you make the filling more than 20 minutes ahead, a little liquid will drain from it; pour this excess off and press the filling to squeeze out any remaining liquid before placing the filling in the dough.

Turn the dough out onto a well-floured surface. Cut it in half and set one half aside. Cut the other half into 6 equal pieces, by cutting it in half and then cutting each half into 3 pieces. Roll each piece into a ball between your lightly floured palms, then lightly flatten into a disk and flour both sides. Set aside while you shape the remaining dough, to give a total of 12 disks.

With your fingertips or a rolling pin, flatten one disk out to a 4-inch round. Repeat with 5 more dough disks. Place 1 slightly rounded table-spoon filling in the center of one round. Fold the dough over to make a half-moon shape and press the edges together to seal in the filling. To ensure that the seal holds, pinch all along the edge, twisting slightly with each pinch. Flatten the bread gently with the palm of your hand, to push the filling out to the seam, and then set on a parchment-lined or lightly floured baking sheet or work surface. Repeat with the remaining rolled-out rounds, then repeat with the remaining 6 dough disks and filling. Set aside while you ready your deep-frying arrangement.

Place a large wok or deep pot on the stovetop (or use a deep-fryer); make sure that your wok or pot is stable. Pour in 1½ to 2 inches of oil (3 inches or more if using a deep-fryer) and heat the oil over medium-high heat. Put out a slotted spoon or mesh skimmer. To test the temperature of the oil, hold a wooden chopstick vertically in the oil, with the end touching the bottom of the pot. If bubbles come bubbling up along the chopstick, the oil is at temperature. The oil should not be smoking; if it is, turn the heat down slightly and wait a moment for it to cool, then test again with the chopstick. (A deep-fry thermometer should read 325° to 350°F.)

Slide one half-moon into the oil, wait a moment, and then slide in a second. The oil will bubble up around them. After about 30 seconds, use the slotted spoon or skimmer to gently turn them over. Continue to cook until they are a rich golden brown all over, 50 seconds to 1 minute. Lift them out of the oil, pausing to let excess oil drain off, then place on a plate or rack. Repeat with the remaining half-moons in batches until all are cooked.

Serve hot or warm (we also love the texture of room-temperature half-moons).

Makes 12 deep-fried half-moon filled breads

PARTY HALF-MOONS: To make a large batch of these for a party, enlist some friends to help shape the half-moons ahead of time, up to 2 hours ahead. Let them sit out, uncovered (it's fine if the dough dries out a little before they are deep-fried). Since the pastries take only a minute to deep-fry, you can cook a double or triple recipe very quickly, a great treat to accompany drinks.

A Uighur woman in a colorful ikat-print dress buying samsa *from a street vendor in Turpan.*

GIANT JIAOZI

In most towns in China, there are restaurants or street vendors selling steamed or boiled *jiaozi* (see Savory Boiled Dumplings, page 150), small filled dumplings that come five or ten to a plate, with a dipping sauce alongside. But until my last trip to Lhasa, I had never seen giant deep-fried *jiaozi* like these. They were like large elongated half-moons, more than eight inches long, golden brown, and stuffed with a delectable vegetarian filling.

The woman making them in the market near the Barkhor (the walking route around the Jokhang Temple in the old part of Lhasa) was from Hunan province, in central China. She'd been in Tibet for twelve years and didn't like it, but admitted she was making a good living. Somewhere in Hunan these must be a specialty, a common treat, but in Tibet they were very exotic, as well as delicious.

This recipe gives instructions for the original giant breads I encountered in Lhasa, but we've also included instructions for a smaller version that is more manageable for the home cook. The larger breads can be a little tricky to cook if you don't have a big deep-fryer, but they are fun to try.

Make the dough first and let it rest while you make the filling and allow it to cool. Shape the breads just before you wish to cook and serve them. Final shaping and cooking will take only about 15 minutes.

Make a batch for lunch and serve them with a fresh salad and a soup, or with grilled meat, such as Oasis Chicken Kebabs (page 247). Allow 2 small or 1 large bread per person.

DOUGH

2 cups all-purpose flour, plus extra for surfaces

¾ teaspoon salt

About ¾ cup lukewarm water

FILLING

4 dried shiitake mushrooms

About 2 tablespoons dried tree ears (see Glossary)

One 100-gram package cellophane noodles

About 6 leaves Napa cabbage

1 small square pressed tofu (see Glossary)

2 tablespoons peanut oil or sesame oil

1 tablespoon minced ginger

2 scallions, cut lengthwise into ribbons
   and then into 1½-inch lengths

2 dried red chiles, or to taste

¼ teaspoon salt

1 tablespoon soy sauce

Peanut oil for deep-frying (2 to 4 cups)

Place the flour and salt in a food processor or bowl. *If using a food processor*, with the blade spinning, slowly pour the lukewarm water through the feed tube until a ball of dough forms. *If working by hand*, make a well in the center of the flour and add ¾ cup water. Stir with your hand and gradually incorporate the flour. If the dough is very stiff or dry, add a little more water and stir and turn in the bowl until all the flour is incorporated and you have a kneadable dough.

Turn the dough out onto a lightly floured surface and knead for 3 to 4 minutes, until very smooth and elastic. Cover with plastic and let rest for at least 1 hour or as long as 4 hours, whatever is convenient.

Meanwhile, start soaking the various dried ingredients for the filling: Place the dried shiitake in a small bowl and add about 1 cup hot water. The mushrooms will float, so place a small plate on top to keep them submerged. Soak for about 15 minutes, or until softened. In another small bowl, soak the tree ears in about a cup of hot water for about 15 minutes, until softened. Drain. Soak the cellophane noodles in lukewarm water to cover for 15 minutes; drain.

When the shiitake are softened, lift out of the soaking water, reserving it. (Some will go into the stir-fry; the rest can be used to flavor a broth.) Trim off and discard the stems. Thinly slice the mushrooms—you will have a scant ¼ cup. Set aside.

Cut off and discard any tough spots from the tree ears. You will have about ¼ cup. Thinly slice, and set aside. Use scissors to cut the soaked noodles into 1- to 1½-inch lengths. Set aside.

Slice the cabbage leaves lengthwise into 1-inch-wide strips, then slice crosswise into ¼-inch-wide slices. You should have 4 loosely packed cups. Set aside.

Thinly slice the tofu, then cut crosswise into ¼-inch-wide strips. You should have about 1 cup sliced tofu. Set aside.

Heat a wok or large heavy skillet over high heat. Add the oil and swirl gently to coat the bottom of the pan. Add the ginger, scallions, and dried red chiles and cook for 10 seconds. Toss in the cabbage and stir-fry briefly. Add the salt and stir-fry for 3 or 4 minutes, or until the cabbage starts to wilt. Add about 2 tablespoons of the reserved mushroom soaking water, the mushrooms, and tree ears and stir-fry for about a minute. Add the noodles and soy sauce and cook, stirring occasionally to prevent sticking, until the cabbage is tender and the liquid has evaporated. Add the tofu and stir-fry for another minute. Turn out into a bowl; set aside to cool to room temperature. You will have about 3 cups filling.

Working on a lightly floured surface, shape the dough into a cylinder. Cut it in half and in half again, then cut each piece into thirds. Lightly flour your palm and flatten each piece gently. Set aside, loosely covered with plastic wrap.

Place a large wok or deep heavy pot on the stovetop; make sure that the wok or pot is stable. (Or use a deep-fryer.) Pour oil into your wok or pot to a depth of 3 inches and heat the oil over medium-high heat. Put out a slotted spoon or mesh skimmer. To test the temperature of the oil, hold a wooden chopstick vertically in the oil, with the end touching the bottom of the pot. If bubbles come bubbling up along the chopstick, the oil is at temperature. The oil should not be smoking; if it is, turn the heat down slightly and wait a moment for it to cool, then test again with the chopstick. (A deep-fry thermometer should read 325° to 350°F.)

Once the oil is at temperature, turn the heat down slightly and shape your first *jiaozi*, leaving the remaining dough loosely covered. Use a rolling pin to roll one piece of dough out to a 7-inch round. Scoop up ¼ cup of the filling and place it in the center of the dough, leaving an inch clear all around the edges. Fold the dough over the filling to make a mounded half-moon shape. Press down lightly to push out air bubbles, then crimp the edges together: Start by pinching the edges together at one point, then twist the bottom over the top. Repeat at ¼-inch intervals to seal closed. The dough is moist and will stick to itself (if for some reason it doesn't, wet a fingertip and use it to moisten one edge of the dough so that it sticks well).

Raise the heat under the oil again. Pick up the filled dough and stretch it gently, elongating it so it becomes more of a banana shape, a little more than 8 inches long, and then slide it gently into the hot oil. The bread will sink and then slowly rise back up in the hot oil. Use the slotted spoon or skimmer to encourage it to turn over after about a minute. It will turn golden and will develop darker brown bubbles in patches. Once it is a richer golden brown, after another 2 to 3 minutes, use the spoon or skimmer to lift it out of the oil, pausing to let excess oil run off, then transfer to a paper-towel-lined plate.

Repeat the shaping and cooking with the remaining dough and filling. Once you have shaped and cooked one bread, you will find it easy to shape one while another is cooking, and then, if you have room, to have 2 or even 3 in the hot oil cooking at once, at various stages of doneness. Cooking time will vary depending on how many breads you have in the oil at once. Serve hot.

Makes 12 elongated filled half-moon breads, about 8 inches long

APPETIZER-SIZED JIAOZI: Divide the dough into 24 pieces by cutting it in half, shaping each half into a cylinder, and cutting each one into 12 pieces as described above. To shape the *jiaozi*, roll each out to a round about 5 inches in diameter, place 2 tablespoons filling on each round, and then fold in half and pinch closed as above. Stretch each filled half-moon to nearly 6 inches long, then slide into the hot oil. You should be able to cook at least 3 of these at a time, shaping more *jiaozi* once the first one is in the oil.

Makes 24 elongated filled breads, 5½ to 6 inches long

VEGETARIAN STIR-FRY: The filling on its own makes a delicious vegetarian stir-fry for 3 or 4 people. Serve with rice and a soup, or over freshly cooked noodles.

A Tibetan woman buys strands of dried cheese cubes at the market near the Barkhor, in the old part of Lhasa. She will probably use them in a stew or a noodle soup. They take long soaking in hot water to soften, but then add good flavor and texture.

CHEESE MOMOS

With the rise of Tibetan restaurants in Lhasa, deep-fried cheese *momos* have become standard fare, a great snack for friends having a beer or hot tea together.

Cheese is a staple in many parts of Tibet, just as it is in Bhutan, across Tibet's southern border. Tibetan-style cheese starts as a soft cheese, made from cooked-down milk (see Yak in Glossary), but it is most often dried, so that it can be easily stored and transported. My first taste of dried Tibetan cheese was long ago in the hut of some Tibetan herders in the mountains of Nepal. The cheese consisted of small off-white cubes, less than an inch square and hard as a rock, that had been strung on a piece of twine and dried in the smoke of the family fire. They had a definite cheesy-fermented flavor like a smoked aged goat cheese.

These days, dried cheese is still made by nomads but it is also widely available for sale, either in cubes or already grated, in the street markets of Lhasa and other Tibetan towns. The town of Shigatse specializes in a sweetened version—the cheese cubes are soaked in sugar water before being dried—but most are savory. People eat the cheese cubes as a snack or add them to *thugpa* (noodle stews), and they use the grated dried cheese to flavor breads.

We improvise the filling for these delicious deep-fried breads by using any one of several nontraditional dry-textured firm cheeses. Our favorite option is to start with a goat's-milk feta and air-dry it over several days, until it becomes more dried out and crumbly. A good last-minute cheese choice is Pecorino-Romano.

We serve cheese *momos* as a snack or appetizer. You can also make a meal of them, accompanied by a soup and perhaps a salad. We love serving them with an acidic condiment such as Market Stall Fresh Tomato Salsa (page 18) or Lhasa Yellow Achar (page 28). Allow 1 cup sauce to accompany 16 *momos*, and put the sauce out in one or two small bowls with a spoon in each so guests can spoon on a little as they eat. Other good complements to *momos* include tart salads such as Napa and Red Onion Salad (page 86) or Cucumbers in Black Rice Vinegar (page 83).

DOUGH

1½ cups all-purpose flour, preferably unbleached, plus extra
    for surfaces

½ teaspoon salt

About ½ cup lukewarm water

FILLING

¼ pound dry-textured goat's-milk feta or similar cheese
    (see headnote), crumbled or minced (1 packed cup)

¼ cup minced scallions (white and tender green parts)

Peanut oil for deep-frying (2 to 4 cups)

Place the flour and salt in a food processor and pulse briefly to mix. With the blade running, slowly add the water through the feed tube until a ball forms. Turn out onto a lightly floured surface and knead briefly. The dough should be soft and elastic. Cover with plastic wrap and set aside to rest for 30 minutes to 2 hours, whatever is most convenient.

Mix together the cheese and scallions in a medium bowl. Set aside.

Use a dough scraper or a sharp knife to cut the dough in half. Set one half aside, covered. On a lightly floured surface, shape the other half into a cylinder by rolling it under your palms. Cut the cylinder crosswise in half, then in half and half again, to give you 8 equal pieces. Work with one piece at a time, leaving the others loosely covered with plastic wrap.

On the lightly floured surface, roll one piece out to a nearly 5-inch round. Place 1 packed tablespoon of the cheese mixture in the center of the round and fold over to make a half-moon shape. Press down lightly with a floured palm, to get rid of air bubbles, and then pleat the edges closed: Start at one end and pinch the edges together between your thumb and forefinger, then twist the pinched place over, rolling the edge. Move along about ¼ inch and repeat, then continue until the edge is completely sealed. This pinch-and-roll technique works well with soft doughs such as this; if you find the dough is not sticking to itself, make sure to brush off any excess flour, and then brush the edge with a very little water to help it stick. Set aside on a lightly floured surface, and repeat with the remaining 7 pieces of dough, and then with the remaining dough and cheese, to give you 16 *momos* in all. Set aside.

Place a large wok or deep heavy pot on your stovetop; make sure the wok or pot is stable. (Or use a deep-fryer.) Pour 2 inches of oil into the wok or pot and heat over high heat. Put out a slotted spoon or a wire skimmer and a rack or plate lined with paper towels. To check the temperature of the oil, hold a wooden chopstick vertically in the oil, with the end touching the bottom of the pot. If bubbles come bubbling up along the chopstick, the oil is at temperature. The oil should not be smoking; if it is, turn the heat down slightly and wait a moment for it to cool, then test again with the chopstick. (A deep-fry thermometer should read 325° to 350°F.)

Once the oil is at temperature, slide one *momo* into the hot oil, taking care not to splash yourself. Add another, and repeat until you have 4 frying at once (if your pot is small, stop before the pot is crowded). Use the slotted spoon or skimmer to move the *momos* around and gently turn them. They will quickly turn golden brown, with darker brown bubbled spots. After 1 to 2 minutes, when they are a rich golden brown and crisped looking, use the slotted spoon or skimmer to transfer them to the rack or plate. Repeat with the remaining *momos*, cooking them in batches.

Serve hot.

Makes 16 deep-fried half-moon filled breads; serves 4 as part of a meal, or 6 as a snack or appetizer

SAVORY TIBETAN BREADS

We've seen griddle-cooked versions of *sha-pa-le* (prounced "shah-pa-láy"), as these breads are called in Lhasa dialect (*sha* is meat and *pa-le* is bread), made by Tibetan women in the market in Darjeeling, in northern India. But in Lhasa (and later, as we had them in Amdo, in the far northeastern edge of the Tibetan world), they're deep-fried. You can order them for lunch in small Tibetan restaurants and then sit comfortably as you dip them into chutney and eat them bite by bite, a satisfying pleasure.

Traditionally the meat that fills these breads is yak meat, chopped finely and flavored with ginger and a little onion and perhaps some fresh Chinese celery leaf (see Glossary). We substitute beef, though you could also use lamb or goat.

Serve the breads hot, as they are done, accompanied by chopped fresh tomatoes or cucumbers, or with pickled radish or a tomato chutney (for example Quick Tomato-Onion Chutney, page 24).

DOUGH

3 cups all-purpose flour, plus extra for surfaces

1 teaspoon salt

About 1¼ cups lukewarm water

FILLING

½ pound (1 packed cup) lean ground beef or ½ pound boneless
   lean beef, such as round steak, cut into 4 or 5 pieces

½ cup minced onion

2 teaspoons minced ginger

1 teaspoon salt or ½ teaspoon salt plus 2 teaspoons soy sauce

1 tablespoon minced Chinese celery leaves (see Note)

Peanut oil for deep-frying (2 to 4 cups)

Combine the flour and salt in a food processor and pulse briefly to mix. With the blade running, add the water in a slow stream until a ball of dough forms. Turn out onto a lightly floured surface and knead for about a minute. The dough should be soft and supple and very smooth. Let rest, covered with plastic wrap, for 30 minutes to 1 hour.

If using ground beef, mix all the filling ingredients together in a bowl. If using steak or another cut, place the meat, onion, ginger, and salt (or salt and soy sauce) in the food processor and pulse repeatedly to make a coarse paste. Transfer to a bowl and stir in the herb, if using. You will have about 1¼ cups packed filling. Set aside, covered with plastic wrap (refrigerate if the wait will be longer than 30 minutes).

Dust your work surface lightly with flour. Use a sharp knife or a dough scraper to cut the dough in half. Set one half aside, loosely covered with plastic wrap. Divide the remaining dough into 12 pieces by cutting it in half and in half again, then cutting each piece into thirds. Roll each piece into a ball under the palm of your hand. On the lightly floured surface, press each round flat under your palm, then flip over and press once on the other side.

Cover 10 of the rounds and roll out the first 2: roll each one out to a 5-inch circle, rolling first one and then the other, to give the gluten a moment to relax. Repeat with the remaining rounds.

Scoop up a rounded tablespooon (about 1 tablespoon plus 1 teaspoon) filling and spread it onto one round with the back of the spoon or with a spatula, leaving a nearly ½-inch border all around the edges. Place another dough round on top of the filling, then crimp the edges all around: Start by pinching the edges together at one point, then twist the bottom edge over onto the top. Move along about ¼ inch and repeat. Continue until you have a rolled edge all around that seals in the filling. Set aside on a lightly floured surface. Repeat with the remaining rounds.

Place a large wok or deep heavy pot on the stovetop; make sure the wok or pot is stable. (Or use a deep-fryer.) Pour 3 inches of oil into the wok or pot and heat the oil over medium-high heat. Put out a slotted spoon or mesh skimmer. To test the temperature of the oil, hold a wooden chopstick vertically in the oil, with the end touching the bottom of the pot. If bubbles come bubbling up along the chopstick, the oil is at temperature. The oil should not be smoking; if it is, turn the heat down slightly and wait a moment for it to cool, then test again with the chopstick. (A deep-fry thermometer should read 325° to 350°F.)

Place 2 filled breads on a lightly floured surface. Flatten each of them gently with a lightly floured rolling pin or with your palm, just to ensure the edges are sealed, then slide one into the hot oil. The bread should sink to the bottom and then slowly start to rise to the surface. Use the slotted spoon or skimmer to flip it over. The side now on top will have some browned patches. Let cook for another 30 seconds, then flip the bread again. It will now be somewhat brown on both sides and starting to puff a little. Let cook for another 30 to 60 seconds, until it is a strong golden brown on both sides, then lift it out carefully and transfer to a paper-towel-lined plate. Repeat with the second bread.

Once you are accustomed to the timing and have a feel for deep-frying the breads, you can easily cook 2 at a time if your wok or pot is large enough. Slide in the first, then after turning it over the first time, slide in the second. Repeat with the remaining shaped breads, then turn down the heat while you shape the remaining 6. Raise the heat again several minutes before you start to deep-fry the remaining breads.

Makes 12 deep-fried filled breads about 5 inches in diameter; serves 6 as a snack, 3 or 4 as a small meal

NOTE ON CHINESE CELERY: Chinese celery can be difficult to find if you don't have access to an East Asian grocery store. We often substitute finely minced mint, especially in summer, when mint is flourishing in our garden. Or simply omit the herb.

LARGE SHA-PA-LE: The breads we usually make are the smaller version we had in Labrang, in Gansu. Smaller breads are easier to handle if you're deep-frying at home. To make larger ones, like those in Lhasa, make 8 rather than 12 breads: Cut each half of the dough into 8 pieces, and roll them out to 8- or 9-inch rounds; use 2 tablespoons filling for each bread.

Serves 4 to 8 for lunch with a side salad, or for a substantial snack

In the village of Labrang (the Chinese name is Xiahe), on a lane leading to the nunnery, we came upon this small mill, a place where roast barley is ground into tsampa and wheat berries into flour.

THE HUI PEOPLE

Acording to China's 2000 census, there are nearly 10 million Hui (pronounced "hway") living in the country. They are officially classified as a "minority nationality" (*minzu*), one of the fifty-five different groups with that designation (Tibetan, Mongol, Miao, etc.). But the Hui are the only people who have the designation as a result of religion, not as a result of language and/or ethnicity.

The Hui are Muslim. Although they are not the only Muslims in China (the Uighurs, Kirghiz, Kazakhs, and Tajiks are also Muslim), they have for centuries considered themselves a separate people, even though ethnolinguistically they are not. They live all across China (with much larger concentrations in the provinces of Ningxia, Gansu, Henan, Xinjiang, and Yunnan), and wherever they live, they speak the local Chinese dialect (as well as Mandarin). At the same time, they incorporate Persian- and Arabic-influenced terms into their vocabulary, so that they speak in a way that is distinctive, whatever the local language they are speaking.

Hui women cover their heads with kerchiefs or scarves and tend to be rather austere in their choice of clothing. Some Hui men grow beards, and most wear small caps as a mark of their religion. We've read that some Hui are more strictly observant than others, and that there are a

number of different forms of Islam followed by the various Hui communities.

One of the ways Hui culture clearly sets itself apart is through food. There are two Chinese characters that are closely associated with the Hui, the characters for *qing* (prounced "ching"), meaning pure, and *zhen* (pronounced "jen"), meaning true. *Qing zhen* is written outside every Hui restaurant, much as the Arabic word *halal* is outside Muslim restaurants in other places. This means the restaurant does not serve pork or cook with lard, both prohibited by Islam. Instead the meat is lamb or goat or sometimes beef.

We always go out of our way to find Hui markets and small restaurants, whether in Lanzhou or Xining, or in smaller towns such as Dali, in Yunnan. There we'll find flatbreads of many kinds, grilled lamb, and inventive soups served over wheat noodles (see Hui Tomato-Lamb Noodle Soup, page 59, for example).

Hui history, culture, and food in China make a fascinating, complicated story. An excellent book on the subject is *Muslim Chinese: Ethnic Nationalism in the People's Republic* by Dru Gladney (see the Bibliography). We strongly recommend it for anyone wanting to learn more about the Hui.

LEFT: *A Hui woman at a market stall in Linxia, in Gansu province, with braids of dried garlic hanging behind her.* RIGHT: *A fine-looking Hui man who runs a shop in Labrang, also in Gansu. The town is predominantly Tibetan, and historically so, because of the monastery (also called Labrang) that is located there. However, there is also a fairly large Hui population who have filtered down from the Hui Autonomous Region in the neighboring province of Ningxia, seeking business opportunities. This man sells saddlery and other kinds of useful equipment and tools.*

FISH

China, freshwater fish mostly, except near the coast, but we confess we're not good at identifying them. We ask for the local name, make a note of it, perhaps even take a photo of the fish lying gleaming on a banana leaf or swimming in a basin at the market. But it all seems a little abstract to us, for fish, especially freshwater fish, are so local—once we get home, we're dealing with a whole different world of fish. Consequently, for the dishes in this chapter, we have used species of fish that are available in North America and that seem to us to be reasonable substitutions for the local fish we've eaten and seen in China.

The regions beyond the Great Wall that we talk about and explore in this book are all far from the ocean. In eastern Guizhou province, small freshwater fish are a staple. They live in the ponds and rivers of the well-watered landscape, there to be gathered when needed. The Miao and the Dong both use them in soups; they may also be grilled or fried or deep-fried, most often after being rubbed with chile paste and dusted with salt. Similarly, in the well-watered areas of Yunnan, fish means fish from small ponds near the house.

Included in this chapter are two different approaches to grilled fish, one stuffed and one salt-rubbed (see pages 222 and 228); a deep-fried chile-hot fish (see page 234) that makes a wonderful accompaniment to drinks; a simmered fish in red sauce from the Miao people of Guizhou (see page 229); and a steamed whole fish, aromatic with ginger, a festive party dish (see page 232). Eating these fish dishes, so different from one another, we are transported to places far away, connected to people who live very different lives.

OPPOSITE: *A streetside version of Dai Grilled Fish (page 222), photographed at a bus stop in southern Yunnan. Each fish is held in a holder of split bamboo that is tied together to pinch the fish tightly.* ABOVE: *Chinese celery, also known as celery leaf.*

Two Dai women and their textiles, in southern Yunnan. The woman in the town of Menghan (top) is stitching a seam on a traditional triangular cushion. The cushions, also found in Laos and Thailand, are used as pillows and support, for most people sit on the floor rather than on chairs. The woman below is seated at her loom on an open verandah that is sheltered from the elements by the large overhanging eaves of the house. She is in a small village across the Mekong River from Menghan.

DAI GRILLED FISH

The Dai region of southern Yunnan province is one of our favorite places to travel and to eat. Here it feels as if good food is available almost everywhere, and at any time of the day. For example, I first tasted these small grilled fish at a bus stop while on a long trip from Jinghong to Yuanyang (see "Yunnan Bus Ride," page 313). The bus had only been traveling about an hour and a half (with a ten- to twelve-hour journey ahead) when we stopped at a small rural junction for a bite to eat. A dozen different vendors were grilling and stir-frying, and there was also sticky rice and fruit and ice-cold drinks, everything a traveler needs.

I was particularly drawn to these fish. The method of grilling was unique, and the filling of chopped scallion and fresh coriander looked particularly good. It was indeed delicious, as was almost everything I tasted at the junction. Then we got back on the bus and headed on down the road.

When I got home weeks later, I was eager to try out the grilling technique. Traditionally each fish is held in a bamboo stick that has been split partly open. The fish goes into the cleft of the stick and the open end is tied together before the bundle goes onto the grill (see photo, page 220). We've worked with various ways of imitating the split bamboo, and the easiest we've found is to use two strong wooden chopsticks tied together tightly at one end with kitchen string (we wrap it round and round about five times before tying it). Wet the string and the chopsticks by soaking them in water for several minutes. You will need four holders. If you are using four small half-pound freshwater fish, you will need only one holder per fish; if using two one-pound fish, you'll want two holders per fish.

To grill the fish, simply place it in the "mouth" of the pair of chopsticks, then tie the other ends of the chopsticks together to help pinch the fish tightly. Serve with the chopstick holder(s) still embracing the fish.

Serve as a main dish with rice or sticky rice (pages 166 and 162) and a salsa such as Dai Tart Green Salsa (page 22). [PHOTOGRAPH ON PAGE 224]

4 white perch or other small freshwater fish (about ½ pound each), or substitute 2 larger fish such as bass or bream or tilapia (about 1 pound each)

FILLING

¼ cup coriander leaves

1 cup finely chopped scallions (white and tender green parts)

1 teaspoon chile pepper flakes

2 tablespoons lard

1 teaspoon salt

Soak 4 pairs of wooden or bamboo chopsticks (8 pairs for larger fish) and about 4 feet of kitchen string in water for 10 minutes. Using the string, tie each pair of chopsticks together *at one end only*, as described in the headnote. Set aside.

If starting with whole fish, clean and gut them. We leave the heads on, because the presentation is more attractive, though the Dai in Yunnan cut the heads off (probably to use them to make fish broth).

The fish need to be split open, to make a wide flap on one side: one at a time, lay each fish down on a cutting board with the head end toward you, the tail pointing away, the spine of the fish to the right, and the open belly to the left (reverse the instructions as appropriate if you are left-handed). With a sharp knife, starting at the base of the tail, on the belly side, cut across the base of the tail, slicing into the fish just down to the bone. Slice almost all the way over to the spine. Now cut toward you along the length of the backbone, again cutting through the flesh just down to the bone. Stop before you reach the gills and then slice toward the belly side, stopping before you reach the edge, so the rectangle you have cut stays attached. Lay your knife almost horizontally into the backbone cut and slice along the ribs to detach the flesh from them, as if filleting the fish—but do not cut all the way through to the belly edge.

Open the rectangular "flap" of one of the fish, and pull it back to keep it open. Place the fish diagonally in the open mouth of a tied chopstick "holder" so the flap of fish is held open, then press the other ends of the chopsticks together and tie them with string so the fish is held tightly. If using larger fish, place a second holder across the open flap and tie tightly, so the fish is held securely. Set aside. Repeat with the remaining fish and chopstick holders.

Prepare a fire in a charcoal grill or preheat a gas grill.

Meanwhile, make the filling: combine the coriander, scallions, chile pepper flakes, lard, and salt in a bowl and mix well. Divide the filling into 4 portions (or in half if using larger fish), and spread it onto the open exposed areas of the fish. Set aside.

Grill the fish over medium-high heat, placing them filling side up on the grill. After 1 minute, cover the grill and cook for 8 to 9 minutes. Check for doneness by looking at the fattest part of the fish and testing for firmness; it should feel tender to the touch. The flesh should flake easily with a fork. Transfer to a serving platter and serve.

Serves 4 as part of a rice meal

OPPOSITE: *Dai Grilled Fish (page 222)* LEFT: *Red chiles at the market in Turpan, in Xinjiang.* RIGHT: *Wall frescoes and a doorway at the Jokhang Temple in Lhasa.*

If I were going to have a job in China and could pick anywhere to work, I think I would choose Jinghong in southern Yunnan. It's a big enough city to have a sense of action on the street, but small enough that a bicycle would be all that I would need to get around. Of course a motorcycle would be better, because then I could easily ride down to Menghan and have lunch at my favorite Dai guesthouse, or I could ride up to the Hani rice terraces and photograph to my heart's desire (and stop overnight in a village somewhere along the way).

Then, of course, there's the weather. I'm sitting here in my hotel room with the windows wide open in February, and I'm looking out at tropical green coconut palms and listening to birds in all directions. Two months from now, Jinghong, like northern Thailand (200 miles south of here), will be hot, hot, hot, but then the rains will come. I like wearing flip-flops and sleeveless T-shirts, and I like it when other people around are wearing them too. I know it's China, but I'd almost call Jinghong "laid-back."

I was thinking the other day about how it must feel for tourists from the other parts of China who come here to visit. (Jinghong is not a place you want to be on the three "golden holidays" when it's thronged with tourists [see "Golden Weeks," page 194].) First of all, although Jinghong has a large Han population, it's still a Dai town (see page 237). The main streets look much like main streets everywhere else in China (except for the palm trees), but when you go behind the concrete buildings, there are narrow lanes and Dai houses, wooden houses, just as in any Dai village to the west or south of here. Last night I was walking back from the night market and a rickshaw guy asked me, "Pai nai?" *Pai nai*— "where (are you) going?"—is Thai, not Mandarin.

Dai women wear sarongs and walk in that certain Southeast Asian way, the way that comes perhaps from wearing a sarong one's whole life. How this must look to a visitor from Xi'an, or Tianjin, where winter is mean and miserable, I can only imagine. Here there are fields of pineapple and plantations of bananas. When I was a child growing up in Wyoming, where winter and even spring are monsters, my family would drive in December all the way to southern California, where people were wearing shorts and T-shirts. I remember thinking how unfair it was.

Jinghong, by the way, is going to change a lot in the next short while, short even by Chinese standards today. If you travel south from here toward the Lao border, the landscape is punctuated by a surreal super-highway being built high up in the sky, not yet open but soon to be. It will connect southwestern China and Southeast Asia, cutting down through northern Laos into north Thailand. Massive concrete pillars rise up from the jungly terrain, and an even more massive amount of concrete has made a highway on top of the pillars. Why are they building the highway in the sky, as opposed to on the ground? Maybe they want to keep the international bus and truck traffic separate from the locals. We don't really know, but we do know which country is using a lot of concrete these days. J

OPPOSITE: Young Buddhist monks congregate on the open verandah of a monastery building near Menghan, in southern Yunnan, not far from Jinghong. Monasteries and temples were closed during the Cultural Revolution and many were destroyed, but now some have been rebuilt. The Dai, like the Thai and the Lao, follow the Hinayana ("lesser path") school of Buddhism.

GRILLED PICKEREL FROM BURQIN

The town of Burqin (pronounced "boor-chin"), in the far north of Xinjiang province, is a hard place to make sense of upon first arrival. All the major buildings in the center of town have been built, or perhaps renovated, with architectural facades that look like a cross between Southern U.S. "plantation" architecture and nineteenth-century Moscow. It's very strange. There are whitewashed stuccoed walls and wildly elaborate pale gray and sky blue lines of trim. Getting out of an overnight bus from Urumqi, Xinjiang's bustling capital city, you suddenly feel as if you are on a movie set, but it's hard to tell where the movie set ends and real life begins.

So why the strange architecture? One person told me it was because of all the tourists they hope to attract, coming from all across China and sleeping here overnight on their way to Kanas Lake (see "Golden Weeks," page 194). Others told me it was because Burqin has become an important market town in the growing trade between China and Russia, while still others said it was "oil pipeline" money. Whatever it is, if you visit Burqin, be prepared to be surprised!

And also, if you're there, be sure to check out the night market near the two or three main hotels. The whole market centers around freshwater fish, and it is a good place to eat. This recipe is a version of the grilled trout I ate there.

Serve with rice and several side dishes, a soup such as Hui Vegetable Soup (page 48), and a green like Pea Tendril Salad (page 66).

Two 1¼- to 1½-pound pickerel or trout, cleaned and scaled
2 teaspoons chile pepper flakes or crushed dried red chile
2 teaspoons coarse sea salt

Prepare a fire in a charcoal grill or preheat a gas grill.

Rinse the fish and make sure they have been completely scaled (use a sharp knife to scrape off any remaining scales). Lay the fish on a cutting board and cut 3 or 4 deep parallel slashes in both sides of each one, spacing them about 1 inch apart and cutting all the way down to the bones.

Mix the chile flakes and salt together in a small bowl. Rub the mixture on the fish, into the slashes and over the skin.

Grill the fish over medium-high heat, about 4 to 5 inches from the flame, for approximately 2 minutes on the first side, then use tongs to turn them over. Cover the grill and cook for approximately 8 minutes. Take off the lid and let the fish cook for 1 more minute, then check for doneness. The flesh should be firm to the touch and should flake with a fork (test next to the bone in one of the slashes at the thickest part of each fish).

Transfer to a platter and serve.

Serves 4 as a main course

NOTE ON SERVING: Put out the whole fish on two plates or a platter and invite guests to lift pieces off; turn each fish over when the first side has been cleaned. *Alternatively*, lift the flesh off the fish before serving, and serve it on individual plates; this way guests avoid having to deal with bones.

MIAO RED-SAUCED FISH

The day I spent in the village of Xijiang, the weather was variable—typical of Guizhou province, in other words. Hits of intense sun were followed by dull light and the threat of rain, then once again the cloud cover would part and the day would brighten. After climbing up steep flagstone paths to the top of the village, the largest Miao village in China, and admiring the views of the sloping roofs below, I found a different route down. At the bottom of the hill was a small "main street" with a little family-run restaurant/café, a man sitting under a tree with some fresh pork for sale, a post office, and a bank.

I was starving after my morning of climbing and exploring the village, and perhaps that's what made the food I ordered for lunch taste so great, but I don't think so. The fish was fresh from the river, the vegetables locally grown. This is the fish I had, fish cooked in an intensely flavored sauce. I don't know what species the fish was; we've tested the recipe using white bass and white perch, and both worked well, though we preferred the white bass. Use whatever small white-fleshed fish you prefer.

You can prepare the dish in the kitchen, or instead cook it at the table, hot-pot-style, as described below. Serve as part of a rice-based meal, accompanied by a simple mild-tasting vegetable dish, perhaps one with some crunch such as Jicama–Tofu Sheet Stir-Fry (page 105), or a fresh cucumber salad. [PHOTOGRAPH ON PAGE 231]

One 1½-pound freshwater fish, such as white bass,
 white perch, or tilapia, cleaned and scaled

2 tablespoons peanut oil or vegetable oil

1 generous tablespoon sliced garlic

1 tablespoon thinly sliced Pickled Red Chiles (page 34) or store-
 bought pickled chiles, or ½ red cayenne chile, seeded and sliced

½ teaspoon ground dry-roasted Sichuan peppercorns

1 teaspoon chile bean paste (see Glossary)

1 cup water

½ cup diced fresh or canned tomato

½ teaspoon salt, or to taste

¼ cup minced Chinese celery leaves for garnish (optional)

Wash the fish and then cut it crosswise in half or into wide steaks. Set aside.

Heat the oil in a wide heavy saucepan (8 to 10 inches in diameter) over medium-high heat. When it is hot, add the garlic and stir-fry for a moment. Toss in the sliced chiles and cook over medium heat until the garlic has softened, about 1 minute. Add the Sichuan pepper, the chile bean paste, and the water, stirring to dissolve the flavorings in the water, and bring to a boil. Add the tomato and boil gently until it is well softened and falling apart, about 3 minutes. Lower the heat and simmer for 10 minutes. Stir in the salt, then taste and adjust if you wish. (*The broth can be prepared ahead and set aside until you are ready to cook the fish. Bring back to a boil before proceeding.*)

To cook the fish at the table, family-style, place a portable stove (an electric hot plate or a small propane stove) on the table and set the pot of broth on it. When everyone is seated and the broth has come back to a boil, slide the fish into the broth, being careful not to splash. *To cook the fish on the stovetop,* slide it into the broth. In either case, once the broth comes back to a boil, cook the fish for about 3 minutes. Use a slotted spoon or chopsticks to turn the pieces over and cook for another 3 to 4 minutes; the flesh should be firm to the touch. Use a slotted spoon to lift the fish out of the broth. Transfer to a wide serving bowl.

Invite guests to help themselves by pulling pieces of fish off the bone with their chopsticks and then spooning the hot sauce over their fish or their rice as they eat.

Serves 3 or 4 as part of a rice meal

NOTE ON SERVING: You can lift the flesh off the bones before serving. Place it in a wide serving bowl, pour sauce over, and serve as above.

NOTE ON LEFTOVERS: We've discovered that both fish and broth are wonderful eaten at room temperature, as leftovers. The texture of the fish becomes firmer as it cools, and the flavors blend happily together.

LEFT: *Three Ge women in the town of Chong'an, in Guizhou province. The Ge are considered by the Chinese authorities and by many Miao/Hmong to be a subset of the Hmong culture, though the Ge disagree.* RIGHT: *An example of Miao embroidery, a band of decoration on an indigo-dyed coat.* OPPOSITE: *Miao Red-Sauced Fish (page 229).*

DONG FESTIVE STEAMED WHOLE FISH

The Dong in Guizhou and Guanxi provinces live far from the sea, and most of their fish is fresh from local streams and ponds. But for this dish, which I had at a party in Zhaoxing, in eastern Guizhou, we like to ignore tradition and use red snapper, a beautiful ocean fish. The head and tail are left on, so that when the fish is presented, freshly steamed and then flavored with a drizzle of hot oil, it looks like a painting, beautifully vivid, and appetizing too. Use whatever fish you like but try to find one that fits in your steamer (see Note).

To steam the fish, you will need a 12- to 14-inch-wide bamboo steamer and a wok or a wide pot with a bamboo or metal steamer insert. You will also need a deep heatproof plate (there will be some pan juices) that just fits into the steamer and is wide enough to hold the fish.

> One 1½-pound red snapper, cleaned and scaled
>
> ¾ teaspoon salt
>
> 1 tablespoon minced ginger
>
> 2 scallions, cut lengthwise into ribbons and then into 2-inch lengths
>
> 1 red cayenne chile, seeded and cut into thin strips
>
> Generous 1 tablespoon peanut oil or vegetable oil
>
> 5 or 6 Sichuan peppercorns, lightly crushed

Wash the fish well and dry it. Check that the fish fits onto the plate you are using in the steamer (see headnote and Note below); you can curve the fish a little on the plate, or trim off the end of the tail or even the head if necessary to make it fit.

Place the fish on a cutting board and cut 2 or 3 parallel diagonal slashes in each side of it, cutting down to the bone. Rub all over lightly with the salt. Rub the minced ginger into the slashes and into the fish cavity. Place the fish on the plate and sprinkle the scallion ribbons into the cavity and over the fish. Sprinkle any remaining ginger over the top of the fish and then sprinkle on the red chile strips. Place the plate with the fish in the steamer basket or insert.

Place the wok or pot on the stove and add about 2 inches of water. Place the steamer basket in the wok or pot (make sure the water is below the level of the steamer) and bring the water to a boil over high heat. Cover the steamer tightly and cook for 10 or 11 minutes, until the fish is firm and the flesh in the slashes is opaque and flakes when pulled with a fork.

Meanwhile, just before the fish is done, at about the 9-minute mark, heat the oil in a small wok or skillet. When it is very hot, toss in the Sichuan pepper, lower the heat to medium, and cook for 30 seconds. Remove from the heat.

Uncover the cooked fish and pour the hot oil over it. Lift the steamer out and onto a work surface, then remove the plate from the steamer. Serve the fish on the plate, with its pan juices, hot or at room temperature.

Serves 4 as part of a rice meal

NOTE ON STEAMERS: There's a limit to the size of fish that a round bamboo steamer can hold, but you can improvise a steaming arrangement in a large roasting pan for a larger fish: Place two trivets in the pan. Place the fish on a long deep heatproof platter and put the platter on the trivets. Add water to the pan, making sure it is below the level of the platter, then cover and steam.

Two older Miao women at the weekly market in Chong'an, in Guizhou. Their long hair is pinned up and covered. The woman on the left is wearing a headscarf that has been indigo-dyed a deep purple-brown, and you can see the head of her silver hair ornament through the folds.

snails

As I sat there in the open-air night market eating area, with stalls at the edges and tables in the center, almost Thai-style, I was very pleased to be in Kaili (a small city in Guizhou). The market was on a hill at the top of a sloping street lined with stalls selling fruit and sunglasses and cheap clothing, and lots besides. The air was soft, and I was about to eat some tiny snails, which looked delicious.

The stall where I sat sold hot-pot sorts of things and also stir-fries to order, but the woman cooking, Lulu, had a pot already bubbling. When I looked closely, I had seen there were small snails simmering away in a chile-red liquid, so I had ordered a plate.

I was her first customer of the evening (the food stalls really get going only after eight). She brought me a bowl of the snails in their sauce, a small bowl of rice, a plastic bag, some toothpicks, and some tissues. She showed me how to put the plastic bag over my hand so I could hold each hot snail while I used a toothpick to ease off its little protective lid and then pull out the moist, pleasantly chewy creature. It takes some doing. Lulu watched me struggle a bit, then came over and showed me the technique again, coming back a few minutes later to check that I'd made progress. The sauce had large tender chunks of garlic in it, slices of ginger, and lots of Sichuan peppercorns, as well as a hint of fennel and plenty of chopped dried red chiles. It was very intense.

Two kids from the next stall came by to have a look at me. Soon they got confident enough to try some English—single vocabulary words, with good pronunciation—as I went on working my way through the pile of snails. They were a brother and sister. They'd never spoken English before, they told me, and it was sweet seeing them take the chance to engage.

When I finally made it to the last snail, Lulu came over. Did I want to wash my hands? "Yes," I said, and so she poured clean water over my hands, until all traces of chile-tinted oil were gone. As I left, the kids called out "good-bye, good-bye . . ." **N**

DEEP-FRIED WHITING

This take on deep-fried fish, which I had in a rural market in a small Dong village in eastern Guizhou, is surprisingly easy. We use whiting, which looks similar to the local fish, long and slender (about 1 inch across at its widest point and about 10 inches long). If you have no access to whiting, use a slender fish or part of a fish, such as the tail end of a cod. The fish is cut crosswise into 1½-inch pieces, smeared with chile paste, and quickly deep-fried. The fish is succulent and mildly hot. The deep-frying tightens the flesh, so it slides off the bone when you pick the fish up with chopsticks, making it very easy to eat.

Like many deep-fries, this can be a main course, but it also makes a great snack to serve with beer, especially, we find, if your guests are hanging around the kitchen waiting for supper. Put it out hot from the pan, perhaps with some slices of cucumber for a contrast of texture and temperature and some (nontraditional) lemon wedges if you wish; guests can eat with chopsticks or with their fingers. If you're serving it as part of a meal, serve with rice, a cooling salad or mild soup, and a green vegetable.

> 1½ to 2 pounds (7 to 9) whiting or other slender fish,
> cleaned, scaled, and fins, head, and tail cut off
> About ¼ cup Bright Red Chile Paste (page 18) or Guizhou
> Chile Paste (page 35) or store-bought chile paste
> About 2 teaspoons salt
> 3 tablespoons cornstarch
> Peanut oil for deep-frying

Wash the fish and dry well. Using a cleaver or sharp heavy knife, cut the fish crosswise into approximately 1½-inch pieces and place in a wide bowl. Add the chile paste and 1 teaspoon of the salt and mix well to distribute the flavorings. Sprinkle on the cornstarch and again mix. The fish will not be coated but just smeared with flavoring. Set aside.

Place a large wok or deep pot on your stovetop; make sure the wok or pot is stable. (Or use a deep-fryer.) Pour 2 inches of oil into the wok or pot and heat the oil over high heat. Put out a slotted spoon or a mesh skimmer. To test the temperature of the oil, hold a wooden chopstick vertically in the oil, with the end touching the bottom of the pot. If the oil bubbles up around it, it has reached temperature. The oil should not be smoking; if it is, lower the heat slightly and wait for it to cool. Then test again. (A deep-fry thermometer should read 325° to 350°F.)

Carefully slide in one piece of fish. The oil will bubble around it, but it should not brown immediately, just start changing color. A little of the chile paste will come off in the oil; don't worry. Add 3 or 4 or 5 more pieces of fish (if you have a large pot or deep-fryer, you will probably have room for more). Use the slotted spoon or mesh skimmer to move the fish around in the oil and turn it occasionally, handling it gently so it stays intact. The fish will be cooked in about 2 minutes, perhaps 3, depending on how much you cook at one time; when done, the flesh will be firm and opaque and will slide easily off the bone. Use the spoon or skimmer to lift out the pieces, pausing to let excess oil drain off them, and transfer to a paper-towel-lined plate. Repeat with the remaining fish (see Note). Serve hot.

Serves 4 to 6 as an appetizer, 4 as part of a rice meal

NOTE ON FRYING: Because some of the paste flavoring the fish will come off as it fries, you may want to skim the chile debris out of the oil partway through cooking. Use a fine-mesh sieve to clear it out of the oil, then discard it.

OPPOSITE: *Deep-Fried Whiting, made instead with the tail ends of several cod.*

LEFT: *A traditional Dai house in Menghan, southern Yunnan. On stilts and built of bamboo, it has an airy long porch and kitchen, and underneath, at ground level, large clay pots brewing rice liquor are stored.* RIGHT: *A Dai woman in traditional sarong, blouse, and hat, with her Chinese bicycle and carrying basket, outside Menghan.*

THE DAI PEOPLE

The label "Dai" in China is given to people from several Tai cultures, primarily the Tai Lü but also the Shan and Tai Koen people. The Dai live in southern and southwestern Yunnan and speak a language related to Thai, Lao, Dong, Zhuang, and others, all of which are members of the Tai-Kadai group of languages. The Dai are the majority culture in the area called Xishuangbanna (in Mandarin, or Sipsongpanna in Dai), at the southern tip of Yunnan, where it borders Burma and Laos. There are also large groups of Dai farther west in the Ruili area of Yunnan, near the Burma border. In all, they number over twenty million people in China.

The Dai were originally animists, and some of those beliefs and practices linger (a respect for trees and for the natural world, a fear of ghosts and other supernatural beings), but the Dai have been Buddhist for over a thousand years, following Theravada Buddhism. Most Dai villages have a Buddhist temple (*wat*), usually with a small monastery attached. Many of these were damaged or destroyed during the Cultural Revolution, then rebuilt in the 1980s and 1990s.

Dai houses are large, graceful wood structures built high on wooden stilts. Under a wide sloping roof is the area for living, cooking, and sleeping. Often there is an open deck where washing is hung to dry and vegetables may be dried before pickling. The kitchen is usually an airy, open-sided roofed area at the back of the house. The space under the house is the work area, for weaving (Dai women, like Dong and other Tai women, are known for their handwoven fabric), for pounding dried chiles, for brewing rice liquor, and for grinding soaked rice paste to make rice noodle batter. It also shelters chickens and pigs and is used for storage.

Like other Tai peoples, the Dai are lowland rice cultivators whose traditional staple is sticky rice (though plain rice is also eaten). Most village households have a small pond behind the house or access to a nearby pond. The ponds are stocked with freshwater fish and are also home to small frogs and crayfish, all of which find their way into the cooking. Fresh uncooked greens and leaves are a part of most meals. Like people in northern Laos and northern Thailand, the Dai gather river weed, sometimes called river moss, air-dry it, and then stir-fry it with flavorings or mix it with sticky rice, wrap it in banana leaves, and grill it.

Grilling is an essential cooking technique that is also used to impart flavor. Vegetables are grilled, then pounded in a mortar to make salsas, and tofu, meat, and fish are all simply grilled. Rice or fish or combinations of foods are often wrapped in banana leaves and steamed or grilled.

Flavorings include salt, as well as chiles (both fresh and dried), black pepper, Sichuan pepper, and an array of herbs, roots, and rhizomes: coriander, mint, scallions, shallots, garlic, ginger, galangal, and wild herbs.

CHICKEN AND EGGS

CHICKEN IS SUCH AN EVERYDAY DISH FOR MANY people in North America that it is difficult for us to imagine a meat-eating culture where chicken is not considered an acceptable food. Tibet, especially rural Tibet, is a place where people traditionally consider chicken inedible, and they tend not to eat eggs either. Perhaps that's not surprising, given that hens don't lay very well at higher elevations—most of Tibet lies at more than 10,000 feet above sea level.

As a result, the recipes in this chapter come from else-where: delectable chicken kebabs from the oases of Xinjiang, where chicken is a special treat, much less common than lamb or goat (see page 247); another take on grilled chicken, from the Dai of southern Yunnan (see page 252); a warming chicken and vegetable stew from Guizhou (see page 250); and a homey version of chicken with noodles from the Altai Mountains of northern Xinjiang (see page 246).

Though we've seen duck for sale at rural markets in Yunnan and Guizhou, we've rarely eaten it there, perhaps because it's a bird for a special occasion, not for everyday eating. Consequently we haven't included any recipes for duck.

We will always have a fondness for omelets, especially when we think of traveling in hardscrabble places. Even when there's not much available in a truck-stop restaurant, there will usually be eggs, as well as oil, salt, and a few vegetables, fresh or dried, to toss into the wok. That image of the omelet as the traveler's friend is why you will find omelet recipes here: eggs cooked in a hot wok with simple local flavors. And they always taste so good!

OPPOSITE: *A kebab cook at a night market in Altai, in northern Xinjiang.*
ABOVE: *Amaranth greens: they can be green all over, green tinted with reddish purple, or even mostly purple.*

MARKET-DAY OMELET

After a long day at a rural market in Chong'an, in Guizhou province,
a day spent photographing the pigs, dogs, chickens, ducks, and horses
for sale, and also the noodle vendors, the Miao and Ge women in their
market-day finery (see page 183), the flower sellers, the tofu makers,
and more, I was almost blind with tiredness. On the way back to my
guesthouse, I stopped in at a small café-restaurant perched above the
river. There were no other customers around, so I waited in the kitchen
chatting with the owners, a Miao couple, while they made me a quick
supper: rice, stir-fried pork with stem lettuce (see Pork with Napa
Cabbage and Chiles, page 298), and a fabulous light-as-air tomato
omelet quickly cooked in the wok.

At home, we use our wok almost every day, often for several of
the dishes in a meal. Many dishes that we associate with European
tradition are transformed when they are cooked in a wok, and omelets
are an outstanding example. The eggs are whisked well, oil is added to
the hot wok and swirled around, and then the foaming eggs are poured
in. They cook untouched, apart from a slight tilting of the pan, for about
a minute, browning beautifully on the bottom; then the omelet is turned
over to cook briefly on the other side. The essentials are thorough
whisking and enough very hot oil.

1 scallion

3 large or extra-large eggs

½ cup finely chopped tomato (1 medium)

½ teaspoon salt, or to taste

2 tablespoons peanut oil or vegetable oil

Trim the scallion and smash it with the side of a cleaver or knife. Thinly
slice lengthwise, then mince the white and tender green parts. Set aside.

Break the eggs into a medium bowl, add the tomato, and whisk
until very foamy. Set aside.

Put out a serving plate.

Place a large well-seasoned wok over high heat. When it is hot, add
the oil and swirl the oil slightly to coat the sides of the wok. Add the salt
to the eggs and whisk. Add the scallion, then pour the egg mixture into
the hot oil. It will bubble and sputter a little. Let it cook for 10 seconds
or so, then tilt the wok slightly in several directions to encourage the
liquid eggs to flow over the cooked edges of the omelet; do not stir.
Continue to cook for 45 seconds to 1 minute, then use a spatula to turn
the omelet over (the bottom should be well browned) and lower the heat
very slightly. Cook for another 20 to 30 seconds, then turn out onto the
serving plate and serve hot.

Serves 1 as a main dish, 2 as part of a rice meal

OMELET WITH TREE EARS

On our first few visits to Tibet, we ate a lot of tree ear fungus. For some reason it was one of the few "vegetables" commonly available in Lhasa and other towns. Perhaps it came in with the Sichuan cooks who traveled out to Tibet in the mid-1980s and started tiny private-enterprise restaurants, or maybe it was in Tibet long before then. It has the advantage that it stores very well in dried form and rehydrates well. In the cold winter months in Tibet, where vegetable choices were few, it was a welcome taste of the plant world.

Tree ear fungus is inexpensive and easy to cook with. In Chinese medicine, it is considered to be very good for the heart. It has a very distinctive texture, slightly chewy, but not at all tough. You can buy tree ears (dark) or their cousins, cloud ears (paler), and either will work fine in this recipe (see photo, page 65). Tree ears look like shriveled little lumps before they are soaked. These days, you can also buy sliced tree ears (sometimes labeled tree fungus), but the texture is not as good, so we suggest that you buy only the whole ones.

We've found that a pinch of cayenne powder or freshly ground black pepper works well in this omelet. If you want to add this spike of heat, add it to the eggs with the salt.

4 to 5 pieces dried tree ears (see Glossary)

3 large or extra-large eggs

½ teaspoon salt

2 tablespoons peanut oil

1 teaspoon minced ginger

1 tablespoon minced scallion

Rinse the tree ears, then place them in a small bowl and pour boiling water over to cover generously. Set aside to soak for 20 minutes.

Drain the tree ears and rinse well. Slice them into thin strips, discarding any tough patches. You should have about 2 tablespoons. Set aside.

In a small bowl, whisk the eggs and salt together until very foamy. Set near your stovetop.

Put out a serving plate.

Heat a wok over high heat. When it is hot, add the oil, then, 10 seconds later, add the minced ginger and the tree ears. Cook for about 20 seconds. Toss the scallion into the eggs and give them a final whisk, then pour them into the pan. There will be a sizzling and bubbling as the egg mixture meets the hot oil. Tip the wok to allow the eggs to spread out to a wider circle. Repeat in another direction. Use your spatula to gently fold several edges of the eggs in toward the center, then again tip the wok so that liquid eggs flow onto the hot pan. Within about 1 minute, most of the egg will be cooked, leaving a liquid center. Use your spatula to turn the omelet over gently and let it cook for another 10 to 15 seconds. Turn it out of the wok onto the plate.

Serves 2 as part of a rice meal; 1 as a main course over rice or with bread

In the frozen snowy expanses of the Changtang, the high-elevation plateau of western Tibet, a Tibetan man tries to steady his horse so he can mount and get traveling again.

It's autumn, a chilly time of year in northern Mongolia. The wind blows constantly. The summer-lush-green grasslands are now bare beige and pale yellow, frozen, dried out, and ready to be covered with snow. The *gers* (the Mongol version of yurts) look like small bumps on the plain and blend right in. Seen up close, there is a little vividness to them, a painted window frame, a colorful door, but from afar, their medium-brown to pale-dun felt covering is just another natural color in a pale landscape. Horses and cattle, too, disappear in the vastness of the prairie, dark and lighter-colored dots. Closer, I can see their heads are down, searching out the scarce blades of grass, until suddenly, perhaps with a change in the wind, something alerts them, and all heads come up.

The other day I met a young Mongol woman called Saren, who lives in the Hulun Buir grasslands with her mother. I asked her how she felt about the summertime and the two-month tourist season. Did her family earn money from tourists? "Yes," she said, "the money is pretty good. We often slaughter a sheep for a group, then cook and serve it Mongol style. Now the tourist season is over, we have money saved to get us through the winter."

She and her mother had moved their *gers*, two of them, one for living and cooking, one for storage, down from the hills to a site near the winding river, whose sky-reflecting intense blue is the only color in the landscape. Neighboring *gers* are a walk or short horseback ride away. Through the winter, until May, Saren and her mother will carry water from the river for drinking and washing. They'll heat their *ger* with a small wood-fired stove, and themselves with endless cups of milk tea or butter tea, and with meals of simmered lamb. (Before summer, they'll move back up to the hilltop, to catch the breezes.)

To get to town, they can walk or hitch a ride down the five-mile track to the highway. One of the buses that come by on the highway every hour or so will take them into Hailar, in about an hour. A trip to town to buy staples (tea, flour, salt, anything but dairy products or meat, which they get from their herd) is an all-day affair.

"Do you like it in town?" I asked Saren.

"No, too noisy, too many people. Here we can speak our language and take care of ourselves and our animals. The cows need to be milked, the young animals cared for. . ." **N**

OPPOSITE: *The Hulun Buir grasslands are dull-colored after the first frost, and Mongol herders move their* gers *down into the valleys to be closer to the streams and rivers. Here one* ger *has already been set up, while the new-style metal frame for the other awaits its covering of wood and canvas and felt; a dog keeps careful watch.*

CHICKEN AND NOODLES TUVAN-STYLE

We don't know if this dish is actually Tuvan or Kazakh. I had it in the village of Hom, in the far northern part of Xinjiang province. The village itself was Tuvan, but many of the people in the small hotel where I was staying were Kazakh, as were several of the cooks. I should have been more alert and asked more questions, but the night I had this chicken with noodles, I was exhausted, cold and wet, and a little shaken up (see "Motorcycle," page 300). It was all I could do to watch them make it, first chopping the onions and carrots, then putting in the chicken to cook, making the dough for the noodles, and rolling them out.

When the bowl of noodles with chicken at last arrived at my table, it tasted not only very good, but also amazingly familiar: it was just like the chicken and noodles my Grandmother Jesse used to make for all my birthdays as a child. Chicken, homemade noodles, bay leaf, black pepper—simple and direct.

CHICKEN

One 2½-pound chicken, or 2½ pounds chicken legs or breasts

1 large onion (¾ pound), diced

2 medium carrots, peeled and diced

3 quarts water

2 teaspoons salt

½ teaspoon freshly ground black pepper

3 or 4 bay leaves

NOODLES

1½ cups all-purpose flour, plus extra if needed

½ teaspoon salt

2 medium eggs

About ½ cup warm water

Wash the chicken. If using a whole chicken, use a cleaver to cut into about 6 large pieces. Put the chicken in a large pot along with the diced onion and carrots. Add the water, salt, black pepper, and bay leaves and bring to a boil, then reduce the heat and simmer for about 1½ hours.

While the chicken is cooking, make the noodles. Mix the flour and salt in a bowl, and then turn out onto a work surface. Make a well in the center of the flour, break the eggs into the well, and add the warm water. With your fingers, start mixing the flour into the liquid ingredients, incorporating more and more of the flour until a dough forms. If the dough seems too dry, add a little water; if it seems too moist, add a little flour. *Alternatively*, place the flour and salt in a food processor and pulse to mix them. Add the eggs and process to mix. Then, with the blade running, gradually add the water and process until a ball of dough forms.

Turn the dough out onto a lightly floured work surface and knead for 5 minutes. It should be very smooth. Cover with plastic and let rest for 30 minutes.

On a well-floured surface, roll the dough out quite thin, to a square about 20 inches by 20 inches. Let sit for 10 minutes, then liberally flour the top of the dough. Roll the dough up into a long cylinder. Using a sharp or a serrated knife, cut the dough into ½-inch-wide noodles. You can let them sit as is until needed, or you can unwind them and use your hands to stretch them even more. If you unwind them, hang them on the back of a chair.

When the chicken is cooked, lift it out of the pot and let it cool just a bit. Remove the skin, then take the meat off the bones and discard the skin and bones. Shred the meat into smaller pieces with your fingers, and put it back into the pot.

Bring the broth to a rolling boil, then add the noodles. They will cook in about 5 minutes, but keep checking, because the cooking time depends upon how much the noodles have dried out. You want them cooked through but still a little firm to the bite.

Put out large pasta bowls or soup bowls. Use tongs or long chopsticks to lift the noodles out of the broth and distribute them among the bowls. Ladle the broth over the noodles and distribute the chicken on top.

Serves 4 as a main course

OASIS CHICKEN KEBABS

Lamb and goat are much more common than chicken in Uighur cooking (see "The Uighur People," page 90), so these kebabs are a special treat. The frugal way of making them is to buy a whole chicken (3½ to 4 pounds), cut off the meat for the kebabs, and then use the rest of the chicken to make soup. Alternatively, you can start with packaged boneless breasts and/or thighs. If you can, use free-range or organic chicken, so you have lots of flavor to work with, as people do in the oases.

Traditionally seasoning is rather spare—a light sprinkling of salt, cumin, and cayenne, added as the grilling starts and again partway through cooking—and that's the style we use here. In Xinjiang, grilling is done slowly, over relatively low heat, and the skewers are turned frequently so all sides are exposed to the heat. We mimic the slow-cooking technique by covering our charcoal grill during cooking, which keeps the meat moist and the coals at a low heat; if you are using a gas grill, set the flame to a lower setting than usual.

Serve the kebabs with flatbreads, such as Uighur Nan (page 190) or Home-Style Tajik Nan (page 191), with store-bought flatbreads, or with rice, and accompany with a fresh salad or simple sliced tomatoes or cucumber, lightly salted.

> 2 pounds boneless, skinless chicken breasts and/or thighs
>
> ½ teaspoon salt
>
> 1 teaspoon crushed or ground cumin seeds
>
> ¼ teaspoon cayenne

If using wooden skewers, soak 10 to 12 long (12-inch) skewers in water for 30 minutes.

Prepare a fire in a charcoal grill or preheat a gas grill. You want a well-developed bed of charcoal or a medium to low flame in a gas grill (see headnote). Place a rack about 5 inches from the coals or flame.

Meanwhile, cut the chicken into ¾- to 1-inch cubes. (Cut breasts lengthwise into 3 pieces and then slice crosswise.) Slide the pieces onto wooden or metal skewers, leaving a tiny space between pieces and at least 2 inches clearance at either end of the skewers. We find it's easier to cook the meat evenly if each skewer is not too loaded down. Set aside on a tray.

Once the grill is ready, place the skewers on the rack. Sprinkle on about one-third of the salt and cumin and a pinch of cayenne. Cover the grill and cook for about 4 minutes. Use tongs to loosen the meat from the rack and turn the skewers on their sides. Cover and grill for another 3 minutes. Give the skewers another quarter turn and sprinkle with the remaining flavorings. Cover and grill for another 3 minutes. Turn the skewers and give the final side another 2 or 3 minutes, covered. Check the chicken at the center of one skewer for doneness (timing will vary with the heat of your fire and also with the type of skewers you use; metal skewers conduct heat, making cooking time a little shorter), and remove the skewers when cooked through.

Serve on the skewers, or slide the chicken pieces off the skewers onto a central platter, so guests can help themselves.

Serves 4 to 6 as a main course

ABOVE: *A Dong woman heads to a small weekly market in eastern Guizhou, with baskets of dried greens on her carrying pole.* OPPOSITE, LEFT: *Dong Chicken Hot Pot (page 250) with condiment bowls of Bright Red Chile Paste (page 18) and pickled mustard greens.* OPPOSITE, RIGHT: *Two young Dong women chat in the evening in Zhaoxing.*

DONG CHICKEN HOT POT

In the Dong village of Zhaoxing, in eastern Guizhou, it is taken for granted that every evening meal includes a soup or stew. When they were speaking Mandarin with me, the Dong people I met called this kind of dish *huo guo*, or hot pot. Placed in the center of the family table, the pot always felt to me like the symbol of home: shared sustenance.

This one is a generous chicken stew, thick with carrots and potatoes and subtly warmed with ginger, Sichuan pepper, and chiles. The broth has a pleasing depth of flavor and complexity, with no one taste dominating. The whole dish comes together in just over an hour, most of that simmering time. It can be made several hours ahead, then reheated just before you wish to serve it.

In the recipe, we suggest a fairly standard Dong fall or winter vegetable combination of potato, carrot, and daikon radish. In another season, you could substitute thinly sliced zucchini and other summer squash for the potato and carrot. (Cooking time will be a little shorter, so the daikon should be added at the same time as the zucchini.) There were also leafy greens stirred into the family hot pot when I was in Zhaoxing, which make a lovely splash of bright green, but you can omit them if you wish.

All the vegetables are thinly sliced. A cleaver is the easiest tool for the job, but a Benriner or other vegetable slicer or a large sharp chef's knife also makes quick work of it. The carrots should be sliced on a diagonal, to make larger medallions. The potatoes and daikon are sliced lengthwise in half and then into thin half-moons. Cut this way, the vegetables cook quickly and are very attractive in the broth.

Serve with rice as a substantial main course. Put out a tart salad, such as Cucumber–Tree Ear Salad (page 79), to balance the warm, slightly sweet richness of the stew. You could also put out side condiments: some chopped pickled mustard greens or Tenzin's Quick-Pickled Radish Threads (page 25), as well as a chile paste (page 18 or 35), for those who like intense flavors. [PHOTOGRAPH ON PAGE 249]

3½ to 4 pounds chicken legs and/or breasts

8 cups water

2 tablespoons ginger cut into small matchsticks

3 garlic cloves, smashed

¼ teaspoon Sichuan peppercorns, lightly crushed or coarsely ground, or more to taste

3 or 4 red cayenne chiles or 5 to 8 dried red chiles

2 tablespoons Shaoxing wine (see Glossary), or substitute balsamic vinegar

2 tablespoons soy sauce, or to taste

2 teaspoons salt, or to taste

1 pound potatoes (4 medium), peeled, cut lengthwise in half, and thinly sliced

1 pound carrots, peeled and thinly sliced on a long diagonal

½ pound daikon radish, peeled, cut lengthwise in half, and thinly sliced (about 1 cup)

2 packed cups spinach or other tender greens, coarsely chopped (optional)

Wash the chicken. Leave the skin on while the chicken cooks, for it adds a lush smoothness as well as flavor to the stew, which contains no other fat. Use a cleaver to chop the chicken into smaller pieces (cut whole legs into 3 or 4 pieces, half-breasts into 2 or 3 pieces). Rinse the pieces again and place in a wide heavy pot (we use our 4-quart Le Creuset pot). Add the water and bring to a boil. Let boil for about 5 minutes, skimming off and discarding the foam that will collect on the surface.

Add the ginger, garlic, Sichuan pepper, and chiles, then lower the heat to maintain a strong simmer. Cook, uncovered, for about 35 minutes, turning the chicken pieces occasionally if they are not completely immersed in the water. Add the wine, soy sauce, and salt and bring back to a boil. The chicken pieces should now be cooked through; cook a little longer if they are not. (If you wish, lift the skin off the chicken and discard.)

Add the potatoes and carrots, stir in, and bring back to a boil. After 5 minutes, add the daikon. Cook until the vegetables are just done, another 5 to 10 minutes. Taste for seasoning and adjust if you wish. (*The stew can be made ahead to this point and set aside for up to 3 hours; refrigerate if for more than 1 hour. Bring back to a strong simmer before proceeding.*)

Add the greens, if using, and stir in. They will turn bright green and be cooked almost at once. Serve hot.

Serves 6 to 8 as a main course with rice

DONG CHICKEN-VEGETABLE SOUP: For the soup version of this stew, use the same amount of water but cut the quantity of all the other ingredients approximately in half. Prepare as above, but simmer the chicken partially covered, and cook the vegetables partly covered as well. Once the vegetables are just barely cooked through, remove the chicken pieces. Let cool for a moment, then lift the meat from the bones and shred or chop into bite-sized pieces. Return the meat to the broth and discard the bones and skin. Taste for seasoning and adjust (you'll probably need to add at least ½ teaspoon salt).

Add the greens, if using, or instead garnish the soup with chopped coriander leaves before serving. Bring back to a strong simmer. Serve hot, distributing the chicken, vegetables, greens, and broth among individual bowls, or put out the pot of soup and a ladle and invite guests to help themselves, family-style. You could also, if you wish, soak 1 pound rice sticks (see Glossary) in warm water for 10 minutes while the soup cooks. Drain and distribute the noodles among individual soup bowls before pouring the soup over.

Serves 6 to 8 as a soup course

Two older Dong men play Chinese chess on a wide wooden bench on one of the covered bridges in Zhaoxing village, in Guizhou. They are sheltered from the rain and the hot sun, but the wide wooden slats on the side of the bridge allow a refreshing breeze to flow.

DAI GRILLED CHICKEN

Like their cousins the Lao, the Dai are brilliant at grilling. Here chicken on the bone is slowly grilled over low heat until succulent. It's rubbed with a blend of crushed garlic and pepper-salt before grilling, so it has a moist spiced crust when it comes off the grill. Absolutely delicious, and any leftovers are wonderful the next day.

Serve on a platter, so guests can help themselves. Accompany with sticky rice (see page 162) or jasmine rice (see page 166), as well as Dai Tart Green Salsa (page 22) or Green Papaya Salad with Chiles (page 78), and Dai Carrot Salad (page 83).

3 pounds whole chicken legs and/or breasts

3 tablespoons crushed garlic

1 tablespoon salt

1½ teaspoons dry-toasted Sichuan peppercorns, ground

1½ teaspoons coarsely ground black pepper

Use a cleaver to chop the legs into 4 pieces each, whole breasts into 4 to 6 pieces. Rinse and place in a wide bowl. Set aside.

Place the garlic in a mortar or a small bowl, add the salt, and mash with a pestle or the back of a wooden spoon to blend. Add both peppers and blend together.

Add the flavor rub to the pieces of chicken and use your hands to rub it all over them. Set aside, covered, while you prepare your grilling arrangement (refrigerate if the wait will be longer than half an hour).

Prepare a low fire in a charcoal grill or preheat a gas grill to medium-hot.

Place the chicken on the grill, cover, and cook for about 20 minutes, or until cooked through; turn occasionally, working quickly and replacing the lid as soon as possible to keep in the moisture and heat. Serve hot.

Serves 6 as a main course

DAI ROAST CHICKEN: This rub of mashed garlic with pepper-salt makes a wonderful coating for roast chicken. Wash and dry the chicken. Stir a tablespoon of oil into the flavor blend and then rub it all over the chicken before roasting at 400°F. This amount of rub will do for a small chicken (under 3 pounds); scale up in proportion if cooking a larger bird.

LEFT: *A view of the Tuvan village of Hom, in the Altai Mountains, with its wooden bridge and wooden houses.*
RIGHT: *Tuvan men on horseback, in Hom. Notice the Kazakh yurt behind them. In this village, Tuvan houses are solid log structures, while the Kazakhs live in yurts.*

THE TUVAN PEOPLE

There are approximately two million Tuvans (sometimes referred to as Tuvinians) in the world today. The majority live in Tuva, a small Central Asian republic east of Kazakhstan; formerly known as Tannu Tuva and part of the USSR, it is now a member of the Russian Federation. Approximately 4,500 Tuvans live in China (another, much larger population lives in present-day Mongolia). The Tuvans in China live in the far north of Xinjiang province. They are concentrated in three large villages located not far from one another in the Altai Mountains: Ak-khabane, Khanas, and Hom.

(In the West, Tuvans are famous for their extraordinary "throat-singing" tradition, but when we asked about it in the Altai region, the Tuvans there told us there were no throat-singers in the small Tuvan population in Xinjiang.)

What's known of Tuvan history in China comes primarily through oral transmission, as there was no written Tuvan script until the twentieth century. We do know, however, that these communities have existed for generations because there is record of them in Chinese government accounts from the Qing Dynasty. The Tuvan language is part of the Siberian branch of the Turkic language family. In China today, Tuvans (referred to in China as Tuwa) do not have their own "minority people"

category (see Glossary) but are classified as Mongol.

Tuvan culture is traditionally based upon hunting and herding. The Altai Mountains are heavily forested with conifers and poplars on their lower slopes and in the valleys, and there is still wild game for hunting. Because of the high elevation and northern latitude, there are only about eighty frost-free days a year, making agriculture difficult. Herds of cattle, sheep, and horses are kept at high pastures in the summer and lower pastures during the long winter. Like their Kazakh and Mongol neighbors, Tuvans are superb when it comes to riding and breeding horses, and horses can be an important part of personal wealth.

Barley, corn, and potatoes are now a significant supplement to the meat and dairy of the traditional Tuvan diet. Kanas Lake, a long, beautiful body of water in the heart of the Tuvan region of the Altai Mountains, has become a popular destination for Chinese tourists. Tourism has brought cash and seasonal work to the area, but the huge scale of the tourism and of the hotels and other infrastructure being built to support it risks totally overwhelming the Tuvan communities. (See "Genghiskhanistan," page 274.)

LAMB AND BEEF

over a wood fire or charcoal, we're always transported instantly to Central Asia: nomads, desert sands, and clear night skies. The recipes in this chapter come from the wide-open spaces— that is, from greater Tibet, Inner Mongolia, Xinjiang, and neighboring Qinghai. Yaks, goats, and sheep are raised in open grasslands, often by nomads—the yaks in colder climates, in mostly Tibetan areas and in the Pamir Mountains, the sheep and goats in the hills and the oases of Xinjiang. (Recipes from the more settled mild-climate areas beyond the Great Wall are found in the Pork chapter.)

Nomads cook meat either by grilling it over an open fire or by simmering it in a pot. You'll find two classic Central Asian grills here: small pieces of lamb threaded on skewers (Uighur Lamb Kebabs, page 260) and spiced ground lamb wrapped around skewers (Keshmah Kebabs, page 262), both succulent and transporting.

With the growth of towns and cities and improved transportation and communications, traditional ways of cooking have evolved in various ways. The simple Mongolian hot pot of the nomad *ger* (yurt) has been adapted in towns to include an array of condiments and vegetables, and it is a very delicious and interesting way to entertain guests (see page 266). So is Mongolian Barbecue (page 263), with meat quickly cooked at the table, then eaten with a delicious array of side dishes and flavorings. In Tibet, Chinese stir-frying techniques have been adopted by many townspeople, and a greater access to vegetables has also changed traditional meat cooking (see Beef with Mushrooms and Cellophane Noodles, page 280, and Beef and Green Chile Stir-Fry, page 287).

OPPOSITE: *A Uighur man grills lamb streetside in Kashgar, in western Xinjiang. He sprinkles on seasonings with his right hand and fans the charcoal with the board in his left.* ABOVE: *Two varieties of bok choi: regular bok choi (left) and Shanghai bok choi (right). Both varieties are also sold when smaller as "baby bok choi."*

UIGHUR LAMB KEBABS

The Uighur people of Xinjiang speak a Turkic language, and the connection with other Turkic peoples comes through clearly with the food as well. Because of the pomegranate juice, these marinated lamb kebabs have a tart-edged garlicky taste that could almost have come straight from Istanbul. The meat is very succulent, and the grilling straightforward. If you have any left over, it is as tasty as can be the second day.

Serve with flatbreads or rice or noodles, accompanied by a salsa and one or more salads: Cooling Oasis Salad with Tomatoes and Herbs (page 89), Onion and Pomegranate Salad (page 89), and/or Cucumbers in Black Rice Vinegar (page 83).

1 pound boneless lamb leg or shoulder

MARINADE
1 medium onion, coarsely chopped
2 tablespoons vegetable oil
¼ cup pomegranate juice, or substitute ¼ cup fresh lemon juice
    mixed with 1 teaspoon sugar
1 teaspoon salt
1 teaspoon freshly ground black pepper
1 tablespoon finely chopped garlic
¾ teaspoon cayenne

Cut the lamb into small pieces, approximately 1 inch square, leaving on a little fat. Set aside.

Process the onion to a paste in a food processor. Transfer to a medium bowl and stir in the remaining marinade ingredients. Add the lamb pieces and stir so they are all coated with marinade. Cover and let sit for 2 hours in the refrigerator.

Prepare a medium-hot fire in a charcoal grill or preheat a gas grill. If using bamboo skewers, soak 8 skewers in water for 30 minutes.

Thread the pieces of meat onto 8 bamboo or metal skewers (the latter are used in the photograph). Don't crowd them; the pieces of meat should barely touch one another.

Place the skewers on the hot grill, about 4 to 5 inches from the coals. Grill for 2 minutes on the first side, then turn. Cook for 7 to 8 minutes more, turning periodically to ensure good color and even cooking. Cooking times will vary somewhat depending on whether you use bamboo or metal skewers and on the heat of your grill, and whether you wish to leave the lamb pink in the middle or to cook it right through.

Serve on the skewers, on a platter.

Serves 4 to 6 as a main course

KESHMAH KEBABS

These kebabs from Xinjiang, made of ground lamb, resemble the ground meat kebabs found all the way from Turkey to Pakistan. But ground meat is not always easy to work with for a kebab, at least it hasn't been for us. First there is the problem of getting the meat to stay on the skewers, and then there's the problem of the kebabs sticking to the grill. So we started to experiment, and here are a few techniques that have worked well for us.

If you have wide flat metal skewers, the meat will hold its shape well, but if not, you can improvise. We use cheap wooden chopsticks, the kind you often get with Chinese take-out, that come stuck together in pairs and wrapped in paper. We use the two sticks as one skewer, without pulling them apart; the added surface area helps the ground meat adhere better.

With regard to the meat sticking to the grill, we came up with a system where the meat cooks above the grill, not on it, so it can't stick. In Xinjiang, grilling is done over a long narrow metal box that holds the coals. The ends of the skewers rest on either side of the metal box, so the meat is suspended over the heat (see photo, page 258). We used this idea as our starting point: We lay two long metal bars across the grill (rebar, available at Home Depot and other building supply stores, works fine, or use any other metal bars you can find), parallel to each other and about 8 inches apart. We rest the ends of the chopstick-skewers on the metal bars, so the meat is suspended above the grill and doesn't touch it. The arrangement is like a tiny rotisserie. A little improvisational, but it works—and the kebabs taste great!

Serve the kebabs with flatbreads or rice or noodles and a salad such as Pea Tendril Salad (page 66) or Silk Road Tomato–Bell Pepper Salad (page 72).

1 pound boneless lamb or goat leg or shoulder, trimmed
    of membranes, cut into chunks, and chilled
About ½ cup minced lamb or goat fat (see Lamb in Glossary)
1 medium onion, diced
2 large eggs
1 teaspoon salt
½ teaspoon freshly ground black pepper
¾ teaspoon ground cumin, preferably freshly ground
Leaf lettuce and/or sprigs of mint or coriander for garnish

Combine the chilled meat, fat, onion, eggs, salt, pepper, and ground cumin in a food processor and process until the ingredients form a paste, several minutes. Transfer to a bowl, cover, and refrigerate for 30 minutes.

Divide the meat into 8 portions. Shape it into oval patties about 4 inches long and place them on 8 wide metal skewers or chopstick-skewers (see headnote). Lay them on a plate, cover, and refrigerate for 30 minutes.

Arrange two metal bars on your charcoal or gas grill (see headnote), so the kebabs will be 4 to 5 inches above the flame, and prepare a medium-hot fire in the charcoal grill or preheat the gas grill.

Place the skewers on the bars and cook for 8 to 10 minutes, turning regularly to ensure even browning.

Serve hot from the grill, on the skewers, with leaf lettuce and/or fresh herbs.

Serves 4 to 6 as a main course

MONGOLIAN BARBECUE

Thinly sliced lamb is now widely available at Korean groceries and some other East Asian groceries. When we first saw it for sale, beautifully thin slices of lamb lying pink and perfect under cellophane wrapping, we couldn't imagine what the market for it was. But in fact barbecuing at the table ("Mongolian barbecue"), as well as Mongolian hot pot, is starting to become very popular. Thin slices of lamb or beef are an essential ingredient for both.

At its origins, Mongolian barbecue is a way of cooking slices of meat on hot metal over a fire. The name in Chinese, *kao rou*, means just that: cook meat. Once you figure out your at-the-table cooking arrangements, the rest is easy. The special Mongolian barbecue pan (called a *tan guo* in Mandarin) used in homes and restaurants in Inner Mongolia is a convex cast-iron skillet, with a surface 12 inches across that slopes gently from the dome down toward the sides. The pan is placed on an electric hot plate or a small propane stove on the table. We have not seen these pans for sale here, but we find that a wide, well-seasoned cast-iron griddle or heavy skillet makes a great barbecue pan, and we use a small portable propane stove to heat it. Whatever your heat source, make sure you are cooking in a well-ventilated room.

The meat cooks directly on the metal surface. Rather than oiling the pan, we lightly oil the meat slices, because they get better color that way. If your pan starts to accumulate liquid, drain it off into a small pitcher; guests can use the juices to flavor their condiment blends if they wish. The important thing is that the meat not boil in liquid, but instead sear on the hot metal.

Once you've figured out your equipment and bought thinly sliced meat, or sliced it yourself, all you need to prepare are the sauces and condiments. You might also want a side dish of salad as a nontraditional accompaniment (Green Papaya Salad with Chiles, page 78, is a nice option, as is Silk Road Tomato–Bell Pepper Salad, page 72) along with plain rice, or Home-Style Tajik Nan (page 191) or pita breads, cut into wedges.

At each place at the table, put out a small plate, two pairs of chopsticks (one for cooking and one for eating), and several small condiment bowls. As with Mongolian hot pot, we feel that a group of four is the largest number that works easily with this centralized way of cooking. Any more, and the cooking surface gets crowded and hungry guests can start to feel frustrated.

> 1 pound boneless beef or lamb, trimmed of fat and chilled, then thinly sliced and cut into approximately 2-by-1-inch pieces
> 1 teaspoon salt
> About 1 tablespoon peanut oil

CONDIMENTS AND DIPPING SAUCES

> ½ cup soy sauce
> ½ cup Jinjiang (black rice) vinegar
> ¼ cup ginger cut into small matchsticks
> 3 tablespoons Guizhou Chile Paste (page 35), Bright Red Chile Paste (page 18), or store-bought chile paste
> Grasslands Herb Salsa (page 23)

Put the beef or lamb slices in a bowl, add the salt, and toss, then add the oil and toss to coat. Transfer to a platter. Put out the condiments and sauces.

Set a cast-iron skillet or flat cast-iron griddle over a small table-top stove. Heat over medium-high heat until hot. Call your guests to the table and invite them to place a little of one or two condiments into their condiment bowls and to mix flavors if they wish. Then show them how to proceed: Place several slices of meat on the hot skillet or griddle. Cook briefly on the first side, less than a minute, then turn them over with chopsticks and cook on the other side. Lift off onto your plate, or serve to guests to get them started. Dip a slice of meat lightly into some flavoring, then eat. Cook and season and eat at leisure, mixing and matching flavors.

Serves 4 as a main course

Some kind of especially wonderful traveler's luck seemed to be with me on my last trip to Lhasa. The two different places I stayed (the Kyichu Hotel and the Snowland Hotel) were converging points for foreigners and ex-pat Tibetans who were in Lhasa pursuing a variety of interesting projects, from establishing a wildlife preserve to discovering and cataloguing centuries-old Tibetan texts. I'd find myself listening to discussions about bear species, or overgrazing issues, or about the Mongolian invasion of Tibet in the fourteenth century.

But the luckiest encounter of all took place in the courtyard of the Ramoche, a temple in the old city. During the Cultural Revolution, the Ramoche was ransacked, and when I first visited it in 1985, there were still slogans on the walls and unrepaired damage everywhere. These days it's a lively place, humming with prayer, aromatic with the scent of butter lamps (the wick floats in melted butter, which is the lamp oil) and butter offerings, and very well cared for. Outside the gates are stalls selling prayer flags and incense, just as there are vendors of votive candles near cathedrals in Europe.

I was watching the comings and goings in the Ramoche courtyard when I met Nima Dorje and Elisabeth. They were waiting for Nima's cousin, who is the monk-manager there and who was going to escort them around the temple. Nima invited me to join them. As we walked, I learned that Nima had fled Tibet as a young man in 1959 along with many others, including the Dalai Lama. He and Elisabeth had met and married in the United States, where they now live.

Nima is originally from a very old village in Chamdo (sometimes written Qamdo), the large region in eastern Tibet that now is divided between the Tibetan Autonomous Region and the province of Sichuan. It's an area of high mountains and deep river valleys, where people have eked out a living for centuries by herding animals and cultivating a few hardy vegetables, such as carrots and turnips and, more recently, potatoes. Staples of the diet are dried yak meat, butter (added to tea), dried cheese, yogurt, and tsampa, with the odd dried or pickled radish or other green. Nima still has family in his home village. Starting in 1984, when he made his first trip back to Tibet since fleeing so long before, he and Elisabeth have made a visit every three years to his village. Each time, they need to get special permission from the authorities, for the area is closed to casual travelers. The trip from Lhasa, which used to take several months in the fifties on foot or horseback, before there were roads, can now be done in three days by car.

Afterward, we went up to the cousin's apartment for lunch. There we feasted on a variety of dishes (yak meat stir-fried with potato, yak with eggplant and tomato, and more) all served with rice, and we drank tea, sweet milk tea or salty butter tea, as we chose. Elisabeth told me that every time they come to Lhasa, Nima's many friends and the family members who live there all want them to share a meal. Their room at the Snowland Hotel is like a permanent open house.

For the next few days, until Nima and Elisabeth left for eastern Tibet, I watched the stream of visitors bringing gifts of tea and food. And I learned a great deal as I sat in their room watching and listening, not only by asking questions and having the chance to taste a lot of home cooking, but, more important, by seeing how people related to one another. It was a rare privilege. N

OPPOSITE: *A young monk carries a Buddha statue at Sera Monastery, not far from Lhasa in central Tibet. Starting in the 1980s, the monasteries and temples in Tibet began to rebuild and repair images and structures that had been damaged or destroyed during the Cultural Revolution (1966–1976). The work still goes on.*

Near a Mongol village in the Altai Mountains of northern Xinjiang, two Mongol men on horseback, with a camel, head out into the mountains.

MONGOLIAN HOT POT

Hot pot (see "Hot Pot at Home and Away," page 269) is a communal meal, a way of sharing food from the same pot. It's most practical with no more than four people, so you can keep track of your pieces of meat and vegetables and not feel crowded. This way of eating together is rather intimate, so share your hot pot with relaxed good friends, and enjoy!

The recipe here is a kind of deconstruction of the Mongolian nomad original. It's how lamb hot pot is commonly served in restaurants in Inner Mongolia, a way of cooking and eating at the table, a form of fondue, if you like. The broth is made ahead from lamb or goat bones (the easiest way is to buy a leg or shoulder, cut the meat from the bones, use the bones to make the broth, and slice the meat for use in the hot pot). Then the broth is used to cook the meat and the vegetables at the table.

BROTH

About 2 pounds lamb bones (from a 4½- to 5½-pound lamb leg
    or shoulder) or 1 pound lamb shank, cut into pieces

10 cups water

3 slices peeled ginger

2 scallions, cut into 2-inch lengths

HOT POT

One 1-pound package thin rice sticks (dried rice noodles)

1½ to 2 pounds boneless lamb leg or shoulder, trimmed of excess
    fat and chilled, then very thinly sliced into approximately
    1-by-2-inch slices

2 cups thinly sliced mushrooms

12 leaves romaine or leaf lettuce, coarsely torn (about 2 cups)

1 cup frozen tofu (see Glossary), cut into 1-inch cubes (optional)

8 Chinese red dates (optional; see Glossary)

¼ to ½ cup coarsely chopped coriander

CONDIMENTS (choose at least three)

½ cup Guizhou Chile Paste (page 35) or Bright-Red Chile Paste
   (page 18), or store-bought chile paste

Cucumbers in Black Rice Vinegar (page 83)

1 cup Soy-Vinegar Dipping Sauce (page 151)

1 cup chopped pickled mustard greens (see Glossary)

½ cup Mongolian Roasted Garlic Paste (page 28)

Grasslands Herb Salsa (page 23)

3 tablespoons minced ginger

Wash the bones or the shank. Place in a large pot, add the water, and bring to a vigorous boil. Skim off any scum, then add the ginger and scallions. Lower the heat to maintain a simmer and cook, partially covered, for 2 hours if using bones, 45 minutes if using shank. Strain the broth through a colander into another pot. If you wish, you can strain the broth a second time through a cheesecloth-lined sieve.

Discard the bones and flavorings; if you used shank, cut the meat off the bone and set aside. If you have the time, cool the broth and then refrigerate it, covered. The fat will rise to the surface and congeal, and it will be easy to remove. In either case, skim off the fat, or remove and reserve for another purpose if desired. (See Cooking Oils and Fats in the Glossary for instructions on rendering and storing fat.) You should have 6 to 8 cups broth; if necessary, add water to bring it to 8 cups. (*The broth can be made ahead and stored well sealed in the refrigerator for up to 2 days or frozen for up to 1 month.*)

Place the dried rice noodles in a large bowl. Add warm water to cover, and set aside to soak for 10 minutes. Drain the noodles and set aside in a bowl.

Arrange the meat, vegetables, and tofu on a platter. Put the condiments on the table. For each guest, put out a plate, two pairs of chopsticks (one for cooking, one for eating), two condiment bowls, and a small soup bowl.

Bring the broth to a boil. Add the dates, if using, and ¼ cup chopped coriander. Transfer to a hot pot or place the pot on a small stove or hot plate in the center of the table. Call your guests to the table. Invite them to take several condiments, and to blend and mix—for example, adding a little chile paste to the chopped cucumbers in vinegar. Then suggest they add several mushroom pieces each and some greens to the pot and wait for them to cook and soften before lifting them out and eating them, plain or dipped in a condiment. Then have them try the other ingredients, cooking a small amount each time, then lifting them out to their plates before seasoning them and eating. (If the broth runs low, add a cup or more of hot water to it and bring back to a boil.)

Once everyone has eaten his or her fill, add the soaked noodles to the broth and cook until softened and heated through, about 3 minutes. Use chopsticks to distribute the noodles among the soup bowls, then ladle broth over and sprinkle on the remaining ¼ cup coriander leaves, if you wish.

Serves 4 as a main course

Driver Lin (see page 307) took me to a small eatery by a dirt road out in the grasslands north of Hailar in Inner Mongolia. There were several rough tables inside, with three or four guys seated at each, all eating their way through mountains of cooked lamb and washing it down with beer. We sat down to a huge late lunch of boiled meats: lamb, heart, lung, liver, kidney, and tongue, as well as several sausages— blood sausage, a kind of lamb boudin blanc, and a lamb sausage green with aromatics—all accompanied by the lamb broth. It was like a meat marathon, that meal. I imagined that in earlier times when an animal was killed for a feast, the meal the Mongols ate would have been like the food in the restaurant: platters piled high with various parts of the animal, all simmered until done, and the sound of bones being gnawed and tossed on the ground when chewed clean. It reminded me of medieval feasts I'd read about.

This one-dish way of cooking, which most nomadic people have developed in some form, is very practical, for it requires just one pot and one fire. The Mongols who live out in the grasslands in *gers* still cook this way, and Mongolian hot pot is the precursor of hot pot traditions in many parts of Asia. We've eaten hot pot in Sichuan, in Beijing, and in Guizhou and Guangzhou, as well as in Cambodia and Vietnam. Each version reflected the local ingredients and the local palate. The basic idea is that all the elements of the meal are cooked at the table in a hot broth, like a fondue, each person cooking pieces of meat and vegetables and then eating them plain or flavored with an assortment of condiments, as he or she wishes.

There are several ways the central pot and broth can be kept hot at the table. Doughnut-shaped hot pots can be found in large Chinese grocery stores. The pots have a central cone in which solid fuel or a gas flame burns, and the soup is in the ring around the heated central cone. Another method, used in hot pot restaurants, involves a specially built table with a hole cut out of the center, in which a pot can rest. The pot is heated by a gas or electric burner underneath it. This design is also found in homes in Inner Mongolia and elsewhere in China. Several of the households I ate at in eastern Guizhou kept the family soup hot using a similar hole-in-the-table arrangement, with a gas burner underneath.

If you don't wish to mess with cutting a hole in a table (!) or setting up a traditional hot pot, you can just use a low-tech little portable gas stove or electric burner placed in the center of a low table. (Another option is to use a deep electric frying pan.) It all becomes very simple: Bring the water or broth to a boil on your stovetop, then transfer the heated pot to the portable stove set at low to medium heat (or transfer the hot liquid to the electric frying pan). We suggest a low table because that way guests can easily see into the pot and reach in with chopsticks. As the meal progresses, the level of the broth will drop; add a little more hot water if you need to in order to have enough cooking liquid. N

OPPOSITE: *Tibetan-style Buddhist monastery and prayer flags in Inner Mongolia, not far from the Russian border at Manzhouli. The monastery is in good repair but there are very few monks so it feels more like a museum than a place of prayer.*

OPPOSITE: *Mongolian Lamb Patties (page 272) with Lhasa Yellow Achar (page 28).* ABOVE: *The food-prep area at the small open-air restaurant in Turpan Zheng, with greens, lamb, and soy sprouts, and three plates of cooked stir-fry, ready to be served with flatbreads.*

silk road lunch

On a trip along the Silk Road long ago (see "Kashgar, 1986," page 112), we made a stop in Turpan Zheng. We had a long all-day wait for the overnight train that would take us west to Kulcha, so we stored our bags and bicycles at the station and went poking around, looking for something to eat and a good way to pass the day.

Turpan Zheng is the station for the Turpan oasis twenty miles away (see "Turpan Depression," page 200), so it has an improvised air to it, as junctions and border towns often do. It caters to people passing through, just as the oases of yesteryear did good business selling food and supplies to the merchants and travelers moving along the Silk Road. There was a long, dusty crooked street with little shops selling everything from saddlery for ponies to rope and twine to lengths of fabric. And everywhere there were small eateries hustling for business. Each one consisted of a woven roof to provide shade from the intense desert sun, a clay tandoor oven for baking nan (see Uighur Nan, page 190), and a counter where noodle dough could be rolled out or bread dough kneaded. All of them had a gas burner too, for wok cooking, and beside it were piles of uncooked food, whatever was available that day: a heap of chopped lamb, a tumble of green vegetables, perhaps some tomatoes or peppers, and, in several places, soybean sprouts in a pale gleaming-white pile dotted with yellow.

We stopped at one little eatery, sat down at a table in the shade of the trellis, and ordered lamb with sprouts (see Silk Road Lamb Stir-Fry with Sprouts and Greens, page 276).

MONGOLIAN LAMB SAUSAGES
AND LAMB PATTIES

Here is our version of the herbed lamb sausages I ate with pleasure out in the Hulun Buir grasslands (see "Hot Pot at Home and Away," page 269), flavored with generous amounts of minced scallions, coriander leaves, ginger, and garlic. Lamb sausage casings can be hard to find, so we use pork casings. Make the sausages 24 hours before you wish to cook them, so they have time to dry a little and firm up.

To serve the sausages, cut into slices and present on a plate along with one or more condiments, such as Quick Tomato-Onion Chutney (page 24), Lhasa Yellow Achar (page 28), Mongolian Roasted Garlic Paste (page 28), and/or Guizhou Chile Paste (page 35). You could also include them in a Mongolian Hot Pot (page 266), cooking them in the broth.

If you prefer not to make sausages, the mixture makes delicious lamb patties for grilling or frying. They are less traditional but much easier and quicker. Serve with slices of cucumber and with lettuce leaves, accompanied by some of the condiments above.

Instructions for both patties and sausages are below. [PATTIES PHOTOGRAPH ON PAGE 270]

1 pound boneless lean lamb shoulder or leg, well chilled,
    or 1¼ pounds ground lamb

¼ pound (about ½ cup packed) coarsely chopped lamb fat
    (if not using ground lamb; see Note)

1 cup coarsely chopped garlic chives or 4 large garlic cloves,
    coarsely chopped

1 cup coarsely chopped scallions (white and tender green parts)

2 cups coriander leaves and stems

3 tablespoons minced ginger

1½ teaspoons salt

1 teaspoon freshly ground black pepper (optional)

About a 3-foot length of pork casings if making sausages

Vegetable oil or peanut oil if panfrying

If using lamb shoulder or leg, cut the chilled meat into thin slices. Place the lamb fat in the food processor and process to a paste. Add the meat and process just until a springy pink ball forms. Turn out into a bowl and set aside. If using ground lamb, place in a bowl and set aside.

Place the garlic chives or garlic in the processor and pulse to finely chop, then add the scallions, coriander, and ginger and pulse to mince them. *Alternatively*, mince the garlic chives or garlic, scallions, coriander, and ginger by hand.

Add the flavorings to the meat, along with the salt and the pepper, if using, and use your fingers to blend the greens into the meat (we find this results in a better texture than mixing the two in the processor). Cover well with plastic wrap and refrigerate for 30 minutes.

TO MAKE SAUSAGES: Untangle the sausage casing and rinse well under cold water. Open one end with your fingers and place it under a gently running tap so that the water flows through the casing and rinses it. Squeeze the water out of the casing, and tie a simple knot in one end.

Unless you have a mechanical sausage maker, the easiest way of stuffing the sausages is to use a 2-quart plastic soda bottle. Cut it crosswise into two pieces, about 6 inches from the bottom. The top half is your new sausage-making tool.

Pick up the sausage casing and fit the open end over the top of the soda bottle, then slide it along the neck of the bottle as far as it will go (about 1 inch). With the top pointing away from you and the cut edge braced against your torso, use both hands to slide the rest of the sausage casing up onto the neck of the bottle; it may seem at first as if it won't fit, but it will, and the work goes quickly. Once it's all on except the knotted end, hold it firmly on the neck with the fingers of one hand.

Take the sausage mixture out of the refrigerator. With your free hand, scoop up a small handful of the mixture and place it inside the top of the bottle, then use your index finger to push it through the neck of the bottle into the casing. It's easiest to fill the casing if you're working very close to the bottle, so hold tightly to the casing and bottle top with the fingers of one hand to maintain tension as you stuff the casing, gradually releasing a little more of it until you have 4 inches of tightly stuffed casing. The stuffing is soft, so force it tightly into the casing; try to keep air out of the casing. Twist the casing to seal off the first sausage, twisting it 4 or 5 times to make a space before the next one. Continue to make sausages, maintaining tension and trying to fill each one full without air bubbles. Your hands will soon get comfortable, and you'll be surprised at how quickly you reach the end of the length of casing. (*Note:* As you twist later sausages, make sure the earlier ones don't come untwisted. If they do, twirl them again.)

Tie a knot to seal off the last sausage (like tying off a balloon) and lay the sausages on a plate in a loose coil. (If you have any filling left over, you can use it for patties to fry or grill; see below.) Cover loosely and refrigerate for 24 hours. The sausages will give off a little liquid, which you should pour off, and they'll firm up.

You can fry the sausages in a little oil in a large heavy skillet over medium heat or grill them over a moderate flame. Prick them all over with a fork, toothpick, or fine skewer before cooking. Panfry or grill for about 10 minutes, turning them to expose all sides to the heat.

To serve, cut into long diagonal slices and set out on a plate, along with a condiment or two.

TO MAKE LAMB PATTIES: Scoop up a scant 3 tablespoons (a golf-ball-sized clump) of the chilled meat mixture and shape into a firm patty about 2½ inches across and ¾ to 1 inch thick. (This size is easy to handle in the pan or on the grill.) Set on a plate, and repeat with the remaining mixture, to make 16 patties.

Place a large heavy skillet over medium-high heat and add about 1 tablespoon oil. Add the patties in batches and panfry for about 4 minutes on each side to cook them through, less for a pinker interior; add a little more oil if necessary. *Alternatively,* prepare a medium-hot fire in a charcoal grill or preheat a gas grill. Grill the patties for about 4 minutes per side, or until done as you like. Serve with your choice of condiments.

Makes about 8 sausages, serving 4 to 6 as a main course with rice or potatoes or noodles, and a vegetable side dish, or 16 patties, serving 5 to 6 as part of a meal

NOTE ON LAMB FAT: You can ask your butcher for lamb fat, or else trim it from roasts and chops. Store it in the freezer so you have it on hand.

I don't know why Albeyat did it, asking me to drive, but I think it made him happy. I think it gave him as much pleasure as it gave me, maybe more. We had a Kazakh version of the theme song from *Titanic* blasting on the tape player, and we had the windows down. Each of us had an arm hooked at the elbow stretched outside. I'd drunk a beer just a short time before, sitting in the midday sun in the crisp alpine air of Kanas Lake, sitting with Tuvan and Kazakh friends, but I wasn't too worried about my driving. With potholes the size of Xinjiang watermelons and a sea of humanity walking on the road, I wasn't going to reach ten miles an hour, let alone twenty. But I had to use my horn a lot, and I think that's the reason Albeyat wanted me to drive.

Kanas Lake is a newly discovered hot spot on the domestic tourist circuit. People come here by the thousands from Shanghai, Hong Kong, Shenzhen, Chengdu, Guangzhou, Beijing—all of China's newly rich. They come especially in September, same as me, for the autumn colors, the brilliant yellow of the poplars and larches. Just like people from the West, they come with brand-name backpacks, Gore-Tex jackets, and hiking boots, and, of course, digital cameras, video cameras, and cell phones. It's just like being in Yellowstone National Park, only in China.

The night before, I'd slept in a yurt with a Kazakh and two Tuvans. We'd stayed up late at night, working our way through an English-Kazakh phrasebook, finding ways to keep our conversation going. I had a list of Kazakh words from the Internet, from a site for families in North America who had adopted Kazakh babies. We laughed at phrases like "Do you have to pee-pee?" (*See es-in-pah pee pee?*) and words such as bunny (*koy-an*) and hamster (*tish-kan*). We drank beer and *baijiu* (white liquor; see "Beer, Etc.," page 340), of course, and we ate a Kazakh *pulao* with shreds of carrot and big pieces of goat shank, gnawing away, bone after bone, as we laughed.

"Do you like China?" I asked at one point, and then, "Would you rather live in Kazakhstan?" It was a complicated question, I knew, but our conversation had already touched on all these things. They conferred a bit, and then wrote out on a piece of paper: "Genghiskhanistan."

"That's what we would like," they said, "Genghiskhanistan: Mongols, Kazakhs, Tuvans, Tatars."

Honk, honk, honk.

Kanas is a Tuvan town, but the Tuvans are now a tourist attraction. The Kazakhs live on the periphery, with no bathroom facilities, without running water. They take tourists on horseback rides and hear karaoke music blaring at night.

Honk, honk, honk. ᴊ

OPPOSITE: *Kazakh yurt and Tuvan wood house near Kanas Lake, northern Xinjiang.*

SILK ROAD LAMB STIR-FRY
WITH SPROUTS AND GREENS

This is our version of the dish that came to the table one day in Turpan Zheng (see "Silk Road Lunch," page 271). It was served on large plates, with a stack of flatbreads alongside. We could have had it over noodles, and that's an option for this stir-fry, though we usually serve it, non-traditionally, with rice.

> 1 tablespoon peanut oil or vegetable oil
>   or rendered lamb fat (see Glossary)
>
> 1 tablespoon minced garlic
>
> ¼ teaspoon ground cumin
>
> About ½ pound boneless lamb, trimmed of most fat,
>   and cut into small bite-sized pieces (about 1 cup)
>
> ¾ pound (about 4 cups) soybean sprouts
>   (see Note on Soybean Sprouts)
>
> ⅔ to ¾ pound Taiwan bok choi or other leafy green, cut
>   crosswise into 2-inch-wide strips (see Note on Greens)
>
> ½ teaspoon salt
>
> 2 tablespoons soy sauce
>
> 2 tablespoons Jinjiang (black rice) vinegar

Place a large wok or wide heavy skillet over high heat. Add the oil and swirl to coat the pan. Toss in the garlic and cumin and stir-fry briefly, then add the lamb and stir-fry until all surfaces have changed color, a couple of minutes. Add the bean sprouts and stir-fry for about a minute. Add the greens and salt and stir-fry for 2 to 3 minutes, then test the sprouts for doneness. When the beans at the ends of the sprouts are beginning to soften, add the soy sauce and vinegar. Continue to cook, stirring occasionally, for 2 more minutes, or until the beans are tender (timing will vary with the size of your pan).

Turn out onto a platter and serve.

Serves 3 or 4 as a main course

NOTE ON SOYBEAN SPROUTS: Unlike the finer-textured mung bean sprouts, which are most commonly available, soybean sprouts come with the bright yellow or green soybean still attached. They take longer to cook than mung bean sprouts, but they never turn soft or mushy, and their resilience is a boon when you are cooking for a crowd. Classic Chinese practice is to break off the beans before cooking the sprouts, but that is not how things are done in more remote places. Cooking the sprouts with the beans still attached results in a lovely contrast in texture between the tender sprouts and firm beans. If you can't find soy sprouts, substitute mung bean sprouts, but add them with the greens and cook until just tender.

NOTE ON GREENS: There's a huge array of Chinese greens grown in the oases of Xinjiang. What's available depends on the time of year. We imagine that in winter this dish would be made with sprouts alone, or perhaps with some pickled greens as well, instead of the fresh greens that were on offer in late May. (A little later in the season, some cooks would toss in a chopped tomato or two for color and reduce the vinegar a little.) Taiwan bok choi looks like long tender romaine, with long medium to narrow leaves growing from a small compact green base. To prepare it, wash it well and then cut crosswise into approximately 1½- to 2-inch-wide strips. The stems have a little crunch and the leaves wilt quickly. Substitute any leafy green you wish—romaine lettuce, for example.

KAZAKH STEW

During the time that I was in the northern part of Xinjiang province, primarily with Kazakh and Tuvan people, I don't recall a single long conversation when the subject of horses didn't come up at least once.

"I have sixteen horses," I was told by Albeyat.

"I have twelve horses," said Serik.

"I have twenty-two horses," said another.

Horses are everywhere, and people ride horses as if they were born on one, effortlessly and gracefully. It's beautiful to watch, especially for someone like me, who can't ride at all. Upon leaving the Kazakh regions of Xinjiang, I promised myself that I would return only once I'd learned to ride a horse, but now I'm wondering how that's going to happen. I grew up in Wyoming, where a lot of people know how to ride, yet every time I tried riding as a child, something went wrong. Horses are so big and they can run so fast!

I'll probably just stick to cooking Kazakh dishes, like this slow-cooked goat stew. It reminds us more of a Moroccan tagine than it does a stew, its reduced broth so full of flavor. Accompany with boiled potatoes, or rice, or Kazakh Family Loaf (page 195) to help sop up the gravy.

MARINADE

2 tablespoons vegetable oil

¼ cup rice vinegar

½ teaspoon freshly ground black pepper

STEW

1¼ to 1½ pounds goat shank or lamb shank, cut into 2-inch pieces (you can have the butcher do this)

2 tablespoons vegetable oil or rendered lamb fat (see Glossary)

1 large onion, diced

3 carrots, peeled and cut into ½-inch chunks

2 tomatoes, cut into ½-inch chunks

2 cups lamb or other light broth or water

1 teaspoon salt

2 or 3 bay leaves

½ cup or more coriander leaves, chopped arugula, or minced scallion greens for garnish

Silk Road shave: a Uighur barber and a customer checking the fineness of his work, streetside in Kashgar, western Xinjiang.

Mix the marinade ingredients in a small bowl. Place the meat in a wide bowl or nonreactive pot and pour the marinade over. Cover with plastic wrap or a lid and refrigerate for 2 hours.

Heat the oil or lamb fat in a heavy pot with lid over medium-high heat. Remove the meat from the marinade and add it to the pot (discard the marinade). Add the onion and cook for 10 to 12 minutes, turning the meat occasionally to expose all sides to the hot pot. When the meat is nicely browned, add the carrots and tomatoes, then add the broth, salt, and bay leaves and bring to a boil. Reduce the heat to a low simmer, partially cover, and cook for 1 hour.

Remove the bay leaves and serve hot, in the cooking pot or in a serving bowl, garnished lavishly with fresh green herbs.

Serves 4 as a main course

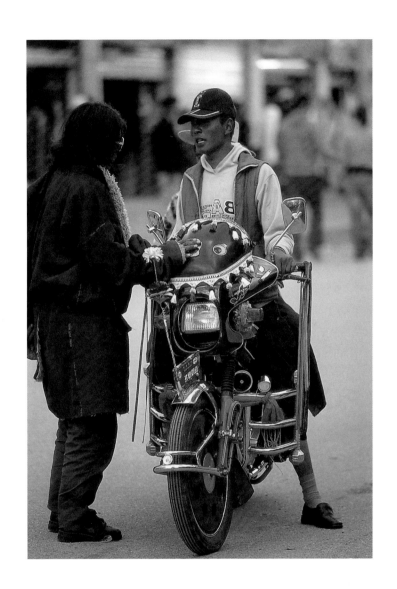

The bus creaked to a stop in the center of the village. We were on the border of Qinghai and Gansu, in the majority-Tibetan area formerly known as Amdo. A woman in long traditional Tibetan dress hurried up to the bus and climbed on, carrying a tray of cups of homemade yogurt to sell to the passengers. It was thick and creamy, irresistible. I got down from the bus, yogurt in hand, to have a look around. The spring wind swirled dirt into the air and rattled windows in the low shops that lined the wide bare street. The village was on a ridge in the middle of rolling soft-green grasslands, the horizon bounded by snow-covered rounded mountains.

A narrow track headed straight out across the green. Far in the distance I could see two motorcycles heading toward town, trailing a puff of dust behind them, a modern version of horsemen on the plain. A few minutes later, they rode up the hill onto the main street, two nomad couples in heavy sheepskin coats (*jubas*), the women, with long braids and with colored sashes belting their coats, riding behind the men.

Nomads in Qinghai and Gansu, as well as in western Tibet, have been making the switch from horses to motorcycles for a while, as soon as they have the money to do so. In the snow, of course, motorcycles are not as flexible as horses, but the rest of the year the nomads prefer them, whatever romantic notions outsiders may have: they are relatively inexpensive (about $600), they can go faster than a horse over a long distance, and they require less daily care.

The day after I saw those nomad motorcyclists, I rode out into the grasslands south of Labrang, in southern Gansu. I was on a sure-footed gray Tibetan pony, sharing the cost of the two amiable Tibetan men who came along as guides with a well-traveled young Tibetan-speaking guy from Maine named Galen. We spent the day riding up into the hills. We saw a fox and its den, yellow Himalayan ducks, and plenty of rolling countryside framed by snow-covered hills. We picnicked on bread and cheese, lounging on fresh green grass by a stream. The ponies grazed nearby. It was a spectacular excursion.

But soon after we started to head home in late afternoon, it began to rain hard, and a strong wind from the north blew the rain straight into our faces (see "Tsampa in a Storm," page 179). Labrang was about fifteen miles away, three hours or so at a walk or slow trot, which was all our horses could manage after our long day's ride. There was no magic to it; we just had to put in the time it would take to get back. As we rode, getting colder and colder, several motorcycles passed us, also heading into town. Their riders were cold and wet too, but they could get there much more quickly than we could.

It made me realize just how liberating motorcycles must be for many nomads, not to speak of the intoxication of machinery for the young men. We've heard that many nomad women complain that their men do no work and instead spend all their time tinkering with their motorcycles or going for joyrides across the grasslands.

Can't say I blame them. **N**

OPPOSITE: *Two Tibetan men talking in the middle of a road in the town of Litang, in western Sichuan.*

BEEF WITH MUSHROOMS AND CELLOPHANE NOODLES

This dish is called *ping sha* in Tibetan: *ping* is the word for cellophane noodles, and *sha* is meat. We substitute beef for the yak meat that is used in Tibet. *Ping sha* always includes mushrooms, either fresh or dried, and is served with plain rice. The slippery pale noodles and succulent pieces of meat and mushroom are richly flavored by the ginger-warmed broth.

> 1 pound oyster or white mushrooms, cut into ½-inch-wide strips
> (about 5 cups), or 2 cups dried mushrooms (shiitake or
> porcini, for example)
> About 2½ cups water
> ½ pound cellophane noodles (see Glossary)
> 3 tablespoons peanut oil or canola oil
> 3 tablespoons minced ginger
> 1 large or 2 medium scallions, sliced lengthwise into thin ribbons
> and then into 1½-inch lengths
> ¾ pound boneless beef, round steak or tenderloin, thinly sliced
> and cut into pieces about 1 inch by 2 inches
> 1 teaspoon salt, or to taste
> 3 tablespoons soy sauce, or to taste
> 1 cup light vegetable, beef, or chicken broth or water

If using dried mushrooms, place in a bowl, add hot water to cover, and place a small lid or plate on the mushrooms to keep them submerged. Let soak for 15 minutes. Drain, reserving 1½ cups of the soaking water.

Slice the mushrooms into ¼-inch-wide strips, discarding any tough stems, and set aside.

Place the noodles in a wide bowl, pour hot water over to cover, and soak for 10 minutes. Drain and cut into long lengths (about 12 inches). Set aside.

Place a large wok or heavy skillet over high heat. When it is hot, add 2 tablespoons of the oil and lower the heat to medium-high. Toss in the ginger and scallions and stir-fry for about a minute, or until softened. Add the meat and salt and stir-fry for about 2 minutes, until the meat has changed color all over. Turn the meat and flavorings out of the pan and set onto a plate. Rinse the wok out with ½ cup water and add to the reserved mushroom soaking water, if you have it, or pour into a small bowl and add another 1½ cups water; set aside. Dry the wok.

Return the wok to medium-high heat. Add the remaining 1 tablespoon oil, swirl it a little, and add the fresh or dried mushrooms. Stir-fry for several minutes, pressing the mushrooms against the hot pan, until they are starting to soften and give off their liquid. Add the reserved water, the cellophane noodles, and soy sauce and cook for another minute, pressing the noodles against the hot wok. Add the 1 cup broth or water and bring to a boil. Boil hard for 1 minute, then lower the heat to medium and add the reserved meat and flavorings. Stir to incorporate them, taste for salt, and adjust if you wish. Turn out into a wide shallow bowl. Serve hot or warm.

Serves 4 as a main course, 6 as one of several dishes with rice

OPPOSITE, LEFT: *Beef with Mushrooms and Cellophane Noodles.* OPPOSITE, RIGHT: *A small village near Gyantse in central Tibet, in winter. The* dzomo *(yak-cow crosses) are coming in to be milked.*

BEEF HOT POT

One step more citified and elegant than Mongolian Hot Pot (page 266), this convivial meal begins with meat and vegetable and ends with soup. Toward the end of the meal, rice noodles are dropped into the hot pot broth to cook, then noodles and broth are ladled out into small soup bowls. (You could also offer quail eggs, which each guest can swirl into his or her bowl of broth; see page 283.) Guests can then top the bowls of broth with a sprinkling of minced ginger, scallion, and coriander leaves, to taste. It's a calming finish to the meal, and satisfying too.

BROTH

6 cups water

2 tablespoons dried shrimp

4 slices peeled ginger

4 slices peeled carrot

About ½ cup coriander leaves

2 tablespoons minced ginger

2 tablespoons minced scallions (white and tender green parts)

HOT POT

1½ pounds beef tenderloin, chilled and then very thinly
    sliced into approximately 1-by-2-inch slices

About 1½ cups thinly sliced white or oyster mushrooms

12 leaves (or more) romaine or leaf lettuce, or a mixture,
    torn in half

2 cups frozen tofu cubes, thawed and drained (optional;
    see Glossary)

1 package thin rice sticks (dried rice noodles), soaked in
    warm water for 10 minutes, then drained

4 quail eggs (optional)

CONDIMENTS (serve some or all)

Cucumber-Vinegar Sauce (page 83)

Soy-Vinegar Dipping Sauce (page 151)

¼ cup chopped pickled mustard greens (see Glossary) or
    Tenzin's Quick-Pickled Radish Threads (page 25)

Mongolian Roasted Garlic Paste (page 28)

Grasslands Herb Salsa (page 23)

½ cup Guizhou Chile Paste (page 35), Bright Red Chile
    Paste (page 18), or store-bought chile paste

Place the water in a medium pot and bring to the boil. Add the shrimp and slices of ginger and carrot, reduce the heat, and simmer for 10 minutes.

Meanwhile, divide the coriander leaves in half, and put one portion aside. Place small piles of the ¼ cup of the coriander, the minced ginger, and minced scallions on a small tray and put out on the table. Arrange the meat, vegetables, and tofu, if using, on a platter. Set the noodles

A Tuvan man on horseback with a small herd of goats, in Hom, a village in the Altai Mountains.

and optional quail eggs aside. Put the condiments out on the table. For each guest, put out a plate, two pairs of chopsticks (one for cooking and one for eating), two condiment bowls, and a small soup bowl.

Transfer the broth and flavorings to a hot pot and place in the center of the table. Or use the heating arrangement that works best for you (see "Hot Pot at Home and Away," page 269). Sprinkle on the remaining ¼ cup coriander leaves and bring back to a boil.

Call your guests to the table. Invite them to take several condiments, and also to blend and mix—for example, stirring a little minced ginger into their soy-vinegar sauce. Then suggest they add several mushroom pieces each and some greens to the pot and wait for them to cook and soften before lifting them out and eating them, plain or dipped in a condiment. Then have them try the other ingredients, cooking a small amount each time so they can keep track of it, then lifting it out to their plates before seasoning it and eating. The beef slices should simmer only very briefly in the broth, so make sure your guests remove their slices of beef while the meat is still a little pink. (If the broth runs low, add a cup or more of hot water to it and bring back to a boil.)

Once everyone has eaten his or her fill, add any remaining meat to the broth, bring it to a boil, and skim off any foam. Add the soaked noodles and cook until softened and heated through, about 3 minutes. Use chopsticks to distribute the noodles among the soup bowls, then ladle broth over.

If you have the quail eggs, invite your guests to break an egg into their hot broth and swirl it around, if they wish. Pass around the small tray of coriander leaves, ginger, and scallions so they can add a sprinkling of each, as they please, to their bowls of soup.

Serves 4 as a main course

CLASSIC LHASA BEEF AND POTATO STEW

This Lhasa classic, traditionally made with yak meat, can be found in every Tibetan household and in many restaurants too. The Tibetan name is *sha-dire* (pronounced sha-di-RAY; *sha* is meat and *dire* is rice), for the dish is always served over rice. We've eaten several versions of it over the years. The recipe here is our distillation of advice from many people, but it is mostly based on insights from time spent with our friend Tenzin (see page 25) in his kitchen in Lhasa.

There are several interesting elements to the cooking method, the most noticeable being the addition of spice (celery seeds) mixed with water to the hot cooking oil. The process feels strange to us, but it's the way Tenzin does it. (Some ground spice is also added later, with the ginger; sometimes it's a curry powder imported from Nepal, sometimes it's just cumin seeds. Here we call for ground cumin and coriander seeds.) Precooking the carrots and potatoes avoids having to cook the stew too long and leaves the meat more tender. We serve the stew over rice, as Lhasa people do.

3 pounds potatoes, well scrubbed

1 pound carrots, peeled

5½ cups water, or as needed

3 tablespoons vegetable oil or peanut oil

1 tablespoon crushed or minced garlic

1 tablespoon coarsely ground celery seeds

2 medium or 3 small scallions smashed and cut into
    1-inch lengths

1 pound boneless stewing beef (beef chuck), cut into 1- to 2-inch
    pieces, or 1¾ pounds bone-in beef shank, cut into 2-inch
    pieces (you can have the butcher slice the shank)

About 2 teaspoons salt

2 tablespoons butter

2 teaspoons minced ginger

1 tablespoon Cumin-Coriander Powder (recipe follows)
    or garam masala (see Glossary)

(continued)

Place the potatoes and carrots in a large pot, add 5 cups of the water, and bring to a boil. Cook until the potatoes are just barely cooked through, then drain, reserving the cooking water. Set the vegetables aside to cool.

In a large heavy pot, heat the oil over medium-high heat. Add the garlic and stir-fry briefly, until fragrant. Stir the celery seeds into the remaining ½ cup water, and then add it to the hot oil: it will make a "whoosh" sound and will spatter, so be careful. Toss in the scallions and stir-fry until softened, about a minute. Add the meat and 1 teaspoon of the salt and cook over medium heat, stirring occasionally, for about 5 minutes.

Meanwhile, strip off the potato peels and chop the potatoes into approximately 1½-inch pieces. Cut the carrots into 1-inch lengths. Set aside.

Add the butter to the meat mixture and stir to blend it in. Add the ginger, the spice powder, the potatoes and carrots, and the reserved vegetable cooking water. Add extra water if necessary to cover the meat completely. Bring to a boil, then reduce the heat and simmer gently, partially covered, for 10 minutes, or until the potatoes are very tender and the broth has thickened with their released starch. Taste for salt and add the remaining 1 teaspoon, or to taste. Serve hot over rice.

Serves 4 to 5 as a main course

Cumin-Coriander Powder

You can make this simple Lhasan spice blend as you need it, or else make up a small batch and store it in a well-sealed glass jar, so it's there when you reach for it.

3 tablespoons cumin seeds
3 tablespoons coriander seeds

Place a medium cast-iron or other heavy skillet over medium-high heat, add the cumin seeds, and stir with a wooden spatula or shake the pan to prevent them from scorching as they heat up. Soon they will be aromatic and starting to change color. Continue to dry-roast for another 15 seconds or so, then remove from the heat and continue to stir for another minute. Transfer to a spice grinder or clean coffee grinder and grind to a powder. Set aside in a bowl to cool.

Place the skillet back over medium-high heat and toast and then grind the coriander seeds. They also need to be dry-roasted until they have changed color, which will take a little longer than the cumin; grinding takes longer too, because coriander seeds have a fairly tough outer husk. Once they are ground, add them to the ground cumin and stir to blend together. Let cool completely before transferring to a clean, dry glass jar with a tight-fitting lid. The mixture will lose intensity when stored, so renew your blend about every 3 to 4 weeks.

Makes a generous ¼ cup

Tibetans waiting outside the locked door to the Norbulingka, formerly the summer palace of the Dalai Lamas, in Lhasa.

Cooks in Lhasa have cosmopolitan tastes, probably because Lhasa has long been a center for trade with China, Nepal, and India. Spices have traveled into Tibet from all directions, along with people with different culinary preferences and knowledge. The result is that Lhasa cooking, like the cooking of city people in most parts of the world, is different from the cooking of people in the countryside. A wider range of ingredients is used, and flavorings are more diverse too.

We've talked elsewhere about the taste for condiments and salsas in Lhasa (see page 24), flavors that seem to have traveled in from the Indian Subcontinent. Another element from the Subcontinent is the use of masala powder in meat dishes as a last-minute addition to enhance flavors. Cooks can buy whole and ground spices in the market, and now packaged garam masala made in India or Nepal is being imported and is finding a place in kitchen cupboards in Lhasa.

jerky khampa-style

When we were in Lhasa years ago preparing for a long trip to western Tibet, we bought some yak meat in the market, then cut it into strips, rubbed the strips with salt and spices, and put them out in the sun. The air was so dry that soon we had jerky, strong-tasting and lightweight. Later we were very glad we'd made ourselves a supply—it was a huge treat when we were bicycling in western Tibet.

But, in fact, we'd never known exactly how Tibetans dry their yak meat. It's something that nomads, herders, and people in remote villages do whenever an animal is butchered. The feet will be simmered in a stew, the intestines will go for sausage casings, and so on. But a yak is a huge beast, and a good portion of it will usually be dried for long storage.

When I asked recently in Lhasa about drying meat, I was given very clear, simple instructions (with no explanation why): Never dry it in the sun, only in the cool shade. Cut the meat into long slices and rinse it with salted water. Put it in a basket, or put a loop of string through a hole in one end of each slice, and hang it in the shade on the north side of the house, preferably in fall or winter. Bring it in at night. It will dry in several days.

Dried yak meat was the original ingredient in most of the recipes for Tibetan dishes in this book that call for beef, though in the cities fresh yak meat is now easily available. The dried meat has a slightly more intense flavor than fresh, and yak meat in general stands up to long simmering better than beef.

Yak meat jerky photographed at a Khampa family house in Lhasa.

BEEF AND GREEN CHILE STIR-FRY

Like many of the meat and vegetable dishes now made in Lhasa, this is a fusion dish: the long green chiles that go into it would not have been available in Tibet before the development of intensive greenhouse horticulture in the area. In Litang, in the heart of the Tibetan area of western Sichuan, Jeffrey had another version of this stir-fry. There the cook tossed in some tomato too, which we list as an option here.

This recipe calls for twisted green chiles, which have a medium heat and beautiful color. You can substitute 4 or 5 Hungarian wax chiles (pale green) or banana chiles (pale yellow). Their hotness varies, but usually banana chiles are less hot and Hungarian wax more like the twisted green chiles. Another alternative is green cayenne chiles (use 6), which will make a hotter dish. Tomatoes, either ripe or semiripe, give a little acidity and very attractive color.

If you can buy beef that is already cut and labeled "for stir-frying," then do so. Otherwise, use boneless sirloin and slice as directed in the recipe.

½ to ⅔ pound beef for stir-frying (see headnote)
    (or boneless beef sirloin)
5 twisted green chiles (see headnote)
2 tablespoons peanut oil or vegetable oil
½ medium onion, thinly sliced
1 tablespoon minced or crushed ginger
2 medium ripe or semiripe tomatoes, coarsely chopped
    (optional)
¼ cup water or light beef or chicken broth
½ teaspoon dry-roasted Sichuan peppercorns, coarsely ground
1 teaspoon Cumin-Coriander Powder (page 284)
¾ teaspoon salt, or to taste

If you have beef for stir-frying, rinse it and cut any larger pieces in half, so that all the pieces are no longer than 1½ inches and about ¼ inch thick. If you are starting with sirloin, rinse it, then slice it into ¼-inch-thick slices and cut crosswise into pieces between 1 and 1½ inches long. Set aside.

Cut the stem ends off the chiles. Cut a slit partway down each chile from the stem end and strip out the seeds and membranes. Cut the chiles crosswise into 1-inch lengths. You will have about 2 cups loosely packed. Set aside.

Place a large wok or wide heavy skillet over high heat. When it is hot, add the oil and swirl slightly to coat the bottom of the pan. Add the onion and stir-fry for about 20 seconds, until starting to soften, then toss in the ginger and stir-fry briefly. Add the chiles and, if using, the tomatoes, and stir-fry until all the chiles have been exposed to the hot pan and are starting to soften a little, 2 to 3 minutes. Add the water or broth and bring to a vigorous boil. Cover and boil for 2 minutes, then uncover and boil briefly so most of the liquid evaporates. When it's almost gone and the peppers are softened, add the meat, Sichuan pepper, spice blend, and salt. Stir-fry for about 1 minute. When all the meat has changed color, taste for salt and adjust if necessary, then turn out into a shallow bowl or serving plate.

Serves 2 as a main course, 4 as part of a rice meal

THE KIRGHIZ PEOPLE

Most of the four million Kirghiz worldwide live in Kyrgyzstan and in neighboring ex-Soviet republics, as well as in northern Afghanistan, but about 150,000 live in China's Xinjiang province, in the Pamir Mountains. Like the Kazakhs (see page 157) and Uighurs (page 90), the Kirghiz are a Turkic people, and their language is a part of the Turkic language family.

In China, most Kirghiz live seminomadically. Moving with the seasons, traditionally they live either in low stone houses (especially in winter) or in yurts made of wool felt (especially in the milder months), surrounded by their grazing animals. They keep herds of sheep, goats, camels, horses, donkeys, and yaks, all of whom seem to be able to survive the rough climate and strong winds of the Pamirs. The Kirghiz also occasionally work as traders, bringing loads of firewood and wool from the high mountains to the oasis markets at the edge of the Takla Makan Desert. You'll see them at the markets, wearing high leather boots and fur-trimmed hats, looking like mountain people compared to the lowland Uighurs.

Kirghiz seasonal dwellings, like those of the Tajiks (see page 343), have a clay tandoor oven in the center and bedding in the form of folded quilts and blankets stacked high against the walls. Tandoor breads are an important part of Kirghiz cooking; the ovens are used for baking flatbreads and to warm the house or yurt.

When riding our bicycles through the Pamir Mountains in the summer of 1986, we came upon several Kirghiz camps. Two or three yurts would be set up together, and outside there would occasionally be a woman sitting at a traditional backstrap loom weaving woolen fabric. Yaks and camels were often tethered or grazing near the yurts, and it never ceased to amaze us, the sight of yaks and camels together. We'd always thought of the two animals as living in such different locations, yaks in high-altitude snow and camels in desert heat. But in the Pamirs they live side by side. The landscape has similar amazing contrasts: At one point high in the mountains we came upon an incredible sand dune almost a thousand feet high, and just behind it, a glacier!

One evening during our trip, just as the sun was setting and we were washing up in our campsite after our meal, two Kirghiz horsemen came riding up. They splashed their way through the nearby stream, then dismounted, hobbled their horses, and left them to graze while they came over to talk to us. We were a little intimidated, for though they were friendly enough, they were also very inquisitive. It was only natural: we were strangers camped in their territory and they wanted to know who we were. They assumed we were from some other part of China, so they asked to see our work papers and travel permit. We showed them our passports but wouldn't hand them over. We tried to explain that we were from a faraway country, but they didn't understand. We offered them tea and bread, looked on as they fingered our mountain bikes, our nylon tent, and our fleece jackets, and were quite relieved when they rode off without giving us any trouble.

LEFT: *A young Kirghiz boy named Sok stands outside his house, which lies beneath Mount Kongur, a 25,325-foot peak in the Pamirs. At his mother's invitation, we camped near the house for a night on our bicycle trip through the Pamirs in 1986.* RIGHT: *Just south of where Sok and his family live, we passed by these huge dunes, made of sand that is blown up the valley by the fierce winds of the Pamirs. Behind the mountains lies Tajikistan; camels graze in the foreground.*

PORK

forage widely if given the chance. They do best in hot-to-warm climates where there is adequate water. They are not suited to deserts or to cold high-altitude climates.

Consequently, the regions and cultures featured in this chapter are the complement of those in Beef and Lamb. Instead of recipes from the grasslands of Inner Mongolia, the oases of Xinjiang, and high-altitude Tibet, there are mainly dishes from many of the peoples of the well-watered subtropical hills and valleys of Yunnan and Guizhou.

In Mandarin Chinese, the word for meat, *rou* (pronounced "roe"), is also the word used for pork, which mirrors the importance of pork in Chinese tradition. The various peoples of Yunnan and Guizhou also depend on the pig. Pork is used to flavor vegetable dishes and soups and is also eaten on its own. It may be dried into jerky (see Hani Slow-Baked Pork Jerky, page 294) or rubbed with a simple spice paste and slow-roasted over coals (see Lisu Spice-Rubbed Roast Pork, page 314). Both the Lisu and the Hani depend on the meat of pigs, as well as wild game, to accompany their meals of rice and vegetables. The pigs run free, so the meat has good flavor.

The Dong and Miao of Guizhou and the Dai of Yunnan also depend on pork. They stir-fry sliced pork with vegetables in simple and delicious combinations: see Miao Pork with Corn and Chiles (page 298), Stir-Fried Pork with Pickled Greens (page 303), and Stir-Fried Pork and Potato Ribbons (page 304). We've also included one Tibetan dish of pork stir-fried with spinach (see page 305) and a delectable deep-fried pork from rural Guizhou (see page 310).

OPPOSITE: *A Miao man carries home a piglet bought at a weekly market in eastern Guizhou.* ABOVE: *Tomatillos.*

HANI SLOW-BAKED PORK JERKY

I was a very happy person the first time I tasted this thin-cut, jerky-like pork. I was standing outside a bus station with my backpack on, very early in the morning in the junction town of Jiangcheng, deep in the big hills of Yunnan just a few miles north of the Lao border. I'd arrived in Jiangcheng late the night before, after a very long, slow, crowded bus ride. I was expecting a tribal center of sorts (Jiangcheng is the largest town in a predominantly Hani and Yi area; see page 316), but the town looked new and sterile, all the buildings veneered with white tiles, just like any one of a hundred different small cities anywhere in China. At the hotel, people had confirmed that the town was indeed a Yi and Hani town, but it sure didn't look like it to my uneducated eye. For dinner I found a *jiaozi* (dumpling) place, but that was it. My hotel room had a television with the usual cast of sixty primarily awful stations, and by my bed there were packages of condoms (and a pamphlet with helpful advice).

I was feeling a little let down by Jiangcheng the next morning as I waited for the bus. Then I spotted a Hani woman with a woven basket sitting on the sidewalk at the entrance to an alleyway. She was serving sticky rice, first putting some rice in the middle of a big green leaf, then adding a piece of pork and a little preserved vegetable, and finally wrapping up the leaf package to be carried away. I went over, bought two, and began eating. Suddenly my long trip into Jiangcheng began to feel good. I was eating local food, food that tasted more like Laos than China. And everything got better from there on.

This Hani pork jerky isn't at all difficult to make. And it probably keeps pretty well, but we always eat it too quickly to find out. We like it with sticky rice, accompanied by a side salad or sauce such as Dai Tart Green Salsa (page 22) or Hani Soy Sprout Salad (page 73) and a clear soup. It also makes a great appetizer served on its own, to accompany drinks.

About 2 pounds boneless pork butt, fresh ham,
    or other pork roast
About 1 tablespoon coarse salt
About 2 teaspoons freshly ground black pepper

Place a rack in the upper third of the oven and preheat the oven to 350°F.

Slice the meat against the grain into slices ¼ inch thick or less. Lay on one or two broiling pans, stretching the slices to make them even thinner. Sprinkle on the salt and black pepper.

Bake for 1 hour, turning the pieces of meat every 20 minutes or so. The pork will become light, like jerky; it should be a little chewy and completely dried out.

Serves 6 as a main course, 8 to 10 as an appetizer

Pork jerky to go, with sticky rice and preserved vegetables, photographed in Jiangcheng, Yunnan.

PORK WITH CHIVES

Having small pieces of pork stashed in the freezer can be a great safety net, especially when company arrives unexpectedly, or when you've lost track of time and need to get supper on the table quickly. You can slice the meat still frozen (a cleaver does a better job than a chef's knife), to help it defrost more quickly, and then stir-fry it with whatever combination of flavors and ingredients you like.

This pork stir-fry from Yunnan uses chives for flavor and color. The strands of green are very pretty among the strips of pork. You can substitute garlic shoots if you wish, or else scallions, cut into ribbons.

Serve the stir-fry with a soup such as Dai Chile-Fish Soup with Flavored Oil (page 54); a salad or vegetable dish, such as Dai Carrot Salad (page 83); and, as a condiment, Guizhou Chile Paste (page 35) or Bright Red Chile Paste (page 18) if you wish.

½ pound boneless lean pork, such as loin or trimmed chops,
    thinly sliced into 1½-by-½-inch pieces

1 tablespoon cornstarch

2 tablespoons peanut oil or vegetable oil

3 or 4 dried red chiles

1 garlic clove, minced

½ teaspoon salt, or to taste

A large handful of chives or garlic shoots, cut into 2-inch
    lengths (1 cup), or 4 medium scallions, smashed, cut
    lengthwise into ribbons and then into 2-inch lengths
    (about 1 cup)

½ cup mild broth or water

1 tablespoon soy sauce

¼ cup coriander leaves (optional)

In a small bowl, combine the pork and cornstarch and mix to coat the meat well. Set aside for 30 minutes to 2 hours (refrigerate, covered, if letting stand for longer than 30 minutes).

When ready to proceed, place a wok over high heat. When it is hot, add the oil and swirl a little. Toss in the chiles and cook briefly, until they puff, 20 to 30 seconds. Lift them out so they don't scorch and set aside, then toss in the garlic and stir-fry briefly, until starting to change color, about 10 seconds. Toss in the pork and the chiles and stir-fry vigorously until all the pork has changed color, about 3 minutes. Add the salt and chives or other green and stir-fry for another minute. Add the broth or water and bring to a boil. Add the soy sauce and stir briefly, until the sauce thickens. Taste for seasonings, and adjust if necessary.

Turn out onto a serving plate and garnish with the coriander leaves if desired. Serve with rice or rice noodles.

Serves 4 as part of a larger meal or 2 as a main course in a simple meal with rice or noodles

OPPOSITE: *Miao Pork with Corn and Chiles (page 298).* LEFT: *In the beautiful Miao village of Lande, south of Kaili in Guizhou, lengths of newly indigo-dyed cotton are hung to dry, and under the eaves of the tall graceful wooden house hang bunches of bright yellow corn.* RIGHT: *A Miao woman in Lande—dressed in traditional silver head dress, jewelry, and clothing—has just participated in a dance performance in the open piazza-like space in the center of the village.*

MIAO PORK WITH CORN AND CHILES

In Jenny's family's apartment (see "Jenny," opposite), her mother made a delicious and attractive Miao stir-fry of corn kernels cut from the cob, small pieces of thinly sliced pork, and chopped red chiles (rather like cayennes, which we substitute here), which gave a fairly chile-hot flavor. [PHOTOGRAPH ON PAGE 296]

⅓ pound pork loin

3 or 4 large ears corn (to yield 3 cups kernels)

1 tablespoon lard or peanut oil

2 teaspoons minced garlic

¼ teaspoon coarsely ground Sichuan pepper

2 red cayenne chiles, thinly sliced, or 3 tablespoons thinly sliced
    Pickled Red Chiles (page 34)

1 teaspoon salt

Thinly slice the pork, then cut into small slices, about ½ inch by 1 inch. Set aside. Cut the kernels from the corncobs: one at a time, stand each cob on a cutting board and use a cleaver or chef's knife to slice the kernels off the cob; set aside.

Place a wok or large skillet over high heat. Add the lard or oil, and when it is hot, toss in the garlic. Stir-fry for a moment, then add the pork and Sichuan pepper. Stir-fry for several minutes, then add the chiles and ½ teaspoon of the salt and stir-fry until the pork has changed color all over, another minute or so. Add the corn and stir-fry for about a minute, then add the remaining ½ teaspoon salt. Stir-fry until the corn is cooked through and tender, another 3 to 4 minutes.

Turn out and serve hot or at room temperature, with rice.

Serves 2 as a main course, 4 as one of several dishes with rice

PORK WITH NAPA CABBAGE AND CHILES

Jenny's mother made this stir-fry, hot and beautiful with freshly minced red chiles, and pleasantly crunchy with barely cooked stem lettuce (celtuce) strands, the first time I ate supper with them (see "Jenny," opposite). Later, in a Miao household outside Chong'an, I had another version of the same dish, just as delicious, cooked in lard rather than in the vegetable oil Jenny's mother used. We substitute Napa cabbage for the stem lettuce; see Glossary for more on celtuce.

We have made this dish with fresh red cayenne chiles and with minced pickled chiles. The pickled chile version has a nice little vinegar edge to it, very characteristic of the pickled and soured flavors in many Miao dishes.

About 1 tablespoon lard or peanut oil

2 tablespoons minced ginger

2 or 3 red cayenne chiles, seeded and minced, or 3 tablespoons
    minced Pickled Red Chiles (page 34) (see headnote)

½ pound boneless pork loin, butt, or tenderloin, thinly sliced

About ½ pound Napa cabbage, preferably from the stem end,
    thinly sliced (4 cups loosely packed)

1 teaspoon salt, or to taste

1 large or 2 small scallions, smashed, cut lengthwise
    into ribbons and then into 1-inch lengths

Place a wok over high heat. When it is hot, add the lard or oil and swirl to coat the bottom of the wok, then toss in the ginger and chiles. Stir-fry for about 30 seconds, to a well-blended bright red mass, then add the pork slices and stir-fry until they have all changed color, 1 to 2 minutes. Toss in the cabbage and stir-fry for about a minute. Add the salt and stir, then cover and cook for about 1 minute. Remove the lid and stir-fry a little longer, just until the cabbage is softened but not limp.

Toss in the scallion ribbons and stir-fry for another 30 seconds or so. Turn out into a wide shallow bowl and serve.

Serves 3 to 4 with rice and a side dish

She's so valiant, Jenny, with her straight back and determined stride, her jacket a fashionable denim number with a little embroidery on it. She navigates cultural divides and the rapid changes in her world with style and grace. Jenny is Miao, the name given in China to a culture that in North America is known as Hmong (see page 183).

Jenny and her family now live in two rooms facing a small courtyard in the middle of Kaili, a small city in Guizhou. A number of other families, all Miao, also live around the courtyard. It's the place where the women do laundry and prepare soured cabbage, a delicious staple (it's soaked in a bath of fermented rice overnight), while their children play. There's a constant coming and going through the covered passage that leads to the small street outside. Many of the other families live from selling textiles on the street; some have vegetable stalls or small street-food stands.

Jenny's family is from a village about two hours from Kaili. They've led a nontraditional life for many years: "My family doesn't have enough rice fields, so we can't grow enough rice to feed ourselves. My father decided we should go to the city. . . . We lived in Shanghai and then in Guilin. We go back and visit the village sometimes. Now we've been in Kaili for six years. My father decided to start a business selling textiles. Then he got sick and needed help. I had to leave school when I was fourteen to help him."

Now she's a street-savvy nineteen, trolling near the main hotels for tourists who might want to buy textiles ("At least have a look!"). Her English, mostly learned from foreign tourists, is amazingly good. Jenny's mother also works selling textiles, but her style is different. She has a very traditional Miao look: her hair is pulled up smoothly into a bun and anchored with a decorative pin. Her calm, almost regal demeanor declares her traditional Miao roots, whereas Jenny's look declares her participation in the new modern China of money and ambition. **N**

Jenny and her mother, photographed in the courtyard outside their rooms in central Kaili, Guizhou.

MOTORCYCLE

All I remember clearly about our motorcycle crash is coming around a corner, probably a little too fast, hitting a patch of gravel and spinning, then hitting the ground and skidding while trying to keep my head and body up as best I could. Serik, who was driving, held on to the bike, and I held on to him. Lucky for us both we didn't go off the road and down the steep mountain slope, or we'd probably have died.

We got right up, looking at each other, looking at ourselves. Serik's face was badly cut, and so were my hands and knees, but we were okay. One of my two cameras, which I had hanging around my neck, was smashed, and the motorbike was twisted and bent, but we yanked the steering column back in line. We got back on and headed on our way, both of us shaking badly.

Twenty minutes or so down the road, we came upon a Tuvan-style log house, and Serik stopped to ask for help. The young couple living in the house, a tall thin Chinese man and a Kazakh woman, took us in and fed us salted and lightly buttered Kazakh tea. They washed our wounds and applied a Chinese topical powder. Their daughter, two years old, watched every move. Serik and the man shared cigarettes. Serik was still very shaken.

By evening, we had arrived in Hom (marked on maps as Hemu, its Mandarin name), a beautiful mountain village, one of three Tuvan villages in this far northwestern corner of China. Rain was falling when we arrived, and there was a mist so heavy it felt as if we were traveling through a cloud. We pulled into a compound with a large canvas yurt and a Tuvan log house. There was smoke coming out of the chimney of the house, and as we drove up, several Kazakh and Tuvan men and women came out, friends of Serik. They took us inside around the fire, and again there was salted butter tea, tasting as good as anything could possibly taste.

For the next few days, Serik and I were companions. We had been strangers, the two of us, having met just the day before, but after our crash, we trusted each other absolutely. We drove back along the same mountain road, five hours on the motorbike, driving slowly and so cautiously that we were probably more at risk. But by evening we made it to his sister's yurt, and then to his, and finally, in the dark of night with a large September full moon, he drove me to a friend's large yurt near Kanas Lake. There, shivering with cold, we said good-bye and hugged before he got back on the bike and rode home. J

OPPOSITE: *Serik's motorcycle, with Jeffrey's pack strapped on the back, parked on the road outside the house of a Han-Kazakh couple, shortly after the accident.*

LEFT: *Miao and Ge people travel across the river to the market held every five days at Chong'an, in Guizhou.* RIGHT: *A Dong woman in Zhaoxing pounds indigo into cloth using a wooden mallet. The pounding makes the cloth shiny and forces color into the fibers.*

STIR-FRIED PORK WITH PICKLED GREENS

The Dong (see page 120) preserve vegetables, meat, and fish by pickling, so there's often an enticing tart or sour note in the flavor balance of their dishes. This simple take on stir-fried pork and greens tastes like the best kind of peasant cooking, a Dong version of a dish from Italy's Abruzzi or from Southwest France, earthy and direct.

I watched it being cooked in a wok set over a wood fire in the kitchen of a Dong family in Zhaoxing village. The temperature was medium-hot, so the initial frying of the shallot and ginger was gentle, rather than the high-temperature frying of many stir-fries. The cook's job also involved keeping an eye on the fire and adjusting the heat by using tongs to move small pieces of wood around, but she made it all look seamless and effortless.

The pickled greens (*suan cai* in Mandarin, meaning sour vegetable) she added after the meat had browned were locally made and delicious. We substitute store-bought pickled mustard greens, a favorite of ours, moist-textured and widely available in Chinese grocery stores. They keep well in the refrigerator and are a useful pantry staple.

The dried chiles and ginger in the finished dish give some heat, and the mustard greens give a cooling hit of sour to balance the sweetness of the shallots and pork. Serve with rice, and perhaps with a clear soup on the side.

½ pound boneless pork shoulder or loin

¼ pound pickled mustard greens (see Glossary)

1 tablespoon lard, peanut oil, or vegetable oil

2 tablespoons minced shallots

1 tablespoon minced ginger

3 dried red chiles, or to taste

½ teaspoon salt

1 scallion smashed, then cut lengthwise in half and
   crosswise into 2-inch lengths

1 teaspoon soy sauce

Thinly slice the pork, then cut into bite-sized slices, about ½ inch by 1 inch. Set aside.

Rinse the mustard greens well in cold water, then chop into medium dice; you'll have about 1 cup. Set aside.

Place a wok or large heavy skillet over medium-high heat. Add the lard or oil and swirl gently. Toss in the shallots, ginger, and chiles and stir-fry for about a minute. Add the pork and sprinkle on the salt, then raise the heat and stir-fry vigorously, tossing the pork and pressing it against the hot wok. Once most of the pork has changed color, add the mustard greens and stir-fry for 2 minutes. Add the scallion and stir-fry for another 30 seconds or so. Add the soy sauce and stir-fry to blend it in.

Turn out into a wide shallow bowl and serve hot or warm.

Serves 4 as part of a rice meal, 2 as a main course

STIR-FRIED PORK
AND POTATO RIBBONS

People all over the world work with potatoes in amazing ways. I thought I knew potatoes pretty well, but in Guizhou I discovered how different they can taste and look, depending on how they are cut and cooked.

This dish is from a large Miao village called Xijiang in rural Guizhou. The potatoes are peeled, sliced, and then cut into strips, rather like fettuccine-width julienne. The pork is also sliced into ribbons, ¼-inch-wide strips about 2 inches long. Though we call this a stir-fry, it's a bit of a hybrid, stir-fried and then simmered. There's an amazing depth of flavor here, a bonus for the cook in a hurry.

4 medium-small potatoes, preferably waxy (about ¾ pound)

½ pound boneless pork loin or butt, thinly sliced

1 teaspoon salt, or to taste

3 tablespoons peanut oil or lard

1 tablespoon sliced garlic

2 dried red chiles

½ cup water

1 tablespoon soy sauce

Peel the potatoes, thinly slice, and then cut the slices into strips about ¼ inch wide (this goes more quickly than you might think, fewer than 5 minutes in all). You'll have 2½ to 3 cups. Set aside.

Stack several pork slices at a time and cut them into ¼-inch-wide strips about 1½ to 2 inches long. Place the pork in a bowl, add ½ teaspoon of the salt, and toss; set aside.

Heat a wok or large heavy skillet over high heat. Add about 1 tablespoon of the oil or lard and swirl a little, then toss in the sliced garlic and stir-fry for 10 seconds. Add the pork and stir-fry for another minute, or until the meat has just changed color all over. Turn out onto a plate or into a bowl and set aside.

Add the remaining 2 tablespoons oil or lard to the pan and swirl around. Toss in the chiles and potatoes and stir-fry for about a minute. Add the remaining ½ teaspoon salt and cook, stirring occasionally, for another minute or two. Add the water and bring to a boil. Cover and cook for about 1 minute. Remove the cover, add the pork, and stir-fry to mix, then add the soy sauce. Cook, stirring occasionally to prevent sticking, until the potatoes are just cooked through but still firm. Taste for salt, and adjust if you wish.

Turn out and serve hot or warm with rice.

An older Miao man herds his geese along a pathway in the large Miao village of Xijiang, in eastern Guizhou.

Serves 2 as a main course, 4 as part of a rice meal

TIBETAN PORK AND SPINACH STIR-FRY

Though the most traditional meat animal by far in Tibet is yak, in one region east of Lhasa, around Gonbo, pigs are also raised for meat. Gonbo pigs are black, with long snouts, and are known for the exceptionally good flavor of their meat. Because the market for them has grown (probably because of the rapidly growing Han population in central Tibet), there are now so many pigs in the Gonbo region that they have rooted up trees and shrubs and are making rather a mess of the local environment. Or that's what the locals told me when I was last in Lhasa—we haven't yet been to Gonbo to see for ourselves.

Meanwhile, here is a Lhasa recipe for stir-fried pork with spinach. It's a fusion dish, spiced with Sichuan pepper as well as with ginger, the familiar Tibetan flavor. The spinach provides a nice balance with the pork and gives a touch of mild sweetness to the dish. There's a little pan sauce too. Serve with rice.

½ pound boneless pork loin or shoulder

5 cups spinach (about ½ pound)

1 tablespoon peanut oil or vegetable oil

2 teaspoons minced ginger

2 tablespoons minced scallions (white and tender green parts)

¼ teaspoon coarsely ground Sichuan pepper

1 teaspoon salt

½ cup water

Thinly slice the pork and then cut into bite-sized pieces (no larger than 1 by 1½ inches). Set aside.

Wash the spinach well in several changes of water, drain, and set aside.

Place a large wok or skillet over medium-high heat. Add the oil and immediately toss in the minced ginger, scallions, and pepper. Stir-fry for about a minute. Add the pork and ½ teaspoon of the salt and stir-fry, pressing the meat against the hot pan to brown it, until almost all of it has changed color, about 1 minute. Toss in the spinach and begin stir-frying it. It will seem voluminous and may feel a little unmanageable at first, but after several turns of your spatula, it will start to reduce in volume. Once it starts to wilt, add the water and the remaining ½ teaspoon salt. Stir-fry until the spinach is cooked, another 30 seconds to a minute, then turn out into a shallow bowl and serve.

Serves 2 as a main course, 4 as part of a rice meal

BEEF AND SPINACH STIR-FRY: If you'd like, use ½ pound boneless beef (round steak or tenderloin works well) instead of pork. Increase the minced ginger to 1 tablespoon, the water to ¾ cup, and the salt to 1¼ teaspoons. Follow the directions above; once the beef has changed color all over, lift it out of the pan and set aside. Add the spinach and stir-fry, then add the beef again once the spinach has started to wilt, when you add the water and the remaining salt.

DRIVER LIN

Lin was a wild character. I knew it the moment I saw him heading toward me, shouldering others out of the way. I'd just arrived at the little airport in Hailar, a small town in the north of Inner Mongolia not far from the Siberian border. He wore the standard taxi-driver's uniform, a black leather jacket and dark pants, and he had the usual taxi-driver's voice, gruff and raspy with cigarette smoke. But in his alertness and solidity, he stood out from the crowd of other drivers, each beckoning to me to choose him for the drive into town.

Lin and I spent a lot of time together over the next seven days. Though my Mandarin is not great and his had a heavy local accent, we had long conversations. He was so smart, and such a good driver, that even the longest days were a pleasure. He quickly understood what I was interested in: local food, material culture, good light (for photography), anything that helped me understand how people lived. One day we drove to Manzhouli, on the Russian border, taking a looping route through miles of grassland dotted with grazing animals so we could stop in to visit a huge Tibetan-style Mongol Buddhist monastery (see photo, page 268). Another time we headed north out of town looking for yurts, herds, and food. We ended up drinking tea and chatting with a Mongol mother and daughter who had just moved their ger (yurt) to its winter site, near a stream in the valley bottom in the Hulun Buir grasslands.

Later we feasted on platters of lamb at a small eatery in the grasslands. Lin ate with the same gusto and physical confidence that he had when he drove, slicing the meat and sausages into easy mouthfuls for us both, and urging me to have more of everything to keep him company.

Lin knew no fear. He drove his small black stripped-down VW Jetta across the grasslands as if it were a horse. Once when we were driving south of Hailar, he abruptly headed off the road, without slowing down at all, and straight up a grassy untracked hill. He was showing me Japanese gun emplacements, there since the ten-year Japanese occupation of the area (at the westernmost edge of Manchuria) in the 1930s. Later the same day, he again headed cross-country, this time to get us to several low domed gers, home of an Evenki family. (The Evenki [sometimes written Ewenke] are a Siberian aboriginal people who live from their herds and from hunting and gathering.)

The next day, Lin took me to the airport and insisted on waiting around until I got on the plane. "What if they cancel the flight?" he said when I urged him to head off. "And anyway, when the plane lands, I'll have passengers to take to town." I couldn't argue. N

OPPOSITE: *This Evenki ger south of Hailar is framed by traditional fencing. In a region that has few trees, the Evenki gather the low-lying willows that grow along the streams and rivers and braid or weave the branches to make barricades and fences that are used to reinforce their gers and, when necessary, to fence off young livestock.*

OPPOSITE: *Delectable Deep-Fried Pork (page 310) with Tribal Pepper-Salt (page 36), served alongside Pea Tendril Salad (page 66).* ABOVE: *Women chop large pieces of deep-fried pork in preparation for a funeral feast in Chong'an. Notice the ginger waiting to be sliced.*

In the small market town of Chong'an, an hour up the road from Guiyang, capital of Guizhou province in the semitropical hills of southern China, I had a small lesson in fats and oils. My teacher was a Miao man who ran a small café. He was making supper, several stir-fries, including stir-fried pork with stem lettuce (see Pork with Napa Cabbage and Chiles, page 298), and an omelet flavored with a little tomato (see page 242). His wok was well used, seasoned, and gleaming, nearly black. Like every other wok cook, he was careful each time he turned out a finished dish to rinse the wok with water (which heats quickly on the hot surface) and scrub it a little, then toss the water into a slop pail (that in rural households would go to the pigs or the hens) and wipe out the wok before placing it back over the hot flame to start cooking the next dish.

"You see," he said, as he cleaned the wok and then began again, this time to make the omelet, "with meat stir-fries, we cook with lard, but for cooking eggs, we use vegetable oil." He passed me the oil so I could smell and taste it. It was a mild oil with no distinctive odor.

We've learned, watching wok cooks from China to Thailand to Vietnam, that rendered pork fat, lard, makes the most delicious and stable cooking oil. We also know that the idea of using lard is not to everyone's taste, and that it can feel like too intimate a dance with saturated fats, especially for people doing a lot of stir-frying. Our own compromise is to use peanut oil for stir-frying most of the time and lard occasionally. Many of the stir-fries in this book call for either peanut oil or lard; the choice is yours to make. If you want to try the pleasures of lard, then you will want to render your own. It takes very little time and effort, and the resulting fat can be stored in the freezer, well sealed. We find that store-bought lard can have an intrusive smoky taste. Also, we like to know where our lard comes from. Pure rendered lard has almost no flavor, but it gives a depth of flavor to whatever is cooked in it. For instructions on rendering lard, see Cooking Oils and Fats in the Glossary.

DELECTABLE DEEP-FRIED PORK

A funeral pig feeds a lot of people. One morning in Guizhou, in the town of Chong'an, I came across a funeral in preparation at the edge of town. A tall white pole marked the household, and outside the house sat mourners wearing white armbands, chatting and smoking. (The deceased was in her eighties, so there was not a sense of tragic loss.) On the other side of the narrow street, several tables were loaded with meat and vegetables. Seated on low benches by the tables, five or six women chopped steadily, cutting carrots on the diagonal into long careful slices, meat into chunks. There was a brazier set up near the house and over it was placed a huge wok full of rendered lard, the preferred cooking medium there. Pork cracklings were simmering their way to crispness in the wok, then were lifted out with tongs. Nearby a man was using a blowtorch to singe the hair off a pig's head, readying it for cooking.

Four hours later, I passed by the house again. The women were still working away, chopping and slicing. They waved at me to sit down with them, then passed me a platter loaded with pieces of deep-fried pork and urged me to eat. It was just fabulous, clean-tasting and lush at the same time. Here's a simple version of the deep-fried pork I ate that day. (There the meat was on the bone and the pieces were larger, then were cut up after cooking; we worked with the proportions below to make the frying easy and as foolproof as possible.)

Serve hot or warm as part of a meal, or as a snack or appetizer with drinks. If serving as part of a meal, include a salad such as Pea Tendril Salad (page 66) or Cucumber–Tree Ear Salad (page 79) and a soup or other moist or well-sauced dish such as Miao Red-Sauced Fish (page 229), as well as rice. [PHOTOGRAPH ON PAGE 308]

About 1 pound boneless pork butt or loin or fresh ham

1 teaspoon salt

BATTER

¾ cup rice flour

¼ teaspoon salt

About ½ cup lukewarm water, or as needed

Peanut oil or lard, for deep-frying (2 to 4 cups)

ACCOMPANIMENTS

3 tablespoons Tribal Pepper-Salt (page 36)

2 limes, cut into wedges (optional)

About an hour before you wish to serve the meal, cut the pork into slices about ¾ inch thick, then cut into approximately 1-inch squares. Place in a wide bowl, sprinkle on the 1 teaspoon salt, and mix with your hands or a spoon to distribute the salt. Cover and set aside for 45 minutes to marinate.

Meanwhile, make the batter: place the rice flour and the ¼ teaspoon salt in a medium bowl. Stir in the lukewarm water to make a loose batter and continue stirring until the batter is very smooth. Set aside.

Set up your deep-frying arrangement: Place a large wok or a large deep pot on the stovetop; make sure the wok or pot is stable (or use a deep-fryer). Pour 2 inches of oil into the wok or pot and heat the oil over high heat. Put out a slotted spoon or mesh skimmer. To check the temperature of the oil, hold a wooden chopstick vertically in the oil. If the oil bubbles up vigorously along the chopstick, it is hot enough. If the oil is smoking, it is too hot; lower the heat a little and wait a minute before retesting the temperature. (A deep-fry thermometer should read about 350°F.)

Pick up several slices of pork, using chopsticks or your fingers, drag them through the batter, and slip them into the hot oil, being careful not to splash yourself. Repeat several times, then use the slotted spoon or mesh skimmer (or chopsticks) to keep the pieces moving in the oil and to ensure that they stay separate. Cook until golden brown all over, about 2 minutes. Use the spoon or skimmer to lift them out of the hot oil, pausing a moment to let them drain, then set on a platter. Repeat with the remaining meat and batter.

Serve the pork hot or warm. Put out condiment dishes of the pepper-salt, so guests can help themselves to seasoning as they wish. We also like to put out (nontraditional) lime wedges; a little squeeze of fresh lime juice complements the pork beautifully.

Serves 4 as a main course, 6 as an appetizer

WEEKNIGHT PORK AND BEAN SPROUTS

This family supper dish from the Dong people (see page 120) in south-eastern Guizhou province is a delicious addition to the weeknight repertoire. You might accompany it with Dai Carrot Salad (page 83) or Pea Tendril Salad (page 66).

I had it on my first evening in the village of Zhaoxing, with a family made up of a nineteen-year-old daughter whose name in English is Kyrra, her parents, and her grandfather. After supper, we waited for Kyrra's parents to change into their finest clothing, then walked along narrow lanes and over a covered wooden bridge to the base of the nearest drum tower (see photo, page 121), which belonged to their neighborhood.

There were rows of wooden benches set up, and Kyrra and I perched on one, along with many people from the village, under the midnight blue sky. In the open piazza beside the tower, the neighborhood troupe assembled quietly, men and women dressed in extraordinary indigo-dyed clothing, the women's full pleated skirts shiny with pounded indigo, the men in short jackets and long indigo trousers; among them were Kyrra's parents. They gave a mesmerizing performance of traditional singing, the harmonies dense and beautiful. They danced too, moving in long lines to the sound of the wooden pipes called *lusheng* (see photo, page 182). At the end of the performance, everyone watching got up and joined the dancers, stepping rhythmically in a long coiled circle beneath the stars: such hypnotic dancing, so timeless.

2 tablespoons peanut oil or lard

1 tablespoon minced garlic

1 tablespoon minced ginger

About ⅓ pound boneless pork butt or shoulder,
  thinly sliced and cut into bite-sized pieces

¼ teaspoon salt

1 to 3 dried red chiles, broken into 2 or 3 pieces each (see Note)

2 cups (about ½ pound) bean sprouts, well washed

2 teaspoons soy sauce

Heat a wok or large skillet over high heat. Add the oil or lard, and when it is hot, toss in the garlic and ginger and stir-fry for about 10 seconds. Toss in the pork slices, salt, and chiles and stir-fry, tossing and turning to expose all surfaces of the meat to the hot wok. When the pork has changed color all over, add the bean sprouts and stir-fry for about 30 seconds, then cover and let cook for about 2 minutes. Remove the lid, add the soy sauce, and stir-fry briefly.

Turn out into a shallow bowl or onto a plate.

Serves 3 to 4 as part of a rice meal

NOTE ON CHILES: With 3 dried chiles, the dish has a definite hit of heat that seems to bring out all the other flavors; if you want a milder flavor, use only 1 or 2 and leave them whole rather than breaking them.

My seat number was 26. It said so right on my ticket, but when I got onto the bus and found the seat (the second single seat on the side opposite the driver, a very good seat), there was a young Miao guy already sitting there. I showed him my ticket and pointed to the number 26, and then pointed to the number 26 right beside his seat, but he didn't budge. I couldn't really blame him for playing clueless. It's worked for me a couple of times too.

Right then the driver climbed up and into his seat, and in an instant he read the situation. He smiled, slapped the seat directly in front of the young Miao—the very front window seat, the best seat in the bus (and for some reason unoccupied), and motioned for me to sit. And so I did. Then the rest of the bus filled and off we went.

Jiangcheng to Jinghong, in southern Yunnan. It took eleven hours the first time I came this way, much of it dirt road, fifteen miles per hour, switchbacks and washouts. The driver this time is Han, maybe older than me, maybe not. He's a cautious driver. He isn't going to rush. Before starting out, he put old-style Chinese music in the tape player, and got comfortable in his seat, his jar of tea beside him. He's going to take whatever time it takes.

Two or three hours in, everyone else on the bus is asleep. The driver pulls up alongside a simple single-story house by the road. Without stopping the engine, he scrambles into the back of the bus and grabs a long narrow wooden bench, then jumps out and runs up to the house. An old man is already coming to meet him, and he beams when he sees the bench. The driver hands it over with a smile, then rushes back onto the bus, and away we go.

My driver has friends all along the way, like a much-loved postman. People wave and he honks back. And I watch him watch his route, taking note of everything, a fallen tree that shouldn't have been cut down, a section of road that is about to give way.

His route is not just any old route. In our bus we have Miao, Hani, Yi—the entire bus is tribal. We pass through Dai villages, and Yao villages, and resettled Hans, tea pickers I think. Every once in a while I ask the driver, "*Shenme minzu?* (What ethnicity?)," and he answers without hesitation. The bus moves along slowly, deliberately, around one switchback, up another, down another. The mountains here are big, covered with tropical hardwoods, or planted with tea or rubber trees, or terraced with rice. The area feels sparsely populated, but I know it's not. There are people living throughout, though sometimes a day's, sometimes several days', walk from the road.

Finally we reach a checkpoint, and we all get checked by the police. Then on we go, but a mile or so down the road the driver stops the bus. A few new passengers appear from nowhere and get on, and then a few more, and then a few more, until finally the bus is absolutely packed, seats doubled up, aisles without a square inch of open space. The driver orchestrates it all, happily, thoughtfully. There's a rule about one seat, one person, but now we're past the checkpoint.

There's money to be earned, of course, by packing the bus, a lot of money. But I think there's more to it than that, at least for the driver. There are two very different worlds, the country and the city, and his bus connects the two.

Nine hours it takes us this time. Slow and steady. ⅉ

OPPOSITE: *A house built around a courtyard in traditional style, in southern Yunnan.*

LISU SPICE-RUBBED ROAST PORK

The Lisu are one of many distinctive cultural groups who live in the mountains of southwestern Yunnan province, high above the valleys of the Mekong and Salween Rivers. Their language is Tibeto-Burman and they follow the Chinese calendar (celebrating Lunar New Year, for example, when the Chinese do, in late January or early February). Traditionally they live by raising pigs and cultivating rice.

At New Year's and other celebrations, pork and sticky rice are the main foods. The pork is roasted over coals or cooked in broth, then served on a large communal platter to accompany mounds of steamed sticky rice or grilled sticky rice cakes. We adapted this recipe for spice-rubbed pork, originally cooked over glowing coals, for cooking as a roast in an oven; we call for a little lard to compensate for the leaner pork that is now standard in North America.

The combination of peppery fresh nutmeg and Sichuan pepper makes a knockout spice rub for pork (you can also use it on lamb). The pork comes out of the oven with a delicious salty spiced crust and moist interior. Serve with sticky rice or plain rice, and a vegetable dish such as Tibetan Ratatouille (page 101) or Market Stall Fresh Tomato Salsa (page 18). Put out a condiment or salad as an accompaniment, such as chopped pickled mustard greens, Tenzin's Quick-Pickled Radish Threads (page 25), or Hani Soy Sprout Salad (page 73).

> About 2 tablespoons lard or bacon drippings
>
> About 1½ pounds boneless pork butt or loin,
>   no more than 2 inches thick at its thickest
>
> 2 teaspoons freshly grated nutmeg
>
> 1½ teaspoons dry-roasted Sichuan peppercorns, ground
>
> ½ teaspoon freshly ground black pepper
>
> 1 teaspoon salt

Place a rack in the center of the oven and preheat the oven to 350°F. Use a little of the lard or bacon drippings to grease the bottom of a roasting pan.

Rinse off the meat and dry thoroughly. Set aside.

Put all the spices and the salt in a small bowl and stir to mix well. Use your fingertips to rub the spice blend all over the meat. Place the meat in the roasting pan with its largest surface facing up. With your fingers or a spoon, dab the remaining lard or drippings all over the top of the meat.

Roast for 50 minutes to 1 hour, until cooked through (timing will vary with the thickness of the meat; if it is 2 inches at its thickest point, it will take closer to an hour). Remove and let stand for 5 minutes.

Thinly slice the meat. If you wish, deglaze the pan with a little water and pour the pan gravy over the slices of meat.

Serves 5 to 6 as a main course

GRILLED SPICE-RUBBED PORK: You can come closer to the original fire-cooked pork of the Lisu if you cook the meat over a charcoal grill. Use pork butt or loin cut crosswise into ¾- to 1-inch-thick slabs. Rub on both sides with the spice blend, then grill slowly (over medium heat), turning the meat once partway through, and basting it with a little lard or oil to keep it moist, until it is cooked through (20 to 30 minutes). Thinly slice before serving.

OPPOSITE: *Lisu Spice-Rubbed Roast Pork, served with Hani Soy Sprout Salad (page 73).*

THE YI PEOPLE AND THE HANI PEOPLE

The Yi are one of the largest non-Han populations in present-day China, with approximately seven to eight million people. They live over a wide area, in towns and villages in the mountainous regions of four different provinces: Yunnan, Sichuan, Guizhou, and Guangxi. There are also Yi populations in Vietnam and in Laos. The Yi were at one time referred to as Lolo, but it's not a term the Yi use, and it is in fact a derogatory name.

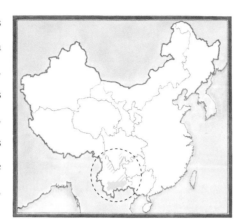

Both the Yi and the Hani languages are in the Tibeto-Burman language family, but the Yi have by far the larger population and are spread out over a much greater area. Much of what we have learned about the Yi comes from the work of American anthropologist Stevan Harrell of the University of Washington. Harrell writes about the concept of ethnicity in China, and those writings have helped us understand what are often very complicated issues.

The mountain town of Yuanyang in southeastern Yunnan seems to be primarily Yi, while the surrounding terraced hillsides are home to the Hani, the people who built and still work the terraces. (For rice-terrace fanatics like us, the Yuanyang terraces are as awe-inspiring as any we have ever seen.) A large town farther south, Luchen, is predominantly Hani, as is another district center, Jiangcheng, still farther south.

The total Hani population in China is approximately 1.3 million. The Hani live mainly on the high southwestern plateau of Yunnan and in the mountains and valleys between the Red River (whose delta is near Hanoi) and the Mekong River. We have always understood that the Hani in China are closely related to the Akha people in Laos and northern Thailand; the distinctive textiles and clothing of the village people in all three countries are very similar.

The Hani and Yi of Yunnan live in a subtropical region, mountainous and forested. There they grow corn, rice, and potatoes, as well as a wide variety of other vegetables. Hani markets in southeastern Yunnan, such as those in the towns of Jiangcheng and Luchen, are colorful and extremely interesting. As in markets in neighboring Laos, there's always a section where you can eat breakfast, lunch, or simply a snack, sitting on a little stool. (The Hani have a particularly beautiful style of low stool with bamboo supports that curve up like buttresses.)

The markets have an almost jungly feel, with much of the produce very specific to this mountainous region of Yunnan. Some of the produce was familiar to us from markets in northern Laos, but many other fruits and vegetables we'd never seen before. There was also a large part of each market for vendors selling tobacco, and always a vendor or two selling three-foot-long bamboo pipes, for smoking the tobacco.

Particularly remarkable to us were the enormous quantities of fresh sprouts that we saw for sale in the Hani markets of Luchen and Jiangcheng. An entire long aisle of each open-air market was full of soybean sprouts, chickpea sprouts, and mung bean sprouts, all in vast quantities. There was also a kind of tofu that we had never seen before (which was also available in the Yi markets in Yuanyang), a little "package" about one and a half inches square, and somewhat firm. It was commonly grilled by street vendors, together with chunks of potatoes, and then dipped in chile sauces. Delicious.

LEFT: *A small Hani market in southeastern Yunnan; the woman on the left is wearing a modern version of traditional Hani clothing.* RIGHT: *In the town of Yuanyang, in southeastern Yunnan, a Yi woman carries her child in an embroidered baby carrier.*

DRINKS AND SWEET TREATS

but at some point midway through this project, we looked at each other and agreed that "Desserts" wouldn't do as a title for this chapter. It's not that sweet foods don't exist beyond the Great Wall, because they do, but not as a separate category of prepared foods.

Fresh fruits—melons, pomegranates, mulberries, and other tender fruits of the Xinjiang oases; apples; and the sub-tropical fruits of Yunnan—are treasured as sweet treats. Kazakhs and Tibetans enjoy sugar added to yogurt. And dried fruits are available almost everywhere. But dessert as we know it in Western countries is a relatively foreign concept beyond the Great Wall.

When we first started traveling here in the 1980s, we would go to great lengths to find tins of peaches, or we'd stand in long queues to buy apples. It wasn't necessarily that we were craving something sweet, it had more to do with the scarcity of fruit in general. In Tibet in the mid-1980s, we discovered packaged Chinese army rations (see "761s, 1985 to 2006," page 331), shortbread-like bars that were semisweet and filling, and great with tea and coffee.

A lot has changed since then, of course. Restaurant culture has blossomed, and there are now many open-air markets and street-food vendors, but desserts (or at least what we can find as travelers) remain few and far between: sweet sticky rice with fruit, cookies of various kinds, and deep-fried doughnuts are about it.

When it comes to "indulgences," tea, beer, and liquor (and, for many people, tobacco) have always been available and much loved. Tea is a way of life beyond the Great Wall and is also a cultural marker: different peoples drink their tea in distinctively different ways (see "Tea, Tea, and More Tea," page 324). Beer is also common. We don't know its history, or how it first arrived in China, but bottles of beer, and bowls of beer, can be found almost everywhere. We like the beer, generally. It tastes like real beer, not having been "lightened up" or "calorie-reduced."

A cup of tea or a glass of beer, some rice pudding or deep-fried sesame balls: welcome to "dessert" beyond the Great Wall.

OPPOSITE: *Pomelos for sale by a Miao villager near Congjiang, in southeastern Guizhou.* ABOVE: *Rock sugar.*

SESAME BALLS
WITH SWEET BEAN PASTE

Sesame finds its way into many savory dishes, often in the form of roasted sesame oil, or as sesame paste (see Noodles with Sesame Sauce, page 149), but it is also an important flavoring for sweets. Here, in a Chinese classic that we've also seen in bakeries beyond the Great Wall, balls of dough puff up in hot oil as they deep-fry, and the sesame seeds that coat them cook to an aromatic golden brown in the hot oil.

These treats are a delight to the tongue—they're about texture as well as flavor. All they require from you is a little patience while you get familiar with the frying technique. Read through the instructions carefully before you start cooking, then enjoy. The balls have a slightly crisp exterior, which collapses as you bite in to a tender interior partly filled with sweetened red bean paste.

1 cup glutinous rice flour

⅓ cup sugar

⅓ cup boiling water

About ½ cup Sweet Red Bean Paste (recipe follows) or
    store-bought red bean paste

Scant ½ cup sesame seeds

Peanut oil for deep-frying (2 to 4 cups)

Mix the flour and sugar together in a bowl. Pour the boiling water over and stir to mix and form a dough. Let stand until cool enough to handle.

Place the filling by your work surface. Divide the dough into 18 pieces (cut in half and then into thirds, and into thirds again). Flatten one piece of dough to a 2-inch round. Place 1 teaspoon filling in the center, pleat the dough up around the filling, and pinch to seal. Roll between your palms to make a rounded ball, then set aside on a lightly floured surface. Fill and shape the remaining balls.

Place the sesame seeds on a plate. Spritz the shaped balls with water. One by one, roll in the sesame seeds to coat and then place them on a tray. Cover the balls loosely with plastic wrap.

Place a large wok, or a deep heavy pot on the stovetop; make sure the wok or pot is stable. (Or use a deep-fryer.) Pour 2 inches of oil into the wok or pot and heat over medium-high heat. Set out a slotted spoon or a mesh skimmer and a paper-towel-lined tray near your stovetop. To test the temperature of the oil, hold a wooden chopstick vertically in the oil, touching the bottom of the pan. If the oil bubbles up around it, it is at temperature. If it starts to smoke, the oil is too hot; lower the heat slightly and test it again. (A deep-fry thermometer should register 250° to 270°F.)

Start by frying just one ball, to get used to the technique. Later on, you can cook 3 or more at a time, depending on the size of your wok or pot. Slide the ball into the oil and cook, using your spoon or skimmer to move the ball around so it colors evenly, for 2 minutes, or until golden. (If it is golden in under 1½ minutes, your oil is too hot; reduce the heat slightly.) Then use the back of your slotted spoon or skimmer to push the ball down firmly, smushing it slightly. It will puff up and then pop back to the surface and turn over; if it doesn't turn over, turn it over with the spoon or skimmer. After another 30 seconds or so, press down again firmly and turn over; repeat several times more, until the ball is puffed and richly golden, a total of about 5 minutes cooking time, then remove to the paper-towel-lined tray. *Do not be impatient!* If the ball browns too fast (in less than 1½ minutes), it won't expand/puff up, and if there are dark brown spots on it (if you don't keep it moving in the initial 2 minutes), they will prevent it from puffing fully. Cook the remaining balls in batches in the same way, allowing about 5½ minutes cooking time per batch.

Serve hot or at room temperature. The sesame balls are of course best fresh from the deep-fryer, but they are surprisingly good even 12 hours after cooking.

Makes 18 filled sesame balls

Sweet Red Bean Paste

Bean paste is used as a filling in many Chinese and Japanese sweets. Use it to fill the Sesame Balls, above, or as a sweet filling for flatbreads.

You can buy red bean paste in Asian grocery stores, but it's very easy to make your own. The cooked pureed beans are sweetened with sugar and blended with a little lard or oil, so the paste has a silky-smooth texture.

1 cup azuki beans (see Glossary)

¾ cup sugar

¼ teaspoon salt

2 to 3 tablespoons lard, melted, or peanut oil

Soak the beans overnight in water to cover by several inches.

Drain the beans and place in a heavy pot with enough water to cover by 1 inch. Bring to a boil, then reduce the heat and simmer, partially covered, until the beans are soft, about 30 minutes.

Transfer the beans and cooking liquid to a food processor and process until smooth. For a very smooth paste, press through a coarse sieve. Place back in the pot and cook over medium heat, stirring frequently with a long-handled spoon to prevent sticking, for 20 minutes. (The mixture will be thick and may "burp" steam; be careful not to get spattered.)

Stir in the sugar and salt and cook for another 5 to 10 minutes. Remove from the heat and stir in the lard or oil, beating to incorporate it completely. Let cool to room temperature. The filling can be stored in a sealed container in the refrigerator for up to 1 week or in the freezer for up to 3 months.

Makes about 2 cups

TIBETAN SWEET TEA

These days in Lhasa, more and more people are drinking sweet tea (*cha la-mo* in Tibetan). It's a style of tea like that in northern India and in Nepal, made with black tea and only medium strong, sweetened with a little sugar, and made pale with milk. With more open borders, enabling slightly easier travel between Tibet and Nepal and India, it seems to have become very popular, especially among the young people.

Tibetan sweet tea is drunk on its own at any hour, stored in thermoses that keep it hot and that can be brought out whenever a guest arrives. The heat and sweetness are very welcome in the cold, dry air. This recipe is for Lhasa-style sweet tea, shaken just before serving to put a little air into it. If you prefer a stronger brew, increase the amount of loose tea you use, and increase the steeping time too.

2 heaping teaspoons loose tea leaves
    (Pu'er, Assam, or Darjeeling)

6 cups water

About ½ cup milk, or to taste

About 1 tablespoon rock sugar or regular sugar, or to taste

Place the tea in a teapot or a saucepan with a lid. Bring the water to a vigorous boil in another pan. Pour it over the tea, and let steep, covered, for 5 minutes. Meanwhile, heat the milk until almost at the boil. Remove from the heat.

Pour the tea through a strainer into a large thermos or a well-sealed large container. Add the hot milk and sugar, cover tightly, and shake to blend well. Pour into individual cups.

Serves 4

We've come to think that tea-drinking traditions are a good way to describe cultural differences. While we associate central China with clear tea (green or oolong or black), the people living beyond the Great Wall drink tea in many different ways.

In Inner Mongolia, the standard tea is milk tea, often served from a samovar (perhaps because of proximity to Russia, but we don't know for sure). There even Han Chinese drink milk tea; it's like a marker of place and belonging. The milk is from local cattle. Mongol nomads and herders add butter and salt to their tea, much as Tibetans do.

In the Xinjiang oases, you'll see men sitting in open-air tea shops called *chai khana* (*chai* is the word for tea), chatting and sipping bowls of clear slightly salty tea, either green tea or black, and again often served from a samovar-like pot (or else from a teapot; see photo, page 176). Up in the Altai Mountains of Xinjiang, Kazakhs and Tuvans drink a lightly salted butter tea. In Guizhou, the Miao and the Dong have a drink known in English as oiled tea. It's a blend of green tea, puffed rice, soybeans, and peanuts, a small meal in a bowl.

Tea is grown on hillsides in many places in Guizhou province by many different kinds of people, including the Miao and the Dong, but the most famous area for tea beyond the Great Wall is in southern Yunnan. Tea (*Camellia sinensis*) seems to have originated near here as a wild tree. The slopes of Yunnan's southern valleys are like a sculpture garden of carefully shaped and tended tea bushes. In early spring, pickers move slowly along the rows of bushes, carefully harvesting young leaves. Later, after the rains of summer, there's another harvest period. (In their encyclopedic book about tea, *The Story of Tea*, Mary-Lou and Robert Heiss tell us that in some areas of Yunnan, tea is harvested from tall old trees deep in the jungle.) The traditional variety of tea grown here is the same as that in Assam (in northeastern India), whereas at higher elevations or in the cooler climates of central China's tea-growing regions, the tea trees are like those of Darjeeling or Fujian.

There's a long history of tea production in southern Yunnan. Green and black teas are produced, but the Dai and Bulong people are especially famous for another style of tea, known as Pu'er tea (Pu'er is a town south of Kunming). The tea leaves are fermented and pressed into bricks or rounds; the best of these are then aged and command high prices. When brewed, Pu'er tea has a dark color. (It's known as black tea in China; what we in the West refer to as black tea has a reddish color when brewed and is consequently known as red tea in China.)

A less refined version of fermented tea, made of twigs and stems and coarse leaves, has for centuries been pressed into bricks and transported over the passes to Tibet by horse caravans. A similar tea is shipped to Mongolia. These days the transport is by truck, but coarse-textured dark brick tea is still sold in the markets in Tibet. Butter tea (*cha po cha* in Tibetan), the classic staple in Tibet, is made of brick tea mixed with hot water, butter, and salt and traditionally churned together. In central Tibet, soda powder (which is like baking soda) is also added to bring out the tea's color. Butter tea is more like a meal than a drink and is still the staple for many Tibetans. Nomads, rural people, and monks and nuns rely on it to keep them warm and fed. It becomes a very filling meal-in-a-bowl when thickened with tsampa (see "Tsampa in a Storm," page 179).

OPPOSITE: *A woman picking tea in southern Yunnan in early spring.*

OPPOSITE, LEFT: *A valiant older nun, photographed outside the Jokhang Temple in Lhasa, where she goes every day to pray; the top of her handheld prayer wheel is on the left.* OPPOSITE, RIGHT: *Eight-Flavor Tea (page 328), with dried pineapple, dried mango, goji berries, Chinese red dates, golden raisins, dried apricot, and rock sugar.* ABOVE: *At every hour of the day and night there are people—lay people and monks and nuns—praying and prostrating by the entrance to the Jokhang Temple.*

wednesday morning in lhasa

Many Tibetans in Lhasa walk to the Potala Palace every morning at dawn and then make a circumambulation of the palace and the hill on which it stands. Some take the time to turn the prayer wheels that are mounted on the whitewashed walls of the route; others just stride briskly along, saying prayers as they work their way through a rosary of prayer beads or spin their handheld prayer wheels.

But the crowd is much heavier on Wednesday mornings, thick like at a country fair. People are more dressed up, in a version of "Sunday best." When I returned to Lhasa recently and saw the crowd on my first Wednesday there (I was out taking photographs), I had no idea what the story was. There was a huge throng of people prostrating to the Potala or fingering prayer beads and praying as they walked. Later someone at my hotel explained it to me: the Dalai Lama was born on a Wednesday, so now Wednesday has become the day of the week that almost everyone makes the Potala circumambulation. It's a quiet form of pro–Dalai Lama expression.

Once they've completed their circuit or two of the Potala (each time around takes about half an hour), many people stop in for a hot tea and a sweet bread twist (see Tashi's Doughnut Twists, page 334) at one of the small food stalls by the circuit route. I stood there sipping my own tea, warming my hands on the cup (the air was chilly at that early hour), and watching the absorbed faces of the Wednesday-morning crowd. N

EIGHT-FLAVOR TEA

This treat is refreshing in the heat and warming in the cold. I first tasted eight-flavor tea on a sunny cool morning in Xining and was delighted by it. It looked so beautiful in the tall glass it was served in, the various dried fruits colorful and intriguing.

These days there's an instant version of eight-flavor tea that is widely sold in China. We prefer to make our own, easily done since all the ingredients are long-keeping pantry items. The ingredients have good flavors and many also have medicinal properties. The dried fruits are there for both sweetness and tartness. We've suggested substitutions here, for there are actually more than a dozen possible ingredients that can make up the eight flavors. What you include depends on what is available and your own preferences.

The less familiar dried fruits, such as dried lychees, wolfberries (known as *goji* in Tibetan), and Chinese red dates (also known as jujubes), can be found in Chinese groceries and Chinese herbal food stores. Wolfberries are orange-red, small (the size of a raisin), smooth-skinned berries with a slightly sweet taste; they are traditionally thought to be good for the eyes and the blood. You'll notice that they are also an optional ingredient in the water used to boil savory dumplings (*jiaozi*; see page 150). Red dates are sometimes included in soup (see Black Rice Congee, page 167); unlike regular dates, they are not eaten raw. They have a mildly sweet taste and are thought to be good for circulation and for the skin.

The water in the desert areas of western China is always a little salty tasting. The salt is welcome in the dryness, and in this drink in particular, salt seems to intensify all the other flavors. We call for a pinch of salt in each serving; try it this way, or do without, as you please.

Serve the tea in tall glasses, to show off the different colors of the "flavors," with long-handled spoons or swizzle sticks, so guests can stir the sugar as it melts in the hot tea. It's pleasant to drink the tea through a wide straw. The recipe is written for 1 serving; if serving 4, for example, put on a large pot of water, multiply the amounts by four and then distribute the tea leaves and flavorings among the glasses. And, as your guests drink their tea, bring another pot of water to a boil, so that you can top off each glass. Surprisingly enough, in our experience the second glass tastes as pleasing as the first. [PHOTOGRAPH ON PAGE 326]

FOR EACH SERVING

1½ cups water

1 teaspoon green tea leaves, or black if you prefer

5 to 8 wolfberries (see headnote)

3 Chinese red dates (see headnote)

2 dried lychees

2 to 5 golden raisins

1 slice dried pineapple, dried mango, or dried peach

2 dried apricots or dried plums

A pinch of salt

1 lump rock sugar (see Glossary), or to taste,
  or regular sugar to taste

Bring the water to a boil. Meanwhile, place the tea leaves and then all the other ingredients in a tall glass or in a glass cup.

Place a metal spoon in the glass (to prevent the glass from cracking when you add the hot water), and add the boiling water. Stir, then let stand for 5 minutes to allow the tea to steep and the dried fruits to soften.

Sip through a straw if you wish, stirring occasionally to help dissolve the sugar.

GREEN TEA SHORTBREAD
WITH POPPY SEEDS

Cookies of various kinds have long been available in China, and packages of cookies find their way to remote corners beyond the Great Wall. Our dear friend Dawn-the-baker, an intrepid cook and traveler, came across shortbread with poppy seeds when she was in Yunnan in the spring of 2000. We asked her to figure out a version of it for this chapter, and here it is, delectable and attractive shortbread, flavored with ingredients local to southern Yunnan: poppy seeds and green tea.

The recipe calls for butter, but in Yunnan lard is the more available and local shortening; substitute lard for the butter if you wish. Use any green tea you like, and grind it to a powder in a food processor or spice grinder, or using a mortar and pestle. The tea gives the rich sweet shortbread an enticing bitter edge.

½ pound (2 sticks) unsalted butter, well softened and
    cut into small chunks

½ cup sugar, plus 2 tablespoons for topping

Generous ¼ teaspoon salt

1¾ cups all-purpose flour

½ cup plus 1 tablespoon rice flour

2 tablespoons finely ground green tea (see headnote)

¼ cup poppy seeds

Position a rack in the center of the oven and preheat the oven to 325°F.

Using a mixer on medium speed, cream the butter, the ½ cup sugar, and the salt until pale and fluffy. With the mixer on low speed, gradually add the all-purpose flour, rice flour, tea, and poppy seeds. The dough should start to come together like moist pie pastry and form into clumps. *Alternatively*, if using a wooden spoon, cream the butter, ½ cup sugar, and salt in a bowl until pale and fluffy. Gradually add the flours, tea, and poppy seeds, beating well after each addition, until the dough is well blended and forming clumps.

Press the dough into a 9-inch square baking pan, removing any air pockets. Prick with a fork, pricking right through to the pan, making rows of marks spaced ½ inch apart. Then cut into fingers 1½ inches by ½ inch or into 1-inch squares.

Bake until the edges of the shortbread pull away from the sides of the pan and the top is touched with brown, 30 to 35 minutes.

Cut the shortbread again while still in the pan. Sprinkle on the 2 tablespoons sugar, then carefully lift the shortbread out and place on a rack to cool.

Makes about 100 shortbread fingers or about 80 small squares

Stalks of sugarcane.

I didn't quite believe it at first when I saw them for sale in the Jinghong market in spring 2006: 761 bars! They are now labeled 781, but there was no mistaking the packaging, no mistaking the contents. We'd practically lived on 761s over the course of five long trips in Tibet in the 1980s, and we'd once seen them for sale, bizarre as it was, in Vietnam (Vietnam and China were at war at the time). But 761s don't otherwise travel all that much.

We never learned the full story about 761s. The picture of the army man on the label was a quick giveaway that 761s are Chinese army rations, but their contents have always been a bit of a mystery. Inside each package are four extremely dense shortbread-like bars, only less sweet. Ingredients are wheat flour, sugar, fat, and not much else. They're good, but not necessarily something we'd put out for guests at home. They are, as I said, very very dense.

In Tibet, we would eat them in the morning with instant coffee that we'd make from the thermoses of boiled water provided in each room, even in the most remote truck-stop hotels. And we'd have 761s as midday snacks, sometimes even for lunch if there was nothing else around.

I can't remember how we first thought to buy them in the Lhasa market, because the packaging doesn't automatically register as food. They also weigh a lot, more like a bar of yellow laundry soap than something you would eat. But however we discovered them, they became an important part of life.

On our first bicycle trip in 1985, we ate them all day long, as we were almost always low on calories. Eating a 761 was like eating four granola bars compacted into one, and sometimes we'd open a package thinking we'd eat just one bar and then end up eating all four. There was a little wrinkle about the manufacturing date, because each package had a date—maybe 1982 or 1983. But they never tasted stale, and we'd always buy up as many as we could find, no matter what the date. I don't know what we'd have done without 761s.

So anyway, there in the Jinghong market, twenty years later, I bought two packages of 781s. I resolved to eat one and take the other one home to show Naomi. A few days passed. I was no longer in Jinghong, and I was having a coffee. I opened a package and had a bite, then another bite.

It had been a mistake, buying just two packages. J

OPPOSITE: *A portrait of 781 bars, taken in Yunnan.*

Kaili, Guizhou: Here I am in the next-to-last seat in the bus. It's a familiar feeling. We won't leave until the bus fills, and we're still five or six people short. Meanwhile, I write in my journal and watch the scene. There's a Miao mother across the aisle nursing her baby, and a pair of leather-jacketed young men just in front of me, smoking away. It's supposed to be a six- to eight-hour ride to Congjiang, the town I'm aiming for tonight, and then tomorrow I'll have another two hours on bad roads to get to Zhaoxing, the big Dong village where I want to spend a chunk of time.

Ah, the driver's starting the bus. At last, we're off. . . .

No, not yet, after all. The bus driver turns off the engine, climbs down from the bus, lights a cigarette.

Stragglers hustle into their seats. Parcels get stowed in the small racks overhead.

I have a window seat, and the window is a large one that opens wide: such a treat, the fresh air, the clear view, and the chance to escape most of the cigarette smoke.

Now, once again, the driver starts the engine. This time we really are leaving.

We make our way through the streets of Kaili. My neighbor, a young guy dressed in black, offers me a hard candy. We begin to head south through the steep green landscape. A child waves to the bus from the side of the road. I wave back, and my heart lifts. Good-bye bus-stand blues. N

ABOVE: *Young children, hardy and lively, in the bright cold air of Tingri village, in early November. Across a wide open plain, Mount Everest and its neighboring peaks, including Cho Oyu, are dazzlingly visible when the sky is clear.* OPPOSITE: *Tashi's Doughnut Twists (page 334), with a glass of sweet tea.*

TASHI'S DOUGHNUT TWISTS

In Lhasa, and in smaller Tibetan towns in Sichuan, Gansu, and Qinghai, you'll see stacks of these deep-fried treats for sale, especially in the morning. Bakers make them and sell them by the handful. The Tibetan name for them in Labrang is *gori maro*. Our younger son, Tashi, has loved them since the first time we made them. They're slightly sweet, a rich golden brown on the outside, and tender in the center, a pleasure with morning tea or coffee.

The shaping puzzled me until I spent time hanging out at a Tibetan bakery in Labrang watching the dough get transformed into double coils. The instructions look long, but once you've shaped one, you'll understand the sequence and then it will all happen easily. Each piece of dough is rolled out to a long, thin snake that then gets twisted on itself twice before being slipped into the hot oil. We often shape and bake half the dough one day, leaving the rest for the next day (see Note on Timing below).

Make these for breakfast or for brunch, or as a late-afternoon snack for a hungry crowd. [PHOTOGRAPH ON PAGE 333]

3 cups all-purpose flour, plus extra for surfaces

½ cup sugar

½ teaspoon salt

1½ teaspoons baking soda

About 1¼ cups lukewarm water

Peanut oil for deep-frying (2 to 4 cups), plus extra for surfaces

If using a food processor, place the flour, sugar, salt, and baking soda in the processor. With the blade spinning, slowly pour the lukewarm water through the feed tube until a ball of dough forms. Continue to process for 15 or 20 seconds. *If working by hand*, combine the flour, sugar, salt, and baking soda in a large bowl. Stir to mix. Make a well in the center and add 1 cup of the water. With your hand or a wooden spoon, stir the water into the flour mixture until all the flour is moistened; add more water if necessary. Knead in the bowl until you have a dough.

Turn the dough out onto a lightly floured surface, then knead it for several minutes, until it is very smooth and elastic. Cover with plastic wrap and let stand for an hour or so. The dough will soften and expand a little as it rests.

Lightly flour a work surface. Lightly oil a nearby surface.

Using a dough scraper or a large sharp knife, cut the dough in half. Set half aside, loosely covered. Working on the floured surface, cut the remaining dough into 8 equal pieces, cutting it in half and then in half and half again (each piece will weigh about 1¾ ounces). Roll one piece under your flattened palms, pressing outward slightly as you do so, into a long rope. The rope will gradually lengthen under your hands; once it is about 10 inches long, set it aside for a moment and start to roll and stretch a second piece in the same way. Come back to the first piece (the dough will have had time to relax a little) and roll it until it is 18 to 20 inches long.

Move the long rope onto the oiled surface. Anchor one end of it on the work surface with one thumb and roll the length of it under the palm of your other hand, rolling always in the same direction, so that gradually it twists more and more. When it is well twisted, pick up one end of the rope in each hand and bring the ends toward each other. The loop of rope will coil on itself. Pull on the bottom loop of the coiled dough to lengthen it slightly, then lightly press it flat on the oiled work surface. Once again anchor one end of it, the one with the two ends of dough, and use your other palm to roll the dough in the same direction as the coils that are already there, in order to twist it further. Lift up both ends and bring them toward each other. The loop will again coil on itself, slowly, making about one and a half twists. Bring the ends together and tuck the open end into the loop of the other end, then pinch to secure it.

The double-twisted dough will be about 4 inches long. Place it back on the oiled surface and press down lightly. Set aside on an oiled baking sheet while you shape the remaining 7 pieces, then divide and shape the other half of dough into another 8 twists (see Note on Timing). Set the sheet of shaped twists near your stovetop.

Place a large wok or deep heavy pot on your stovetop; make sure the wok or pot is stable. (Or use a deep-fryer.) Pour 2 inches of oil into the wok or pot and heat the oil over high heat. Set out a slotted spoon or mesh skimmer. To test the temperature of the oil, hold a wooden chopstick vertically in the oil, touching the bottom of the pan. If the oil bubbles up around it, it is at temperature. If it really sizzles or starts to smoke, the oil is too hot; lower the heat slightly and test it again. (A deep-fry thermometer should read 325°F to 350°F.)

Slide in one shaped twist. It will sink, then slowly rise back up. After about 30 seconds, use the slotted spoon or skimmer to gently turn it over. It should be golden, not dark brown. (If the doughnut darkens more quickly, your oil is too hot, so lower the heat slightly; see Note on Troubleshooting.) Let cook for another 30 seconds, then turn it back over. The second side should now be a medium brown. Cook for another 20 seconds or so on each side, or until the doughnut is medium to dark brown. You will see attractive pale lines where the twists cross over. Use the slotted spoon or skimmer to lift the twist out onto a paper-towel-lined plate.

Repeat, this time starting with one twist and then adding a second if your pot is large enough, when you turn it over for the first time. Cooking times will be a little longer when you cook 2 or more at a time. Cook the remaining shaped twists in the same way. Allow to cool for several minutes before serving.

Makes 16 twists, 4 to 5 inches long; serves 8 as a snack or for breakfast

NOTE ON TROUBLESHOOTING: If the oil is too hot, the outside of the twists will quickly turn a rich dark brown and crust over before the center has cooked; if this happens, lower the heat slightly before putting in the next dough twist.

NOTE ON TIMING: You can shape and cook half the dough, then refrigerate the remaining dough, wrapped in plastic, for as long as 24 hours. The process of dividing and shaping the dough will eventually warm it to room temperature, but the cool dough ropes will probably take a little longer to stretch.

In the village of Labrang, not far from the monastery, there's a small bakery. Every day the baker shapes and cooks stacks of doughnut twists. Here some of the dough has already been shaped and is ready to be dropped into the hot oil, while at the lower left, the baker's hands are shaping yet another twist.

OPPOSITE: *Tibetan Rice Pudding (page 339), made with small pieces of dried apple.*

LEFT: *A monk outside one of the large temples at Labrang Monastery in Gansu.*

RIGHT: *A traditional Tibetan house in western Sichuan, set in fields where cattle graze.*

"No, there's no mare's milk in this region," said Ma Yun Da Lai, an expert in Mongolian milk products. "That's only in the western regions. Here we have cow's milk." I met Mr. Ma in the small city of Yakishi, in the northern part of Inner Mongolia, where he has a small laboratory. He was working to develop a liqueur made from milk.

As a person who happens to dislike the taste of milk, I had a feeling of dread when he poured me a wineglass of the milk liqueur. Oh no, I thought, another of those moments when you just have to hold your breath. I took a cautious sip. . . . It was a delicious surprise, mildly alcoholic, and definitely not milky tasting. I was reminded of Bailey's Irish Cream and said so. Mr. Ma smiled broadly. I asked if *koumiss*, the traditional Mongolian drink made from fermented mare's milk, had inspired the liqueur. "No, not really. *Koumiss* is fermented and this is distilled. In fact, I was more aiming for the taste of Bailey's," he said, pulling out a bottle. We laughed, then tasted the Bailey's and the milk liqueur side by side. The Bailey's was sweeter and more alcoholic; the milk liqueur was more aromatic, and definitely my favorite of the two.

It had been a day of new tastes and new ideas. Earlier, at lunch, I'd been offered a local berry wine, pale pink, light (about 5 percent alcohol), slightly aromatic, and not at all sweet. It's called *lam mei cu* (pronounced "lam may tsu") and known by its initials, LMC. I was with some people from Yakishi who had generously decided to take me to lunch.

Every once in a while someone would raise a glass. Then we'd all raise our glasses and drink together, not in a "bottoms-up" way, but sipping as we wished, the wine a good accompaniment to the simmered elk and other local dishes on the table. The wine is made from cloudberry-like berries that grow in the mountains nearby. So far it's not available except in Yakishi. To my regret, I couldn't even find a bottle in Hailar to take home with me. **N**

The contents of a Mongol home, a ger, waiting for the frame and covering to be erected around them. The Mongol families who live out here on the Hulun Buir grasslands (north of Hailar in Inner Mongolia) move every fall to be closer to the river.

TIBETAN RICE PUDDING

This delicious version of rice pudding, known as *de-sil* in Tibetan, uses broken rice (the lowest grade of rice; see Glossary), which is ideal for the pudding because the broken grains release starch as they cook, creating a thicker, smoother texture.

In Tibet, there's a little brown root, rather like a miniature yam, that is gathered in the wild and then dried. Small piles of it are for sale in the markets, and it is traditionally used as a sweet flavoring in this rice pudding, sometimes in combination with raisins from Xinjiang. We substitute dried apple, chopped into small pieces, for the Tibetan root, and we skip the raisins, as we prefer to let the subtle perfume of the apple stand on its own. Do feel free to substitute golden raisins for some or all of the dried apple if you wish. The other sweet flavoring is honey. Use a pale, clean-tasting flower honey.

Serve the pudding in small bowls for dessert or as a snack, either plain, or drizzled with a little more honey or butter or yogurt, or a combination. Leftovers make a welcoming breakfast (see Note).

[PHOTOGRAPH ON PAGE 336]

3 cups water

1 cup broken rice

Pinch of salt

3 cups whole milk

½ cup packed dried apples, preferably organic, chopped into
 ½-inch or smaller pieces

3 tablespoons clover honey or other flower honey,
 or more to taste

2 tablespoons butter, or to taste (optional)

Bring the water to a boil in a small heavy pot. Place the rice in a sieve and rinse with cold water to clean it, then sprinkle into the boiling water. Bring back to a boil, then lower the heat to medium-low and cook, covered, until most of the water is absorbed and the rice is soft, about 15 minutes.

Add the salt, then stir in the milk and apples. Raise the heat and bring back nearly to a boil, then reduce the heat to very low, cover, and simmer for 45 minutes to 1 hour, stirring occasionally with a wooden spoon to make sure the rice is not sticking; after about 30 minutes, add the honey and stir in. When cooked, the pudding will be very thick.

Just before serving, stir in the butter, if using.

Makes about 6 cups; serves 6

NOTE ON REHEATING: If left to stand for any time after cooking, the pudding will thicken even more. To reheat it or to loosen the texture, place over low heat, and stir in up to 1 cup more milk (as well as the optional butter). Stir frequently as the pudding warms, to prevent sticking.

BEER, ETC.

In our travels beyond the Great Wall, we can't remember a time when we wanted a beer and couldn't find one. We could be in a village at 15,000-feet elevation in far western Tibet, and there'd be beer to drink with dinner. Or we could be in a small predominantly Muslim village in Xinjiang, and sure enough there'd be beer, tall brown or green glass bottles of beer. Beer is almost everywhere, which is remarkable, but how it gets there might be even more remarkable.

Once we were traveling by truck through the Changtang, the high desolate region of western Tibet, a region where you can drive all day and never see another vehicle. Late one afternoon, we reached a tiny "truck stop," where we were going to spend the night. Far in the distance we could see a large old truck making its dusty way across the landscape, traveling about ten to fifteen miles per hour, bumping, shifting gears, lurching along. Finally it got to the truck stop and came to a shuddering halt in the middle of the road. People suddenly started to appear from nowhere. Soon boxes of beer were being tossed off the truck and money was changing hands. We too rushed to the truck, grabbed several cases of beer, and paid the wild-eyed driver for it. A few minutes later, he got back in his cab and the truck drove off, slowly grinding its way along the dirt road, bottles clinking and clanking.

There's booze other than beer beyond the Great Wall, but most of it's local. We once stayed in a guesthouse in Menghan, in southern Yunnan, sleeping on a mattress on a slatted wood floor in a beautiful Dai post-and-beam house built on stilts. It was a great place to stay, and the food served at the guesthouse was some of the best food we've ever eaten in Southeast Asia. The only problem was that we had a hard time sleeping because we could hear constant commotion all night from chickens perched on the wooden beams just beneath our room. One morning, when we went to look at them, we realized that, apart from the chickens, we were sleeping over the brewing area: twenty or thirty enormous earthenware vats of local rice liquor, rather like sake, were down there fermenting by the hour in the tropical heat.

Liquor made from rice and other grains is common throughout Guizhou and Yunnan. Like *lao khao* (rice liquor) in neighboring Thailand and Laos, it is fermented but not distilled; it has a very easy, nice taste and seems to have a little less alcohol than wine. The same is true for the common local drink in Tibet, *chang*, which is most often homemade from barley and usually served in bowls.

Guizhou is famous as the home of China's most well-known distilled liquor, Mao Tai. Mao Tai, like many types of Chinese commercial liquor, is made from sorghum and is extremely strong, much stronger than Western whiskeys. We can tolerate Mao Tai, but just barely. It tastes too much like *baijiu* (white liquor), a generic Chinese firewater that is almost as ubiquitous as beer but much more lethal. One kind of Chinese liquor we like a lot, a dark medicinal drink made from millet, is called Wu Jia Pi. If you ever see it for sale, buy a bottle and try it, a taste of far away.

OPPOSITE: *In the rural markets of Guizhou, there's always a laneway or alley where men buy and sell tobacco. Since before buying one must sample the tobacco on offer, the men are couched on their haunches smoking small stone pipes of tobacco as they examine the cured leaves of tobacco for sale.*

FROM LEFT: *A mother and child in the village of Dafdar, along the Karakoram Highway in the Pamirs; a weathered man in Kashgar; a Tajik family who welcomed us into their small house in Dafdar. (The sunlight is coming in through the open smoke hole in the roof, which is right above the family's tandoor oven.)*

THE TAJIK PEOPLE

The Pamir Mountains at the far western edge of Xinjiang province are home to the small population of Tajik people who live in China. They number approximately 42,000 and live in a small area that extends from just north of the old frontier village of Tash Kurgan south to the Pakistani frontier. In neighboring Tajikistan, Afghanistan, Uzbekistan, and the upper Hunza Valley of Pakistan, there are about fifteen million Tajiks. Unlike the other peoples in Xinjiang, who speak Turkic languages, the Tajiks speak an Indo-European language that is related to Persian. The Pamir Tajiks include smaller groups who speak Wakhi and other Iranian languages.

Younger Tajik women wear their hair in many long braids down their backs, decorated with buttons down their length. It's a striking and attractive look. A Tajik woman in the small town of Tash Kurgan told us that once a woman has had a number of children, she has no time for the elaborate braiding required and then just keeps her hair in one or two braids, with no decoration. The women's brightly colored cotton dresses are worn over leggings or pants, and they cover their heads with colorful caps or scarves.

The Pamirs are high snow-capped mountains separated by broad U-shaped valleys. Because of the elevation, and the winds that blow nearly year-round, the agricultural season is short and not much can be cultivated. The Tajiks keep herds of sheep, goats, and camels, which graze on the sloping treeless pastures on the flanks of the mountains. These days, in winter most Tajiks live in small hamlets or villages in houses built of stone, but in summer many live in yurts and move with their herds from grazing ground to grazing ground.

The town of Tash Kurgan is an overnight stop for trucks and buses traveling the Karakoram Highway (between Kashgar and Pakistan's Hunza Valley). It's the modern version of the role the town had for centuries as a frontier post on the old Silk Route. There's an old fort at the edge of town (see photo, page 5); you can climb up to the ruins, get a view of the valley, and imagine the era of Marco Polo. Because of the business generated by the road, we suppose, Tash Kurgan has several bakeries, run by Uighurs, and restaurants and inns, run by Han or Uighur people.

The Tajik houses and yurts that we have seen are very inviting spaces. The houses are rectangular or square and the yurts round, but both usually consist of one large room divided into separate spaces by different floor levels. In the center is a tandoor oven, below a smoke hole in the roof that also lets in light. A higher floor is built to one side of it as a sitting and living area, and against the far wall are stacked folded quilts and blankets. Another area, at yet a different floor level, is the food preparation/kitchen space, where sacks of flour and other staples are stacked against the wall.

The staples of the Tajik diet are breads made of wheat flour; goat's or sheep's milk; yogurt and butter made from the milk; tea; and, on rare occasions, meat. The other outstanding Tajik staple in our experience is hospitality (see "The Pamirs, June 1986," page 141).

Two young nuns in Lhasa.

AFTERWORD

In the stories and essays scattered throughout this book, we describe the amazing food, the remarkable people, and the unforgettable places that lie beyond the Great Wall. But by far the best way to appreciate them all is to travel there yourself, whether independently or as part of a group tour. All you really need to get started is a passport, a visa for entering China, and a plane ticket. Well, and perhaps a sense of adventure!

Travel beyond the Great Wall is not like a holiday in the South of France or a cruise through the Greek Isles, and we don't expect it to be. What enchants and fascinates us are the extraordinary cultures of the people who live in the far reaches of what we think of as the Chinese empire, and the dramatic landscapes in which they live.

The regions beyond the Great Wall were inaccessible to foreign travelers for so long, enticingly out of reach, that perhaps the most remarkable aspect about traveling there is simply the fact that we can. There are various ways to get started. You can fly directly to Beijing, Shanghai, or Hong Kong, then fly or take a train from there. We often enter through Thailand, flying up to Kunming or Jinghong from Bangkok or Chiang Mai. You can also enter by land (see "Border Crossings," page 348). You can cross into Yunnan from Laos or Vietnam, but both these options take more time. People come across on the Trans-Siberian railway from Europe, and then down through Mongolia. Or you can enter through northern Pakistan over the Khunjerab Pass, or from Nepal through the Himalaya, or from Kyrghyzstan or Kazakhstan into northern Xinjiang, but all of these land border crossings depend on the season, and, to some extent, on which way the political winds are blowing. (For the most current information, we always check the Lonely Planet website called The Thorn Tree, at http://thorntree.lonelyplanet.com.)

Many people coming from abroad choose to travel with an organized tour, which is a good option if you don't speak any Mandarin, are tight for time, and don't mind touring in a group. But do some research ahead. There is a great website called the Oriental-List, and we highly recommend subscribing to it in the months or weeks leading up to a trip—or for that matter, anytime (www.members.shaw.ca/pnhpublic/China.html). It's free, and the person who makes it happen, Peter Neville-Hadley, has been traveling to remote parts of China for years. Other people frequently add postings to pass along the name of a particularly good tour operator (or a particularly bad one) and information about interesting places to visit, places off the beaten path. As we've tried to convey in some of the essays in this book, there can still be nowadays, to some extent, a Wild West quality to travel in central China and beyond the Great Wall, a sometimes rocky ride between scam artists and people who are salt-of-the-earth. One of the best ways we know to prepare for navigating the unexpected, and to be a little more travel-savvy, is to read the postings on the Oriental-List and on The Thorn Tree.

Everyone is different when it comes to traveling, but a few strategies have worked well for us over the years in our travels beyond the Great Wall. First of all, when you find a great hotel or guesthouse, or a small town or village where you really feel comfortable, if you have some time, stay put. Make yourself at home. Rent a bicycle. Find a place to eat that you like returning to and become a "regular." It makes a world of difference.

Second, not all places are created equal. Certain towns and villages, such as Yuanyang, Menghan, Zhaoxing, and Gyantse, are extraordinarily beautiful, while others are dismal, ugly, or just awful. And while dismal, ugly, and awful can be interesting, a small dose is better than a big dose.

We try to plan trips that allow us to spend as much time as we can in remarkable places or on bus journeys through beautiful landscapes.

Third, don't try to do it all in one trip. Distances are big beyond the Great Wall. Plan a trip to Tibet, or to northern Xinjiang, or to Yunnan. Don't try to hit them all. See "Suggested Itineraries," below.

Pay attention to time of year, and, if possible, avoid the three big holiday weeks in China (see "Golden Weeks," page 194). If you can, try to visit or stay in remarkable places when they're at their peak. Look at temperature and rain charts for different areas; they can give you a good idea about what to pack as well as which season will suit you best. We were in Tibet in December once, and while we appreciated the chance to see Lhasa in pilgrim season, our days were very short. We spent a lot of time snuggled in our warm sleeping bags drinking hot drinks, and not much time walking around outside. Summer and early fall are beautiful in northern Xinjiang, Qinghai, and central Tibet, for example, but very rainy in Yunnan and Guizhou.

If you are traveling independently, you want to leave room for serendipity. Don't overplan your itinerary, but do research the region(s) you hope to visit. Before you go, spend a few long evenings on the Internet. With so many people teaching English in out-of-the-way places and writing blogs, it is unparalled as a traveler's tool.

Finally, we recommend travel books (see the Bibliography) and photography books. Check out a stack from the library. Lose yourself in the stories of early travelers and in the images—a donkey cart in a desert oasis, a snow-capped mountain and a team of yaks, a drum tower in a Dong village. It's not only okay to romanticize, to let images reverberate in your head long before you go, it's important. And when you're there, once you've traveled all the way around the world to get to your destination, drink a big bottle of beer and pinch yourself: you're actually there. Have fun!

You can't do everything at once, and in fact slowing down and concentrating on one area or region makes travel more rewarding. Here are some possible itineraries for your travels beyond the Great Wall, followed by suggestions about border crossings.

CULTURAL DIVERSITY IN YUNNAN

timing: Anytime but the rainy season (June to September).

note: Yunnan is so complex culturally that we recommend close reading of guidebooks, the Internet, and ethnographic texts to give you more ideas.

- You can fly or travel by bus to Jinghong and then do a loop through Sipsongpanna on the Lao and Burma border, where the majority population is Dai, and where there are also Lahu, Jingpo, and other villages. Great local markets and good trekking possibilities; ask around in Jinghong.
- If you start in Jinghong and head northeast, to the Red (Yuan) River Valley, you come into Yi and Hani country with amazing rice terraces and lively markets; by bus or car and driver.
- West of Kunming lies Dali, a travelers' mecca in a majority Bai area on Lake Er Hai. From there you can get to Lijiang, a Naaxi area. Good trekking in the Tiger Leaping Gorge area nearby.
- Northwest of Kunming, in the hills that border Sichuan, around Lake Mugu, are villages of various cultures, including Yi; read Stevan Harrell's books (see the Bibliography) for more.

TIBETAN LANDSCAPES OUTSIDE TIBET

timing: Best from May to November.

- Western Sichuan and Yunnan: Make a loop, starting in Chengdu going west to Litang, then heading southwest through Chagcheng (sometimes written Xiangcheng) and Derong toward the Tibetan towns in western Yunnan (Deqen, Zhongdian, etc.). You can do this trip in a series of buses or, more expensively, by hiring a car and driver in Chengdu. Allow at least two weeks. You could also start in Kunming, in Yunnan, and do the trip in reverse. Horse trekking possibilities.

- Qinghai, western Sichuan, and Gansu: Starting in Chengdu or in Lanzhou (in Gansu), you can take a circular route through mostly Tibetan towns, and through some wild and wide open landscape; several of the great rivers of Asia rise in this region, including the Yellow, the Yangtse, and the Mekong. Allow three weeks. Much of this area has been open to outside travelers only a short while. Plan to spend extra days in Litang, Dege, Yushu, Madoi, Tongren (Reting), and Labrang. You might try going trekking or on a horse trek in the Amne Machin Mountains or near Zoige, in northern Sichuan. Try the local Hui specialties as well as Tibetan dishes.

TIBETAN ITINERARIES WITHIN THE TIBETAN AUTONOMOUS REGION (TAR)

timing: Best from May to December.

note: You now need special permits for travel outside the Lhasa area, and you must have a car and driver or travel with a group—either option is expensive.

- Central Tibet: Fly to Lhasa and travel by bus or hired car with driver past Yamdrok Lake (Yamzho Yumco) to Gyantse and then on to Shigatse (Xigazê); you could then loop back to Lhasa or continue to Sakya Monastery before looping back to Lhasa. Allow at least three or four days. If you continue past Shigatse, the road leads to the Everest region, now being developed for tourism, and then over the mountains to the Nepali border.
- Excursions from Lhasa include a day or two camped at Nam Tsho (sometimes Nam Co), a lake northwest of Lhasa; a one- or two-day trip to Reting Monastery, north of Lhasa; a one- or two-day trip to Samye Monastery; an arduous three-day hike to Samye, and much more. Study a guidebook or ask on The Thorn Tree for more ideas.
- Pilgrimage to Mount Kailas and area, including Lake Manasarowar and the border town of Burang, in far western Tibet (only until late October). You will need to hire a vehicle and driver, or go with a group; allow three weeks. Allow three days or more for the *parikrama* (circumambulation) of Mount Kailas. Unless you are with a group tour, bring your own camping supplies.

SILK ROAD

timing: Best from May to late October.

- Northern route: Take the train or fly to Jiayuguan or Yumen (the western gate of the Great Wall), or fly or go by bus to Dunhuang, then travel west from one oasis to the next by train or bus or with a car and driver. Allow three weeks. You'll pass through, and hopefully spend time in, Hami, Turpan, Korla, Kulcha, and Aksu, and eventually reach Kashgar (Kashi), far to the west near the Pamirs. From there you can fly back east to central China, or else continue to Pakistan through the Pamirs. See "Border Crossings," page 348, for other branchings off from this itinerary.
- The southern route is a rougher, less traveled option. As above, fly or go by bus to Dunhuang or Yumen. Or travel to Golmud by train, plane, or bus. Take buses or go with a car and driver along the route between the southern oases, including Kargan, Hotan (famed for its silk for centuries), and Kargilik (also known as Yecheng). Eventually you'll have circled round far enough to connect with the northern route at Kashgar—see above for options from there. There's also a road connection between the north and south routes that links Korla to Ruoqiang.

CULTURAL DIVERSITY IN GUIZHOU AND GUANGXI

timing: Guizhou is often rainy; February, July, and August are the wettest in both provinces.

note: As with Yunnan, the cultural complexity of Guizhou demands that you look carefully at guidebooks and ethnographic writings before you travel.

- Fly to Guiyang and then travel by bus to Kaili. Use Kaili as a base for Ge and Miao towns and markets nearby, then travel by bus southeast to Dong areas in both eastern Guizhou and western Guangxi.
- From Guiyang head west and south to Boyei areas, and from there continue by bus into Yunnan (see page 346).

INNER MONGOLIA: GRASSLANDS AND STEPPE

timing: The grasslands are green and lush only from mid-June to September, and that is when there are festivals and also crowds.

- Take the train or fly to Hohhot and then travel by bus or car and driver, or in a group, to the grasslands about three hours north. There are possibilities for horse trekking and more.
- Travel by train from Lanzhou, in Gansu, into Ningxia and the Ordos region (in the loop of the Yellow River), and get out at one or more towns such as Yinchuan or Wuhai along the way. Genghis Khan is buried in the region—check guidebooks for details.
- Fly or take a bus to Hailar, in northeastern Inner Mongolia, then travel an hour north to the Hulun Buir (sometimes Hulanbir) grasslands.

border crossings

Check for visa requirements before you leave. Some border crossings can be done in only one direction (in other words, you can leave but not enter by that route, or vice versa) and the rules change from time to time.

INTO/OUT OF XINJIANG

- Across the Khunjerab Pass, from Pakistan's Hunza Valley, along the Karakoram Highway to Kashgar (May to October only).
- Across the Tian Shan Mountains from Aksu into Kyrgyzstan.
- Across the Tian Shan Mountains from Kashgar to Kyrgyzstan.
- In the far north, the crossing at Yachung into Kazakhstan.
- West of Urumqi, the crossing into Kazakhstan at Korgaz.

INTO/OUT OF TIBET

- Across the border with Nepal, north of Kathmandu. Note that this road is subject to washouts in rainy season and to heavy snow in early spring.
- Across the border to western Nepal. Nepalese authorities control access to the other side closely. The closest town on the Tibet side is Burang. (This crossing is possible only in the warmer months.)

INTO/OUT OF INNER MONGOLIA

- By the trans-Siberian railroad, via Ulaanbaatar (Ulan Bator) in Mongolia, crossing at Erenhot in Inner Mongolia.
- By road or train through Manzhouli, at the Russian (Siberian) border.

INTO/OUT OF YUNNAN

- There used to be a train between northern Vietnam and Kunming, a spectacular journey, but for the moment that is closed. The only option now is travel by local buses.
- There is a border crossing to Burma (Myanmar) from Ruili, in southwestern Yunnan, that is sometimes open to foreigners.
- The border with northern Laos is changing with the building of a new superhighway from Kunming through Laos to Thailand. The border has been open for some years to allow foreigners to leave; entry has been more difficult, but this could change at any time.

A NOTE ON SINICIZATION AND CULTURAL SURVIVAL

In the 1950s, the Chinese government embarked on a system of classifying all the peoples living within the borders of its country. It was an inventory of people and culture, conducted by anthropologists employed by the government. The original classification identified fifty-four "minority nationalities" as well as the Han majority, and since then there has been some fine-tuning of the categories.

The idea seems slightly distasteful to us, this classification or categorizing of people, but in one sense it does represent an acknowledgment of the existence of many distinctive cultures within China. What it doesn't highlight, however, is the overwhelming numerical and political advantage of the Han majority, and the power it has to influence or overwhelm the other smaller cultures, a process referred to as sinicization.

Sinicization has been taking place for centuries. For example, after the Manchus conquered China in 1644 and established the Qing Dynasty, they adopted many aspects of Han Chinese culture, abandoning their nomad traditions and eventually losing their language. The Zhuang, a large group living in Guangxi Province, have now so assimilated that in many areas they are practically indistinguishable from their Han neighbors.

Sinicization occurs in different ways. As part of the process of nation-building, shortly after the Revolution, the central government imposed a standard Chinese language on the whole country (the language chosen was Beijing dialect, known in English now as Mandarin) and embarked on a massive literacy campaign. In many areas beyond the Great Wall, schooling is given only in Mandarin. In some places such as Tibet and Xinjiang, there are also schools that teach in the local language, but these are generally of lower quality. Children who attend Chinese-language schools are at an advantage when it comes to higher education and good jobs. This creates pressure on minority-culture parents to send their children to Chinese-language schools, which in turn puts their own language and culture at risk.

Another threat to minority cultures is the movement of Han people from central China to the areas beyond the Great Wall. There was movement of this kind before, but on a very small scale compared with now. After the Revolution in 1949, the Beijing government deliberately moved troops and settlers into non-Han areas in order to assert sovereignty and to control local populations, especially in Xinjiang and Tibet, where nationalist feelings were strong. Over the last twenty years, the government has invested in tourism and also in mining and manufacturing in areas beyond the Great Wall, encouraging Han Chinese settlers to migrate there in an effort to stabilize the areas politically. The expansion of the railway network (including the completion of the railway to Kashgar in 1999 and to Lhasa in 2006) is dramatically accelerating the process.

The media, of course, also plays an important role in cultural change. In the past, the Beijing government communicated with people via loudspeakers in every town and village, broadcasting slogans, rules, and reminders of political orthodoxy, all in Mandarin. The growth of television gave Beijing even greater access to people on the periphery, with more than sixty channels, all closely monitored by the government for political correctness and all but a few broadcasting only in Mandarin.

GLOSSARY

AMARANTH: See GREENS.

AZUKI BEANS: These small red beans, rather like miniature kidney beans, are from the plant *Vigna angularis* and are sold in East Asian groceries and health food stores. They can be cooked, like other beans, for savory dishes, but are most often used in China to make sweet bean paste, a filling for pastries.

BARLEY: Barley (*Hordeum vulgare*), one of the earliest cultivated grains, originated somewhere in the Tigris and Euphrates Rivers area. Barley can tolerate dry heat and cold and drought, and it is relatively salt-resistant. It is a staple crop in desert areas of western Asia, in western Europe, and in Tibet, where several varieties are grown. The whole grains, often referred to as barley berries in North America, can be milled to make **barley flour**. The berries, like the flour, can be found at many health food stores. In Tibet, barley is usually roasted in hot sand, then ground into a fine flour-like powder called tsampa (see Tsampa, page 180).

BEAN SPROUTS: Many seeds will sprout if kept moist and warm. Legumes such as soybeans and mung beans are widely used in their sprouted form. Sprouting makes the hard seeds more tender and sweeter. The sprouts have less protein, fat, and carbohydrate than the beans and more B vitamins and vitamin C. They can also be cooked more quickly. In this book, both mung bean (*Phaseolus aureus*) sprouts and soybean (*Glycine maximus*) sprouts are called for. To sprout mung beans or soybeans, use about ¼ cup organic beans, wash well with water, place in a wide-mouthed 2-quart jar, and cover with a damp paper towel or damp cotton cloth. Rinse with water twice a day. The seeds will start sprouting in three to four days and will be ready to eat, or cook and eat, on the fifth day. You will get about 10 times the volume of beans you started with: ¼ cup beans yields a generous 2½ cups sprouts. **Mung bean sprouts** are the most com-monly available, found in the produce sections of most grocery stores, and they are usually referred to simply as bean sprouts. They are a pale almost-white and 2 to 3 inches long, with a small seedpod at one end. When fresh, they are crisp-tender. They should always be thoroughly washed before using. They can be stir-fried or simply blanched in boiling water for a moment to soften them before being dressed (see Index for recipes). **Soybean sprouts** are more robust and longer, often 4 inches long; they are available in Asian grocery stores and specialty produce markets. (Photograph on page 92.)

BEAN THREADS: See CELLOPHANE NOODLES under NOODLES.

BROKEN RICE: See RICE.

CELERY SEEDS: The seeds of the celery plant (*Apium graveolens*), greenish and aromatically celery-tasting, with an edge of bitterness, are available in supermarket spice sections and in South Asian groceries (usually under the name *radhuni*). They are used in some Tibetan dishes. See also CHINESE CELERY, CELERY LEAVES.

CELLOPHANE NOODLES: See NOODLES.

CELTUCE: A species of lettuce (*Lactuca sativa* var. *augustana*), sometimes called Chinese stem lettuce or asparagus lettuce, celtuce originated in China and was introduced to Europe and the United States. (In Tibet it is known as *osun*.) It has a fat pale green stem like a long thick broccoli-like stalk, about a foot long, with a tuft of tender lettuce leaves on top. We have only seen green-leaf celtuce but have read that there are also white and purple-leafed varieties. It grows as a winter crop in warm areas of China, and in temperate climates it grows like leaf lettuce, for harvest in the fall. Celtuce seeds are available in North America but it is rarely sold here as a vegetable. If you do find some or grow your own, prepare it as you would kohlrabi or broccoli stalks: peel the stem, then thinly slice it and stir-fry it. The top leaves can be cooked as greens or eaten as a salad green.

CHICKPEAS: Chickpeas (*Cicer arietinum*) are large round legumes, like outsized green peas; in North America they are widely known by their Spanish name, *garbanzo*. They grow in pods and when fresh are a strong green color. They're most widely available (in supermarkets as well as health food stores and South Asian groceries) in dried form, when they are an off white to pale yellowish beige. Like other legumes, they can be sprouted, as we saw in the Yi and Hani markets in southern Yunnan (see Hani Soy Sprout Salad, page 73).

CHILES: Chiles originated in Central and South America and were taken to Europe and Asia and Africa during the era of European exploration and colonial expansion. In some regions, they displaced the traditional local heat-giving ingredients, such as ginger and black pepper; in others, they supplemented them. Most chiles are the fruit of an annual bush, *Capsicum annuum*, but they vary widely in color, shape, and degree of chile heat. Even within a single variety, there may be wide variation in the amount of chile heat. One well-traveled chile, the bird chile, is the fruit of a perennial, *Capsicum frutescens*. Chiles are rich in vitamin C and seem to have antibacterial properties. They can bring not only warmth but also distinctive flavor to a dish. The "heat" in a chile is a measure of the amount of capsaicin in the fruit. The membranes and the seeds tend to have a higher level of capsaicin than the flesh. After handling chiles, be sure to wash all surfaces, knives, and your hands thoroughly; wear gloves if you have sensitive skin. Avoid rubbing your eyes.

BANANA CHILE: Mild, about 8 inches long and 3 inches across at the top, and tapering to a soft point, banana chiles have only mild to medium chile heat (though this can vary). They are a pale green to pale yellow color.

Hungarian wax chiles or cubanelles, both in the pale yellow, long, wide chile category, can be substituted.

BIRD CHILE: Unlike other chiles, which are the fruit of an annual, *Capsicum annuum*, bird chiles are the fruit of a perennial, *Capsicum frutescens*. They are small, from ½ inch to 2 inches long, narrow, and sharply pointed with an intense chile heat. They are sold green, a solid medium dark green, or brilliant red, the color they turn when completely ripe. They are sometimes referred to as Thai chiles.

CAYENNE CHILES: Cayennes are the workhorse chiles of India and the Subcontinent and common in many parts of the Caribbean as well as in Southeast Asia. They are green when immature and then ripen to a brilliant red. Cayennes are elegant looking, long and narrow and smooth; they are from 5 to 8 inches long and under 1 inch across at the top, tapering to a narrow point. They have medium heat. Cayennes are used fresh or pickled. The chiles we have seen laid out to dry and most of those that we have eaten in Yunnan and Guizhou are cayenne chiles or very like cayennes. A second chile we saw there was more rounded, with a slightly sweet flavor and milder heat, like the Spanish *pimentón*. (Photograph on page 16.)

CAYENNE PEPPER: Cayenne pepper (sometimes known as cayenne powder) is made of dried red cayenne chiles that have been ground to a powder. A rich reddish brown, it is generally intensely chile-hot. Cayenne peppers vary, so proceed with caution when you buy a new batch. Store as you would any other ground spice, well sealed in a glass jar away from light and heat.

CHILE BEAN PASTE/CHILE BEAN SAUCE: A very versatile seasoning paste, widely available in Chinese grocery stores (in small bottles; we look for Lee Kum Kee brand), and used as a flavoring in many dishes from Sichuan, as well as in some Miao and Dong dishes—

and elsewhere, we're sure. The basic flavors are chiles, Sichuan pepper, salt, and garlic, in a base of cooked mashed soybeans, with no sweetness. The paste gives some heat, but not an overwhelming amount. It is added to hot oil or hot cooking liquid as a seasoning and flavor base. Store, once opened, well sealed in the refrigerator.

CHILE OIL: Chinese and Southeast Asian grocery stores sell chile oil, made with dried red chile flakes in oil, usually cottonseed oil. We suggest that you make your own chile oil; see recipe, page 29. It takes little time, tastes far better than commercial versions, and keeps well in the refrigerator. It is used to give heat and flavor both as a table condiment and as an ingredient in cooked dishes.

CHILE PASTE: Made of dried red chiles ground and cooked in oil, usually with additional flavorings such as garlic and salt and sometimes other spices (star anise, for example), chile paste is sold in Chinese and Southeast Asian groceries and is a useful pantry staple. As with chile oil, you can easily make your own (Guizhou Chile Paste, page 35), with better oil than is usually used in manufactured pastes (where cottonseed oil is common). Fresh chile paste (see Bright Red Chile Paste, page 18) is made from fresh chiles and seasonings, with no cooking.

DRIED RED CHILES: Autumn is harvesttime for chiles, as for many other crops, and it's thus the time when large woven mats are spread with fresh chiles and laid in the sun to dry. They're a beautiful sight in many villages in Guizhou, Guanxi, and Yunnan. Dried red chiles keep well and can be used instead of fresh chiles to give heat to cooked dishes. Look for dried red chiles from Thailand or India. Once you find a brand you like, stick to it, so you know the heat and can adjust for it; like most other products of the vegetable kingdom, dried red chiles vary in heat and flavor.

Spices for sale in Lhasa: chile flakes and (on the left) star anise.

CHINESE CABBAGE: See NAPA CABBAGE.

CHINESE CELERY, CELERY LEAVES: Chinese celery is also known as leaf celery, as opposed to pale-stemmed leaf-stalk celery, the more common form of celery in the West; both are varieties of *Apium graveolens*. Chinese celery is a more intense green in color, with tough, fibrous green stems and tender leaves that look like enlarged coriander leaves at first glance (see photo, page 221). It is pungently aromatic and strong tasting. Celery leaves are chopped and used as an herb in parts of China and Southeast Asia. The whole plant can also be used as a vegetable, in soups or in stir-fries, though its stems are tough and stringy and must be finely chopped; lovage is a good substitute for the leaves. See also CELERY SEEDS.

CHINKIANG VINEGAR: See VINEGAR.

CHINESE RED DATES: Also known as jujubes, Chinese dates are the fruit of a small tree (*Zizyphus jujuba*) that has been cultivated for millennia in China. When fully ripe, the fruit is a dark orange-red, the size and shape of a date, with a large stone inside. The skin is edible. When relatively fresh, the fruit is plump and smooth looking, with firm flesh; when it is more dried out, the skin is

Duck at the market in Chong'an, Guizhou.

wrinkled looking and the flesh softer. The fruit has a mild sweet taste, and it is used cooked, not raw, as a flavoring in tea or soups or stews (see Eight-Flavor Tea, page 328; and Black Rice Congee, page 167). In traditional Chinese medicine, jujubes are used as an energy tonic; they are believed to be good for circulation, the spleen, and the skin, and are considered to be warming.

CHIVES, CHINESE CHIVES: Chives are all members of the onion family, *Allium*. In North America, the most common chives are fine green, hollow, round stems that grow in bunches, *Allium schoenoprasum*. Perennials that grow well in cool moist well-drained soil, they have a tender texture and strong oniony taste and aroma. They are sold in small bunches and used as a fresh herb. In Asian groceries, you are more likely to find flat green leaves, not as tender as regular chives, sold in fairly large bunches; these are Chinese chives, *Allium tuberosum*, sometimes referred to as *garlic chives*. Sometimes they are sold as *chive flowers*: flower buds on long stems. The leaves and bulbs may be cooked and eaten as a vegetable; the leaves can also be used fresh in place of regular chives, if finely minced (see photo, page 43).

COOKING OILS AND FATS: For stir-frying and deep-frying, we almost always use cold-pressed Chinese peanut oil. We buy it in large cans; it also comes in plastic bottles. It has a good clean taste and is more stable at high temperatures than other oils. You can substitute canola oil if you wish, or if you have people in your life who are allergic to peanuts; canola oil is less stable at high temperatures. The other cooking fat that is widely used in China is rendered fat, rendered pork fat (lard) in Yunnan and Guizhou and Sichuan, and rendered lamb or goat fat in Xinjiang and other predominantly Muslim areas.

To render your own fat, start with good clean fat, preferably from organically or naturally raised animals. Trim fat off the meat whenever you buy it, then store, well wrapped, in the freezer until you have accumulated a pound or more. (If you buy pork belly, for example, it comes with a thick edge of fat that you can trim off easily before using the meat.) When ready to proceed, chop the fat into ½-inch cubes or smaller pieces and place in a wok or heavy skillet over medium heat. Use a spatula to move the pieces around until they start to give off a little liquid fat. Once they do, raise the heat a little to speed up the melting process and continue to move the pieces around to prevent scorching. After 10 to 15 minutes, all the fat will have melted, leaving small cracklings. Use a mesh skimmer or slotted spoon to scoop up the cracklings and drain them on a paper towel. (Use like croutons in salads or as a topping for rice, lightly tossed with a little salt if you wish.) Remove the melted fat from the heat and let cool for several minutes, then pour into a clean, dry glass jar. (If you wish, you can strain it through cheesecloth to remove any debris.) Let cool, then cover tightly and store in the refrigerator. Half a pound of chopped fat yields about ½ cup rendered lard or lamb fat.

CORIANDER: The coriander plant (*Coriandrum sativum*) is a temperate-climate annual that also grows well in the subtropics. It yields an herb (its tender leaves and stems) and a spice (its seeds). **Coriander leaves**, also known by their Mexican name *cilantro*, are used as an herb and a garnish in many of the cuisines beyond the Great Wall. Sometimes, instead, Chinese celery leaves are used, es-

pecially with meat dishes. **Coriander seeds**, round and pale and about ⅛ inch in diameter, are used, ground, as a spice by some cooks in Tibet. As with all spices, dry-roasting them before grinding them brings out their flavor. Bunches of fresh coriander are now available in most produce sections; coriander seeds are sold in the spice sections of grocery stores.

DAIKON: See RADISHES.

DEEP-FRYING: A method of cooking that is really very easy if you are set up for it, but that many home chefs avoid. The food cooks immersed in hot oil, and because oil can be brought to a much higher temperature than water, it can be a very quick way of cooking both savory and sweet foods. The essentials are a large stable pot, either a large wok or a wide pot about 4 inches deep (or a deep-fryer); a slotted spoon or a mesh skimmer for lifting food out of the oil and letting excess oil drain off it; and peanut oil, lard, or another oil that is stable at high temperatures. (We like having a good strong ventilation fan.) You may also want a thermometer, but we suggest you use "the chopstick test": The oil should be at about 350°F. To test, hold a wooden chopstick vertically in the oil with the end touching the bottom of the wok or pot. If bubbles rise up the side of the stick, the oil is hot enough. The oil should not smoke; if it does, turn down the heat a little and wait a minute before testing again for temperature and cooking. Individual recipes give detailed instructions for deep-frying. Just remember that the oil needs to stay hot, so do not add too many items at once.

DRIED SHRIMP: Sold in clear cellophane packages in Chinese and Southeast Asian stores, dried shrimp are used to add depth of flavor to a number of dishes. Look for bright-colored shrimp, and choose smaller ones over larger ones. Once you open a package, seal very tightly (to keep the pungent odor from wafting out) and store in the refrigerator.

EGGPLANT: While the most familiar eggplant to North Americans is large with a dark black-purple skin, eggplants (*Solanum melongena*) come in many different shapes, sizes, and colors. In China, the most common varieties are long, slender, and pale or medium purple. This type of eggplant, often referred to as **Asian eggplant**, **Japanese eggplant**, or **Chinese eggplant**, is now sold in well-stocked produce sections as well as in Asian markets. It does not need salting and rinsing, as some large Mediterranean eggplants do, to wash away bitterness. Just slice it or chop it, without peeling it, and use as directed. Eggplant can be grilled or roasted or used in stir-fries and simmered or braised dishes.

FAGARA: See SICHUAN PEPPER.

GARAM MASALA: Literally "hot flavor powder" in Hindi, garam masala is made of roasted spices ground to a powder. It's widely sold in South Asian groceries, as well as in gourmet markets. Use as a last-minute flavoring, to give a hint of cinnamon, cumin, and coriander.

Yi woman in Yuanyang, Yunnan.

GARLIC: In the last few years, China has begun exporting large quantities of garlic to other countries in Asia, such as Thailand, as well as to North America. The low price seems to have pushed many North American garlic growers out of the market. We encourage you to buy local garlic whenever possible.

GARLIC CHIVES: See CHIVES, CHINESE CHIVES.

GINGER: A rhizome, ginger (*Zingiber officinale*) can be grown in tropical to temperate climates. It is available in most supermarkets. It has a pale yellowish tan outer skin and crisp yellowish flesh that can be fibrous and tough in mature ginger. Buy ginger that is firm to the touch; the finer and smoother the skin, the fresher the ginger. Young ginger, very fine-skinned ginger with pinkish knobs on it, is available only at some times of the year (usually June to August). It is the most tender of all.

To use, peel off the outer skin with a knife or peeler. To mince, cut into slices, then stack the slices a few at a time, cut into sticks and then cut crosswise into small pieces. To cut into matchsticks, slice lengthwise, stack the slices, and cut lengthwise into narrow batons. Store ginger in the refrigerator, loosely covered in plastic. As it ages, ginger becomes softer and the skin wrinkles, while the flesh becomes fibrous. (Photograph on page 17.)

GLUTINOUS RICE, GLUTINOUS RICE FLOUR: See RICE.

GOAT MEAT: We enjoyed getting more familiar with goat meat while working on this book. Goat meat is sold at many kosher butchers, in Caribbean groceries, and at South Asian groceries, especially at halal butchers. We were told by a butcher that regulations require that the tail be left on sheep and goat carcasses so that they can be told apart: goats have narrow tails, sheep tails are wider. In North America, goat is generally much less expensive than lamb and yet it has a very similar good flavor.

GOAT'S MILK, GOAT'S MILK YOGURT, GOAT CHEESE: Goat's milk is increasingly available in large grocery stores and in health food stores, as is goat's milk yogurt.

The protein structure of goat's milk means that stabilizers or thickeners must be added to get a thick creamy texture in the yogurt. Goat cheese, particularly aged goat cheese, is very like the aged or dried cheese that is used in Tibetan cheese-filled breads and cheese *momos*.

GOJI: See WOLFBERRIES.

GREENS: Leafy green vegetables have an important place in most central Chinese cuisines and in many of the cuisines beyond the Great Wall. Of the numerous greens used in China, an increasing number are becoming available in markets and produce sections in North America. We've listed the ones that we refer to in this book below, but if you come across an unfamiliar Asian green, do try it. The easiest "first try" approach is to wash it well, drop it into a pot of boiling salted water, and cook until just tender, then drain and dress with rice vinegar, soy sauce, and a dash of roasted sesame oil. Or, instead, you could substitute it in one of the recipes that calls for greens. See also NAPA CABBAGE and CELTUCE.

AMARANTH GREENS: These attractive greens have become more available here recently. They may be bright green or else pink-red with green. The stems of all but the youngest plants are quite tough, so trim off the tougher stems and then wash and chop up the remaining tender stems and the leaves. Use in stir-fries or soups, or simply parboil and dress for a salad. (Photograph on page 241.)

BOK CHOI: Sometimes spelled *bok choy*, this is perhaps the most common Chinese green. There are actually several varieties and they are sold in several sizes. **Regular bok choi** has white stems and dark green leaves. **Shanghai bok choi** is a medium matte green color all over. The vegetable has wide, tender, flat stalks with long rounded leaves, growing from a short stem to create a loose green head; both stems and leaves are eaten. **Baby bok choi** are about 3 inches long; regular bok choi may be a foot long. To use, cut lengthwise in half and place in a bowl of water to rinse well. Lift out, drain and use as is, or chop. See also TAIWAN BOK CHOI. (Photograph on page 259.)

MUSTARD GREENS, PICKLED MUSTARD GREENS: Mustard greens are leafy greens in the *Brassica* family. They are sold in Asian grocery stores and in produce markets. Most versions available in North America look a little like a loose head of lettuce, with bright or dull green leaves attached at the bottom of the stems to make a loose head. They have a pleasing touch of bitterness and a suggestion of mustard in their cabbage-family flavor. They are best used in soups or in stir-fries with pork. Pickled mustard greens, a useful addition to the pantry, are a dull khaki green in color. They are sold in Chinese and Southeast Asian groceries, usually in clear plastic packages, and are often labeled sour mustard greens. They consist of a wedge of a head of greens, a thick piece of stem with attached leaves. The mustard is parboiled, then soaked in a brine of just salt and water, so flavors are simple and clean. To use, turn out into a bowl, with the brine, then lift out a piece, rinse in fresh water if you wish, and chop off the amount you want. Use in stir-fries to give a tart or sour note. Or finely chop and set out as a condiment or topping (see the congee recipes on pages 167 and 173, for example). Store leftover pickled greens in their brine in a sealed nonreactive container in the refrigerator (as you would other pickles) and use as needed; they keep well.

PEA TENDRILS/PEA SHOOTS: The growing tips of the vines that produce sugar snap peas or green peas are widely used as a vegetable in Southeast Asia and in parts of China. Tender, with a mildly sweet flavor, they are a real favorite in our house. They're now sold in most Chinese and Southeast Asian groceries, as well as in many specialty produce markets. Two main versions of pea tendrils are available in North American markets, both of them delicious. The more traditional kind have strong twining stems and tender tips; each stalk is about a foot long. These are sold loose, by weight, or in large bags. They must be chopped into shorter lengths before being used in stir-fries, or parboiled and dressed, or added to soups. The smaller, finer version, tender stems with fine leaves, is sold in small clear plastic bags and is best prepared as a very quick stir-fry, on its own, simply flavored with garlic and salt. (Photograph on page 66.)

TAIWAN BOK CHOI: This is the name given to a green that is almost like a small, more tender romaine lettuce, with long, flat, medium-green leaves growing from a short stem. It is relatively new to us; we like its tender texture and delicate flavor.

HOG PLUM: A sour green fruit that is very occasionally available in Asian produce markets in North America, hog plums (*Selaeocarpus madopetalus*) are oval and usually 2½ to 3 inches long. The fruit has a large pit, thin dull-green skin, and crisp or hard flesh. It is used in Southeast Asian cooking, including Dai cooking, to give a sour note in savory dishes. Its name in Dai and in Thai is *makawk*. We find that tomatillos are the best substitute.

JINJIANG (BLACK RICE) VINEGAR: See VINEGAR.

JUJUBES: See CHINESE RED DATES.

KELP: See KOMBU.

KOMBU/KONBU: *Kombu* is the Japanese name for dried kelp. The plant it comes from is a seaweed, *Laminaria*, that grows in large fronds in the ocean. It is sold in dried rectangular sheets about 3 by 5 inches. To use, soak in lukewarm water until softened. Kombu can be eaten uncooked, or chopped and stir-fried, or used to deepen the flavor of soups or other dishes. It is a natural source of MSG. Known in Mandarin as *hai dai*, kombu is sold in East Asian groceries and in many health food stores.

LAMB, LAMB FAT: Lamb is the meat of young sheep; the meat of older sheep, usually referred to as mutton, is not called for here. You can substitute goat meat for lamb in any of these recipes, if you wish, as people seem to do in the regions beyond the Great Wall. In Central Asia, from Xinjiang to Afghanistan, the preferred variety of sheep is fat-tailed sheep. The animals have large, heavy tails, which is where they store extra fat, presumably an adaptation that has enabled them to survive in unpredictable and harsh environments. Small cubes of lamb fat are often included in kebabs and in meat-filled breads to enrich them. Until recently, when vegetable oils became more easily available in Central Asia, dairy and meat fats were the only ones available, especially for nomadic peoples, and there's still a preference for animal fat over vegetable oils. See also COOKING OILS AND FATS.

LARD: See COOKING OILS AND FATS.

MAKAWK: See HOG PLUM.

MATCHSTICK CUT: To cut ginger or carrots into matchsticks, first peel and then slice lengthwise or on a long diagonal, to give a large surface area. Stack several slices and cut into narrow matchsticks.

MEAT: Though many meats unfamiliar to North Americans are eaten beyond the Great Wall, in this book we call for only those meats that are readily available and acceptable to most people in North America. This means that we have omitted dishes that involve dog meat or camel or horse meat. Dog meat, from a special variety of dog bred for the purpose, is eaten in some parts of southern China, by the Miao and Ge people as well as by the Han. Camel is a staple meat (and a treat) for Uighurs, some Mongols, and others who live in arid areas and raise camels. (In specialty Uighur restaurants in Shanghai and Beijing, you will see menus offering braised camel's foot and other unfamiliar delicacies.) Similarly, horses have long been a staple for some Mongols and Kazakhs and for Tuvans. The horses provide milk and then meat for nomads and seminomads living in the western part of Inner Mongolia and for Tuvans in the northern tip of Xinjiang.

MILLET: Millet is actually the name of a family of grains in the genus *Panicum*. Millets can be grown in dry, hot areas and so are important traditional food crops in desert regions—for example, in parts of Inner Mongolia and in Rajasthan in India, as well as in sub-Saharan

Africa. The millet eaten in parts of Europe and northern China, *Panicum miliaceum*, also known as common millet, has small round pale yellow grains. It's called *xiao mi*, or small rice, in Mandarin. Most health food stores sell whole millet. To use, place in a sieve and rinse well under cold running water before cooking. Millet cooks best in plenty of water; once cooled, it solidifies into a mass; to reheat, add a little water and stir.

MINORITY PEOPLES: "Minority peoples" is the English translation of the Mandarin term used by the Beijing government to describe all the non-Han peoples within the People's Republic of China. At the moment, there are fifty-five recognized minority peoples. (Both anthropologists and some of the peoples themselves would argue about some of the categories; for example, in some cases, smaller groups have been lumped into a larger one, without distinction. For a complete list of the government's approved minority peoples, go to www.china.org.cn/e-china/population. Thirteen of the non-Han peoples living in China are discussed in more detail in this book: Tibetans, Mongols, Uighurs, Dong, Kazakhs, Miao, Hui, Dai, Tuvans, Kirghiz, Yi, Hani, and Tajiks. Several others are mentioned or appear in photographs: Bai, Lisu, Ge, Zhuang, and Manchu.

MONOSODIUM GLUTAMATE/MSG: A white powder that is added to cooked dishes by many cooks in China, both in central China and beyond the Great Wall, to deepen or bring out the flavor of the dish. On its own it tastes not of salt, as you might expect, but meaty, the flavor known in Japanese as *umame*. In Tibet it's known as *vechin*, a version of its name in other parts of China, *vetsin*. If you want to try using it, use roughly in the same quantity as you use salt in the dish. See also KOMBU/KONDU.

MUNG BEAN THREADS: See CELLOPHANE NOODLES, under NOODLES.

MUSHROOMS: Gathered **wild mushrooms** are widely used in Tibetan cooking and wherever they are available in other places beyond the Great Wall. **Dried mushrooms** and **fungus** are a staple of Chinese cooking, practical in difficult climates because they can be transported and stored easily. **Dried shiitake mushrooms** are widely available in Chinese groceries and health food markets, sold in clear cellophane bags. The best are those with a cracked pattern on the caps. The mushrooms must be soaked in warm water until they soften, then can be used in simmered dishes and in stir-fries; the mushroom soaking water is usually added to the dish (or saved for a soup stock) so no flavor is lost. **Dried tree ears**, sometimes called **wood ears**, and **dried cloud ears** are a dried fungus, **Auricularia**. They are used in stir-fries, mostly for their texture. Tree ears are dark, almost black, lightweight, and crumpled looking; cloud ears are paler. Both are available in Chinese and Southeast Asian groceries. They keep indefinitely if well sealed in plastic. To use, soak in warm water for 15 minutes or so, then drain, trim off and discard any tough bits, and thinly slice the smooth, slightly gelatinous fungus. They have little flavor but add a pleasing soft crunch. You may also come across presliced tree ears or cloud ears; we find they don't have as good a texture as the whole ones, but they can be substituted if necessary. (Photograph on page 65.)

NAPA CABBAGE (BRASSICA RAPA, SUBSPECIES PEKINENSIS): Also known as Chinese cabbage, Tientsin or Shantung cabbage, or celery cabbage, Napa cabbage is a large long cabbage with tightly wrapped crisp flat white stems topped with pale yellow-green leafy edges. In Mandarin it is *bai cai* (prounced "bai tsai"), meaning white vegetable. It has a slight mustard flavor. It can be cut crosswise into slivers or separated into leaves and chopped; both techniques are used in this book. The cabbage can be eaten raw or blanched, as salad, but it is often stir-fried or simmered or braised. It is the main ingredient in the most common form of kimchee, the Korean chile-hot pickled condiment. In many parts of China it is also pickled by simple brining: it is usually sun-dried for a few days, then placed in a heavy crock, layered leaf by leaf with salt, and weighted down. Once the leaves soften and ferment, they keep well, a useful food and source of flavor for the long winter months. (Photograph on page 95.)

NOODLES: Check the Index for a listing of recipes for handmade wheat flour noodles and rice noodles. Many other noodles are sold, fresh or dried, in Chinese and Southeast Asian grocery stores; we list here the ones we mention in this book.

CELLOPHANE NOODLES/BEAN THREADS: A commercial product made from processed dried mung beans, also known as Lungkow green bean threads or bean vermicelli, these noodles are an extremely handy and long-keeping pantry staple. Cellophane noodles are sold in 500-gram (1-pound) cellophane packages and in 100-gram packages in East Asian grocery stores and well-stocked supermarkets. The thin translucent-white strands, which look like shiny string, are very tough when dried and are best cut with sharp kitchen scissors. The larger packages may be divided into four bundles, each tied with white string, or the noodles may be in just one large tangle. To divide a bundle, pull it apart and snip with scissors to separate a section of noodles. They must

A woman and her daughter, grilling in Yuanyang, Yunnan.

be soaked in hot water for 10 to 20 minutes before being cut into lengths and cooked. Once soaked, they are tender but still firm, so they keep their shape even when simmered in soup or after they are tossed with a dressing or sauce. (Photograph on page 56.)

EGG NOODLES: As the name suggests, egg noodles contain some egg, which gives them strength. Chinese egg noodles usually are yellowish in color and are sold dried, looking like fettuccine, in 500-gram (1-pound) packages.

FRESH RICE NOODLES: Fresh rice noodles are sold in Chinese and Southeast Asian groceries in larger cities. They come cut or in folded wide sheets, in which case they are usually labeled *sa-ho* noodles, and they can be cut into strips. They should be rinsed in warm water

A Uighur woman working at her outdoor kitchen, Kashgar oasis, Xinjiang.

before being stir-fried or added to soup. They require little cooking.

RICE STICKS: Rice sticks are noodles made of a paste of soaked ground rice and water, cut into either narrow or wide noodles, and dried. They are brittle when dried and must be softened in lukewarm water for about 15 minutes before they are stir-fried or added to soups or simmered dishes. Rice sticks can be found in Chinese and Southeast Asian grocery stores, usually in 500-gram (1-pound) packages (allow about 1 pound dried noodles for 3 to 4 people). They keep indefinitely in the pantry if well sealed in plastic. (Photograph on page 56.)

NUTMEG, MACE: The seed of the fruit of the nutmeg tree (*Myristica fragrans*) is the source of two spices: nutmeg and mace. Nutmeg is the seed itself, about 1 inch long and shaped like an elongated sphere; mace is the net-like outer covering (the aril) of the seed. When added in small amounts, both spices give a warm, aromatic flavor to both sweet and savory dishes. You can buy ground nutmeg, but it's better to buy whole nutmeg and to grate it when you need it.

OIL: See COOKING OILS AND FATS.

PEANUT OIL: See COOKING OILS AND FATS.

PEPPER: Black and white pepper are the dried fruits of a tall climbing vine (*Piper nigrum*) that thrives in tropical climates. For black pepper, the peppercorns are picked unripe, then placed in the sun to dry and to ferment. For white pepper, the ripened fruits are soaked and the outer layer is stripped off before the peppercorns are dried. Black pepper has a more aromatic flavor; white pepper is sharper in taste. See also SICHUAN PEPPER.

PICKLED MUSTARD GREENS: See MUSTARD GREENS under GREENS.

POMEGRANATE: An ancient fruit that grows on a small tree, *Punica granatum*, the pomegranate may be red or

yellow or a blend of the two, and it may be sweet or sour. Inside the tough leathery skin are nested groups of white seeds covered in soft pink-red pulp. The seeds can be eaten raw as a refreshing fruit or pressed for juice, sweet (which has some tartness to it) or sour. If the sour juice is cooked down and concentrated, the result is **pomegranate molasses.** Both the juice and the molasses are used as souring agents in meat cookery across Central Asia, as well as in the Caucasus and Turkey. Lime or lemon juice or unsweetened cranberry juice can be used as a substitute. Pomegranates are in season from late September until about February. They are cultivated from the Eastern Mediterranean to the Caucasus, across central Asia, and south through Iran and Afghanistan into northern India.

QUINCE: The fruit of the tree *Cydonia oblonga*, and related to apples and pears, quinces are large, yellow, and oddly lumpy looking. They are available in fall. They are hard and sour when raw, but with a sweet fragrance. When cooked, they are still tart, but pleasing, and their flesh turns pink. They are used in Turkish and Persian cooking, and in Central Asia, to add a tart-sweet note to meat dishes and *pulaos*.

RADISHES: Radishes that are very like the European radish—small and rounded, with a cherry red or pink exterior and bright white crisp interior—are grown across Central Asia, including in Xinjiang, where they are used raw in salads. In Tibet we've seen pink-tinted radishes, and we have been told that the traditional radishes were pink but have now largely been displaced by varieties of white radish, *Raphanus sativus spp.* **Daikon** (the Japanese name) or **white radishes** are a useful vegetable beyond the Great Wall, for they are hardy and can be grown in very cold climates. They are relied upon in Tibet and parts of Yunnan as a pickled vegetable (see Tenzin's Quick-Pickled Radish Threads, page 25). They are also used in soups and stir-fries. Daikon radishes may be white or pale green, and they vary in size, from about 6 inches long to over a foot; usually they are about 1½ to 2 inches wide at the top with a stubby pointed tip and sometimes a little green still at the leaf end. Buy firm, smooth-skinned radishes and choose smaller ones over larger. Store in the refrigerator. You may see these labeled or referred to as white turnip in Chinese groceries; when they are sold pickled, the label will often read "white turnip pickle" or "preserved turnip." Daikon are hotter tasting in the summer and milder and sweeter in the winter.

RICE: Most of the daily rice in the milder-climate areas beyond the Great Wall (Yunnan, Guizhou, Guanxi, and parts of Sichuan) is locally grown. These local rices aren't exported, so we suggest that you look for a white rice that you enjoy (our household favorites are Thai jasmine and American-grown Japanese-style rice) and adopt it as your staple rice. We list here the rices mentioned in the book as well as others that you may want to try as an accompaniment to dishes from beyond the Great Wall.

BHUTANESE RED RICE: This attractive partially polished rice from Bhutan has been available in North America for more than ten years. It has medium rounded grains, takes about 10 minutes longer to cook than white Mediterranean rices, and has an agreeable nutty flavor. Use it for hearty dishes such as lamb or goat *pulao*.

BLACK STICKY/GLUTINOUS RICE: Though black sticky rice grows in Vietnam and Bali as well as in Thailand and southern China, we have seen only black rice grown in Thailand for sale in North America. Black rice is unpolished rice that has a black bran rather than the more common pale brown bran. Inside the bran is a white grain of glutinous (sticky) rice. Because of the bran, when cooked, black sticky rice does not cling to itself. It is often cooked in a blend with polished rice, and the black in the bran stains the polished rice a beautiful purple color. Like other sticky rices, black rice has a slightly sweet flavor; it is also very aromatic when it is cooking. Also see CHINESE BLACK RICE.

BROKEN RICE: Rice brokens are the broken grains that result from rice milling. Rice is graded in part according to the proportion of broken grams: the fewer there are, the higher the grade. Consequently, brokens are gathered and sold separately. During cooking they release their starch, making a smoother stickier texture, ideal, for example, for rice pudding (see Tibetan Rice Pudding, page 339). Broken rice is widely available in Asian markets.

CHINESE BLACK RICE: Sold in North America under the name Forbidden Rice, Chinese black rice, unlike black sticky rice, is not a glutinous rice. It grows in northeast China and is a brown rice (unpolished rice). It can be served as plain rice to accompany a meal; like all brown rices, it takes a little longer to cook than white rice, 35 minutes, and needs more water: 3½ cups water to 2 cups rice.

GLUTINOUS RICE: See STICKY RICE, below.

JASMINE RICE: An aromatic medium- to long-grain rice from Thailand, jasmine rice is now readily available in North America; American-grown jasmine rice is also widely sold. The cooked rice is tender, with a slightly clinging texture (see Basic Rice, page 166).

MEDITERRANEAN RICES: These short- and medium-grain rices, rounder than jasmine or basmati, can absorb large amounts of liquid. They are ideal for risotto, paella, and *pulaos* because they absorb the flavors of the broth they are cooked in. Look for baldo or arborio or one of the Spanish rices such as Valencia for making the *pulaos* in this book. You can also try using Bhutanese red rice, for it too absorbs flavor and stands up well to being stirred while it is cooking.

STICKY RICE, GLUTINOUS RICE: Sticky rice is a variety of rice. It is called sticky rice, or glutinous rice or sweet rice, because the grains stick together when cooked and it also has a slightly sweet taste. (It contains no gluten: the word "glutinous" refers to its sticky qualities.) It has a very low percentage of amylose and a high percentage of amylopectin, the two basic starches in all rices. (Basmati, in contrast, has high amylose and low amylo-

pectin, so it absorbs a lot of water and cooks to a drier texture, the opposite of sticky rice.) Because sticky rice absorbs very little water when cooking, it is usually prepared by soaking it in water, then steaming it over boiling water (see page 162).

Sticky rice is a staple for many of the minority peoples who live in southern Yunnan, Guizhou, and western Guanxi. The rice grown and eaten there is medium-grain and very like the sticky rice grown and eaten in Laos and Thailand. Thai sticky rice (labeled sweet rice or glutinous rice or *gao nep*) is available in most Southeast Asian and Chinese groceries. Japanese sweet rice is quite different in taste and texture, being short-grain and sweeter tasting.

RICE FLOUR, GLUTINOUS RICE FLOUR: Rice flours are made by grinding polished white rice to a powder. They are available in large supermarkets and in Asian groceries. Regular rice flour, also known as rice starch, is used in shortbread to make it more tender and as a thickening, as well as for making rice noodles. Glutinous rice flour, made from sticky rice (see *rice*), is used for some pastries. Because it is high in amylopectin, it makes a very smooth soft dough. The two kinds of rice flour are *not* interchangeable, so read the package carefully.

RICE VINEGAR: See VINEGAR.

RICE WINE: See SHAOXING WINE.

ROCK SUGAR: This quite refined sugar comes in large pale golden crystal-shaped lumps, usually sold in cardboard boxes. It has a pleasant taste of fruit to it, different from the blandness of regular white sugar. We call for it in Eight-Flavor Tea (page 328), and in Onion and Pomegranate Salad (page 89), though white sugar can be substituted. Look for it in Chinese and Southeast Asian groceries.

SALT: Most salt consumed beyond the Great Wall is gathered from salt lakes or salt springs. We use kosher salt or (nontraditional) sea salt.

SCALLIONS: Also known as **green onions** or **spring onions**, scallions are a member of the onion family (*Allium*) and are widely used in many of China's culinary cultures. To use, trim off the root end, then trim off the toughest parts of the green tops, as well as any outer layers that are damaged (you may not need to trim the greens if the scallions are very fresh and tender). The recipes in this book assume that scallions are trimmed. When a recipe here refers to scallions, we mean both the white and tender green parts; if only one or the other is wanted, it will be specified. For Chinese dishes, scallions may be smashed with the flat side of a cleaver or knife to release flavor. Scallions can be cut lengthwise in half or into ribbons and then cut crosswise, often into 2-inch lengths, before being used as a flavoring in a stir-fry or soup, or minced. Chopped scallion greens are often used as a garnish.

SEAWEED: See KOMBU/KONBU.

SESAME OIL, SESAME PASTE, SESAME SEEDS: Sesame is a bush (*Sesamum indicum*) that is native to the Indian Subcontinent. It produces seeds that are very high in oil. There are two kinds of sesame oil, roasted and nonroasted. Only **roasted sesame oil**, sometimes referred to as **Asian sesame oil**, is called for in this book. It is made from sesame seeds that are roasted before being ground for their oil. The oil is a warm brown in color and aromatic, with a smell and taste of the roasted seeds. It is usually used in small quantities, as a flavoring added at the end of cooking or as a topping. The most widely available brand is Kadoya, from Japan, but there are also good Chinese sesame oils sold in Chinese groceries. Recently we've discovered a delicious seame oil made from black sesame seeds. **Nonroasted sesame oil**, almost clear in color, is used as a cooking oil in parts of India; it stands up relatively well to high temperatures. It is not part of the pantry beyond the Great Wall. Because of their high oil content, sesame seeds should be stored in the refrigerator tightly sealed. Always taste the seeds before using them: they should taste slightly sweet. If there is a bitter edge, their oil has gone rancid and they

should be discarded. Sesame seeds have an outer hull that may be warmish beige or black in color. The seeds we've seen used beyond the Great Wall are mostly hulled, almost white, and tender. They are usually dry-roasted to bring out their flavor. They are used on breads and in sweets, as well as to make sesame paste, which is very like the sesame paste from the Eastern Mediterranean that is known as *tahini* or *tahine*—and which we use as a substitute. The sesame paste in China is made from roasted seeds, so it has a more intense roasted sesame flavor.

SHALLOTS: A member of the onion family (*Allium*), shallots are small bulbs covered in a pale orange-brown to reddish-brown papery skin. They have a mild flavor somewhere between garlic and onion. The large shallots grown in Europe are mild tasting and almost watery. We suggest that you look in Asian groceries for Southeast Asian and South Asian shallots, which are smaller and we think, have a cleaner flavor.

SHAOXING WINE, COOKING WINE, RICE WINE: In Chinese cooking, various rice wines and rice liquors may be added as flavorings to stir-fries and simmered dishes. In this book, we call only for Shaoxing wine, sometimes labeled *shaoxing jiu*. A reasonable substitute is a medium-dry sherry, or look for the Chinese rice wine sold as *shi qi* rice wine.

SICHUAN PEPPER: Also called *fagara* in English, Sichuan pepper (sometimes spelled Szechuan) is an old and very important spice in China. Like black and white peppercorns, the pepper comes from the small berries of a tree. The tree, *Zanthoxylum piperitum*, is a variety of prickly ash; it is a close cousin of the Japanese pepper bush known as *sansho*. The berries are picked and then sun-dried. The resulting peppercorns are reddish brown, lightweight, and hollow. Inside some of them you may find a shiny black seed; it is bitter and should be discarded. Different companies use varying amounts of care in processing their Sichuan pepper; look for pepper that has been well cleaned and is aromatic, and buy whole peppercorns, rather than ground pepper, for better

Main stairs to the Potala Palace in Lhasa.

flavor and freshness. The spice numbs the tongue and makes the mouth tingle in a pleasing way (the numbness may last for a while). There's a woody resinous flavor and a back aroma that resembles some of the elements in the taste and smell of nutmeg. To bring out the full aroma of Sichuan pepper, heat it, either by **dry-roasting** it before using or by adding it early in the cooking so that it gets heated and adds its full flavor to the dish. (Photograph on page 37.)

SOYBEANS, SOYBEAN SPROUTS: Fresh soybeans are large round green peas, larger than chickpeas, the seeds of the plant *Glycine maximus*. In North America, they are most often available frozen both in the pod and shelled, in 1-pound plastic bags, often labeled *edamame*, the Japanese word for soybeans. Fresh or frozen shelled soybeans can be stir-fried (see Chile-Hot Bright Green Soybeans with Garlic, page 103) or boiled, drained, and tossed with a little salt, and then served to accompany drinks. They are a handy freezer item to have on hand, since they cook so quickly and have such a fresh green color. Dried soybeans, like other dried legumes, are very hard and take a long time to cook (in plenty of boiling water); they are not called for in this book. Cooked and processed, they are the essential ingredient in many staples from China and Japan, including tofu in its many forms; some miso pastes; and soy sauce. Soybean sprouts are sturdier looking than the common mung bean sprouts (longer and thicker), and they usually still have the bean pod attached to the sprout; the pod turns from yellow to green as it sprouts. (See photograph, page 92.) Soy sprouts stand up well to stir-frying and keep their crispness much longer than mung bean sprouts do when cooked. You will find them in Chinese and Southeast Asian grocery stores and in well-stocked supermarkets (or ask your supermarket to stock them). They should be well rinsed in cold water before using. See also BEAN SPROUTS.

SOY SAUCE: Soy sauce is traditionally brewed from soybeans, mixed with a grain (usually wheat these days), and cultured with *aspergillus* spores. We still find Kikkoman brand to be the most reliable of the widely available soy sauces, though Superior Soy—especially

Local market in a Hani village in southeastern Yunnan.

their mushroom soy—also has good flavor. As with rice vinegars, we suggest that you go to a Chinese grocery store and buy several different soy sauces. Taste them, and see which ones you prefer. You may be surprised at the variety of flavors. Some are lighter-tasting and more suitable for dipping sauces; others, with more depth, are better for seasoning dishes during cooking. **Thick soy sauce**, sometimes labeled **soy sauce paste**, is a product from Taiwan made of soybeans and wheat, like soy sauce, but it is thickened with potato starch. It has an intense, slightly sweet flavor and a thicker consistency, and it is used as a dressing rather than for cooking. The brand we use is Kimlan.

STAR ANISE: This beautiful star-shaped warm-brown spice (*Illicium verum*) is now widely available in well-stocked grocery stores as well as Chinese and Southeast Asian groceries. It has an aniseed or licorice flavor that is penetrating. Star anise is used whole, rather as cinnamon sticks are, to perfume soups or stews, especially those made with beef. It also finds its way into some pickles and preserves in Yunnan. Don't worry if the stars are broken; just use the pieces in the same way as you would use a whole one.

STIR-FRYING: This method of cooking requires a hot wok or other curved pan (though a large deep skillet can be substituted if necessary) and high heat. All ingredients, including seasonings, should be prepared ahead, for cooking time is short and timing is quite precise. Ingredients are usually cut small or thinly sliced, and they are cut to the same size so that they cook evenly. Those that will cook more quickly are added later in the cooking process. First the pan is heated, then a little oil is added and the pan swirled gently to coat the cooking surface. Once aromatics or other ingredients are added to the oil, the food is moved around the wok with a metal spatula so that all sides of the ingredients eventually come into contact with the hot oiled surface of the pan. The spatula can be used to press an ingredient against the pan, then to lift it away and turn it over, in order to expose a different surface to the heat.

The ideal equipment for stir-frying is a good wok with a long-handled spatula that looks like a metal shovel with a wooden handle (see photograph, page 187.); the best heat source is a hot flame. We stir-fry on our regular gas stovetop; in commercial kitchens, it's done over higher-BTU burners. You can stir-fry on an electric stove if you have a collar to hold your wok stable on the burner or have a flat-bottomed wok. A hot wood stove (rather like the traditional stoves of northern China) also works well for stir-frying: lift off the cover of one burner, and the wok will fit neatly into the hole.

TEA: Originally cultivated in China, and now grown in the hills of northern India and in Sri Lanka, as well as temperate areas of Africa, tea trees (*Camellia sinensis*) are grown for their leaves. The trees are kept trimmed to about 4 feet so that pickers can reach the fresh young leaves at the top. The harvest starts in the spring. Beyond the Great Wall, Yunnan is famous for its tea, and tea is also grown in Guizhou province, on terraced hillsides that have a temperate climate and receive adequate rainfall. The flavor of tea is affected by the quality of the leaves and where they are grown, as well as by how they are processed. **Black tea leaves** have been dried and then fermented; **green tea leaves** have simply been dried, without fermentation. Tea leaves may be rolled or chopped, left loose, or compressed into bricks the way Tibetan brick tea is. See "Tea, Tea, and More Tea," page 324.

TOFU

FRESH TOFU: Tofu (sometimes spelled dofu or daofu, and also referred to as bean curd) is made from soybeans that are boiled, then pressed to release a thick, smooth liquid, which is then mixed with a coagulant that makes it set to a firm texture. (Among the people living in the hills of Yunnan and Guizhou and Guangxi, and in neighboring parts of Southeast Asia, we've seen a number of other coagulated tofu-like foods, mostly made of rice or mung beans, cooked and processed like soybeans with a coagulant.) Fresh tofu is widely sold, usually in 2- to 3-inch-square white blocks that are immersed in water. It comes in various textures, from fairly firm, the standard

Chinese style, to smooth and closer to the texture of barely set custard (known as **silky tofu**, which is not called for in this book).

Tofu should be stored immersed in water in a sealed container, in the refrigerator. The water should fill the container to the brim and should be changed every day. Properly stored, fresh tofu will keep for 4 days. Rinse it before using it.

If you have too much fresh tofu on hand, you can freeze it: Cut it into 1-inch cubes, stack them on a plate or small tray, and freeze them. Once frozen solid, they can be transferred to a plastic bag, well sealed, and kept in the freezer until ready for use. **Frozen tofu** is porous, with an open spongy texture, ideal for absorbing flavor. Let thaw, squeeze out excess water, then toss it into a hot soup or stew. (Photograph on page 74.)

PRESSED TOFU: When fresh tofu is pressed under a weight (rather as you can press fresh cheese under a weight for the same reason), it gives off liquid and firms up to a cheese-like texture. Pressed tofu, known in Mandarin as *doufu gan*, is sold at Chinese grocery stores. It comes in small cellophane packages, usually about 4 inches square and ¼ to ½ inch thick. Sometimes the tofu is pale, sometimes it is tinted dark brown because it has been flavored with anise and soy sauce.

You can also make your own pressed tofu by wrapping cubes of fresh tofu in cheesecloth, placing them on a plate, and putting a weight (another plate with a weight on it) on top. The pressure will force water out of the tofu—drain it off occasionally—until it has shrunk and become firmer and more cheese-like in texture. Pressed tofu does not keep well; once opened, seal tightly in plastic and refrigerate for no more than 2 days. To use, rinse, then slice or chop into small cubes before combining with other ingredients. See Pressed Tofu with Scallions and Ginger, page 75.

TOFU SHEETS, TOFU STICKS: During the process of making tofu, as the soy liquid is coagulating and setting into blocks, layers or sheets of it may be skimmed off before it sets. These tender sheets are called tofu sheets

or bean curd sheets (*yuba* in Japanese). They can be used as wrappers or chopped and added to dishes. However, fresh tofu sheets are not widely available and so are not called for in this book. **Dried tofu sheets** and **tofu sticks** are available in larger Chinese grocery stores and are handy pantry staples, widely used in vegetarian cuisines and in places where fresh food is not always easy to come by. Both the sheets and sticks are a pale yellowish tan and brittle. The sticks are made of fresh tofu sheets that have been rolled up and dried; dried tofu sheets are the flat version and are very brittle. Both are sold in clear cellophane packages. To use, soak in warm water until tender (about 15 minutes), and remove and discard any tough bits. Break or chop into pieces and add to soups or stir-fries (see Index for recipes).

TOMATILLOS: Also known by their Mexican name, *tomates verdes*, or as Mexican green tomatoes, tomatillos are the fruit of the *Physalis ixocarpa* plant. They are enclosed in papery husks. (See photograph, page 293.) When ripe, the fruits range in color from bright green to yellow to purple. They are used to make green salsa (*salsa verde*) in Mexico, often cooked but sometimes raw. They have a fresh acidic, tart flavor. We use them as a substitute for hog plums (see above) to make a version of grilled hog plum salsa from the Dai people of southern Yunnan (see the recipe on page 22).

TREE EARS: See MUSHROOMS.

TSAMPA: Tsampa (its Tibetan name, sometimes transcribed *tsamba*), is the staple food of Tibet. It is made of whole barley grains that are roasted, traditionally in hot sand, and then ground to a very fine flour-like powder. Because the grains have been cooked before being ground, tsampa is edible and digestible with no further cooking. It is eaten stirred into tea and is also used as a thickener or ingredient in some stews and soups. It can be made at home in your kitchen; see page 180.

VINEGAR: Vinegar is acetic acid that ranges from 3.5 to over 7 percent acidity. It can be made from, and

Hani market in Luchen, Yunnan

flavored with, many different ingredients. In this book, we call for rice vinegar, meaning white rice vinegar, and Jinjiang (black rice) vinegar. **Rice vinegar** is made from white rice, water, and salt. We prefer the vinegars that have about 4 to 4.5 percent acidity. They have a milder, softer flavor than plain distilled white vinegar or most cider vinegars. Our favorites are the Japanese brewed rice vinegars, such as Marukan brand. Look for rice vinegar in a Chinese or Southeast Asian grocery and buy several different brands. They're not expensive, and it's interesting to explore the varieties; make sure the ones you buy are unseasoned (some Japanese vinegars come seasoned, so that they can be used to flavor sushi rice). Taste the vinegars and decide which one(s) you like. In the recipes in this book, we call for rice vinegar as a seasoning and also for making pickled red chiles (see page 34) and pickled radish threads (see page 25). (We also use rice vinegar in vinaigrettes, with olive oil, to dress Western-style green salads.)

Jinjiang (black rice) vinegar, sometimes labeled Chinkiang vinegar, is very dark and has a clean, aromatic taste. It's made of glutinous rice, water, and salt (wheat is sometimes also on the list of ingredients). It's not to be confused with black vinegar or "vegetarian vinegar," both of which are generally metallic tasting or taste of chemicals. You'll find Jinjiang vinegar in Chinese grocery stores. Cider vinegar and a mild balsamic vinegar are reasonable substitutes, though not identical. Jinjiang vinegar is a common table condiment in the northern and western regions beyond the Great Wall, used to flavor bowls of noodles, for example.

WOK: We call for a wok or a wide heavy skillet for the stir-fried dishes in this book (see also *stir-frying*). A wok is a concave pan, a descendant and adaptation of the traditional Indian *karhai*. If you are buying a wok, you may want to have a look at Grace Young and Alan Richardson's book *The Breath of a Wok* (see Bibliography), but here are a few general pointers: Woks work best over a flame rather than on an electric burner, though if you have a metal collar to support yours, you can use it on an electric burner. Look for a carbon steel (spun steel) or a cast iron wok in a Chinese grocery or equipment store. Carbon steel woks weigh less and are quicker to heat up and to cool down; cast iron woks are heavier and hold the heat longer. We prefer our carbon steel wok for quick stir-fries; cast iron is ideal for simmered dishes. Avoid stainless steel, aluminum, or nonstick woks, which don't stand up well to long use and don't distribute the heat properly.

When you bring your new wok home, you will need to clean and season it before using it: scrub it in plenty of hot soapy water, rinse well, and dry. Place the wok over high heat, and when it is almost smoking, remove it. Let it cool a little, then rub it all over with an oiled paper towel or cotton cloth, which will probably become quite black. Place the wok back over high heat. Add a little peanut oil, about 2 tablespoons, and swirl the oil around

as it heats. Just before it smokes, remove the wok from the heat. Let it cool for several minutes, then use a clean paper towel or cotton cloth to rub the oil all over the inside of the wok. Pour off any excess oil, and repeat this step again. Rinse the wok with hot water (no soap or detergent) and wipe dry.

After you use your wok, or when you finish cooking one dish and want to use it again for another, always rinse it out right away with water and scrub it clean, then dry it immediately.

WOLFBERRIES: Widely marketed as *goji berries* or *Tibetan goji*, these raisin-sized orange-red fruits are sold, dried, in health food stores as well as Chinese herb stores. They are the fruit of *Lycium barbarum* and *Lycium chinensis*, species of boxthorn that grow in temperate climates (some have become naturalized in southern England). The dried fruits taste slightly sweet; some are soft, like raisins, while others have dried out more. They have a small inedible seed in the center. Most wolfberries sold in North America seem to come from Ningxia, the Chinese province east of Gansu and south of Inner Mongolia. They also grow in Xinjiang and in Inner Mongolia. Wolfberries have played a role in traditional Chinese medicine for centuries, as a food that is beneficial to the kidneys and liver, nourishes the blood, and is good for the eyes; they are now being marketed as powerful antioxidants, cancer-fighting foods. They can be eaten raw, like raisins, but traditionally they are added to tea or brewed as a tea, or added to broths (see Savory Boiled Dumplings, page 150).

WONTON WRAPPERS: Available in Chinese groceries, these come in packages of 80 to 100, each separated from the other by a dusting of cornstarch. Store well sealed in the refrigerator for not more than a week.

YAK: Technically "yak" is the term for the male of the bovine species *Bos grunniens*, (in Tibetan, the female is called *dri*), but in English it is often used to refer to all yak-like creatures. Yaks are large animals that have adapted to high altitudes and the extreme temperatures of the Tibetan plateau and mountains. They are found in Tibet, Quinghai, Nepal, the Kunlun Mountains, the Pamirs, and in parts of Mongolia. They have long hair, most often black but sometimes brown or partially white; a wide face with long, curved, pointed horns; and a small hump at the shoulder. *Dri* produce a rich, thick milk and are also crossbred with cattle, to produce the yak-like, though smaller, *dzo* (male) and *dzomo* (female). The *dzomo* produces more milk than the *dri*; the milk of both is used to make cheese, yogurt, and butter. These animals are used for agricultural labor and as beasts of burden. Like yaks, they are prized for their meat.

Man plowing in springtime, using a team of yaks, north of Lhasa.

BIBLIOGRAPHY

Allen, Charles. *A Mountain in Tibet: The Search for Mount Kailas and the Sources of the Great Rivers in India.* London: Futura, 1983.

Anderson, E. N. *The Food of China.* New Haven: Yale University Press, 1988.

Bianco, Lucien. *Origins of the Chinese Revolution, 1915–1949.* Stanford: Stanford University Press, 1971.

Bonington, Chris. *Kongur: China's Elusive Summit.* New York: Norton, 1983.

Chang, K. C., ed. *Food in Chinese Culture: Anthropological and Historical Perspectives.* New Haven: Yale University Press, 1977.

Chapman, F. Spencer. *Memoirs of a Mountaineer: Lhasa, the Holy City.* Gloucester, England: Alan Sutton, 1938.

Chunyang, An, and Bohua Liu, eds. *Where the Dai People Live.* Beijing: Foreign Languages Press, 1985.

Corrigan, Gina. *Guizhou.* Chicago: Passport Books, 1995.

Cramer, Marc. *Imperial Mongolian Cooking: Recipes from the Kingdoms of Genghis Khan.* New York: Hippocrene, 2001.

Dahlen, Martha. *A Cook's Guide to Chinese Vegetables.* Hong Kong: Guidebook Company, 1992, 1995.

David-Neel, Alexandra. *Voyage d'une Parisienne à Lhassa [Journey to Lhasa].* Paris: Pocket Edition, 2007.

DeFrancis, John. *In the Footsteps of Genghis Khan.* Honolulu: University of Hawaii Press, 1993.

Di Cosmo, Nicola. *Ancient China and Its Enemies: The Rise of Nomadic Power in East Asian History.* Cambridge: Cambridge University Press, 2002.

Du, Shanshan. *Chopsticks Only Work in Pairs: Gender Unity and Gender Equality among the Lahu of Southwest China.* New York: Columbia University Press, 2002.

Dunlop, Fuchsia. *Land of Plenty: A Treasury of Authentic Sichuan Cooking.* New York: Norton, 2003.

Ekvall, Robert. *Fields on the Hoof; Nexus of Tibetan Nomadic Pastoralism.* New York: Holt, Rinehart & Winston, 1968.

Fleming, Peter. *Bayonets to Lhasa.* Hong Kong: Oxford University Press, 1984.

———. *News from Tartary: A Journey from Peking to Kashmir.* London: Jonathan Cape, 1936.

Foster, Barbara. *Forbidden Journey: The Life of Alexandra David-Neel.* San Francisco: Harper & Row, 1987.

Gladney, Dru C. *Muslim Chinese: Ethnic Nationalism in the People's Republic.* Cambridge: Council on East Asian Studies, Harvard University, 1991.

Goldstein, Melvyn C. *A History of Modern Tibet, 1913–1951: The Demise of the Lamaist State.* Berkeley: University of California Press, 1989.

———. *The Snow Lion and the Dragon: China, Tibet, and the Dalai Lama.* Berkeley: University of California Press, 1999.

Goldstein, Melvyn C., and Cynthia Beall. *The Changing World of Mongolia's Nomads.* Berkeley: University of California Press, 1994.

Govinda, Lama Anagarika. *The Way of the White Clouds: A Buddhist Pilgrim in Tibet.* London: Rider, 1966.

Harrell, Stevan, ed. *Cultural Encounters on China's Ethnic Frontiers.* Seattle: University of Washington Press, 1997.

———. *Ways of Being Ethnic in Southwest China.* Seattle: University of Washington Press, 2001.

Harrer, Heinrich. *Seven Years in Tibet.* New York: Dutton, 1954.

Hayashi, Yukio, and Yang Guangyuan, eds. *Dynamics of Ethnic Cultures across National Boundaries in Southwestern China and Mainland Southeast Asia: Relations, Societies, and Languages.* Chiang Mai: Ming Muang, 1993.

Heiss, Mary-Lou, and Robert Heiss. *The Story of Tea: A Cultural History and Drinking Guide.* Berkeley: Ten Speed Press, 2007.

Herklots, G. A. C. *Vegetables in South-East Asia.* London: Allen & Unwin, 1972.

Hopkirk, Peter. *Foreign Devils on the Silk Road: The Search for the Lost Cities and Treasures of Chinese Central Asia.* London: Murray, 1980.

Jonsson, Hjorleifur. "Yao Minority Identity and the Location of Difference in the South China Borderlands." *Ethnos* 65:1 (2000): 56–82.

Keay, John. *The Gilgit Game: The Explorers of the Western Himalayas, 1865–95.* London: Murray, 1979.

———. *When Men and Mountains Meet: The Explorers of the Western Himalayas, 1820–75.* London: Century, 1977.

Lamb, Alastair. *The McMahon Line: A Study in the Relations between India, China and Tibet, 1904–1914.* London: Routledge & Kegan Paul, 1966.

LeBar, Frank M., Gerald C. Hickey, and John K. Musgrave, eds. *Ethnic Groups of Mainland Southeast Asia.* New Haven: Human Relations Area Files Press, 1964.

Le Coq, Albert von. *Buried Treasures of Chinese Turkestan.* 1925. Reprint, Hong Kong: Oxford University Press, 1985.

Liangwen, Zhu. *The Dai, or the Tai and Their Architecture and Customs in South China.* Bangkok: DD Books,1992.

Lin, Florence. *Florence Lin's Chinese Regional Cookbook.* New York: Hawthorn Books, 1975.

———. *Florence Lin's Complete Book of Chinese Noodles, Dumplings and Breads.* New York: Morrow, 1986.

Macartney, Lady Catherine. *An English Lady in Chinese Turkestan.* 1931. Reprint, Hong Kong: Oxford University Press, 1985.

Maillart, Ella. *Forbidden Journey.* 1937. Reprint, London: Century, 1983.

———. *Turkestan Solo.* 1934. Reprint, London: Century, 1985.

Majupuria, Indra, and Diki Lobsang. *Tibetan Cooking.* Lashkar, Tibet: S. Devi, 1994.

Miller, Luree. *On Top of the World: Five Women Explorers in Tibet.* New York: Paddington Press, 1976.

Nicholson, Barbara et al. *The Oxford Book of Food Plants.* London: Oxford University Press, 1969.

Nightingale, Pamela, and C. P. Skrine. *Macartney at Kashgar: New Light on British, Chinese and Russian Activities in Sinkiang, 1890–1918.* Oxford: Oxford University Press, 1987.

Norman, Jill. *The Complete Book of Spices.* London: Dorling Kindersley, 1990.

Pallis, Marco. *Peaks and Lamas.* London: Woburn Press, 1939.

Phillips, Roger, and Martyn Rix. *The Random House Book of Vegetables.* New York: Random House, 1993.

Pranavananda, Swami. *Kailas Manasarovar.* New Delhi: Swami Pranavananda, 1949.

Ramsey, S. Robert. *The Languages of China.* Princeton: Princeton University Press, 1987.

Rossi, Gail. *The Dong People of China: A Hidden Civilization.* Singapore: Hagley & Hoyle, n.d.

Rudelson, Justin Jon. *Central Asia Phrasebook: Languages of the Silk Road.* Hawthorn, Australia: Lonely Planet, 1998.

———. *Oasis Identities: Uyghur Nationalism along China's Silk Road.* New York: Columbia University Press, 1997.

Salikhov, S. G. *Blyuda: Uzbekskoi Kukhny [Uzbek cuisine].* Tashkent, Uzbekistan: 1991.

Sayavongkhamdy, Thongsa, and Yukio Hayashi. *Cultural Diversity and Conservation in the Making of Mainland Southeast Asia and Southwestern China: Regional Dynamics in the Past and Present.* Kyoto: Center for Southeast Asia Studies, 2003.

Schwartz, Daniel. *The Great Wall of China.* London: Thames & Hudson, 1990.

Shipton, Eric Earle. *Mountains of Tartary.* In *The Six Mountain-Travel Books.* Seattle: Mountaineers, 1985.

Sivin, Nathan, ed. *The Contemporary Atlas of China.* Boston: Houghton Mifflin, 1988.

Skrine, C. P. *Chinese Central Asia.* New York: Barnes & Noble, 1926.

Snellgrove, David, and Hugh Richardson. *A Cultural History of Tibet.* 1968. Reprint, Boston: Shambhala, 1986.

Stein, R. A. *Tibetan Civilization.* London: Faber & Faber, 1972.

Tannahill, Reay. *Food in History.* 2nd ed. New York: Crown, 1988.

Teichman, Eric. *Journey to Turkistan.* 1937. Reprint, Oxford: Oxford University Press, 1988.

Tropp, Barbara. *China Moon Cookbook.* New York: Workman, 1992.

———. *Modern Art of Chinese Cooking.* New York: Morrow, 1982.

Tucci, Giuseppe. *To Lhasa and Beyond.* Rome: Instituto Poligrafico dello Stato, 1956.

———. *Tibet: Land of Snows.* Calcutta: Oxford University Press, 1967.

Waddell, L. Austine. *Buddhism and Lamaism of Tibet.* Kathmandu: Educational Enterprise, 1978.

Ward, F. Kingdon. *The Mystery Rivers of Tibet.* 1923. Reprint, London: Cadogan Books, 1986.

Weatherford, Jack. *Genghis Khan and the Making of the Modern World.* New York: Three Rivers Press, 2004.

Whitfield, Susan. *Life along the Silk Road.* London: Murray, 1999.

Whyte, Robert. *Rural Nutrition in Monsoon Asia.* London: Oxford University Press, 1974.

Wu, Cheng'en. *Monkey.* Translated by Arthur Waley. 1941. Reprint, New York: Grove Press, 1994.

Young, Grace, and Alan Richardson. *The Breath of a Wok.* New York: Simon & Schuster, 2004.

In addition:

The photographs in back issues of *National Geographic* give glimpses of premodern times beyond the Great Wall. Look for April 1925; October 1930; November 1932; and June 1933.

Steppe. Published in England, the magazine focuses on Central Asia.

Helpful websites:

http://thorntree.lonelyplanet.com

The Oriental-List: www.members.shaw.ca/pnhpublic/china.html

For the Chinese government's view of its people, see "China in Brief": www.china.org.cn/e-china/population

ACKNOWLEDGMENTS

This book reflects many encounters with people, many trips and conversations. We are grateful for all we have learned along the way, from people whose names we never knew or have lost track of, as well as from those named below.

From our early travels, huge thanks to Tenzin Namgyal for his help in Lhasa, and to anthropologists Mel Goldstein, Cynthia Beall, and Corneille Jest for their insights. Thanks also to Sok and his mother for their hospitality in the Pamirs and to the Tajik nomads below the Khunjerab pass. We remember with gratitude the hospitality of the schoolteacher in Akmeqit in southern Xinjiang. We thank Yu Jiao and her family in Menghan, in southern Yunnan, for all they taught us when we stayed with them with our sons, Dominic and Tashi; and Oran Field for generously sharing his knowledge of the culinary traditions of the people of Yunnan. And we thank again all our traveling companions from those early days.

Our recent travels beyond the Great Wall have been solo trips, so each of us has a list of special people to thank.

FROM JEFFREY: Serik for taking me on his motorcycle; the wonderful family who helped us (and fed us) after our motorcycle crashed and Serik's sister, who fed us homemade noodles and goat shank after a long hard day. At Kanas Lake, Albeiyat and his Tuvan friends from Altai, who talked late into the night about the Tuvan villages of the region. In Altai, the very nice teacher who went out of his way to help me visit the Mongol village; also, Stephane and Tanya. In Chengdu, Sim and the great staff at Sim's Guesthouse who helped me figure out how to get into and back out of western Sichuan and eastern Tibet. In Litang, the Tibetan long-distance taxi driver who took me to visit his incredible family home along the way from Litang to Kanding. And

thanks to various long-distance bus drivers of southeastern Yunnan for their help.

FROM NAOMI: Tenzin Namgyal and Drolma in Lhasa for their friendship and for their culinary advice; Nima Dorje, his hospitable family and friends in Lhasa, and Elisabeth and Edwina. Monk Kesang, young nuns Lamu Drolma (Julie) and Tashi Tsomo (Nicole), and Tsai Rangding of Labrang, as well as Popo Tserin. Mel Goldstein and Cynthia Beall for answering yet more questions in Lhasa recently. The scholars of Tibetan intellectual history Leonard van der Kuijp, Christoph Cueppers, and Per Sorenson; the environmentalists Derek Martin and Lance Craighead; Ian Alsop; and Galen Murten. In Inner Mongolia, Driver Lin; Lisa, Lily, and Wu Ya Nan for generous hospitality in Hailar and Yakishi; Mr. Ma for sharing information about Mongolian milk products; Saren and her mother. In Kaili, Guizhou, Jenny (Shi Jin Hua) and her mother; Tony; and Liu Zo Cai. In Zhaoxing, the family Lu at the Fu Quan guesthouse; Kyrra (Lu Qin Xiu) and her family; the older women at the drum tower; and Charlie Levin and Maria Moller.

We both feel very lucky to know Rocky Dang of Phoenix Travel in Hong Kong, who has helped us over the years with ticketing, with various emergencies, and, even more important, with his encyclopedic knowledge of life and culture in many parts of China. We thank Rocky and Peter for always making us welcome at their flat in Hong Kong. In Chiang Mai, thanks to Pom at P.M. Travel, and in Bangkok, thanks again to John at Hollywood E-6 for his impeccable film processing.

Loving thanks to Dominic and Tashi, now moving into adulthood, who traveled miles with us in Yunnan when they were much younger, and who now are patient tasters of recipe tests and also hold the fort with great equilibrium when one or the other of us heads out for a long trip.

As always when our work involves China, we are very grateful for Hilary Buttrick's generous help with our endless questions about language and food. Thanks to Richard and Juliet for welcoming Naomi in London. Many thanks to Dawn Woodward for all her recipe work, and to Ed Rek, as well as to Cassandra Kobayashi for recipe testing; special thanks to Dina.

Once again we are grateful to our agent Liv Blumer for all her help and advice, and to Anne Collins, Sharon Klein, and the team at Random House Canada for their strong support.

After we hand in the manuscript and photographs, it takes the work of many people over many months to transform them into a book. Warm thanks to photographer Richard Jung for his wonderful studio shots, and to stylists Linda Tubby (food) and Roisin Nield (props) for their thoughtful contributions to the shoot. We thank Judith Sutton, who has copy-edited all our books, for her care. At Artisan we thank Trent Duffy for shepherding the book through all its stages; art director Jan Derevjanik for her strong, attentive design work; Sigi Nacson for careful fact-checking; Nancy Murray for supervision of the production; Anna Berns, for helping with many details; Rodica Prato for the maps; and publicists Jaime Harder and Nicki Clendening for their help.

The person who makes it all happen is our much-loved editor and publisher, Ann Bramson, at Artisan. She always encourages us to think big (and never as forcefully as with this project) and then has the job of pulling the pieces together into a coherent and beautiful book. We are so grateful for all your care, Ann, and for your friendship.

SOURCES FOR EQUIPMENT AND INGREDIENTS

If you live in a city or town with one or more Chinese or Vietnamese or Thai grocery stores, then you should be able to find all the ingredients called for in this book. (If you live far from an Asian grocery store, then you will need to shop online for a few of the ingredients used in the recipes; see below for sources, or else stock up next time you are in a larger town.) Smaller stores may not always stock tofu sticks or sheets, but you can ask them to order them. Go and have a good look around and ask questions of shoppers as well as of store employees; it's the best way to get familiar with all that is available. Many of these shops also sell specialized cookware such as woks. If there is no Asian equipment store near you, for a wide selection of woks you may want to shop online at The Wok Shop (see below).

EDEN ORGANIC FOODS
WWW.EDENFOODS.COM

For organic soy sauces, rice vinegars, dried seaweed, etc. Eden products are also sold at many natural food stores; ask your local store to order what you need if they don't already carry it.

ETHNIC GROCER
WWW.ETHNICGROCER.COM
For soy sauces, tofu sticks, vinegars.

KALUSTYAN'S
123 LEXINGTON AVENUE
NEW YORK, NY 10016
212-685-3451
WWW.KALUSTYANS.COM

For all dried and packaged ingredients in this book except tofu products, including dried rice of all kinds, soy sauces, rice vinegars, sesame oil; as well as baskets and pots for steaming sticky rice.

TAP PHONG TRADING COMPANY
360 SPADINA AVENUE
TORONTO, ONTARIO M5T 2G5

A very wide choice of cookware, including bamboo cookers, hot pots, mesh skimmers, cleavers, mortars, etc. No mail order.

T&T SUPERMARKETS

Many stores in and around Vancouver and Toronto, as well as stores in Calgary and Edmonton; for store locations go to www.tnt.supermarket.com. Every Asian ingredient imaginable, both dried and fresh, including very fresh fish.

WING YIP SUPERSTORES

At four locations in Great Britain, and expanding; go to www.wingyip.com for store locations. Very like T&T, with a huge array of pan-Asian ingredients.

THE WOK SHOP
718 GRANT AVENUE
SAN FRANCISCO, CA 94108
415-989-3797
WWW.WOKSHOP.COM

For bamboo steamers, cleavers, mesh skimmers, and hot pots of many kinds, as well as carbon steel and cast iron woks.

INDEX

Page numbers in *italics* refer to illustrations; those in **bold** refer to the principal discussion of an ethnic group.

achar:
  Lhasa Yellow Achar, *26*, *28*, *270*
  see also chutney
Afghanistan, 10, 90, 174, 288, 343
Albeyat (driver), 274, 277
Altai, Xinjiang, 189
Altai Mountains, 5, 44, 157, 255, 324
amaranth greens, 208, *241*, 353
Amdo Noodle Squares, 128
Amdo region, 7, 128, 144, 214, 279
azuki beans, 350
  in Sweet Red Bean Paste, 323

Bahargul (Uighur woman), 72
Bai people, **103**
  recipes of, 103, 286
Banak Shol Hotel, Lhasa, 51
barbecue, Mongolian Barbecue, 263
barley, 160, 161, 180, 350
  Roasted Barley Flour, 181
  see also tsampa
bean paste. *See* Sweet Red Bean Paste
beans. *See* mung beans; soybeans
bean sprouts, 350
  Hani Soy Sprout Salad, 73, *315*
  Silk Road Lamb Stir-Fry with Sprouts and Greens, 276

Sprouts and Cabbage Salad Kazakh-Style, 72
  Weeknight Pork and Bean Sprouts, 311
bean threads. *See* cellophane noodles
beef, 258–59, 280–88
  Beef and Green Chile Stir-Fry, 287
  Beef and Spinach Stir-Fry, 305
  Beef Hot Pot, 282–83
  Beef-Sauced Hot Lettuce Salad, 67, *69*
  Beef with Mushrooms and Cellophane Noodles, 280, *281*
  Classic Lhasa Beef and Potato Stew, 283–84
  in Mongolian Barbecue, 263
  in Savory Tibetan Breads, 214–15
  in Steamed Tibetan Momos, *153*, 154
  in Tibetan Bone Broth, 45
  in Tsampa Soup, 46, *47*
beer, 321, 340
Beijing, 21, 269, 274
bell peppers, Silk Road Tomato-Bell Pepper Salad, 72
Best Place to Live, The (Schein), 183
beverages, 321
  see also beer; tea; wine
Bhutan, 212

Bhutanese red rice, 357
black glutinous rice, 357
black rice vinegar. *See* Jinjiang vinegar
black sticky rice, 357
bok choi, 208, *259*, 353, 354
  in Hui Vegetable Hot Pot, *116*, 117–18
  in Lhasa-Style Leafy Greens, 104
  in Silk Road Lamb Stir-Fry with Sprouts and Greens, 276
bones:
  in Kazakh Goat Broth, 44
  in Tibetan Bone Broth, 45
breads, 186–215
  Appetizer-Sized Jiaozi, 211
  Cheese Momos, 212–13
  Flaky Fried Sesame Coils, 202–3
  Giant Jiaozi, 210–11
  Ham Sesame Coils, 203
  Home-Style Tajik Nan, 191–92, *193*
  Hui Green Onion Crepes, 204
  Hui Two-Layer Crepes, 203–4
  Kazakh Family Loaf, 195–97, *196*
  Large Kazakh Fusion Loaf, 197
  Large Sha-pa-le, 215
  Mini-Crepe Alternative, 204
  nail-studded stamping device for, 190, 206
  Party Half-Moons, 209
  Savory Tibetan Breads, 214–15
  Succulent Lamb Samsa, 198–99

Uighur Nan, 190–91, *206*
Uighur Pastries with Pea Tendrils, *207*, 208–9
brick tea, 324
broccoli:
  in Hui Vegetable Hot Pot, *116*, 117–18
  as substitute for celtuce, 103
broken rice, 339, 357
broths. *See* soups
Bulong people, 324
Burma, 237, 348
Burqin, Xinjiang, 228
butter tea, salted, 179, 264, 300, 324

cabbage. *See* Napa cabbage
Cambodia, 54, 269
Campbell, Gabriel, 85
carrots:
  Carrot and Pork Filling, for Savory Boiled Dumplings, 150–51
  Dai Carrot Salad, *80*, 83
  Ginger and Carrot Stir-Fry, 96, *97*
  in Kazakh Pulao, 177
  Silk Road Chickpea-Carrot Fritters, 119
  in Vegetarian Stir-Fry, 211
cauliflower, in Hui Vegetable Hot Pot, *116*, 117–18
cayenne chiles, *16*, 17
  in Pickled Red Chiles, *33*, 34
cayenne pepper, 351

greens (cont.)

    Stir-Fried Pork with Pickled Greens, 303

    see also specific greens

Green Tea Shortbread with Poppy Seeds, 329

grilling techniques:

    Dai method, 222, 237

    for ground meat kebabs, 262

Guangxi province, 3, 10, 12, 120, 232, 349

    travel in, 348

    see also Dong people

Guangzhou (Canton), 9, 194, 269, 274

Guizhou province, 3, 10, 12, 309

    food traditions of, 35, 36, 220–21, 232, 269, 304

    Mao Tai distilled liquor of, 340

    pig raising in, 292

    tea growing in, 324

    travel in, 348

    see also Dong people; Miao people; specific towns (e.g., Kaili)

Ham Sesame Coils, 203

Han Chinese majority, 7, 8, 10, 39, 60, 112, 189, 200, 205, 305, 349

Hani Chile-Garlic Paste, 28

Hani people, 10, 28, 294, **316**, *317*

    recipes of, 28, 29, 36, 73, 114, 294

Hani Slow-Baked Pork Jerky, 294

Hani Soy Sprout Salad, 73, *315*

Harrell, Stevan, 316

Harrer, Heinrich, 129

Heiss, Mary-Lou, 324

Heiss, Robert, 324

herbs, Cooling Oasis Salad with Tomatoes and Herbs, 89

Himalaya, 3

Hmong people, 10, *182*, **183**, 299

    see also Miao people

hog plum (*makawk*), 22, 354

Hom, Xinjiang, 246, 255, 300

Hong Kong, 189, 194, 274

hot pots, 269

    Beef Hot Pot, 282–83

    Dong Chicken Hot Pot, *249*, 250–51

    equipment for, 269

    Hui Vegetable Hot Pot, *116*, 117–18

    Mongolian Hot Pot, 266–67

Hot Sour Salty Sweet (Alford and Duguid), 168

Hui Crepe Wraps, 204

Hui Green Onion Crepes, 204

Hui people, 7, 9, 39, 205, **216**, *217*

    food traditions of, 48, 117, 139, 144, 216

    recipes of, 18, 29, 48, 59, 83, 117–18, 128, 139, 148–49, 151, 174–76, 203–4, 328, 334–35

Hui Tomato-Lamb Noodle Soup, *58*, 59

Hui Two-Layer Crepes, 203-4

Hui Vegetable Hot Pot, *116*, 117–18

Hui Vegetable Soup, 48

Hui Vegetarian Broth, 48

India, 78, 85, 174, 285, 323

ingredients, 13

    sources for, 366

Inner Mongolia, 5, 8, 12, 60, 244

    berry wine of, 338

    food traditions of, 67, 86, 172, 263, 266, 269, 324

milk liqueur of, 338

    travel in, 348

    see also Manzhouli; Mongol people

Iran, 174

jasmine rice, 166, 357

Jenny (Miao woman), 298–99, 299

jerky:

    Hani Slow-Baked Pork Jerky, 294

    Khampa-style, 286

Jest, Corneille, 85

Jiangcheng, Yunnan, 294, 316

jiaozi (dumplings), 150

    Appetizer-Sized Jiaozi, 211

    Giant Jiaozi, 210–11

    Savory Boiled Dumplings, 150–51

Jicama-Tofu Sheet Stir-Fry, 105

Jinghong, Yunnan, 78, 82, 83, 110, 163, 168, 227, 313, 331

Jinjiang (black rice) vinegar, 360–61

    Cucumbers in Black Rice Vinegar, 83

Kaili, Guizhou, 74, 299

    bus-stand blues in, 332

    eating snails in, 233

    minced tofu rice sandwiches, 74

Kanas Lake, Xinjiang, 72, 133, 194, 228, 255, 274

Karakoram Highway, 112, 343

Kashgar, Xinjiang, *108*

    1986 travel to, 112

    post office, 108

Kazakh Family Loaf, 195–97, *196*

Kazakh Fusion Loaf, Large, 197

Kazakh Goat Broth, 44

Kazakh Noodles, *130*, *132*, 133–34

    Dried, 134

    Rolled-Out, 134

Kazakh people, 10, *156*, **157**, 216, 274

    food traditions of, 44, 100, 133, 157, 177, 187, 324

    recipes of, 44, 72, 100, 133–34, 151, 177, 195–97, 228, 277

    yurts of, 72, 133

Kazakh Pulao, 177

Kazakhstan, 10, 90, 157

Kazakh Stew, 277

Kazakh-Style Sprouts and Cabbage Salad, 72

Keay, John, 129

kebabs:

    Keshmah Kebabs, 262

    Oasis Chicken Kebabs, 247

    Uighur Lamb Kebabs, 260, *261*

Khunjerab Pass, 147

Kirghiz people, 10, 141, 216, **288**, *289*

    food traditions of, 187

    recipes of, 151, 191–92

kitchen equipment, 13

    for hot pots, 269

    for Mongolian barbecue, 263

    sand pots, 126, 130

    sources for, 366

    steamers, 13, 154, *155*, 232

    woks, 13, 309, 361

kombu (dried kelp), 354

    Kombu with Dark Soy and Scallion Ribbons, 82

    in Lhasa Seaweed Salad, 82

koumiss (fermented mare's milk), 338

Kratz, Amy, 85

CONVERSION TABLES

Here are rounded-off equivalents between the metric system and the traditional systems that are used in the United States to measure weight and volume.

weights

US/UK	METRIC
¼ oz	7 g
½ oz	15 g
1 oz	30 g
2 oz	60 g
3 oz	90 g
4 oz	115 g
5 oz	150 g
6 oz	175 g
7 oz	200 g
8 oz (½ lb)	225 g
9 oz	250 g
10 oz	300 g
11 oz	325 g
12 oz	350 g
13 oz	375 g
14 oz	400 g
15 oz	425 g
16 oz (1 lb)	450 g

volume

AMERICAN	IMPERIAL	METRIC
¼ tsp		1.25 ml
½ tsp		2.5 ml
1 tsp		5 ml
½ Tbs (1½ tsp)		7.5 ml
1 Tbs (3 tsp)		15 ml
¼ cup (4 Tbs)	2 fl oz	60 ml
⅓ cup (5 Tbs)	2½ fl oz	75 ml
½ cup (8 Tbs)	4 fl oz	125 ml
⅔ cup (10 Tbs)	5 fl oz	150 ml
¾ cup (12 Tbs)	6 fl oz	175 ml
1 cup (16 Tbs)	8 fl oz (½ pint)	250 ml
1¼ cups	10 fl oz	300 ml
1½ cups	12 fl oz	350 ml
1 pint (2 cups)	16 fl oz (1 pint)	500 ml
1 quart (4 cups)	32 fl oz (2 pints)	1 liter

oven temperatures

	°F	°C	GAS MARK
very cool	250–275	130–140	½–1
cool	300	148	2
warm	325	163	3
moderate	350	177	4
moderately hot	375–400	190–204	5–6
hot	425	218	7
very hot	450–475	232–245	8–9